Sentimental Republic

HARVARD EAST ASIAN MONOGRAPH SERIES 475

Sentimental Republic

Chinese Intellectuals and the Maoist Past

Hang Tu

Published by the Harvard University Asia Center
Distributed by Harvard University Press
Cambridge (Massachusetts) and London 2025

© 2025 by the President and Fellows of Harvard College
All rights reserved. No part of this publication may be reproduced, translated, stored in a retrieval system, or transmitted in any form or by any means, electronic, mechanical, photocopying, recording or otherwise, without prior written permission from the publisher.

Published by the Harvard University Asia Center, Cambridge, MA 02138

The Harvard University Asia Center publishes a monograph series and, in coordination with the Fairbank Center for Chinese Studies, the Korea Institute, the Reischauer Institute of Japanese Studies, and other faculties and institutes, administers research projects designed to further scholarly understanding of China, Japan, Korea, Vietnam, and other Asian countries. The Center also sponsors projects addressing multidisciplinary and regional issues in Asia.

Publication of this book was partially underwritten by the Mr. and Mrs. Stephen C. M. King Publishing and Communications Fund, established by Stephen C. M. King to further the cause of international understanding and cooperation, especially between China and the United States, by enhancing cross-cultural education and the exchange of ideas across national boundaries through publications of the Harvard University Asia Center.

Library of Congress Cataloging-in-Publication Data

Names: Tu, Hang, 1990– author.
Title: Sentimental Republic : Chinese intellectuals and the Maoist past / Hang Tu.
Other titles: Harvard East Asian monographs ; 475.
Description: Cambridge, MA : Harvard University Asia Center, 2025. | Series: Harvard East Asian Monograph series ; 475 | Includes bibliographical references and index. | English, with words and phrases in Chinese.
Identifiers: LCCN 2024014015 | ISBN 9780674297579 (hardcover)
Subjects: LCSH: Politics and culture—China—History—20th century. | Politics and culture—China—History—21st century. | Intellectuals—China—History—20th century. | Intellectuals—China—History—21st century. | Emotions—Political aspects. | China—Intellectual life—1976– | China—Politics and government—1949–
Classification: LCC DS779.23 .T83 2025 | DDC 951.05—dc23/eng/20240925
LC record available at https://lccn.loc.gov/2024014015

Index by Cynthia Col

∞ Printed on acid-free paper
Printed in the United States of America

For M.Z.

The dark night gave me black eyes,
I use them nonetheless seeking for the light.
Gu Cheng, "One Generation"

黑夜給了我黑色的眼睛,
我卻用它尋找光明。
顧城,〈一代人〉

Contents

List of Illustrations ix

Acknowledgments xi

Introduction: Emotions after Revolution 1
    The Divided Intelligentsia 7
    Emotion and Intellect 16
    The Post-Mao Generation and the Problem
        of Memory Politics 26
    Overview of the Chapters 34

PART I: EMOTION AS ETHICAL REASONING

1. Pleasure and Guilt: Reason and Emotion
in the Age of New Enlightenment 45
    Enlightened Sentiments 48
    Reason and This-Worldly Pleasure 53
    Emotion and Other-Worldly Guilt 64
    The Convergence of Pleasure and Guilt 76

2. The Liberal Imagination: The Politics of Mourning
in the "Chen Yinke Fever" 80
    The Pathos of Chinese Liberalism 84
    A Cultural Loyalist in Despair 89
    An Apolitical Academician 101
    A Martyr of Liberalism 108
    Debating Chen Yinke's Legacy in Contemporary China 115

PART II: THE FUSION OF EMOTION AND POLITICAL VISION

3. Left Melancholy: A Dialogue between Chen Yingzhen and Wang Anyi — 125
   - Fin-de-Siècle Socialism — 127
   - The Melancholic Intellectual — 135
   - The Vanquished Left — 142
   - Utopian Verses — 147
   - A Chronicle of Revolutionary Shanghai — 150
   - Toward a Melancholic Marxism — 157

4. A Passion for God: Liu Xiaofeng and the Conservative Revolt against Modernity — 166
   - Revolution and Religion — 168
   - Early Romanticism — 178
   - From Cultural Christian to Chinese Straussian — 185
   - A Conservative Revolution — 196
   - Leap of Faith — 206

PART III: THE MANUFACTURED AFFECT

5. *China Can Say No*: Popular Nationalism and the Spirit of *Ressentiment* — 211
   - The Business of Nationalism — 224
   - The Psychology of *Ressentiment* — 230
   - Divided Reception — 240

   Epilogue: Searching for the Chinese Dream — 250
   - The Problem of Ideological Polarization in the Post-Mao Era — 253
   - A Passion for God — 256
   - Between Melancholy and Nostalgia — 260
   - The Pathos of Liberalism — 265
   - From *Ressentiment* to Righteous Anger — 270

Bibliography — 277

Index — 313

Illustrations

1	Li Zehou and Liu Zaifu in Boulder, Colorado, 2018	67
2	The first edition of *An Extended Biography of Liu Rushi* (1980)	96
3	The former residence of Chen Yinke on the southern campus of Sun Yat-Sen University, Guangzhou	100
4	The tomb of Chen Yinke and Tang Yun at Mount Lu Botanical Garden in Jiujiang	116
5	Chen Yingzhen and Wang Anyi at the 1983 Iowa Writing Program	149
6	Front covers of the *Say No* series	214
7	A poster for *Fragrant Youth* (2017) featuring the ballet dancers of Mao's revolutionary art troupe	262
8	The final duel between "Big Daddy" and Leng Feng in *Wolf Warrior 2* (2017)	273

Acknowledgments

This book has been a long time in the making. A prototype was accepted by the Department of East Asian Languages and Civilizations at Harvard University as a PhD dissertation, but its origins can be traced back to my undergraduate years in Guangzhou. Between 2008 and 2012, I was a literature major at Sun Yat-Sen University, where I first began to explore the vehement public intellectual debate about the Mao era. In the academic quarters at the time, there was no open rebellion but instead widespread discontent with the political quietism of Chinese intellectuals, a disquiet that prevailed among many veteran scholars for whom humanities meant more than professional training. As an obscure young man from a modest background, I felt myself to be an outsider in the tension-ridden academia—part neither of the establishment nor of a youth rebellion. Yet even though I stayed outside, the stories and tales about the lives of the defiant few intrigued me, and the polarized debate surrounding the Chinese New Left captivated my mind. The general mood of frustration only added to the nostalgia for the past, especially the 1980s New Enlightenment. I was struck by how so many senior intellectuals remained so "eighties": their hopes, fears, desires, and tastes were deeply rooted in the golden years of the Chinese humanists, whose mentality did not survive 1989 and the subsequent market reform.

During the years of reading and researching, my initial puzzle blossomed into a full-fledged book project. I owe a great debt of gratitude to many colleagues, friends, teachers, and institutions who have shaped this long intellectual journey. At Harvard, my deep gratitude goes to David Der-wei Wang, who has given me his unwavering support through every step of my professional development, from writing grant proposals to surviving the job market. My decision to venture into the study of affect and emotion was no doubt influenced by the important bond between teacher and student: Professor Wang's scholarship on modern Chinese lyricism remains a great source of inspiration. I also thank Elizabeth J. Perry, who introduced me into the field of Chinese politics and invited me to work on a collaborative research project on the Christian colleges of republican China. Professor Perry's exploration of China's revolutionary tradition has been indispensable for my engagement with the intellectual politics of the People's Republic of China (PRC). I am also very grateful for the privilege to study with Jie Li, whose erudite learning in Chinese memory politics has had a direct impact on my work. Under her relentless questioning, I abandoned undefendable theoretical premises one by one, and developed my own authorial voice and theoretical position. Needless to say, I am indebted to Marshall Brown, who took me out to explore New England, edited my writing countless times, and watched my dissertation grow from a shaky seminar paper to a three-hundred-page manuscript. Still, I frequently feel guilty of failing to live up to his standard of good expository writing: simple, informative, and interesting. I was also very fortunate to have conversations with Wai-yee Li, who kindly read my chapters and shared her extensive knowledge of Chen Yinke and Ming loyalism with me. Peter E. Gordon's class on modern European intellectual history also provided me with a comparative lens to examine Chinese social and political thought.

A sustaining network of peers and friends played an essential role during my academic sojourn on the East Coast. Each of my classmates broadened my intellectual horizon with their passion and curiosity: Lei Ying, with her critical rigor and erudite knowledge of Buddhism and late Qing intellectual trends, constantly encouraged me to engage the realm of ideas; Tan Li Wen Jessica's work on Nanyang (Southeast Asian) writers inspired me to examine Sinophone literary productions outside mainland China; Kyle Shernuk and Peng Hai shaped my interest in questions of ethnicity and indigeneity; I benefited immensely from illuminating exchanges with Jannis Jizhou Chen and Dingru Huang on posthumanism and ecocriticism, and with Dylan Suher, Huanruo Wang, and Yedong Chen on Chinese media. My graduate school years were also enriched by the company and friendship of other extraordinary peers, including Jing Cai, Lingjia Xu, Lu Kou, Feiran Du,

Huijun Mai, Mengdie Zhao, Yang Hua, Yi Yang, Menglan Chen, Ming Tak Ted Hui, Fangdai Chen, Mengze Yao, Min Qiao, and many others.

I am further beholden to many mentors and friends who have supported me during my formative years. At Sun Yat-Sen University, my amorphous interests took shape under the caring and inspiring mentoring of Fan Dai, who encouraged me to pursue an academic career. Wenping Gao, Yuyu Liu, Jiaxiang He, Yanni Lei, and Hui Zhou introduced me into the rich tradition of anglophone literary and critical theory, a rigorous training that has remained with me to this day. At the University of Washington (UW), Eva Cherniavsky was a continuous source of scholarly advice and inspiration. In her seminar on critical theory, she patiently helped me navigate notoriously abstruse texts by Derrida, Lacan, and Foucault and spent time reading and commenting on many of my ideas and writings. I survived Marshall Brown's class on *The Phenomenology of Spirit*, where he taught me to appreciate the multiplicities of the Hegelian thinking that have been politicized by his French interpreters. I enjoyed my independent study with Yomi Braester, as we looked into the cultural and intellectual dynamics of the early reform era. This book would not have come together had Yomi not reminded me, more than once, that thoughts and ideas can be approached through the lens of literature and film. I also benefited immensely from the graduate student community at UW. Conversations with Xiao Ma, Xiaonan Wang, Belinda Q. He, Xiaoshun Zeng, Shuxuan Zhou, Katherine Morrow, and many others have greatly shaped my scholarly pursuit. In addition, I am indebted to my roommate Thomas Joseph (TJ) Walker, who spent time reading and commenting on my paper drafts. Kayaking with TJ in Union Bay is one of the best memories of my days in Seattle.

Research for this project was made possible by a number of institutions that provided me with a platform to present my work in progress. These include the Harvard Yenching Institute, the Fairbank Center for Chinese Studies, the Chiang Ching-kuo Foundation for International Scholarly Exchange, Boston University, Hong Kong University of Science and Technology, National University of Singapore, Yale-NUS College, Nankai University, Zhejiang University, and many others. The workshops, conferences, and panels that I organized or attended have pushed me to repeatedly revise and refine my arguments. In March 2017, with the support of the Harvard Yenching Institute and the Chiang Ching-kuo Foundation, David Wang and I organized an international conference titled "Rethinking Intellectual Currents in Contemporary China" at Harvard. I am grateful to Chan Koonchung, Ge Zhaoguang, Qian Yongxiang, Wang Fan-sen, Wang Hui, and Zhou Lian, whose critical commitment to Chinese intellectual history inspired me to join their rank. At the 2018 Association for Asian Studies (AAS) Annual Conference, I organized a panel titled "In Search of Autonomy: Chinese Intellectuals between Politics and Scholarship." I thank the chair, discussants, participants, and audience for their invaluable feedback: Charles Laughlin, Josephine Chiu-Duke, Michael Duke, Sebastian Veg, Dongxian Jiang, and Mengze Yao, among others. Josephine, in particular, has supported me over the long course of writing. I also wish to acknowledge that it was through the 2019 AAS Annual Conference panel I organized with Po-hsi Chen, "Left-Wing Melancholia in Asian History, Culture, and Literature," that my chapter 3 took its initial shape. The criticisms and suggestions made by Paul G. Pickowicz, Paola Iovene, Po-hsi, and Xiaolu Ma substantially helped me hone my analysis. I would also like to extend my deep gratitude to Jianmei Liu for inviting me to present my work at the Hong Kong University of Science and Technology (HKUST) in 2019. Many stimulating conversations with scholars at HKUST, especially Shengqing Wu, Min Qiao, Song Han, and Yijiao Guo, significantly expanded my critical horizons.

This book could not have been completed without generous help from my colleagues and students at the National University of Singapore (NUS). I feel extremely fortunate to be able to start my career at the Department of Chinese Studies at NUS, a collegial, culturally diverse, and intellectually rich environment. Kenneth Dean, Chang Woei Ong, Khee Heong Koh, Sai-Shing Yung, Sin Kiong Wong, and others have offered unstinting support for my professional development. No junior faculty can ask for a better mentor than Lanjun Xu, who tailored my research proposals, offered solid advice, and introduced me to many other aspiring scholars in the larger NUS community. I also appreciate the company of talented peers: Bei Hu, Cheow Thia Chan, Jack Meng-Tat Chia, Ying-kit Chan, Chen Liu, Ruiqing Shen, Charles Kian Hoe Wong, Yan Yang, Yanjie Huang, and many others. I also want to express my appreciation to Susan Ang Wan-Ling, who provided invaluable support for my teaching. Meanwhile, I taught a gradate seminar and two undergraduate courses on modern Chinese literature and culture, and enjoyed the opportunities to interact with many students. I want to thank all my students, particularly my PhD advisee Xinran Wang, a specialist on food culture, for sharpening my thinking.

The publication of this work was facilitated by a number of research grants, including the Harvard University GSAS Dissertation Completion Fellowship, the GSAS Merit and Term-Time Research Fellowship, the GSAS Summer Support Initiative, the Fairbank Center Summer Research Fund, the Yun-Cheng Sa Memorial Fellowship, the China Times Cultural Foundation Young Scholar Award, and the NUS Faculty of Arts and Social Sciences Start-Up Fund. Meanwhile, most of the materials discussed in this book were obtained through hours spent at libraries across the world, especially the Harvard-Yenching Library, the Tateuchi East Asia Library at the University of Washington, the East Asian Library at Princeton University, the McKeldin Library at the University of Maryland, the Wan Boo Sow Chinese Library at NUS, the Lee Shau Kee Library at HKUST, the Library of Congress, the National Archives, and the National Library of China, among others. I thank the library staff for providing me with access to archives and digital databases at their respective institutions.

From manuscript to publication, my heartfelt thanks go to Bob Graham, Kristen Wanner, and Qin Higley at the Harvard University Asia Center for their faith in the value of my scholarship, as well as to the three anonymous readers, whose critical scrutiny helped improved my argument in every way. I extend special thanks to Jianmei Liu, Lei Ying, and Chang Woei Ong for their invaluable feedback in the last stage of my revision.

No words can ever adequately express my gratitude for my family members for their love and support. Special thanks are due to my parents, who worried that I would never secure an "iron rice bowl" for my seemingly idiosyncratic pursuit. This book is also dedicated to my grandfather Liu Xinda 劉欣大 (1934–2017), an ardent literary critic whose admiration for Hu Feng 胡風 (1902–1985) cost him twenty years in the impoverished countryside of Jiangxi.

Introduction

Emotions after Revolution

On the night of May 14, 1989, twelve prominent Chinese intellectuals arrived at Tiananmen Square, a place filled with more than three hundred thousand protestors.[1] Just one day earlier, student agitators in Beijing had started a hunger strike following a series of failed negotiations with the Chinese government. To avoid the continued escalation of the conflict, moderate student leaders invited the "teachers" of the democratic movement to speak directly to the hunger strikers. As a group, these thinkers—writers, literary critics, philosophers, historians, and political scientists—first achieved public fame in the 1980s as critics of high socialism. The catastrophic failure of the Cultural Revolution brought to power a revisionist leadership in 1978 that claimed it would abandon the doctrines of Maoism in search of a human face of socialism. From the crucible of this political transition, a cultural renaissance was born. The next decade became the golden era for the cultural vanguard of the post-Mao generation. Aided by a general enthusiasm for high culture, the liberalization of the ideological sphere, and the intellectuals' strategic efforts to gain access to the

---

1. Dingxin Zhao, *The Power of Tiananmen*, 167.

reform-minded party patrons, those men of belles lettres utilized state-sponsored literary journals, television channels, and public forums to articulate their vision of enlightenment. The Chinese intelligentsia (*zhishifenzi* 知識分子), a moral and political ideal that had crystallized in the May Fourth Movement of 1919, was not a distinct social group with definable characters. Rather, those who identified themselves as the transmitters of culture and ideas imagined the intellectual as the guardian of public good and the opponent of political tyranny. Whereas the Maoist regime arrested, exiled, and silenced millions of educated professionals—those judged by Mao as potentially subversive social elements—Deng Xiaoping's "rehabilitation policy" (*pingfan zhengce* 平反政策) sought to incorporate the alienated cultural elite into the reformist state. Although Deng initially hoped that intellectuals would become partners and advisors to his "reform and opening-up" (*gaige kaifang* 改革開放) program, the Chinese intelligentsia explicitly called for a radical break with China's revolutionary tradition. Hence, the 1989 Beijing student movement was partly inspired by their iconoclastic teaching.

However, the high-flown proposal for a new enlightenment that carried powerful appeal in the discursive battles against the ruling ideology yielded quite different results on the night of May 14. In the wake of the growing antagonism between the demonstrators and the party hard-liners, these twelve intellectuals were invited to the broadcasting center in Tiananmen Square to persuade the students to end their strike and move out of the square. Earlier in the day, the much-anticipated dialogue between government officials and student leaders had ended in chaos, causing confusion and anger among the strikers. Acting as mediators, the intellectuals delivered a statement: "Our Urgent Appeal Regarding the Current Situation" (*women dui jintian jushi de jinji huyu* 我們對今天局勢的緊急呼籲), a mild proposal pleading for "calm rationality" as a corrective to "radicalism and extremism."[2] To their surprise, the students were outraged. Activists were offended by the paternalistic tone of those scholars who "live on the air." Worse, the demeanor of sober reason and the call for incremental

---

2. Dai Qing, "Yetan chunxia zhijiao."

reform may have greatly alienated the hunger-strikers, who were in the unruly affective states of anxiety and fear.[3] In the end, it was the emotionally intense—if not hysterical—speeches made by a radical student activist, Chai Ling (1966–), that moved her followers to tears and action.[4] Chai eulogized the destructive aesthetics of self-willed hunger as the assertion of one's moral and political rectitude against the state, whose inaction signaled "lack of conscience" and "heartlessness."[5] She frequently evoked excessive, rancorous, and apocalyptic tropes of sacrifice and bloodshed—a colorful language that evoked the ideological extremism of Maoist propaganda—to galvanize support for a head-on confrontation. Moreover, Chai interrupted the peaceful conversation between the scholars and the crowd by broadcasting a "hunger strike declaration," instantly fueling the students' moral indignation against the conciliatory stance of the intellectuals. In the end, the twelve scholars had to leave the square, but the protestors did not withdraw. This dramatic event, along with the subsequent crackdown, signified the end of the New Enlightenment movement.

The incident, in capsule form, raises many of the questions explored in this book, which centers on the role of political emotions in the post-Mao cultural and intellectual dynamics. How does emotion—as a constellation of affective intensities, moral sentiments, and political judgments—factor in the post-Mao political debates about China's revolutionary past? In the 1980s, reformist thinkers repeatedly chastised the Maoist regime for inflaming a host of "vehement passions"[6]—hate, fear, and shame—in the service of ideological extremism, resulting in

---

3. Student leaders felt betrayed by the intellectuals who played the role of mediators rather than standing firmly with the student demonstrators. See Lu Li, *Moving the Mountain*, 138, quoted in Dingxin Zhao, *The Power of Tiananmen*, 169.

4. Multiple accounts portrayed Chai Ling as an emotionally intense leader who exerted powerful influence over the student demonstrators throughout the entire movement. Chai's adamant refusal to leave the square despite mounting tensions has been the subject of heated debates. For analyses of Chai's role in the hunger strike, see Calhoun, *Neither Gods nor Emperor*, 61–62; Dingxin Zhao, *The Power of Tiananmen*, 267–96; for Chai's account, see Chai, *A Heart for Freedom*.

5. Chai, "Interview at Tiananmen Square with Chai Ling."

6. Philip Fisher argues that passion breaks off the ordinary flow of experience and creates a state of exception. I use Fisher's definition to describe the aesthetic, emotive, and affective underpinning of Mao's revolutionary mandate that draws deep

the breakdown of basic ethical norms during the Cultural Revolution. Thus, to humanize socialism, they consider it necessary to create new emotional norms—empathy, compassion, and guilt—that could fundamentally transform the moral and affective terrain of a paralyzed society steeped for thirty years in the emotive mode of class hatred. Yet too often, hopes to cultivate stable and democratic emotional norms evaporated in the resurgence of Maoist symbols, rituals, and languages that came to infect the opponents of ideological extremism. The troubling resemblance was evident in the radical student leaders' constant invocations of "the martyr of democracy," culminating in Chai Ling's call to "awaken the Chinese people with blood and death."[7] How, then, to explain the failure of the "sentimental education" envisioned by the enlightened thinkers?

To answer these questions, *Sentimental Republic* looks beyond the 1980s New Enlightenment and puzzles through a surge of emotionally charged debates about red legacies—the ideals and memories of the Mao era—from the late 1970s into the twentieth-first century. It analyzes how post-Mao intellectuals, literati, and writers debated the remainder and reminder of China's revolutionary past in light of its postsocialist transition. Throughout this book, "Mao's revolution" serves as a generic term to designate a constellation of sociopolitical events, values, and memories shaped by Mao's radical theory and practice of socialist utopianism. In historical terms, it refers to a wellspring of mass movements, political campaigns, and utopian social engineering from the founding of the People's Republic of China (PRC) to the Cultural Revolution; in political terms, it points toward Mao's millenarian vision of "permanent revolution" that vowed to eliminate class distinctions, wage war against bureaucratic privileges, and celebrate violent, populist revolt against all forms of social inequalities; in cultural-intellectual terms, it describes the rustication of the educated elite, the cultivation of proletarian consciousness, and radical

---

and intrinsic connections between extreme sentiments and socialist utopianism. See Fisher, *The Vehement Passions*, 1–11.

7. Geremie Barmé argues that Chai's rhetoric bears the brunt of the totalitarian language deployed by the Maoist propaganda in the Cultural Revolution. See Barmé, *In the Red*, 331–33.

experiments in education and cultural production. Although the utopian ideal of revolution had lost much of its erstwhile prestige in the post-Mao era, the magnitude of chaos, violence, passion, and destruction was such that disputing its meaning remains at the center of contemporary Chinese cultural and intellectual life.

Admittedly, to claim that the post-Mao intelligentsia remained haunted by the specters of revolution might initially sound anticlimactic. Since the 1980s, the proposition that China exhibited a deliberate turn away from its socialist past toward revisionism, capitalism, or pragmatic nationalism has become almost a cliché. In the eyes of many, Deng Xiaoping's 1981 "Resolution on Certain Questions in the History of our Party since the Founding of the PRC" (*guanyu jianguo yilai dang de ruogan lishiwenti de jueyi* 關於建國以來黨的若干歷史問題的決議) attempted to impose a historical verdict on the country's unsettling past so as to move beyond the horizon of revolution.[8] With the accelerating pace of market reforms, clamorous voices emerged in the early 1990s to unmake the revolutionary mentality in favor of conservative, realistic, and nationalistic alternatives. On the whole, political thinkers and cultural critics were drawn increasingly away from the Maoist ideal and toward indefinite, but less radical, solutions to Chinese history and politics.

Yet, after decades of social transformation, the vanished revolutionary past continues to haunt contemporary Chinese cultural politics. The Great Helmsman's enshrined body, embalmed and placed into a crystal coffin, is still being displayed for public veneration inside the Chairman Mao Memorial Hall at the heart of Tiananmen Square. Compared to the ideological laxity of the Jiang Zemin presidency (1993–2003), the Hu–Wen Administration (2002–2012) adopted a left-leaning and populist approach to address the mounting social crisis caused by Jiang's coastal-focused reforms, initiating a wave of state propaganda to reassert the spectacular achievements of the Chinese

---

8. The resolution tackles Mao's controversial legacy by separating Mao's contributions—as the founder of the Chinese Revolution—from his "erroneous" ultraleftism in the Cultural Revolution. For a discussion of the reconfiguration of Maoism in official historiography, see Dirlik, "Mao Zedong in Contemporary Chinese Official Discourse and History."

Communist Revolution.⁹ President Xi Jinping's new orthodoxy, offered under the motto "the two thirty years should not negate each other," further stressed the continuity between the Maoist model of revolution and the Dengist market reform.¹⁰ Within the orbit of elite politics, Maoist ideals retained their popularity partly as a powerful alternative to global capitalism and a self-confident assertion of China's unique path of modernization—whether labeled "anti-modern modernity"¹¹ (*fanxiandai de xiandaixing* 反現代的現代性) or "socialism with Chinese characteristics." For instance, in the protracted and bitter discussion surrounding the emergence of the Chinese New Left in 1997, the prominent PRC intellectual historian Wang Hui 汪暉 (1959–) published an extravaganza of essays to expound the emancipatory potential of Maoist mass politics, which provoked virulent infighting for the next decade between the Left and the liberal factions.¹² In 2005, the literary establishment was also treated to a polemical debate about Yan Lianke's 閻連科 (1958–) satirical novella *Serve the People* (*Wei renmin fuwu* 為人民服務), which offered a scandalous depiction of an adulterous affair at the height of the Cultural Revolution between a low-ranking army soldier and the beautiful wife of his general.¹³ Yan's sacrilegious attempt to turn Mao's "holy revolution" into a pornographic romance drew the ire of orthodox socialist realist writers, who were determined the defend the sacred aura of Mao's most memorable slogan. Both incidents signaled the unsettling effects of the Maoist ideals and memories on the Chinese present.

Ideological polarization was also evident in the public memory debates. From the 2000s onward, the country was engulfed in a succession of heated discussions about red legacies, from the elegiac remembrances of socialist egalitarianism to the anguished denunciations of Maoist violence. In the so-called Gao Village incident of 2001, for

---

9. Cheng Chen, *The Return of Ideology*, 96–125.
10. See Weigelin-Schwiedrzik and Cui, "Whodunnit? Memory and Politics before the 50th Anniversary of the Cultural Revolution."
11. For an account of the anti-modern aspect of Chinese socialist modernity, see Wang Hui, "Contemporary Chinese Thought and the Question of Modernity"; for an exposition, see Murthy, "Modernity against Modernity."
12. Wang Hui, *The End of the Revolution*.
13. For an analysis, see David Wang, "Red Legacies in Fiction."

example, the Australian Sinologist Gao Mobo (1952–) published a rosy account of how the Gao villagers of Jiangxi Province enjoyed economic security and cultural dignity in the Cultural Revolution, offering a trenchant critique of the liberals' exclusive focus on elite memory.[14] Whereas left-leaning historians mobilized Gao's subaltern perspective to reverse the liberal verdict on the catastrophic impact that Mao's massive political campaigns had on rural areas, indignant liberals launched a national media campaign to boycott Gao's book and condemn his leftist acolytes for reviving the "poisonous legacy of the Cultural Revolution" (*wenge yidu* 文革遺毒).[15] The peculiar dynamics of public-cum-ideological scandal making thrived in the age of social media. In 2014, when the former Red Guard celebrity Song Binbin 宋彬彬 (1949–2024) openly apologized for having participated in the killing of her deputy principal Bian Zhongyun 卞仲耘 (1916–1966) in the Beijing Red Guard movement, Chinese netizens engaged in passionate debates about the unresolved conflict and hatred rooted in the past. Not surprisingly, the public remorse sparked an emotional backlash from the Maoists, who claimed that revolutionary justice is beyond the scope of fragile humanism. These cases were not isolated events. Instead, the proliferation of controversies that appeared regularly in public reflects the country's schizophrenic relationship to its revolutionary past.

The Divided Intelligentsia

Sentimental Republic chronicles the polarized reactions to the question of a derailed socialist revolution at the center of the post-Mao intellectual life. Understanding political ideas as a fusion of rational argumentation and emotive utterance, it follows a group of liberal, Left, conservative, and nationalist scholars and writers who actively participated in acrimonious struggles about the meaning of the past. Should the Chinese condemn revolutionary violence to bid farewell to socialism? Or would the return of revolution provoke alternative visions of China's future path? Drawing on genres ranging across

14. Gao, "Shuxie lishi: *Gaojiacun*."
15. Xu, Dang, and Jiao, "Zhiyi *Gaojiacun*."

fiction, poetry, memoir, and philosophical discourse, *Sentimental Republic* probes the nexus of literature, thought, and memory, bringing to light the dynamic moral sentiments and emotional excess that structured intellectual discussions and literary representations of the Mao era. Even though persecution and exile have fueled liberal indignation against the atrocities of the Cultural Revolution, the growing grievance at market reforms has nourished a lingering melancholy for the unrealized ideals of socialism. The conservatives' resentment against "modern nihilism," on the other hand, cultivated a quasi-religious yearning for the return of the Maoist sublime. Finally, popular nationalists drew on the narrative of China's victimization by Western imperialism to incite vociferous expressions of patriotic ire. By analyzing how rival memory projects stirred up melancholy, guilt, anger, and resentment, I argue that the polemics surrounding the country's past cannot be properly understood without reading for the emotional trajectories of the post-Mao intelligentsia.

To illustrate the key role of emotion in elite memory politics, it is useful to provide an overview of the historical formation of these four major intellectual clusters in the post-Mao era: the Left, liberals, conservatives, and nationalists.[16] The Maoist regime orchestrated a succession of political campaigns against the Chinese intelligentsia, beginning in 1951 with the Thought Reform (*Sixiang gaizao yundong* 思想改造運動), followed by the 1957 Anti-Rightist Campaign (*Fanyou yundong* 反右運動), and culminating in the Cultural Revolution. The experience

---

16. This book typologizes major post-Mao intellectual camps into a quadruple ideological matrix based on their views on Mao's revolutionary legacy. I model this typology on several pioneering works. Cheek, Ownby, and Fogel divide Chinese intellectuals among three main ideologies: liberalism, leftism, and New Confucianism; using similar categories, Xu Jilin conceptualizes these ideologies based on their views on the 1980s enlightenment tradition, which generates a "liberal-left-conservative" triangular matrix; Fewsmith pits the "enlightenment intellectuals" against advocates of neoconservatism, neostatism, and popular nationalism; Veg and He Li propose a slightly different division (the Left, social democrats, liberals, and advocates of neo-authoritarianism); Ma Licheng conducts an exhaustive analysis of eight social thoughts in contemporary China. See Cheek, Ownby, and Fogel, *Voices from the Chinese Century*; Xu Jilin, *Dangdai Zhongguo de qimeng yu fanqimeng*; Fewsmith, *China since Tiananmen*, 83–162; Veg, "The Rise of China's Statist Intellectuals," 24; He Li, *Political Thought and China's Transformation*; Ma Licheng, *Dangdai Zhongguo bazhong shehui sichao*.

of rampant violence, coerced labor, and mass trials left a deep imprint upon many surviving writers and intellectuals, which in turn gave rise to a liberal consensus in the late 1970s to condemn Mao's ultraleftist revolutionary practices as a series of totalitarian crimes.[17] Throughout the 1980s, Deng Xiaoping's reform unleashed the social and cultural imaginary, giving rise to a remarkably diverse and cosmopolitan atmosphere punctuated by "the debate on humanism," "the high-culture fever," and multifarious practices in modernist literature and film. In the wake of the 1989 Tiananmen crackdown, however, intellectual discourse underwent a dramatic transformation from the consensus politics of the liberal reform to a renewed emphasis on the indigenous sources of China's modernization. From the early 1990s onward, the Chinese Communist Party (CCP) shied away from political reforms, installed a Patriotic Education Campaign, and deployed authoritarian governance to speed up economic growth. In academia, the nascent New Left, guided by a distaste for the widespread inequality and corruption brought by neoliberal capitalism, positioned themselves as defenders of workers and peasants through skillful deployment of Maoist and neo-Marxist theories.[18] On the Right, conservatism emerged

---

17. The use of the term "liberal" in the Chinese context needs further qualification. It covers a wide range of intellectual currents, from the liberal Marxists of the 1980s (who opposed ultra-leftism and favored a humanist version of reformist socialism) to the neoliberals of the 1990s (who believed that a radical market reform would necessarily enhance political rights). Yet, I suggest in chapters 1 and 2 that a common thread that runs through these heterogeneous intellectual dynamics is the call for the condemnation of Mao's revolutionary legacy in particular and the abandonment of radical approaches to Chinese history and politics in general.

18. The Chinese New Left differs greatly from its Western counterpart. In the Euro-American context, the Left serves as a generic name for the succession of political movements since the French Revolution that have placed social equality at the center of their agenda. Although the commonalities linking the Chinese Left and their Western contemporaries (e.g., anti-capitalist critiques) might satisfy Wittgenstein's notion of "family resemblance," left-wing intellectuals in the RPC are notable for their ideological affinity with the party establishment. In general, the Old Left (*lao zuopai* 老左派) refers to China's "establishment intellectuals" who adhered to orthodox Marxism; by contrast, the New Left (*xin zuopai* 新左派) used Western critical theory (e.g., neo-Marxism, postmodernism, and postcolonialism) to criticize China's market reform. Both embraced state socialism (or the "China model") as an alternative to neoliberal capitalism. In addition, these political standpoints were

as a powerful retort to the quixotic fantasy of an overly rational enlightenment. Composed of Confucian revivalists, cultural nationalists, and proponents of realpolitik, this group emphasized the continuity of China's "organic" civilizational tradition against the alien and decadent ideologies of the West.[19] Beyond the elitist cultural circles, popular nationalists looked out at the post–Cold War international order through painful memories of China's "hundred years of humiliations" (*bainian guochi* 百年國恥). This new nationalism pitted itself against liberal cosmopolitanism, eschewed democratic reform, and valorized assertive patriotism as the glue binding the nation together.[20]

As we can see, the post-Mao intellectual debate was severely polarized: each political camp held drastically different, if not diametrically opposed, views of Mao's revolution and its lessons for China's postsocialist transition. Whereas leftist intellectuals struggled to unveil the emancipatory potential of Mao's mass democracy against neoliberal governance, (neo)liberals argued that the failure to purge Mao's

---

always the result of ideological battles. For instance, the term "New Left" was coined by its liberal detractors, who saw no fundamental difference between die-hard Maoists and neoleftist acolytes. See Xudong Zhang, *Postsocialism and Cultural Politics*, 52–62; also see Joseph, *The Critique of Ultra-Leftism in China*.

19. The term "conservatism" has been used to describe multiple intellectual trends throughout twentieth-century China, from the ascendance of right-wing movements under Chiang Kai-shek's rule to the interplay between new authoritarianism and cultural conservative redux in the post-Tiananmen era. I acknowledge the malleable and versatile nature of Chinese conservatism but emphasize that the rejection of secular modernity lies at the heart of the conservative revival in contemporary China. For conservatism in the republican era, see Fung, *The Intellectual Foundations of Chinese Modernity*, 61–95; Tsui, *China's Conservative Revolution*.

20. Extant typologies tend to exclude nationalism for various reasons. Contemporary Chinese nationalism is either treated as an overarching consensus among major intellectual camps across the ideological spectrum or dismissed for its lack of theoretical sophistication and coherent political vision. Such understanding is derived mostly from the conventional literary-historical studies of China's cultural elite that prioritize the realm of high-minded ideals. Meanwhile, recent scholarship has drawn inexorably toward the popular circulation and mass reception of ideas in the post-Tiananmen public space. As chapter 5 demonstrates, even though Chinese nationalism did not possess the utopian, millenarian vision as envisioned in other major ideologies, it is well represented among the commercial media, state propaganda, and, more generally, grassroots thinkers and activists.

legacy—a series of "totalitarian crimes"—has incurred a "return of the repressed."[21] Although conservatives were not infatuated with Communist anti-traditionalism, they sought to remold Mao's socialist legacy as an artificial placeholder for a continuous Confucian-meritocratic tradition. Popular nationalists, meanwhile, deliberately downplayed the internationalist dimensions of proletarian revolution and identified Mao's desire for national rejuvenation as the exclusive core of his revolutionary saga.

My analysis has been enabled, first and foremost, by intellectual historians who provide a wide range of critical perspectives on the post-Mao ideological polarization. In view of the highly contested memory projects inherent in Chinese intellectual debate, many scholars attribute the source of controversies to the fundamentally different values and political beliefs held by divergent intellectual factions. Both Zhang Xudong and Xu Jilin have noted that the intellectual debate of the 1990s revolved around the "binary opposites between liberty and equality": whereas the liberals hoped to advance free-market capitalism and the rule of law to secure civil liberty, the Left urged the party-state to provide more welfare and social protection to honor the principle of socialist egalitarianism.[22] Cultural and political conservatives, by contrast, distinguished themselves from both the liberals and the Left by their desire to restore a traditionalistic social order based on authority, hierarchy, elitism, and heritage. Noting the sharp rightward turn of the post-Tiananmen intelligentsia, Joseph Fewsmith, Els van Dongen, Peter Moody, Yingjie Guo, and John Makeham have identified a diverse set of realistic, neo-authoritarian, and Confucian revivalist political imaginaries that have underpinned the conservative animus against modernity.[23] Chinese nationalists, meanwhile, shared the conservative

21. Xudong Zhang, *Postsocialism and Cultural Politics*, 52–88.
22. Xudong Zhang, *Postsocialism and Cultural Politics*, 52; Xu Jilin, *Dangdai Zhongguo de qimeng yu fanqimeng*, 16–27.
23. Extant scholarship makes a salient distinction between political conservatism (e.g., the advocates of an authoritarian and pragmatic approach to governance) and cultural conservatism (e.g., Confucian revivalists) in the post-Tiananmen era. Yet as Els van Dongen argues, the distinction overlooks the fact that in reality the two trends "coexisted as products of the changing domestic and international environments" (*Realistic Revolution*, 9). Chapter 4 demonstrates that some cultural conservatives

hostility to liberal democracy but prioritized nation rather than tradition as their benchmark. Harking back to a lineage of statist thinking in China, which Peter Zarrow has aptly described as "the view that the state . . . is the ultimate locus of sovereignty, self-legitimating, and the highest source of good," nationalists insisted with escalating vehemence that the "Chinese nation" (*Zhonghua minzu* 中華民族), not a particular political party or social class, was the rightful agent of history.[24]

This book builds upon these provocative analyses that have understood post-Mao intellectual polemics as a manifestation of divergent ideas and ideologies. Yet one can argue that, insofar as intellectual historians are primarily concerned with the life of ideas—that is, the deployment, transformation, and ramification of fundamental concepts[25]—it risks reading the contemporary Chinese mindscape into abstract discourses, ideologies, and worldviews. By separating volatile sentiments, lived experience, and personal memories from codified beliefs and thoughts, the rationalistic-normative approach fails to clarify why and how the supposedly rational debate surrounding Mao's revolutionary legacy has always led to polarized positions and emotional reactions. In the critical discussion of the liberal-versus-Left polemics, for instance, scholars focus on how the two camps mobilized different Western theoretical discourses ranging from neoliberal economics to post-Marxism to serve their political agendas.[26] But by taking the rhetoric of the debates at face value, this reading has reduced the debate into stark polarities: liberty versus equality, modern versus anti-modern, and forgetting versus remembering. In styling the liberal

---

were equally drawn to authoritarian politics. For political conservatism, see Fewsmith, *China since Tiananmen*, 83–112; for Confucian revival and cultural conservatism, see Makeham, *Lost Soul*; Moody, *Conservative Thought in Contemporary China*; Yingjie Guo, *Cultural Nationalism in Contemporary China*.

24. Zarrow, *After Empire*, 4; for a critical analysis of contemporary Chinese statist thinking, see Veg, "The Rise of China's Statist Intellectuals."

25. This mode of inquiry, which developed in dialogue with Reinhart Koselleck's *Begriffsgeschichte* (conceptual history) and the contextualism of the Cambridge School, focuses on how Chinese cultural and political elites articulated, modified, and challenged certain key concepts during a particular period of time. For methodological discussions of conceptual history in the Chinese context, see Carrai, *Sovereignty in China*, 9–14; Van Dongen, *Realistic Revolution*.

26. Xu Jilin, *Dangdai Zhongguo de qimeng yu fanqimeng*, 65–128.

polemics as a pale copy of Isaiah Berlin and the leftist provocation as an invocation of the Frankfurt School, the conceptual analysis has unmoored intellectual polemics from specific historical referents and emotional repertoire, simplified the debate into the clash of political doctrines, and reified ideas as timeless standards by which to measure their practitioners.

Although I cannot pretend to do justice to the rich research available on post-Mao intellectual history, most specialists would agree that, with a few notable exceptions, these works predominantly focus on the rational ideas and political arguments of intellectuals.[27] To be sure, the disagreement between the liberals and the Left was irreducibly ideological, but it was also a vehement disagreement driven by memories, passions, and convictions. The enthusiastic readers of Chen Yinke 陳寅恪 (1890–1969) and Gu Zhun 顧准 (1915–1974) have been drawn not only to their understanding of freedom but also to their moral indignation and political defiance—and, to a large extent, to the turbulent life and tragic fate of the "republican-period intellectuals" (*minguo zhishifenzi* 民國知識分子) under Mao's socialist campaigns. The forces driving the liberals' attachment to Berlin's "negative liberty" were never purely intellectual, but rather were intertwined with moral tales, painful memories, and political desires. Likewise, Wang Hui's quest for the emancipatory potential of Maoism derived as much from neoleftist theory as from his musings on Lu Xun's aesthetics of despair, his reflections on the pathos of fin-de-siècle socialism, and, above all, his provocative attempt to revitalize the demonic power of revolution through "downward transcendence" (*xiangxia chaoyue* 向下超越).[28] Beyond the formal debate over liberty and equality, the liberals and the Left found themselves locked in a bitter and protracted cultural war

---

27. Critical works have been produced by intellectual historians who deal explicitly with the emotional and affective aspects of Chinese intellectual debate. For instance, Gloria Davies discusses the moral obligation of "worrying about China" that has consistently underpinned modern and contemporary Chinese intellectual discourse; Hung-yok Ip analyzes the emotional and aesthetic perspectives of Communist intellectuals' self-construction in the republican period. I stand on their shoulders as I carve out my own reading. See Davies, *Worrying about China*; Ip, *Intellectuals in Revolutionary China*.

28. Wang Hui, *Ah Q shengming zhong de liuge shunjian*, 79–89.

that returned again and again to the lived experience of socialism. Ultimately, the peculiar dynamics of the Chinese memory debate—a dialectic between testimony and propaganda—cannot be grasped at the level of conceptual analysis alone.

Sentimental Republic approaches the post-Mao intellectual debate as a combination of ideas and feelings, theories and experiences, emotive utterances and rational deliberations. Such an approach allows us to see how affect, rather than calm rationality alone, has strongly influenced Chinese discussion and memory of the Mao era. Understanding the Chinese memory debate as a nexus of intellectual deliberation and emotional outpouring also enables us to analyze how it was generated from within the post-Mao ideological and affective landscape rather than simply imported from Euro-American theoretical discourse. Engaging with—but looking beyond—the 1990s formation of the four major intellectual clusters, this book examines the volatile political emotions explicitly manifested or implicitly at work throughout post-Mao ideological contentions, from the liberal politics of mourning and leftist melancholy to conservative and nationalistic resentment. More specifically, I analyze four distinctive political emotions and affective structures that had underpinned Chinese cultural debate and intellectual polemics since the early reform period: first, as anguished remembrances of Maoist violence and destruction; second, as resurgences of melancholy that cleave to something positive about socialist ideals; third, as quasi-religious passion for a mythic narrative to invest post-secular society with a sacred cultural-political tradition; and fourth, as the outpouring of patriotic fever for national rejuvenation in the post–Cold War era. The overall aim is to generate a better understanding of the emotional landscape of the post-Mao intelligentsia that undergirded ideological polarizations.

In seeking to offer an alternative way of "feeling" about Chinese intellectual polemics, I realize that I may have raised thorny methodological questions. As I have located the sources of political controversy at the level of emotions, it is indeed tempting to read every idea as a manifest enactment of certain feelings. But I would like to plead innocent to two charges that I doubt a careful scrutiny would sustain. The first charge is that I have arbitrarily associated each intellectual cluster with one dominant emotion. Although the emotional landscape I discuss is inseparable from existing intellectual divisions, my point is not that the Left is necessarily melancholic or the nationalist angry. Rather, I attempt to show how the underlying structure of feeling among the post-Mao intelligentsia (which emerged prior to the 1990s ideological divisions but was articulated in rival memory projects) offers a unique prism through which to analyze the emotional tenor of Chinese intellectual debate. Second, to the critics who worry that my paradigm merely replaces existing intellectual divisions with a typology of emotions, I clarify that I do not reduce rational-political argumentation to volatile emotions and affective intensities. Nor do I seek to deconstruct or dispute the ideological premises of existing intellectual clusters, which many scholars have admirably done. Rather, my proposal is that the various -isms have not grown solely out of rational deliberation, but also as sensorial, affective, and emotive utterances deeply informed by personal desires, shared feelings, and moral sentiments. In sum, my aim is to enrich our understanding of post-Mao intellectual polemics by adding a careful engagement with the role of affect and emotion in thinking.

In other words, this book examines not emotion per se but the interaction between feeling and thinking. Instead of building a one-way street (where emotion shapes reason), I argue that a balanced approach to the study of post-Mao cultural and intellectual dynamics should mediate the reason-emotion nexus in three ways: (1) by highlighting the extensive parallelism of moral sentiments and ethical reasoning in the Chinese memory debates; (2) by exploring how a variety of feelings shape political convictions and animate personal visions across ideological spectrums; and (3) by illuminating how certain affects are mobilized by divergent agents to imbue political ideas with emotional appeal and moral authority. As I demonstrate, these three interrelated inquiries illustrate the meaning of "sentimental republic" as a dialectic between sense and sensibility, thinking and believing, and, in particular, moral passion and political strategy. But to answer these questions, we must first look beyond the reified dichotomy of reason versus emotion and revisit the Western and Chinese theoretical discourses on the intricate connection between ideas and feelings.

Emotion and Intellect

What is emotion? Why does it affect thinking? How should we read for feelings in supposedly rational arguments? First, my deployment of "affect" and "emotion" entails a critical reflection on the scholarly discussions regarding the "affective turn" across the humanities, social sciences, and cognitive and neural sciences. The term "affect theory" refers to theoretical paradigms ranging from Brian Massumi's Deleuzian-Spinozist notion of the "sensorial body" to Silvan S. Tomkins's psychological blueprint of "basic affects."[29] In contradistinction to the intellectualist mode of thinking, affect is understood as a nonintentional, physiological, and autonomic experience prior to cognitions, intentions, and political judgments.[30] The vindication of the sensorial is said to offer a corrective to the presumptively rationalistic approach to politics and aesthetics proposed by Kantian-Habermasian thinkers. Affect theorists consider how political attitudes and ideological convictions are conditioned by affective intensities and resonances rather than by rational thinking alone. But as Ruth Leys points out, although this post-Cartesian anti-intentionalism exposes the pitfalls of the dichotomous logic of reason versus emotion, it also inadvertently encourages a politically dubious conclusion that intellectual-political orientation is subject to nonsignifying and nonconscious "affective arousals."[31]

In contrast to the radical disjunction between affect and cognition proposed by today's affect theorists, cultural historians and political philosophers have sought to investigate the production of physiological feelings in relation to the social and political regulation of emotions. Utilizing J. L. Austin's notion of performatives, William Reddy argues that "emotional utterance" could be regarded as a form of "speech act" with expressive and cognitive features. In other words, an emotional expression translates and transforms a variety of "loosely connected thought material" into linguistic expressions that describe and act on the world.[32] Likewise, Martha C. Nussbaum states that emotions, as

---

29. Massumi, *Parables for the Virtual*; Tomkins, *Affect Imagery Consciousness*.
30. For a critical review, see Leys, "The Turn to Affect."
31. Leys, "The Turn to Affect," 436–37.
32. Reddy, *The Navigation of Feeling*, 94.

"upheavals of thought," are linked to social norms that are left out of what she calls "the cognitive appraisal or evaluation" of emotive response.[33] Reddy has also echoed Nussbaum's argument by exploring what he calls the "emotional regime," emphasizing the role of emotionally laden rituals and practices in undergirding various types of political systems, from totalitarian regimes to liberal democracy.[34] In his landmark study of political psychology, Theodor W. Adorno asserted that fascist propaganda encourages identification with an atavistic "authoritarian personality," characterized by traits ranging from unquestioning obedience to extreme aggression.[35] Nussbaum argues, on the contrary, that the cultivation of appropriate emotions (e.g., empathy, love, guilt) sustains and inspires strong commitment to liberal democratic values.[36] In sum, these accounts share a reliance on the notion of emotion as a system of ethical and political reasoning that mediates rational and cognitive appraisals with moral sentiments and particularistic feelings. After all, affect is the product of the social world and is not immune to political norms.

My conception of emotion mediates between these two critical explorations of affect. It reckons with the volatile and ambiguous affective intensities that have underpinned cultural debates about the experience of the Chinese Revolution, but also with the conscious mobilization of feelings and emotions toward clear-sighted, coherent, and exclusive ideological designs for China's postsocialist political order. Here, I am indebted to Anna M. Parkinson's attempt to situate emotive utterance at the threshold between fluid affective structures and socially legible emotions. For Parkinson, whereas affect is "diffuse, not yet legible, and often morally ambiguous," emotion as "congealed affect" is subject to social and political regulation.[37] Parkinson's analytical distinction between affect and emotions enables me to focus on the interaction between the physiological underpinning of affect and the "normative valence of particular emotions in their sociopolitical

---

33. Nussbaum, *Upheavals of Thought*, 4.
34. Reddy, *The Navigation of Feelings*, 63–111.
35. Adorno et al., *The Authoritarian Personality*.
36. Nussbaum, *Political Emotions*.
37. Parkinson, *An Emotional State*, 10–17.

context."³⁸ As I demonstrate, the immediate affective responses to the memories of the Mao era are ever-shifting psychological torrents with amorphous and undetermined moral and political connotations that precede political values and beliefs. Yet the outward expression of socially distinct emotions—from nostalgia and melancholy to guilt and shame—is inextricably intertwined with conscious political judgments about the ethical and moral consequences of Mao's revolution. It is the transformative movement between the autonomic "affective constellations" and the politically motivated "emotions" that has significantly shaped memory debates about the Mao era.

Furthermore, my attempt to reconcile the disagreements between the materialist and the socially normative understanding of affect is also informed by the dynamic interplay between *qing* 情 (emotion) and *li* 理 (intellect) in the Chinese tradition. Where the Western philosophical tradition is typically thought to pit reason against emotion, Sinologists propose that the classical Confucian notion of *xin* 心 (heart-mind) unifies the cognitive and emotive capacities of the mind.³⁹ This holistic view has been complicated by a "weak" dualist approach that distinguishes the "higher" cognitive mind from the "lower" bodily impulse in Confucian ethics.⁴⁰ But while mainstream scholarship seeks to excavate the "intelligence of emotions" in traditional Chinese thought, such a romanticized interpretation may prove to say more about our own postmetaphysical discomfort with pure reason than about Confucius's originally naturalistic vision of the heart-mind.⁴¹ Indeed, if we resist the urge to romanticize the harmony of reason and emotion as a Chinese alternative to occidental rationalism, we may find that the

---

38. Parkinson, *An Emotional State*, 27.

39. For instance, Roger T. Ames and David L. Hall argue that "thinking for Confucius is not to be understood as a process of abstract reasoning, but is fundamentally performative in that it is an activity whose immediate consequence is the achievement of a practical result." See Hall and Ames, *Thinking through Confucius*, 44.

40. Slingerland, "Mind and Body in Early China."

41. As both Curie Virág and Edward Slingerland suggest, the Western fascination with the Confucian holist heart-mind is "rooted in a longstanding European interest in reading into the Chinese past a harmony of reason and emotion that was perceived to have been lacking (or lost) in the European tradition" (Virág, *The Emotions in Early Chinese Philosophy*, 3). See also Slingerland, "Mind and Body in Early China."

English term "emotion" falls short of the diverse connotations of *qing* 情, ranging from the objective condition of the material world (e.g., circumstance) to subjective human feelings and dispositions.[42] As scholars have noted, the broad semantic range of *qing* in pre-Han texts indicates that early Chinese philosophers propagated competing ethics of emotion, from Mencius's proposal for the person's natural disposition for "pity and compassion" to Xunzi's advocacy for the suppression of human desires through the artifice of rituals.[43]

Although the diverse ontological layers of *qing* certainly defy the bifurcation of cognition and feeling, the mainstream Confucian tradition still emphasizes the tension between the emotive and cognitive sources of moral direction. Starting with the Western Han thinker Dong Zhongshu's 董仲舒 (179–104 BCE) antithetical framework that pitted *xing* 性 (the inborn nature) against *qing* 情 (the delusionary state), a lineup of Confucian thinkers cautioned that the unbounded outflow of volatile sentiments could lead humanity astray and so must be rectified by a set of normative moral regulations. Song Neo-Confucians further elaborated on the categorical difference between (the good) *xing* and (the evil) *qing* (*xingshan qinge* 性善情惡), culminating in Zhu Xi's 朱熹 (1130–1200) proposition to purge "human desire" (*renyu* 人慾) for the sake of "heavenly principle" (*tianli* 天理).[44] Yet the late Ming and Qing eras witnessed a succession of heterodoxic voices that challenged the monopoly of *li* 理 (rational principle) in Neo-Confucian orthodoxy, such as Feng Menglong's 馮夢龍 (1574–1646) iconoclastic call for the "cult of *qing*" (*qingjiao* 情教) over *li*, and Dai Zhen's 戴震 (1724–1777) deliberate effort to justify private desires against the *li*-centered public morality.

Furthermore, the interaction between emotion and intellect took new bearings in twentieth-century China. The May Fourth cultural

---

42. Virág has listed the extensive semantic range of *qing* in pre-Qin philosophy, including particular emotions (e.g., anger and sadness), preference (e.g., liking and disliking), motivational states (e.g., desire and intention), cognition (e.g., thinking and reflection), moral feelings (e.g., respect and filial affection), and specific moral virtues (e.g., humanness and ritual propriety). See Virág, *The Emotions in Early Chinese Philosophy*, 8–9; Graham, "The Meaning of Ch'ing [Qing]."

43. See Puett, "The Ethics of Responding Properly."

44. Martin Huang, *Desire and Fictional Narrative in Late Imperial China*, 25–29.

movement of 1919 was a Kantian breakaway from the emotional bondage of Confucian dogma, with science and democracy hailed as the master signifiers of Chinese modernity.[45] But the utopian yearnings for enlightenment rationality also rejuvenated waves of cultural and intellectual ferment that sought to recalibrate the poetics of *qing* in the light of radical political transformations, from Zhang Junmai's 張君勱 (1887–1969)'s invocation of "outlooks on life" (*rensheng guan* 人生觀) in the controversy over science and metaphysics (*kexue yu xuanxue lunzhan* 科學與玄學論戰), to Cai Yuanpei's 蔡元培 (1868–1940) and Zhu Guangqian's 朱光潛 (1897–1986) calls for the aesthetic inculcation of enlightened sentiment; from the celebration of the irrational and the intuitive among anarchist-nihilist thinkers, to the resurgence of lyricism in diverse literary and artistic practices.[46] Meanwhile, the engaged revolutionaries were torn by the eternal contestation between emotion and intellect no less paradoxical than the May Fourth liberal progressives. The anti-intellectualism of Chinese Communism remains a thorny matter, but scholars concur that Mao's socialist regime was intensely preoccupied with the management of affect, to the point of neurosis.[47] To live a revolutionary life from the Yan'an period to the Cultural Revolution was to experience continuous psychological shocks caused by extreme emotions: agape, *ressentiment*, and self-purgation. The existential dilemma between *xin* 信 (a profoundly affectionate devotion) and *si* 思 (a detached rational reflection) has impelled different political choices and ideological beliefs among Chinese intellectuals, ranging from self-willed conformity and confession to internal exile and defiance.

---

45. In his examination of Liang Qichao's thought, Joseph Levenson introduces a history/value division, noting that modern Chinese literati, akin to Liang, grappled with a psychological conflict between "value" (a rational adherence to Western values) and "history" (an emotional attachment to the crumbled Confucian tradition). This tension left Liang-like literati "intellectually alienated and emotionally tied to his tradition." See Levenson, *Liang Ch'i-ch'ao and the Mind of Modern China*, 219.

46. For a critical genealogy of the dialectic of emotion and rationality in the May Fourth Movement, see Peng Hsiao-yen, *Weiqing yu lixing de bianzheng*; for Chinese lyricism, see David Wang, *The Lyrical in Epic Time*; Shengqing Wu, *Modern Archaics*.

47. See Perry, "Moving the Masses."

In connection with this, the field of modern Chinese literary and cultural studies has undergone a massive emotive turn, producing a cornucopia of works ranging from the study of particular emotions (such as trauma, pain, love, and sympathy) and artistic styles (such as lyricism and aestheticism) to the exploration of sentimental public space, virulent political discourse, and sensationalist media in twentieth-century China. But in part because of the urgent desire to assert the spontaneous, natural, and emancipatory aspects of feelings suppressed by the earlier scholarly preoccupation with reason, such an emotion-centered perspective fails to explain how fluid feelings embody, enchant, and orient intellectual thinking. Here I am indebted to David Wang, Haiyan Lee, and many others' collective proposition that a paradigmatic rethinking of the reason-emotion nexus must further demonstrate how emotion interacts with intellect. In particular, Wang coins the term "critical lyricism" to describe how the intertwined connotation of reason and emotion enabled various liberal, leftist, and conservative Chinese writers to spell out aesthetic and political responses to the 1949 national divide.[48] In their path-breaking studies of early twentieth-century Chinese discourse of sentiment, Haiyan Lee and Jianmei Liu note how modern Chinese literature began with a "revolution of the heart," identifying "revolution plus romance" as the key literary-affective trope through which a new national community could be articulated.[49] In contrast to the Habermasian ideal of a rational public sphere, Michael Berry, Eric Hayot, Jing Tsu, Eugenia Lean, and Gloria Davies delineate how volatile public sentiments—sympathy, compassion, trauma, humiliation, and what Davies terms "patriotic worrying"—helped shape critical debates on a wide range of political issues throughout twentieth-century China, from the ethical dilemmas of political loyalty and filial piety to the double bind of revolution and reform.[50] Whereas Weihong Bao uses the term "affective medium" to illustrate the centrality of affect in the left-wing agitation cinema, Ban Wang

48. David Wang, *The Lyrical in Epic Time*, 1–40.
49. Haiyan Lee, *Revolution of the Heart*, 255–97; Jianmei Liu, *Revolution Plus Love*.
50. Michael Berry, *A History of Pain*; Hayot, *The Hypothetical Mandarin*; Jing Tsu, *Failure, Nationalism, and Literature*; Lean, *Public Passions*; Davies, *Worrying about China*.

approaches Maoist aesthetics through the "sublime figure" of revolution, a "process of edification and elevation" that sublimated the all-too-human into the superhuman.[51] Together, this collective scholarly endeavor reveals how discourses of sentiment are never merely pure and simple feelings but rather involve ethical judgment and cognitive thinking.

These provocative analyses further enable me to rethink the conceptual-rationalistic understanding of the contemporary Chinese mindscape. In his 1785 essay "What Does It Mean to Orient Oneself in Thinking?," Immanuel Kant argues that, just as a human being needs a sense of direction (e.g., left, right, south, north, up, down) to move in any given space, they also possess a mental orientation (e.g., concept, judgment) as the precondition of thinking.[52] Such an initial orientation, as Kant suggests, is given by human rationality, which "grants our thinking in its original sense of direction."[53] Interestingly, Kant uses the term *Gefühl* (feeling) to describe a priori faculty at the root of our mental capacity to formulate concepts and make judgments.[54] This initial orientation may thus not necessarily be impassioned thinking, but could also take diverse emotive forms, such as conviction, intuition, and moral passion. For example, what oriented Chinese intellectuals to criticize or eulogize Mao's revolutionary legacy was not pure reason or a priori political conviction, but precisely ambiguous *Gefühl*—memories, feelings, passions, and dispositions shaped by the lived experience of socialism. Speaking of the Cultural Revolution, many liberals would immediately think through the anguished memories of persecution—the horrors of Red Guard violence, mass trials, and political exile; the leftist critique of neoliberal privatization, by contrast, was fueled by a nostalgic remembrance of the values, ideals, and realities of everyday life under socialism—community, altruism, collectivism, and revolutionary romanticism. These heterogeneous feelings formed the ground of political judgment and oriented the individual to go Left or turn Right in the post-Mao ideological space. To truly affirm the role of

---

51. Bao, *Fiery Cinema*; Ban Wang, *The Sublime Figure of History*, 2.
52. Kant, "What Does It Mean to Orient Oneself in Thinking."
53. Gordon, *The Continental Divide*, 5.
54. For an analysis, see Packer, "Kant on Desire and Moral Pleasure."

feelings, we must therefore explain how emotion actively shapes the fundamental orientation of intellectual argumentation, including thinking, judging, evaluating, and concept forming.

To this end, this book aims to reconcile the tension between the literary-emotive and the conceptual-rationalistic approach to the study of the contemporary Chinese mindscape. To appreciate the dialogic of emotion and intellect is neither to repudiate the power of feeling nor to substitute rational thinking for a mythic ontology of affect. Rather, it is to understand, in the word of Raymond Williams, "thought as felt and feeling as thought."[55] As Haiyan Lee puts it, Williams's critical concept of the "structure of feeling" "captures social consciousness as lived experience *in process*, or *in solution*, before it is 'precipitated' and given fixed forms."[56] Lee has adapted Williams's paradigm to circumvent the false dichotomy between ideology and feeling and explore the intertwined relationship between new ideas about the self and its emotions during the May Fourth period. Building on Williams's and Lee's approach, I also leave open the causal relationship between thinking and feeling and focus on their mutual interaction in the post-Mao cultural and intellectual context.

More specifically, the reason-emotion nexus takes three distinct forms throughout this book. Taking emotion as part and parcel of ethical reasoning and moral judgment, I am first concerned with the questions of how and why particular emotional responses took on added ethical and political significance in the rancorous ideological arena of the post-Mao era. Why would liberal-minded reportorial investigators painstakingly search for signs of remorse from the former Red Guards, while the Left denounced the discourse of guilt as a deliberate repression of Maoist politics? The second quest understands feeling as the Kantian "initial orientation" that shapes political conviction and animates intellectual argumentation. To what extent did the pathos of persecution and defeat inform the liberals' pursuit of "negative liberty" and the Left's reflection on the crisis of Marxism? The last approach considers affect as the result of conscious ideological

---

55. Williams, *Marxism and Literature*, 131, quoted in Haiyan Lee, *Revolution of the Heart*, 10.

56. Haiyan Lee, *Revolution of the Heart*, 10 (emphasis in the original).

manipulation. How, for example, did Chinese nationalists deploy and distort China's national history to manufacture public resentment against the West? Above all, this tripartite framework strikes a balance between the affective underpinning of political imaginaries and the political tonality of emotions—between the role of human sentiment and affect in orienting intellectual thinking and the power of reason in reflecting the ethical and political connotations of emotion.

Furthermore, the interaction between thinking and feeling enables me to rethink the formation of political ideas as sensorial, aesthetic, and literary practice deeply connected to memories, dispositions, and moral sentiments. Thus, my goal is not to typologize diverse and ambiguous emotions into the well-worn ideological matrix of the liberal-left-conservative-nationalist quadruple mentioned before, but rather to investigate the dynamic sentiments and feelings that endowed liberalism, leftism, conservatism, or nationalism with emotional appeal and moral authority. Instead of arbitrarily associating each intellectual cluster with one predominant emotion, I look beyond formulaic intellectual divisions and explore the amorphous affective syndromes and intense psychic energies at work in post-Mao ideological contentions. Admittedly, Mao's admirers tended to cluster at the left end of political spectrum, whereas most of the critics of China's socialist past adopted a liberal position. But political disagreements often obscured the profound and troubling emotional excess that underpinned different ideological claims about the Mao era—from sentimental outpouring to moral outrage, from resignation and disillusionment to the passions of belief. As my discussion shows, Chinese intellectuals frequently relied on specific memories and manufactured political emotions to construct their visions of the past as authentic and authoritative. Just as both liberals and leftists drew moral passions from the pathos of defeat, the conservatives' quest for a sacred national past also betrayed a nostalgic yearning for a quasi-religious sensation that once energized their earlier pursuit of Maoist utopia. By resorting to quirky feelings and particularistic experience, they invested the rational and abstract principles of liberty or equality with moral sentiments, political desires, and psychological attractions. An affective idea, in other words, may acquire a motivational power that pure -isms could not possess. This means that the root of the post-Mao ideological controversy can never be fully grasped except through a nuanced analysis of the divided emotions toward the Mao era that undergird political argumentations.

Meanwhile, I conceive of my project not as a comprehensive sociopolitical history of the post-Mao emotional landscape but as a selective genealogical investigation into the discursive construction of diverse feelings and sentiments in post-Mao intellectual debate. In my scenarios, emotions are understood less as outward manifestations of the author's psychological interiority and more as narratological constructions of feelings—guilt, shame, melancholy, passion, and resentment—across a variety of literary texts and intellectual discourses. In attempting to read the dialogic of emotion and intellect through the discursive trope, I hope to further demonstrate the interconnectedness of literary experimentations and intellectual reflections in the post-Mao context. Against the conventional wisdom that literary scholars tend to explore feelings, rhetoric, and aesthetics whereas intellectual historians are generally more interested in reconstructing thinking, concepts, and logics, the boundary between literature and thought has always been fluid in Chinese humanities. Building on this tradition, this book pays attention to the peculiar "literariness of ideas" (*sixiang de wenxuexing* 思想的文學性)—that is, ways in which liberal, leftist, conservative, and nationalist thinkers encrypted their thinking by mobilizing an army of figurative language, opaque references, and esoteric teachings.

A full engagement between intellectual history and literary studies is something for the future. Here I propose to rethink how contemporary Chinese intellectual debate is deeply intertwined with the traditional cultural politics of *wen* 文, a classical Chinese term pointing toward diverse forms of discursive practices ranging from ornamentation and civilization to the art of governance and the illumination of history and cosmology.[57] Echoing David Wang's proposal to reconceive "the tradition of literature as manifestation" beyond the Western notion of mimesis,[58] my approach explores how *wenxue* 文學 (literature), so understood, continues to serve as the primary medium for public discussion of, and intellectual engagement with, politics in contemporary China; particularly, it has become a most powerful, yet

---

57. David Wang, "Worlding Literary China," 5.
58. David Wang, "Worlding Literary China," 5.

also paradoxical, form that allows the unremembered and the unspeakable to be inscribed against a state-sponsored politics of amnesia. After all, it is a familiar fact that ancient and modern writers alike—from the unruly Ming Confucian Li Zhi to the outspoken dissident-activist Liu Xiaobo—have been persecuted for holding unorthodox political views. It is also well-known that in the course of Chinese history, those unwilling to be silenced have developed various literary ways to signal their teachings to their intended audiences, such as allegory, allusion, apparent inconsistency, and noticeable omission. Likewise, the heavily censored Chinese public sphere required that intellectuals and writers express their political ideas not in "direct speech" (*zhiyan buhui* 直言不諱) but instead through stylistic and rhetorical artifices, an allegorical mode of writing harking back to the classic poetics of "entrusting (unexpressed) meaning to the words" (*jituo* 寄託). These cases indicate that the inherent meaning of political ideas is not to be located in discourse itself, but in the manifestation of discourse in various literary and aesthetic forms.

The Post-Mao Generation and the Problem of Memory Politics

This book aims to situate individual thinkers and writers within a shared historical horizon to illuminate the manifold interactions and contentions among the post-Mao generation. Historically, the affective (rather than purely intellectual) responses to the unsettling past resulted from the fact that the rival intellectual projects in the reform era were bound up in the shared adolescent experience of the post-Mao generation in the heat of Mao's revolution. Most of the intellectual figures discussed belong to the Red Guard generation (*laosanjie* 老三屆), who came of age in the most turbulent decade of Chinese socialism.[59] This political generation experienced first the eruption of heightened revolutionary passions in the early days of the Cultural Revolution, then the bloody factional warfare among the Red Guards that

---

59. Guobin Yang, *The Red Guard Generation and Political Activism in China*, 5–7.

immediately followed, and finally the debilitating effects of the "sent-down" movement in the early 1970s, which engendered widespread disillusionment with Mao's socialist utopia. Ironically, the crash of Mao's last revolution deepened the emotional attachment to Maoist ideals in the market era. The abandonment of Mao's revolutionary legacy aroused strong sentiments—especially a willful socialist nostalgia—among the post-Mao generation, because revolution and its disavowal had been indivisibly linked with the dilemma of affirming or negating their own "lived experience of socialism."[60] Meanwhile, overseas intellectuals and writers also mingled their reflections on revolution with similarly passionate sincerity, genuineness, and agony. Alienation and trauma, nourished throughout the perilous years of emigration, generated the exiled liberals' strong emotional reactions to the crimes and atrocities of socialist revolution (chapter 2). For devoted Sinophone Marxists, by contrast, Mao's grand revolution has always been a distant mirage, an alien but alluring dream, and an imagined utopia constructed vis-à-vis the materialistic and philistine capitalist reality (chapter 3). Together, these divergent political emotions toward China's tumultuous revolutionary past reinforced the ideological polarizations in the post-Mao era.

However, the fusion of emotion and political vision in these competing memory projects often resulted in aesthetically and politically appealing—if at times anachronistic and controversial—appropriations of the past for radically different future visions. Indeed, Chinese intellectuals have shrewdly presented partial and highly selective memories of the Mao era to justify their millenarian visions of China's transformation and discredit the political agenda of the opposing factions. To explain the (mis)uses of memory in intellectual polemics, my study draws on related scholarship that has focused on three interrelated

---

60. My distinction between the lived experience of socialism and socialist ideology is inspired by Alexei Yurchak's discussion of the last Soviet generation. In Yurchak's perspective, although the Soviet system produced tremendous suffering, many of the fundamental values of socialism were of genuine importance for Soviet citizens. He therefore proposes to make a distinction between socialism "as a system of human values and as an everyday reality of 'normal life'" and socialism as "'the state' or 'ideology.'" See Yurchak, *Everything Was Forever, Until It Was No More*, 8.

quests: retrieving oppositional memories against the hegemonic memory production of the authoritarian state; describing how different social groups remember the Maoist past differently; and examining the contemporary representations of that past in a variety of cultural artifacts.[61] But whereas the factual, sociological, and representational aspects of memory are indispensable grids from which to analyze post-Mao memory ecology, my study departs from the previous emphasis on how societies remember by prioritizing how Chinese intellectual elites revised, transformed, and mobilized the past to legitimatize competing ideological designs for China's postsocialist political order. This presentist approach is inspired by Jie Li's proposal to move beyond the endless controversy over "what really happened" and instead examine "what the past does for and to the present."[62] Drawing on Pierre Nora's celebrated term "sites of memory" (*lieux de mémoire*) and Jan Assmann's conception of "cultural memory," Li and other scholars have explored how "given revolutionary symbols and myths were created in the first place, how their forms and meanings changed in specific historical contexts, and how they have been mobilized by different agents during the past few decades."[63] Yet whereas this scholarly endeavor deals mainly with cultural artifacts,[64] I focus on how "red legacies" could serve as assets or liabilities in the realm of political ideas. To what extent did memories of the Maoist past enable post-Mao intellectuals to justify their ideological visions while imposing powerful constraints upon that very vision? To answer this question, I look at how each intellectual faction actively reshapes red legacies—enshrining some aspects while expunging others—in line with different political scenarios for China's future.

Admittedly, the tendency to present selective memories of the Mao era has provoked moral indignation from critics. In 1990, the political

---

61. For the first approach, see Watson, *Memory, History, and Opposition under State Socialism*; for the second, see Lee and Yang, *Re-envisioning the Chinese Revolution*; for the third one, see Ban Wang, *Illuminations from the Past*.

62. Jie Li, "Discerning Red Legacies in China," 5.

63. Jie Li, "Discerning Red Legacies in China," 5.

64. For museums and memorials, see Denton, *Exhibiting the Past*; for visual and performing arts, see Xiaomei Chen, *Staging Chinese Revolution*; for cinema and the urban environment, see Braester, *Painting the City Red*.

dissident Fang Lizhi 方勵之 (1936–2012) condemned the "techniques of amnesia" deployed by the CCP to purge any oppositional narratives from the Chinese public sphere.[65] Fang's critique has been supplemented by scholars and activists who closely trace how the collective memories of catastrophic historical events—the Anti-Rightist Campaign, the Great Leap Forward, and the Cultural Revolution—have been censored by China's political elite.[66] Understandably, his inquiry adopts an interrogational approach that praises certain intellectual figures for their heroic fight against amnesia while condemning many others for their willful distortion of national history. Yet while this morally driven perspective exposes the deceptive rhetoric and opportunistic intent rampant in Chinese memory politics, it also tends to measure the value of ideas according to political standpoints. Important as these criticisms have been, I fear that moral passion might be behind our eagerness to intervene rather than explain. This book does not offer yet another moralized depiction of how leftists have failed to account for the human cost of revolution in their reckless pursuit of a Maoist alternative, or why liberals have turned their eyes away from the underprivileged masses who retain fond memories of the socialist welfare state. As David Wang contends, the master narrative of "revolution and enlightenment" has framed Chinese cultural modernity in stark polarities, with "a strong sense of historical relevance and political urgency."[67] As a result, the debate over remembering or forgetting follows a circular logic and ultimately replicates the polarized structure of the contemporary Chinese memory politics it strives to explain.

Furthermore, the eagerness to intervene, criticize, and politicize in Chinese memory debates is intertwined with a much older concern surrounding the political responsibility of intellectuals in public. As Benjamin Wurgaft points out, the very notion of the modern intellectual is a cultural and political ideal crystallized in Émile Zola's fierce "J'accuse" at the outset of the Dreyfus affair.[68] The engaged public

---

65. Lizhi Fang, "The Chinese Amnesia"; Yan, "On China's State-Sponsored Amnesia."
66. For a nice literature review, see Jie Li, *Utopian Ruins*, 7.
67. David Wang, *The Lyrical in Epic Time*, xi.
68. Wurgaft, *Thinking in Public*, 10.

intellectual, as the tale goes, speaks not in the service of a specific social group but on behalf of justice and carries a moral responsibility to "bear witness to truth" and to "expose the lies of government."[69] Similarly, that a *zhishifenzi* 知識分子 (intellectual) has a moral imperative to "serve the public good" (*weigong* 為公) is a recurring theme throughout Chinese history, from the fusion of moral learning and public service in the Confucian ideal of "scholar-officials" (*shidafu* 士大夫) to the double bind of enlightenment and national salvation that confronted the May Fourth generation.[70] In the wake of Mao's demise, the urgency of reform demanded that China's cultural elites take a stand on the public implication of their ideas, and that they awaken, educate, enlighten, and mobilize the masses for the purposes of societal enlightenment. Echoing Václav Havel's archetype of Eastern European refuseniks,[71] the fierce critic Liu Binyan 劉賓雁 (1925–2005) thus defines the essence of public engagement as practicing "a higher kind of loyalty" (*di'erzhong zhongcheng* 第二種忠誠), that is, engaging in a truth-seeking criticism that exposes the labyrinth of repression, censorship, and ideological lies fabricated by the loyal disciples of the party.[72]

This oppositional stance has made a deep impact on earlier English-language scholarship on PRC intellectual politics, most notably Merle Goldman's analysis of China's "dissident intelligentsia" stretching from Lu Xun to Hu Feng.[73] Later scholars, especially Timothy Cheek, Joseph Fewsmith, and Carol L. Hamrin, broadened our horizons by turning to the pluralization of the Chinese intellectual field since the early reform years. This critical scholarship, as Cheek neatly phrases it, portrays Chinese intelligentsia not as "living in opposition" but interacting with the party establishment and commercial interests.[74]

69. Chomsky, "The Responsibility of Intellectuals."
70. See Yu Ying-shih, *Shi yu Zhongguowenhua*; Schwarcz, *The Chinese Enlightenment*; Cheek, *The Intellectual in Modern Chinese History*.
71. Havel, "The Power of the Powerless."
72. Liu Binyan, *Di'erzhong zhongcheng*.
73. Goldman, *China's Intellectuals*.
74. Fewsmith discusses the pluralization of Chinese intelligentsia after 1989; Hamrin and Cheek explore "establishment intellectuals"—who were both leading scholars and high-level party cadres; Cheek's recent work situates the post-Mao intellectual ferments within the long arc of the twentieth-century Chinese Revolution

Furthermore, the Habermasian notion of civil society has profoundly shaped the sociological investigation into the "structural transformation" of the post-Mao public sphere, producing seminal discussions on how China's marketization process provided "semiautonomous," "directed," and "grassroots" public spaces for rational-critical discourse.[75] However, even though this collective endeavor has softened the once-stark dichotomy between resistance and conformity, the urgent desire felt by many to discern the seeds of China's future democratization still exerts an impact on our perceptions of Chinese thinkers and writers. Beyond academia, media discourses, popular myths, and cultural baggage continue to portray opposition as the fundamental political ethics of the Chinese intellectual.

The strong moral sentiment invested in the figure of the intellectual, as circulated in Chinese popular and academic discourse, finds echoes in the contemporary West. Since the 1980s, the rise of technocratic elites and the fragmentation of the public sphere have created a sense of crisis among Euro-American scholars,[76] ushering in a wave of elegiac accounts that mourn the decline of the public authority held by the cultural elite in the neoliberal era.[77] Furthermore, the fall of radical politics—including the dissolution of 1960s radicalism and the disintegration of the Soviet Union—have given rise to reflections on the narcissistic attraction of illustrious intellectual figures to radical political experiments throughout the twentieth century, such as the "dangerous liaisons" between Martin Heidegger and the Nazi regime and the alchemy of "tyrannophilia" that compelled Jean-Paul Sartre and his leftist compatriots to fantasize about the Maoist alternative.[78] Yet,

---

and enlightenment. See Fewsmith, *China since Tiananmen*; Hamrin and Cheek, *China's Establishment Intellectuals*; Cheek, *The Intellectual in Modern Chinese History*, 262–314.

75. Cheek, Ownby, and Fogel, "Mapping the Intellectual Public Sphere in China Today"; Veg, *Minjian*; Gu and Goldman, *Chinese Intellectuals between State and Market*.

76. For a comprehensive analysis of the crisis of the intellectuals in the age of postmodernity, see Boggs, *Intellectuals and the Crisis of Modernity*.

77. For representative works, see Jacoby, *The Last Intellectuals*; Posner, *Public Intellectuals*; Bloom, *The Closing of the American Mind*.

78. For a definition of tyrannophilia, see Lilla, *The Reckless Mind*; for a study of the political and philosophical consequences of Heidegger's Nazism, see Wolin, *The*

too often political moralizing has turned a calibrated analysis of intellectuals in politics into a "politicized history of intellectuals."[79] Such melodramatic narratives recount how brilliant and reckless thinkers, obsessed with actualizing their "pure ideas" through political intervention, ended up legitimizing extreme violence and state terror. This template tirelessly harks back to the "lure of Syracuse," when Plato, hoping to realize his philosophical principles, set sail for Syracuse to advise the tyrant Dionysius the Younger on how to produce a perfect regime. But as Wurgaft observes, the moralist view "makes politics the crucial horizon line for all intellectual work, judging the life of the mind purely in terms of the political provocations to which it responds."[80] In the end, the interrogational approach becomes a thinly disguised expression of indignation against the "failure" of certain thinkers to live up to the moral criteria of their predecessors.

Going beyond the apologetic/polemic model, I attempt to explain the origins of ideological polarization by investigating the cultural logic and political thinking that valorized "selective remembering" among the post-Mao political and intellectual elite. To avoid the lacuna of moral reasoning, Anna M. Parkinson proposes that we refrain from asking "whether the past has been overcome or mastered and in which way," and instead pivots to examine "the framework established by the discourse of 'coming to terms' with the past" in the study of memory politics.[81] To understand the metamorphosis of moral emotions, we scholars must, paradoxically, rein in the impulse of political moralizing. Thus, instead of asking whether the socialist past has been either denigrated or romanticized, I look at how Chinese writers and thinkers mobilized specific aspects of the past to solidify divergent political claims about China's future path—including the revanchist liberal call to finish the "incomplete project" of enlightenment, the leftist attempt to fulfill the

---

Politics of Being; for a political critique of Sartre and his leftist followers, see Judt, *The Burden of Responsibility*.

79. See Bourg, "Blame It on Paris," 181.

80. See Wurgaft, *Thinking in Public*, 4.

81. Parkinson, *An Emotional State*, 4; for a discussion of the relationship between political emotions and intellectual discourse in West Germany, see Moses, *German Intellectuals and the Nazi Past*, 1–14.

redemptive promise of revolution, and the soul-wrenching conservative search for China's mythical ancestral roots beyond and before the advent of the modern. After all, Jeffrey K. Olick has pointed out that "national identity and political legitimacy always involve a precarious balance between remembering and forgetting."[82] Similarly, the post-Mao controversialists don't generally forget; instead, they remember differently and thus produce conflicting views on how to reconstruct a usable collective past behind a new, postrevolutionary Chinese national identity.

As revealed by the politics of commemorating China's collective past, disputes over the meaning of revolution were often intertwined with broader reflections on the multiple strains of Chinese modernity: How does one justify the country's past search for utopian socialism in the wake of a rising capitalist mentality? Does the ideational aspiration of Mao's revolution still speak to us? If so, how does one account for the atrocities conducted in the name of revolution? Or should the Chinese nation abandon its misguided search for modern revolution and enlightenment once and for all by returning to its Confucian civilizational origin? Above all, twentieth-century China's prolonged quest for revolution has produced an endless catalog of utopias and dystopias, dramas and traumas, and justices and injustices—all of which weighed heavily on the minds of Chinese intellectuals. To understand and appreciate the profound passions and convictions of the post-Mao generation, one must rein in the desire for outright intervention and follow Chen Yinke's hermeneutics of empathy to "stand in the same realm as the thinkers of the past" (與立說之古人，處於同一境界).[83]

However, my reluctance to criticize from any a priori liberal or leftist standpoints does not mean that I refrain from exposing the moral blindsight, deceptive rhetoric, and opportunistic intent in Chinese intellectual discourse. Rather, I pit the lofty ideals and high-minded visions against the practices of their authors, with the aim of exposing the fissures and inconsistencies between thinking (*vita contemplativa*) and acting (*vita activa*). This move follows Habermas's call to "think with Heidegger against Heidegger," which separates the

---

82. Olick, *The Sins of the Fathers*, 7.
83. Chen Yinke, "Feng Youlan *Zhongguo zhexueshi* shangce shencha baogao," 279.

ideational significance of existential philosophy from its unpleasant ideological (mis)uses.[84] As Peter Gordon forcefully argues, the utopian promise of past ideas may retain a certain validity even though "that promise was broken by the fact of its restricted application."[85] Therefore, it is the responsibility of intellectual historians to "seize hold of" the emancipatory potential of ideas at a moment of danger.[86] In our own time, it is not uncommon for intellectuals to capitulate to power and betray the very philosophical visions they profess. But to indulge in moral condemnation is to deny the deeply contradictory nature of Chinese intellectual thinking as a combination of thinking and believing, defiance and conformity, moral passion and political enchantment. Therefore, I hope that a careful reconstruction of the life of the mind will shine a brighter light on the myopia of Chinese intellectuals better than moralizing ever could.

Overview of the Chapters

Sentimental Republic examines several critical events, figures, and scenarios to map out the emergence of unsettled feelings regarding the nation's past across ideological spectrums, from the liberal politics of mourning and leftist melancholy to conservative and nationalistic resentment. Rather than provide an exhaustive, chronological investigation of major intellectual trends, I devote attention to several key thinkers and episodes that illuminate the broader cultural symptoms and intellectual transformation underway in the contemporary Chinese mindscape. Hence, texts and cultural artifacts are no longer treated as being exclusively owned by individual thinkers or certain intellectual schools, but rather as a barometer of collective aspirations and feelings in the post-Mao era. Still, my exclusive focus on individual characters and cases warrants justification. A thorny question is how to select critical texts and key figures from the vast repertoire of scenarios, discourses, and cultural artifacts pertinent to the post-Mao

---

84. Quoted in Gordon, "A Lion in Winter."
85. Gordon, "Contextualism and Criticism in the History of Ideas," 45.
86. Benjamin, "Theses on the Philosophy of History," 255.

intellectual dynamics: How can the writers, intellectuals, and scholars discussed represent broader intellectual trends? Why are certain important figures and watershed events missing from my reading? What are the criteria for the inclusion and exclusion of texts and authors?

My critics might point out, for example, that the Chinese New Left and mainland Confucians (*dalu xinrujia* 大陸新儒家) are more visible in spelling out leftist and conservative themes than my selected cases. Yet, just as Goethe claims that "clarity is an appropriate distribution of light and shadow," no picture can be drawn without leaving unexplored shades.[87] Therefore, a skillful painter knows how to use the symbiotic relationship between light and darkness to give their artwork a dynamic quality. By "lightening up" these individual cases, my painting illustrates the different ideological visions posed by opposing political camps (such as liberal vs. the Left); shows the contrasts and variations across generations and geographic areas (such as mainland Chinese vs. Sinophone articulations); mediates the tension between elite and grassroots memory politics (such as academic intellectuals vs. populist writers); and elucidates the diverse forms of discursive practices ranging across fiction, poetry, biography, film, and intellectual discourse. With each case having been selected to meet one or more of these criteria, I seek to map out the multiple strains of emotions and affective structures during this period.

Meanwhile, one of the difficult issues that has confronted the intellectual history of the post-Mao era is that of a unified political metanarrative. For some readers, the story of the post-Mao generation gained its aesthetic appeal insofar as it could be narrated according to the larger political tumult of this period, a tragic bildungsroman beginning with the birth of a youth rebellion and ending with the return of authoritarian politics. However, I share Peter Gordon and John McCormick's concern that the impulse to narrate the entire epoch within a single "psychodrama of Oedipal development" is inevitably reductive.[88] This book does use a quadruple ideological matrix to characterize major post-Mao intellectual and political currents, but it also cautions against any impulse to unify the divergent features of each individual case

87. Müller, *A Dangerous Mind*, 9.
88. See Gordon and McCormick, "Weimar Thought," 3–4.

under a common political theme. I have always been fascinated by the diverse modes of inquiry among Chinese liberals that persistently resist containment within a single political camp. When I write about conservative intellectuals, I am equally attracted to the mercurial nature of their thinking: Liu Xiaofeng's 劉小楓 (1956–) circuitous pilgrimage from Jesus to Confucius and then to Mao, for instance, reflects the peculiar politics of ideological conversion and deconversion that has marked the paths of many post-Mao conservatives. And it would be naïve to assume that one could understand the authors of *China Can Say No* without taking cognizance of the conflictual factors—from bourgeois self-hatred to anti-liberalism and from personal desires to public performance—that have shaped their convoluted nationalist conviction. Thus, this project presents post-Mao intellectual history not in its dramatic unity but through distinct vignettes—self-styled figures, sensational events, and unlikely encounters, making them points of reference for my readers to grasp the broader intellectual movements and cultural dynamics in the post-Mao era. The insights and provocations that emerged from these individual figures, as I will demonstrate, help us understand the shared intellectual passion and the structure of feelings of the post-Mao generation.

By fussing about particulars, I also aim to unsettle the dominate narrative that portrays mainland China as the center of the post-Mao cultural renaissance. Despite the predominance of the Red Guard generation in the debate about the fate of Mao's revolution, we need to look beyond the geographic contour of the nation-state to understand the global circulation and transformation of their ideas and beliefs. In conjunction with Edward Said's analysis of "traveling theory"—the migration of discourses and theories from place to place,[89] this book documents how the dynamic interplay between China proper and the global Sinophone communities contributes to the emergence of heteroglossic literary and intellectual currents in the postsocialist era.[90] Here, I deploy the term "Sinophone" to describe a language-based critical lens through which to view the linguistic, cultural, and intellectual dynamics in Chinese-speaking communities across the globe. Yet while

---

89. Said, "Traveling Theory," 226–47.
90. See Shih, Tsai, and Bernards, *Sinophone Studies*.

Sinophone scholars such as Shu-mei Shih prioritize Sinitic-language communities outside China proper to debunk the myth of a (Han-centered) Chinese diaspora, I do not intend to replicate the dichotomous scheme of "China vs. the Sinophone" or "hegemony vs. resistance."[91] To be sure, I endorse the collective endeavor to retrieve the voices of Sinitic minorities and immigrants that lie at the margins and peripheries of the Chinese literary canon. In the study of political ideas, however, John Makeham, Els van Dongen, Weiming Tu, and others have forcefully demonstrated how, since the 1980s, the "ongoing process of intellectual cross-fertilization and rivalry" between PRC intellectuals and overseas Chinese scholars has greatly facilitated the revival of key cultural-intellectual currents in China, especially Confucianism.[92] Therefore, the inquiry conducted in this book asks not how *wai* 外 (outside) excludes, subverts, and deconstructs *zhong* 中 (inside), but rather how *wai* actively shapes, defines, and changes the very connotation of *zhong* (civilization's core). My study of the Chinese liberal imagination, for instance, departs from extant interpretations of Chinese liberalism as an outgrowth of post-Tiananmen intellectual transition inside the territory of the PRC. Rather, I establish the liberals' imaginary nostalgia for republican China within a broader international history of the Chinese diaspora, illustrating how Chinese émigrés and exiled scholars actively participated in public debates about liberal alternatives in the Chinese context (chapter 2). Furthermore, my engagement with leftist melancholy on both sides of the Taiwan Strait shows that the search for the emancipatory potential of Mao's utopian socialism might not necessarily collapse into the Sinocentric political vision of the Chinese New Left (chapter 3). Rather, the interaction between the Chinese and Sinophone leftist literary expressions reveals the value of negative thinking that is lost in much of the muscular undertone of the New Left. In sum, these seemingly marginal perspectives offer an epistemological vantage point to understand the complex and fluid articulations of heterogeneous political currents that unexpectedly,

91. Shih, "What Is Sinophone Studies?," 11.
92. Makeham, *Lost Soul*, 6; Weiming Tu, "Cultural China"; Van Dongen, *Realistic Revolution*, 3–4.

rather than inevitably, gave rise to the dominant intellectual currents in contemporary China.

Finally, there are limitations to my approach. For all that, the selection of these texts and authors may still reflect my own aesthetic taste. Prudence counseled scholars long ago that our obsession with individual figures or schools of thought might inadvertently turn authors into fans, thereby producing a normative effort to celebrate or prosecute the achievements or the crimes of their protagonists. I have rarely allowed myself to write from the position of an advocate or a detractor, but the urge to approach ideas as lived and practiced by particular individuals has grown more powerful in our posthuman age. Throughout the long years of research on Chinese intellectuals, I have always drawn inspiration from writing about those whom I deeply admired—Li Zehou 李澤厚 (1930-2021), Chen Yinke, and others—whose work inspired me to pursue an academic career. When I write about controversial figures, I am equally fascinated by the theatricality of their dark drama. And even when I encounter most unscrupulous figures, such as the authors of *China Can Say No*, my antipathy is no less intermingled with a delight in poking fun at their hyperbole and swagger. From these figures and stories, I see comedies and tragedies, promises and failures, cynicism and sincerity, and most importantly, the dynamism of individual lives and microscenes behind grand master narratives. The goal is to make the world of Chinese intellectuals more vivid, more nuanced, and deeply human through my thick description. This book, therefore, must be read as an alternative or supplementary account to other, more comprehensive works.

Having made these observations, I now outline the contents of each chapter. Taking emotion as ethical reasoning, part 1 (chapters 1–2) is concerned with the question of how certain feelings (e.g., guilt, shame, and mourning) have acquired normative valence and political significance in Chinese liberal thinking. It examines how liberal-minded intellectuals advocated a palette of scenarios for a sentimental education as the emotive underpinning of enlightenment rationality. Turning to the fusion of emotion and intellect, part 2 (chapters 3–4) demonstrates that vehement passions or defeatist pathos stimulate, provoke, and inform literary innovation and intellectual agenda from the Left and the Right alike. Chapter 3 analyzes how left-wing writers grappled with the emotional overlay of melancholy to come to terms with the ruins of Maoist utopia. Chapter 4 investigates how the conservatives' heart-wrenching search for a postrevolutionary cultural identity was paradoxically energized by a similar passion for God—an obsession with the sublime and the eternal—that once enchanted Maoist utopianism. Last, part 3 (chapter 5) focuses on the manufactured nature of emotion and navigates how negative affect was exploited and mobilized by populist intellectuals and sensationalist media for political persuasion. It offers a specific take on the intertwined relationship between *ressentiment* and nationalism through a detailed exploration of the China Can Say No popular sentiment in the post-Tiananmen era. Each episode reveals how various searches for China's revolutionary past were intermingled with feelings and affects, and how psychic energy in turn underlined and framed expressions of competing political visions in the postsocialist present.

Chapter 1 discusses how Chinese aestheticians and literary critics debated emotional cultivation in the immediate post-Mao period. The reformist thinkers condemned the Cultural Revolution for harnessing a host of vehement emotions—hate, fear, and shame—toward vicious political ends, resulting in the breakdown of basic ethical norms. A New Enlightenment would involve the creation of enlightened sentiments that could fundamentally transform the moral and affective terrain of a paralyzed society steeped for more than a decade in the emotive mode of Maoist fanaticism. I center on two salient feelings frequently discussed by enlightenment thinkers: pleasure (*le* 樂) and guilt (*zui* 罪). The veteran aesthetician Li Zehou proposed a Kantian-Confucian "aesthetic education"—the inculcation of "affection" (*qing* 情), "moderation" (*du* 度) and "culture[s] of pleasure" (*legan wenhua* 樂感文化)—to engender and sustain a strong commitment to enlightenment rationality. In contrast to Li, who embraced Confucian this-worldly pleasure, the humanist critics Ba Jin 巴金 (1904–2005), Ji Xianlin 季羨林 (1911–2009), and Liu Zaifu 劉再復 (1941–) advocated for a "culture of contrition" grounded in the Christian notion of guilt. Reflecting on the alleged Chinese "failure" to express shame and remorse at the Red Guard's violence, these scholars underscored the irredeemable sense of guilt to stimulate one's inner conscience as a corrective to the pervasive apathy in the post-Mao public sphere. Li's

Confucian ethics of emotion and the humanistic discourse of "cultural reflection" (*wenhua fansi* 文化反思) represent distinct intellectual movements in the 1980s, and I seek to illuminate their commonalities and their contrasts. Above all, this chapter demonstrates how Li's aesthetics of this-worldly affection and the humanists' search for otherworldly guilt eventually merged into a shared agenda to bid farewell to the myth of revolutionary utopia.

Chapter 2 continues to examine how the culture of apology has profoundly shaped the liberal politics of mourning in the post-Tiananmen era. I analyze the surge of passions and pathos surrounding the life and scholarship of Chen Yinke, a cultural loyalist who expressed his moral indignation against the political reformation of intellectuals in the Mao era. I focus on how liberal-minded intellectuals actively participated in mourning Chen Yinke's tragic fate as a poignant symbol of the aggregating cultural catastrophes caused by Mao's socialist revolution, from Yu Ying-shih's 余英時 (1930–2021) "empathic identification" with Chen Yinke's loyalist resistance to Lu Jiandong's 陸鍵東 (1960–) melodramatic account of Chen Yinke's death in the Cultural Revolution. The liberal pathos transformed Chen Yinke's image from an apolitical thinker into a scholar against politics, a cultural loyalist resisting modernity, and a liberal martyr in defiance of Mao's revolutionary mandate. These tales and stories about Chen Yinke have inspired Chinese liberals to engage with the fin-de-siècle debate over the meaning of liberty in China's revolutionary twentieth century—its dimensions, its power, and the price Chen Yinke has paid to bring it into existence. By illustrating how the debates over Chen Yinke stirred up a constellation of volatile feelings and moral passions, I show that Chinese liberal thinking cannot be separated from the political emotions of the post-Mao intelligentsia.

Yet the liberals' moral repulsion at the crimes of the socialist revolution was challenged by leftist writers who argued that elegiac remembrance—not a sloppy dismissal—provides emotional cultivation to dwell on the specter of the Maoist past. Thus, chapter 3 turns to the aesthetic, affective, and political dimensions of leftist melancholy in Chinese and Sinophone literature following the collapse of Mao's Cultural Revolution. I focus on the literary and intellectual exchanges between the Taiwanese Marxist Chen Yingzhen 陳映真 (1937–2016) and the Shanghai-based novelist Wang Anyi 王安憶 (1954–) to illustrate how left-wing writers on both sides of the Taiwan Strait come to terms with the ruins of socialist utopia. As one of those veteran Marxists whose faith in socialism was shaken by the human costs of Mao's utopian experiment, Chen Yingzhen's melancholic reflections on the failure of radical politics were underpinned by a persistent—one might say outdated—belief in the messianic promise of revolution. Wang Anyi, on the other hand, sought to overcome her sense of exhaustion and ennui in the 1990s by drawing inspiration from Chen Yingzhen's utopian socialism. In delineating the rifts and affinities that both created tensions and nourished the friendship between the two writers, I explore their melancholy efforts to confront disillusionment, resignation, guilt, and forgetting in the postrevolutionary era. Some critics have dismissed such melancholy as a pathological or reactionary approach to left-wing politics, but the dystopian turn among leftist writers like Chen Yingzhen and Wang Anyi is, in fact, still animated by an emancipatory political promise.

Meanwhile, the liberals' attempt to exorcise religious sentiment has paradoxically aroused a muscular yearning for the return of the revolutionary sublime in postsecular China. In chapter 4, I analyze how the Chinese theologian Liu Xiaofeng dismissed Li Zehou's notion of "this-worldly pleasure" as the symptom of a modern nihilism and sought to rekindle a religious passion after the collapse of socialist utopianism. Liu is best known today as the founder of the Chinese Straussian School, a conservative intellectual movement that advocated a quasi-theological form of political leadership in contemporary China. Little attention has been paid, however, to the relationship between Liu's political authoritarianism and his meditation on religion. This chapter traces Liu's lifelong search for an "ultimate value" from his youthful yearnings for Christian redemption in the 1980s New Enlightenment to the utter profanation of the sacred in his recent espousal of the Mao cult. I suggest that Liu's conservative turn should not obscure the profound and troubling continuity between his earlier search for an other-worldly religious ethics and his later obsession with this-worldly political theology. By exploring the entanglement between revolution and religion throughout Liu's zigzagging journey, I consider Liu's transition as part and parcel of a generational endeavor to come to terms with the dilemma between enlightenment rationalism and its theological discontents that beset the post-Mao intelligentsia.

Chapter 5 delineates how the sorcerers of Chinese nationalism mobilized the theme of China as a victim of Western imperialism to critique the liberals' faith in cosmopolitan tolerance and enlightened sentiments. By focusing on the polemics surrounding the 1996 bestseller *China Can Say No* (*Zhongguo keyi shuobu* 中國可以說不), I demonstrate that *ressentiment*—a constantly morphing assemblage of strong and negative emotions—has been the principal psychological motor behind the explosive rise of popular nationalist sentiment since the 1990s. Engaging the Nietzschean critique of *ressentiment*, I aim to explain how the moral psychology of *ressentiment*—the repression of shame, the impulse to detract, and the inversion of values—was diffused through the capillaries of grassroots nationalism. The dynamic interaction between vengeance and vulnerability in the say-no farce conjured up a schizophrenic Chinese identity vacillating between cultural frustration and national pride in the post–Cold War era.

This study concludes with an epilogue reflecting on the surge of intellectual passion toward the Chinese Dream in the Xi Jinping era. I explore how President Xi's millennian vision of China as the new guardian of global order radically reconfigured the rhetoric of intellectual debates and galvanized rival factions into action. Liberal intellectuals, Confucian revivalists, nostalgic leftists, and grassroots nationalists interpreted the Chinese Dream not simply under the rubric of national rejuvenation, but also through ambivalent allegories and conflicting emotive utterances: amnesia, mourning, cynical conformity, and religious piety. All these impulses illustrate the pressures on purely intellectual judgments about the present arising from emotional memories of China's revolutionary past. In the present moment of global right-wing resurgence, Chinese intellectuals have remained deeply divided about the meaning of Mao's revolution for the future direction of China—its demonic power, its moral and ethical implications, and the price Chinese people have paid to bring it into existence. Yet the dynamic feelings and moral passions surrounding the country's past may help us understand the dilemmas of the post-Mao generation caught between revolution and reform.

PART I

Emotion as Ethical Reasoning

CHAPTER ONE

Pleasure and Guilt

Reason and Emotion in the Age of New Enlightenment

> The philosophy of existence is not founded in speculation, faith, or divine grace, but in the fluid and changing emotions themselves . . . Confucius' deep lamentation over running water is representative of the Chinese philosophy and aesthetics he and his disciples inaugurated, in which aesthetic appreciation takes the place of religion, and in which transcendence is placed squarely within the realm of human relations.
> —Li Zehou, *The Chinese Aesthetic Tradition*

> There exists a solidarity among men as human beings that makes each co-responsible for every wrong and every injustice in the world . . . If I fail to do whatever I can to prevent them, I too am guilty . . . that I live after such a thing has happened weighs upon me as indelible guilt . . . Jurisdiction rests with God alone.
> —Karl Jaspers, *The Question of German Guilt*

This chapter is a significantly revised and expanded version of the article "Pleasure and Sin: Li Zehou, Liu Zaifu, and the Political-Theological Motif in Post-Mao Cultural Reflections," *Prism: Theory and Modern Chinese Literature* 17, no. 1 (March 2020): 157–71, published by Duke University Press. Reprinted with permission.

In 1995, the prominent Chinese philosopher Li Zehou 李澤厚 (1930–2021) and literary critic Liu Zaifu 劉再復 (1941–) published a polemical book titled *A Farewell to Revolution* (*Gaobie geming* 告別革命) in Hong Kong. Li and Liu were arguably the most influential thinkers to emerge from the cultural milieu of the 1980s New Enlightenment. The 1989 Tiananmen crackdown and the ensuing wave of arrests and terror left reformist intellectuals disastrously demoralized. In the midst of great uncertainties and anxieties, Li and Liu fled mainland China in haste and took shelter in various places, finally settling down in Boulder, Colorado, in 1992.[1] But their faith in enlightenment had withstood the test of emigration. In *Farewell*, the two exiled intellectuals brought years of philosophical rumination to bear on the tempestuous fate of reason in modern Chinese history and politics. In particular, they criticized the Maoist practice of revolution for fetishizing "a variety of radical and violent actions and mass uprisings that attempt to overthrow extant order and authority."[2] The lure of radicalism, the glorification of violence, and the messianic belief in revolutionary justice have repeatedly interrupted China's incremental reforms and the cultivation of democratic temperament. In their sober—yet impassioned—call to "bid farewell to revolution," Li and Liu envisioned an enlightened, dispassionate Chinese mentality to overcome the dangerous passions, extreme sentiments, and aggressive impulses that once lay at the core of left-wing radicalism in twentieth-century China.

Farewell quickly became a banner for those who still cleaved to the emancipatory ideals of the New Enlightenment. It also led to what Xu Jilin has called "a parting of the ways" (*sixiang fenhua* 思想分化) between liberals and the Left with regard to the legacy of the New Enlightenment.[3] In the 1980s, reformist intellectuals inaugurated a series of "cultural reflections" (*wenhua fansi* 文化反思) to address the human abuses, mass atrocity, and other forms of political violence committed in the frenzy of ideological fanaticism. However, this reformist consensus was shattered by the bloody crackdown in Tiananmen Square. During the subsequent conservative backlash, members of the

---

1. See David Wang, "'Standing Alone Atop the Mountain.'"
2. See Li Zehou and Liu Zaifu, *Gaobie geming*, 60.
3. Xu Jilin, *Dangdai Zhongguo de qimeng yu fanqimeng*, 17.

reformist intelligentsia were caught up in an orgy of compulsory reeducation and self-castigation. Aside from the resurgence of political authoritarianism, the disorienting effects of marketization in the 1990s further alienated enlightenment intellectuals, who observed the rise of massified culture with a mixture of disappointment and disgust. Thus, even though enlightenment had lost much of its erstwhile appeal, the nostalgic liberals were drawn to Li and Liu's political manifesto and its claim that the pursuit of incremental reform remained an "unfinished project" in the new age of "market Leninism."

But the tragic outcome of the 1980s New Enlightenment was also a warning sign for many. The failed liberalization cast its long shadow over China's cultural vanguard and spawned a chorus of leftist outcry against Western models of modernization. In the swirl and wake of the growing grievance at market reforms, the Chinese New Left fulminated against Li and Liu's thesis as a thinly disguised neoliberal schema to "depoliticize" radical thinking and legitimize "end-of-history" liberal triumphalism.[4] For a new generation of scholars playing with postmodern and postcolonial paradigms, this ideological farewell announced not the end of revolution per se but rather the limits of the enlightenment project that prevented Chinese intellectuals from seeing the manifold potential of revolutionary politics. For the advocates of neoliberalism, by contrast, Li and Liu's lukewarm humanism has proved to be not only a flawed bulwark against the intrusive power of the party-state but also an outdated approach to the complex socioeconomic problems generated by global capitalism. Even in the eyes of humanist scholars, Li and Liu's attempt to recuperate the May Fourth liberal ethos from the overpowering mandate of revolution was dubiously Whiggish. Intellectual historians, including Lin Yu-sheng, Wang Fan-sen, and Rana Mitter, have exposed the dangerous liaisons between the May Fourth iconoclasts and the children of Mao's Cultural Revolution: both sought a "cultural-intellectualistic approach" to political ills, fueled by "obsession with youth" and "destruction of the past," and revealed an "arrogance about the superiority of one's own

---

4. See Wang Hui, *The End of the Revolution*, 3–18.

chosen system of thought."⁵ Eventually, the failure of the 1980s New Enlightenment became, in the words of Michael André Bernstein, a "foregone conclusion."⁶

Enlightened Sentiments

Although these critiques furnish a critical rethinking of the paradoxes and conflicts of enlightenment norms, they reduce *Farewell* to a willful, anachronistic manifesto of a naïvely old-fashioned liberal humanism.⁷ In his laudable attempt to recuperate the lyrical dimension of modern Chinese writers, David Wang urges scholars to turn away from the polemics of "revolution versus enlightenment" and focus on the question of "how subjectivity expresses, acquires, and critiques feelings and emotions as nuanced as that ascribed to the studies of either revolution or enlightenment."⁸ Echoing Wang's proposal that "enlightenment can have an impact only when charged with creative sensibilities,"⁹ this chapter redirects attention to Li Zehou and Liu Zaifu's exploration of the emotive dimensions of reason. But while Wang seeks to triangulate the dichotomous narrative of modern Chinese literary history with critical lyricism, I aim to circumvent the tired scheme of enlightenment and counter-enlightenment by directing attention to the discourse of "enlightened sentiments"—the cultivation of aesthetic sensibility and moral emotion—at the center of the New Enlightenment project.¹⁰ Above all, humanist thinkers in the 1980s were intensely preoccupied with the role of emotional cultivation in foregrounding the liberal ideas of freedom and autonomy. For those who lived through "the age of extremes"—the succession of trials, purges, factional warfare, and class

---

5. See Yu-Sheng Lin, *The Crisis of Chinese Consciousness*, 26–27; Wang Fan-sen, "'Zhuyi shidai' de lailin"; Mitter, *A Bitter Revolution*, 208.

6. Michael Bernstein, *Forgone Conclusions*.

7. For instance, Xin Gu reads Li Zehou's philosophy as a pale copy of Hegelian Marxism grounded in the tradition of German idealism. See Xin Gu, "Subjectivity, Modernity, and Chinese Hegelian Marxism," 205–45.

8. David Wang, *The Lyrical in Epic Time*, xii.

9. David Wang, *The Lyrical in Epic Time*, x.

10. For the notion of enlightened sentiments, see Nazar, *Enlightened Sentiments*.

struggles that characterized the Mao era—socialist revolution was charged with hate, fear, shame, and an obsession with violence. From the Yan'an Rectification Movement to the era of high socialism, the party invented, developed, and orchestrated a diverse array of "emotion work" that galvanized the masses to wage ruthless struggles against the real or imagined "enemies" of the people.[11] After 1949, the new socialist nation installed a hierarchy of property-based "class-status" (*chengfen* 成分) system—or what Haiyan Lee calls "class racism"—to institutionalize the dichotomy of friend and foe and sustain the momentum of Mao's permanent revolution.[12] The ritualized practice of "exposure" (*jiefa* 揭發), "confession" (*jiaodai* 交代), and "denunciation" (*pidou* 批鬥) culminated in the Cultural Revolution: the "ten years of madness" that turned husbands against wives, children against parents, and students against teachers, all of which devastated millions of families and led to the breakdown of basic ethical norms among community members. In the immediate post-Mao era, the effort to cast off the "self-incurred tutelage"[13] of humanity thus involved the creation of new emotional norms that could fundamentally transform the moral and affective terrain of a paralyzed society steeped for more than a decade in the emotive mode of Maoist fanaticism.

This chapter illustrates how enlightenment thinkers sought to create multiple and sometimes conflicting emotive norms to address the trauma of the past and cultivate enlightened sentiments at the crucial juncture of China's post-Mao transition. I center two salient public feelings discussed by Li Zehou and Liu Zaifu: "pleasure" (*le* 樂) and "guilt" (*zui* 罪). Returning to the Confucian aesthetic tradition, Li coined the term "culture[s] of pleasure" (*legan wenhua* 樂感文化) to highlight the cultivation of natural, secular emotions at the origin of Confucian civilization. He proposed a Kantian-Confucian "aesthetic education"—the inculcation of "affection," "moderation," and "this-worldly pleasure"—to engender and sustain a strong commitment to

---

11. Perry, "Moving the Masses."
12. For class racism, see Haiyan Lee, *The Stranger and the Chinese Moral Imagination*, 197–242; for class-status system, see Yiching Wu, *The Cultural Revolution at the Margins*, 38–46.
13. Kant, "An Answer to the Question," 17.

enlightenment rationality. In contrast to Li, who embraced Confucian this-worldly pleasure, humanist critics such as Ba Jin 巴金 (1904–2005), Ji Xianlin 季羨林 (1911–2009), and Liu Zaifu advocated a "literature of contrition" (*zuigan wenxue* 罪感文學) grounded in the Christian notion of guilt. Reflecting on the alleged failure of the Chinese people to express shame and remorse at the Maoist violence, these critics underscored the value of guilt in stimulating one's inner conscience as a corrective to the pervasive apathy in the post-Mao public sphere.

Furthermore, I seek to unveil a shared vision of sentimental education between Li Zehou's ruminations on this-worldly pleasure and Liu Zaifu's treatises on other-worldly guilt. Sentimentalism—the doctrine that holds that moral and political thinking originates in refined feelings—was developed by eighteenth-century empiricists such as David Hume and Adam Smith and philosophers such as Jean-Jacques Rousseau and Denis Diderot. Contrasting the Kantian proposal for a dispassionate noumenal self, these intellectuals highlighted the education of the senses, such as the inculcation of human feelings, aesthetic sensibilities, and moral consciousness, to cultivate a passionate commitment to enlightenment rationality.[14] Similarly, the notion of enlightened sentiments became crucial for the May Fourth generation's effort to foster moral sensibility and democratic sentiment among Chinese citizens. This "enlightenment structure of feeling," as Haiyan Lee puts it, "radicalizes the individual as the basic and irreducible unit of moral choice and action" and "breaks with the Confucian structure of feeling in staking uncompromising and nonnegotiable claims for individual freedom and autonomy."[15] In the May Fourth literary field, diverse romantic genres from "Mandarin Ducks and Butterflies" romances to bildungsromans celebrated the reflexive character of the sentimental that creates sympathy, pity, and compassion among Chinese readers. Bergsonian philosophers and Confucian revivalists further sharpened the cultural contours of sentimentalism by endowing sensibility with a distinct Chinese affective lifeworld to critique the hard-nosed, unemotional facade of occidental rationalism. By fusing enlightenment with

---

14. See Frazer, *The Enlightenment of Sympathy*, 4.
15. Haiyan Lee, *Revolution of the Heart*, 95–96.

sentiment, the practitioners of sentimental education suggested that reflexive autonomy rests not solely in pure reason but rather in an interactive process of feeling and judging.

In foregrounding the centrality of emotional norms in the post-Mao cultural reflection, I stage a critical dialogue with the scholarship on May Fourth sentimentalism. As Haiyan Lee, Eugenia Lean, Chen Jianhua, and others have forcefully demonstrated, discourses of sentiment dominated the late Qing and early republican literary and cultural field and participated in the creation of new cultural identity and national community.[16] Turning to Li and Liu's aesthetic theory and political thinking, this chapter asks how two moral sentiments—pleasure and guilt—took on added ethical significance and actively shaped the 1980s liberal-reformist agenda of "farewell to revolution." At first glance, however, Li and Liu derived very different lessons from Maoist emotional excess and projected distinct visions of the postrevolutionary moral renewal. A major figure in the 1980s "aesthetic fever" (*meixue re* 美學熱), Li directed his critique against the "sublime aesthetics" of the socialist era, when sensory and artistic enjoyment was intertwined with a fanatical—one might even say quasi-religious—enthusiasm toward Mao's utopian revolution: the emotional ecstasy of the raging crowd, the awe-inspiring figure of the Great Helmsman, and an unreserved expression of hatred against class enemies.[17] Li deplored how the dehumanizing dogmas of the Cultural Revolution barbarized cultural life, destroyed aesthetic taste, and sanctified ugly violence. To cultivate "new sensibilities" (*xin ganxing* 新感性) for contemporary Chinese humanities, Li sought to reconstruct a Kantian-Confucian aesthetic vista grounded in "this-worldly pleasure" (*cishi zhi le* 此世之樂)—sense gratification, an autonomous mode of contemplation, and delightful but moderate emotions.

In contrast to Li's philosophical optimism, Liu Zaifu (among other humanist critics) castigated the Chinese "inability to mourn"—the alleged failure of his generation to express remorse for the atrocious

---

16. Haiyan Lee, *Revolution of the Heart*; Lean, *Public Passions*; Chen Jianhua, "'Gonghe' zhuti yu simiwenxue."
17. See Ban Wang, *The Sublime Figure of History*, 194–228.

crimes of the past.[18] Above all, the catalog of injustices and horrors committed in the name of revolution—the mass killing of landlords, the systematic abuse of rightist intellectuals, and the atrocities committed by the Red Guards—weighed heavily on the minds of humanist critics. Whereas writers of "scar literature" (*shanghen wenxue* 傷痕文學) condemned the ultraleftist faction Gang of Four for inciting violence and commemorated universal victimhood, Liu and his allies confronted the complicity of Chinese intellectuals who facilitated great crimes during the chaos and violence of Mao's mass campaigns. In diaries, memoirs, and miscellaneous reflections, these humanist writers described how the fratricidal practice of mutual incrimination in the endless criticism and self-criticism tribunals turned victims into perpetrators and perpetrators into victims. To reckon with the vicious imbrication between victimhood and perpetration, Liu proposed that only a biblical notion of guilt could interrogate the soul of the post-Mao generation and foster an innate sense of moral conscience beyond legal and political measures.

Notwithstanding the characteristic tension between this-worldly pleasure and other-worldly guilt, however, Li and Liu offer two distinct, yet closely intertwined, visions of enlightened sentiments. Even though their voices were only two amid a chorus in the sustained post-Mao intellectual reflection on the thorny questions of responsibility, justice, and morality, Li and Liu captured two salient public sentiments in the immediate postrevolutionary years: the excitement of rising from the turbulence of revolution and plunging into the brave new world of cosmopolitan spender and bourgeois sensibility; and the shame of belonging to a contaminated, feudalistic tradition of political despotism and mass violence. The following discussion is therefore divided into three parts. First, I demonstrate how the destruction of the old revolutionary order unleashed unprecedented social imagination and artistic creation in the early 1980s, and how such optimism and hope proved inspirational to Li's deep philosophical rumination on aesthetic

---

18. The morally driven discourse of Chinese humanism bears an affinity with Margaret Mitscherlich and Alexander Mitscherlich's discussion of the German "inability to mourn" in the postwar era. See Mitscherlich and Mitscherlich, *The Inability to Mourn.*

pleasure. The second part turns to examine how the unrelenting political conflict and ideological backlash shaped post-Mao public disputes over transitional justice, and how Liu's compassionate call for a collective guilty conscience resonated with the humanists' call for self-purification and moral regeneration. The concluding part demonstrates that Li's espousal of this-worldly pleasure and the humanists' search for an other-worldly guilt eventually merged into a shared agenda to bid farewell to the Maoist sublime.

Reason and This-Worldly Pleasure

The beginning of the New Era (1976–1989) marked an extraordinary moment in Chinese cultural and intellectual history. With the demise of Mao and his ultraleftist acolytes in 1976, the reformist leadership under Deng Xiaoping began to lift ideological indoctrination and encouraged writers and intellectuals to "liberate their thought" (*jiefang sixiang* 解放思想) and "seek truth from facts" (*shishi qiushi* 實事求是). The waning of the revolution and the dynamism of reforms propelled the thinking of the post-Mao generation, whether they were establishment intellectuals on the conservative Left or cultural iconoclasts and avant-garde artists on the Right. Amid the succession crisis and ideological shifts, a small but growing number of the cultural elites began to revive humanist notions and moral values. Through literary testimonies and philosophical deliberation, the emerging community of dissent directed its energy toward humanist cultural and ethical norms: How should the Chinese people "become human" again and cultivate "human emotions" (*renqing* 人情) after decades of "merciless" (*wuqing* 無情) class struggle and proletarian warfare? How should they create a new language of truth, sincerity, and civic responsibility out of a traumatized, decimated, and fragmented society?

The revival of humanism started in the realm of aesthetics (*meixue* 美學), a discipline that occupied a prominent place in the cultural politics of the PRC. From modernist art to Misty Poetry, from the celebration of the fantastic and the primitive to solemn reflections on "socialist alienation," a full-blown "aesthetic fever" fanned emotional wildfires and aroused nationwide discussions about the nature, function, and significance of beauty.[19] Addressing political problems of the day as an aesthetic issue, the participants of the debate sought a "redistribution of the sensible": a reordering of what can be seen, felt, and appreciated that could empower new forms of political sensibility against the Maoist sublime.[20] Many poignantly felt that Mao's last revolution ("a cultural destruction in the name of cultural revolution")[21] bowdlerized Chinese aesthetics and reduced artistic enjoyment to the most infantile and repetitive expressions of political conformity. When asked why college students were cramming into overcrowded classes on aesthetics in the early 1980s, a respondent recalled that "the Cultural Revolution destroyed beauty and sanctified ugly barbarism . . . and so we study [aesthetics] to search for an ideal human vision."[22] The revolt against revolutionary asceticism also brought back the frozen music from the past: a lineup of Chinese and Western "bourgeois aestheticians" who had been forcibly erased by the Maoist public discourse. The list of cultural heroes ranged from the Crocean aesthetician Zhu Guangqian 朱光潜 (1897–1986)[23] and the Goethean poet Zong Baihua 宗白華 (1897–1986) to Sigmund Freud, Jean-Paul Sartre and Friedrich Nietzsche. Moreover, rebellious youths celebrated the aestheticization of the everyday life as theoretical justification for their obsession with bourgeois fashion: unkempt hairstyles, revealing clothing, Yellow Music, erotic art—the list was endless. Together, these divergent aesthetic vistas grounded in beauty, sensuality, and delightful emotions ensnared hearts, captured minds, and produced a symphony of unmitigated optimism.

The most memorable cry for a "Copernican revolution" in aesthetics came from Li Zehou, whose 1981 magnum opus, *The Path of Beauty*

---

19. See Zhu Dongli, *Jingshen zhilü*, 71–105.
20. Rancière, *The Politics of Aesthetics*.
21. Ban Wang, *The Sublime Figure of History*, 196.
22. Ma Guochuan, *Wo yu bashiniandai*, 54; Li Zehou recalled that "courses in aesthetics were in [high] demand at schools and universities . . . public lectures attracted thousands of students and even common workers." See Li and Cauvel, *Four Essays on Aesthetics*, 22.
23. Despite Zhu's self-willed conversion into a Marxist scholar in the 1950s, it was his earlier republican-era writing that drew enormous attention in the 1980s. For a refined study of Zhu's early aestheticism, see Yeh, *The Alienated Academy*, 270–74.

(*Mei de licheng* 美的歷程), earned him the epithet "the spiritual mentor of the young generation." Li was born in 1930 into a declining gentry family in rural Hunan, the heartland of the Chinese Revolution. Like many who grew up in the chaos of the Second Sino-Japanese War (1937–1945), Li became a zealous Marxist at an early age and participated in underground Communist activities during his stay at Mao's alma mater, the First Normal School of Changsha. After the founding of the PRC, Li studied aesthetics and philosophy at Peking University and then joined the Institute of Philosophy at the Chinese Academy of Social Science as a research fellow. In the years that followed, his reputation grew prodigiously: between 1956 and 1961, Li participated in the Great Debate of Aesthetics (*Meixue dabianlun* 美學大辯論), an academic-cum-ideological campaign targeting Zhu Guangqian's bourgeois idealism. Whereas Zhu understood artistic experience as an intuitive, immediate, and autonomous mode of contemplation detached from extraneous concerns and secular entanglements, his intellectual nemesis Cai Yi 蔡儀 (1906–1992) adopted the Leninist theory of reflection to treat aesthetic appreciation as a passive mirroring of objects in subjective minds.[24] Li, meanwhile, sought to reconcile the antinomy between spontaneity and receptivity by proposing an "aesthetics of social praxis" (*shijian meixue* 實踐美學): humankind, while engaging in remolding external environment through labor, also transforms its inner psychological consciousness. Our capacity for perceiving beauty is thus the result of "sedimentation" (*jidian* 積澱), a historical process by which cultural and aesthetic taste is accumulated and precipitated into collective unconscious.[25]

The Cultural Revolution brought only a short interruption in Li's pursuit of dialectical aesthetics—he was forced to undergo "political

---

24. Rather than insisting on the principle of aestheticism, Zhu offered a trenchant criticism of his own "reactionary, decadent and escapist" bourgeois idealism to align himself with the party's Marxist orthodox. Meanwhile, Cai Yi and others endeavored to prove that Zhu's modified stance was still diametrically opposed to Marxist-Leninist epistemology. See Zhu Guangqian, "Wo de wenyi sixiang de fandongxing"; Cai Yi, *Xin meixue*; for a detailed study of this debate, see Shim, "The Aesthetic Thought of Zhu Guangqian," 153–66.

25. Li Zehou, "Meixue san tiyi"; for an analysis of Li's theory of sedimentation, see Chong, "Combining Marx with Kant."

reeducation" at a rural May Seventh cadre school (*wuqi ganxiao* 五七幹校)—but by the late 1970s, he had returned to Beijing and threw himself into completing his major philosophical treatise, *Critique of Critical Philosophy: A New Approach to Kant* (批判哲學的批判：康德述評), which immediately became a key text in post-Mao intellectual life. Like a number of other humanist scholars dissatisfied with the reigning orthodoxies of socialist realism, Li presented a modified version of historical materialism—or, in his words, an "anthropology of human practice" (*shijianlun de renleixue* 實踐論的人類學)—by combining Marx with Kant. Against the Leninist conception of the human as a passive and obedient subject, Li celebrated Kant's notion of the beautiful as "purposiveness without purpose" and encouraged his readers to be more self-assertive in affirming human autonomy as the categorical imperative. Yet he also reformulated transcendental idealism with Marxist social premises. Instead of acknowledging the spontaneity of the mind as an a priori condition for human experience, Li emphasized the materialist foundation of our consciousness. His neologism "subjectality" (*zhuti xing* 主體性) thus endorsed the Kantian conception of human beings as active agents while constraining human will within a historically formed "cultural-psychological structure" (*wenhua xinli jiegou* 文化心理結構).[26]

To his admirers and his critics, Li stood as the very embodiment of the 1980s New Enlightenment: he exerted his power to form and reflect public opinion through his intervention into Marxist humanism, his treatises on modern Chinese intellectual history, and his ruminations on Confucian aesthetics. In 1986, Li—then at the height of his influence—urged the young protagonists of the "high-culture fever" (*wenhua re* 文化熱) to confront the "symbiotic variations of enlightenment and national salvation" (啟蒙與救亡的雙重變奏) in Chinese modernity. With the ousting of the party's liberal-minded general secretary Hu Yaobang 胡耀邦 (1915–1989) in the same year, the power struggle between conservative and reformist political elites spilled over into cultural circles, suffusing the paranoid intelligentsia

---

26. Li Zehou, "Subjectivity and 'Subjectcality.'"

with bitter factionalism and heightened radicalism.[27] The sense of urgency compelled Li to argue that the overpowering mandate of "saving the nation"—the emotional excess propelled by patriotic ardor—had repeatedly suffocated the rationalist spirit of *Aufklärung* throughout the New Culture Movement in the 1910s and 1920s. Fearing that his generation would again plunge into vicious "line struggles," Li proposed to resuscitate—or "creatively transform"—the May Fourth legacy of liberal pluralism against all forms of ideological zealotry.[28]

Although scholars from various ideological camps have written extensively about Li's macroscopic imagery of enlightenment, little attention has been paid to the intertwined relations between Kantian rationality and Confucian ethics of emotion throughout his philosophical journey. In contrast to the Kantian detached noumenal self, Li's tendency to anthropologize reason led to a different assertion: that the human being is governed by emotive forces and psychological torrents and situated within the social and historical world. In *The Path of Beauty* (1981) and its sequel, Li coined the term "emotional-rational structure" (*qingli jiegou* 情理結構) to describe the harmony of reason and emotion at the heart of Confucian aesthetics. But it was not until the 1990s that Li explicitly rebelled against Cartesian rationalism by affirming the Confucian "original substance of feeling" (*qing benti* 情本體)—the foundational role of "emotion" (*qing* 情) in cultivating human affection and generating moral-political norms for the postrevolutionary age. Many critics took Li's emotive turn to mean he had abandoned his strong commitment to Kantian pure reason and retreated to moral sentimentalism.[29] Yet Li's 1990s espousal of emotion

---

27. For an analysis of the paranoid mentality of intellectual elites in the 1980s, see Dingxin Zhao, *The Power of Tiananmen*, 53–78.

28. Li Zehou, "Qimeng yu jiuwang de shuangchong bianzou."

29. Scholars from a variety of disciplines regard Li's 1990s obsession with Confucian ethics as a deviation from his earlier commitment to Kantian rationalism. Yet even though Li did not spell out his theoretical premises on Confucianism until the nineties, his major exegesis of the Confucian ethics of emotion was already published in the early 1980s. As both David Wang and Jinhua Jia propose, Li advocated complementing Kantian transcendentalism with Confucian aesthetic sensibilities throughout his search for enlightenment. See David Wang, *The Lyrical in Epic Time*, 358–59; Jia, "Li Zehou's Reconception of the Confucian Ethics of Emotion."

as the foundation of Chinese morality exemplifies his sustained concern for complementing Kantian enlightenment with Confucian aesthetic education—an elaborate scheme of inculcating proper emotions toward rational ends—throughout the 1980s.

Of particular importance here was Li's excavation of the "culture of pleasure" as the core feature of Confucian aesthetics. In Confucian classics such as *The Analects*, the Chinese term "pleasure" (*le* 樂) indicates an ideal emotional state of delight gained through cognitive learning and moral cultivation.[30] Whereas Plato condemns hedonistic pleasure for inflicting physical pains and cognitive disorder, Confucius emphasizes the need to release or redirect one's sensual desire toward ethical ends.[31] In *The Chinese Aesthetic Tradition* (*Huaxia meixue* 華夏美學) (1988), Li suggested that, even though *le* is aroused by desires for sex, beauty, food, and luxury, it must be tamed and transformed into virtuous and sustainable delight. For this reason, Li associated Confucian pleasure with a culture of music and aesthetics. Noting that pleasure (*le*) and music (*yue*) are written with the same character 樂, Li proposed that fine music—that which expresses the ideal of harmony, balance, simplicity, and purity—not only stirs up delightful

---

30. I have considered two possible translations for *le* 樂: "pleasure" and "delight." Andrew Lambert and Curie Virág choose "delight" to highlight the moral imperative of *le* in *The Analects* against the short-lived, sensuous *yu* 慾 (desire). By contrast, Michael Nylan uses "pleasure" to capture the widespread preoccupation with the question of immediate sensual gratification in the Warring States Period (481/403 BCE–221 BCE), which included "massive places, terraces, or parks . . . exquisite foods and wines; captivating music; fine rhetoric." Although "delight-like state" might be closer to the Confucian ethical feeling of *le*, I choose "pleasure" to emphasize Li Zehou's central concern with the aesthetic exuberance brought on by joyful encounters with the secular and the sensuous world. See Lambert, "From Aesthetics to Ethics"; Nylan, "On the Politics of Pleasure"; Virág, *The Emotions in Early Chinese Philosophy*, 41–42.

31. As Emily Fletcher's analysis shows, the Platonic conception of pleasure is essentially associated with pain or painful desire. For Plato, pleasure has the power to "distort our perceptions, beliefs, and values." By contrast, Lambert argues that the Confucian notion of *le* encompasses a wide range of virtuous feelings such as "love" (*ai* 愛), "joy" (*yi* 怡), and "happiness" (*huan* 歡). See Fletcher, "Two Platonic Criticisms of Pleasure"; Lambert, "From Aesthetics to Ethics."

emotions but also awakens an inner desire for self-cultivation and moral perfection.³² True delight, in this sense, is not short-lived exuberance brought on by sensuous gratification, but instead achieved only through the fulfillment of one's character—that of a Confucian gentleman (*junzi* 君子) who always behaves in accordance with the moral norms of ritual propriety (*li* 禮).

To understand Li's fascination with the educative function of Confucian aesthetics, it is helpful to recall his antipathy against Mao's "sentimental education," a radical political vision that enshrines unbridled emotions and irrational impulses as the motor force of revolution. The animosities of the earthly Mao toward the Confucian ideal of "subjecting oneself to the rules of ritual propriety" (*keji fuli* 克己復禮) fostered an iconoclastic ideology that hailed the "tiger spirit" (*huqi* 虎氣) and "monkey spirit" (*houqi* 猴氣) of the revolutionary vanguard with devilish glee. In his essay "On Young Mao Zedong" ("Qingnian Mao Zedong" 青年毛澤東), Li showed how Mao's voluntarist psycho-philosophy was littered with agnostic imageries of impulse (*chongdong* 衝動), movement (*dong* 動), conflict (*chongtu* 衝突), and struggle (*douzheng* 鬥爭).³³ Mao's celebration of the romantic, impulse-driven, and emotive "overpowering self" (*guiwo* 貴我), his social-Darwinian vision of a chaotic universe propelled by incessant motions and infinite struggles, and his idiosyncratic mania for unmasking the hidden class enemy through endless purges and trials—all these had a profound influence on the polemic style and extreme behavior of the Red Guard generation. To curb the "violent delights" of Mao's acolytes, Li countered that pleasure can be nurtured only through "proper measure" (*du* 度)—understood as the capacity for restraint and behavior management. Because human nature combines finitude and spontaneity, and is propelled by creativity yet constrained by time and history, it is necessary to adhere to the "doctrine of the golden mean" (*zhongyong* 中庸), a practical reasoning that constantly gauges, modulates, and

32. Li Zehou, *Huaxia meixue*, 16–32; Li's perspective on music and Confucian ritualism might have been inspired by Xu Fuguan. See Xu Fuguan, *Zhongguo yishu jingshen*.
33. Li Zehou, "Qingnian Mao Zedong," 127–49.

controls subjective wishes and desires according to external norms and circumstances.³⁴

Furthermore, Li's search for an ideal disposition of moderation and self-restraint gravitated toward what he termed the "this-worldly" orientation of Confucianism, a secularist "one-world view" categorically different from the Judeo-Christian culture of guilt. In sharp contrast to the Christian thirst for salvation, Confucius refrained from discussing other-worldly creatures and ethics—death, ghosts, spirits, and supernatural beings—for fear that these "mysterious phenomena, feats of force, rebellious conduct, and spirits" (*guai, li, luan, shen* 怪, 力, 亂, 神) might undermine the ethical values of this world.³⁵ For this reason, Li believed that the Confucian "culture of pleasure" connotes a secular-humanistic affirmation of worldly happiness over religious devotion for salvation, martyrdom, or afterlife existence.³⁶ In Li's own words, Confucius celebrates neither Christian guilt nor Japanese shame but instead hails the pursuit of pleasure in this life as the ultimate value:

> In the "culture of pleasure" the spirit cannot be separated from the body and there is a thorough affirmation of human existence in this world. Even in the darkest and most difficult times, people believe that sooner or later, there must be a reversal towards the good. They firmly believe that their future is bright, and that it is not placed in any Heavenly kingdom, but rather in this very reality.
> 「樂感文化」重視靈肉不分離，肯定人在這個世界的生存和生活。即使在黑暗和災難年代，也相信「否極泰來」，前途光明，這光明不在天國，而在這個世界。³⁷

---

34. See Li Zehou, *Lishi bentilun*, 8–16.

35. Although Confucius did not explicitly deny the existence of deities, he stressed that one "would not speak about mysterious phenomena, feats of force, rebellious conduct, and spirits." Confucius's exchanges with his disciples suggest that he feared that speculation about the unknowable and the supernatural might distract people from this-worldly concerns: "Without understanding life, how can you understand death." See Ni, *Understanding the Analects of Confucius*, 203, 266.

36. For an analysis, see Rošker, *Following His Own Path*, 120.

37. Quoted in and translated by Rošker, *Following His Own Path*, 121.

In many ways, Li's advocacy for this-worldly pleasure harked back to the republican education minister Cai Yuanpei's 蔡元培 (1868–1940) iconic 1917 speech "On Replacing Religion with Aesthetic Education" ("Yi meiyu dai zongjiao shuo" 以美育代宗教說). Although Cai shared the iconoclastic urge of the New Culture Movement to overthrow all "divine authorities" (shenquan 神權) and "superstitions" (mixin 迷信), he also believed that religious aesthetics contained a rich repository for Bildung, or achieving a state of transcendence through the appreciation of beauty. As Peter Zarrow's refined study of Cai's aesthetic thinking shows, Cai granted religion its original pedagogic function to cultivate people's aesthetic sensibility. Yet for the May Fourth iconoclast, religion also aroused public emotion in a superstitious way and therefore had to be replaced by modern aesthetic education.[38] Whereas Christian art uplifts sentiments and fosters altruistic behavior, aesthetic education—in Cai's mind, the inculcation of artistic consciousness through music, literature, sculpture, and architecture—could help instill enlightened "knowledge, will, and sentiment" and create "civilized people" without resorting to "primitive and pathological" religious doctrines.[39] Against all forms of theodicy, Cai and other proponents of "ontological aesthetics" (meixue benti lun 美學本體論) suggested that the aesthetic realm of art and beauty alone offers the requisite moral and spiritual remedy for the disenchanted modern society.[40]

Despite their divergence in life paths and methodological premises, Li continued Cai's vision of aesthetic education, expanding its terrain to Confucian secular humanism and endowing it with renewed political relevance. Following the May Fourth predecessors, Li also suggested that, in the absence of a transcendental deity, Confucian aesthetic cultivation played the role of a "nonreligious religion" in terms of its capacity to educate and edify humanity through this-worldly pleasure without recourse to any divine guidance. As he put it, a Confucian affective mind does not "rely upon the salvation of humanity by God" but rather "strives to rectify and nurture manifold

---

38. Zarrow, *Abolishing Boundaries*, 84–85.
39. Cai Yuanpei, "Yi meiyu dai zongjiao shuo," 68–69.
40. See Chen Wangheng, *Ershi shiji Zhongguo meixue bentilun wenti*.

feelings through aesthetic inculcations."[41] Meanwhile, Li further instilled Confucian this-worldly aesthetics with a rational spirit of self-fulfillment. This perspective was evident in his effort to explain the peculiar genesis of a "pragmatic reason" (*shiyong lixing* 實用理性) that distinguished the Confucian this-worldly mentality from Christian transcendence. It is important to note that *shiyong lixing* does not refer to the Western philosophical tradition of pragmatism, but instead points toward a secular mentality that finds pleasure and meaning in the realm of concrete, material, and sensual life against the transcendental. In this sense, Li identified "pragmatic reason" as the ability of a person to cast off the illusion of religious transcendence to become a sovereign creator of their own:

> There was no need for an external God, whose orders, which were based upon irrational authority, had to be blindly followed. On the other hand, people still possessed hope of salvation (humanism) and self-fulfillment (individual sense of mission) without rejecting this world or humiliating themselves . . . Everything could be left to the balanced measure and regulative function of the pragmatic reason.
> 不需要外在的上帝的命令，不盲目服從非理性的權威，卻仍然可以拯救世界（人道主義）和自我完成（個體人格和使命感）；不厭棄人世，也不自我屈辱⋯⋯一切都放在實用的理性天平上加以衡量和處理。[42]

Li's pragmatic reason serves not as a simple assertion of a secular-realistic mentality but as a talisman against all forms of violent and unbridled religious myths. Here, Li's perception that extraordinary myth is the enemy of enlightenment might have been influenced by Ernst Cassirer (1874–1945), whose philosophy of culture served as an important source of inspiration for Chinese humanist scholars and writers throughout the 1980s. In *The Myth of the State* (1945), the antifascist German scholar reflected on the surrendering of rational logic

---

41. Li Zehou, *Huaxia meixue*, 216.
42. Li, "Kongzi zai pingjia," 25, quoted in and translated by Rošker, *Following His Own Path*, 143.

to fascist political mythology that promised to bring back the mythic traditions of the past. Although propagandistic mythmaking was in flagrant contradiction to empirical reality, it provided a simple, direct, and transcendental answer to the problems and anxieties of the secular present. With the regression of rational explanation into mythical configurations, as Federico Finchelstein neatly summarizes, "demonstration was replaced with fabrication; the sacred took the place of the secular; extraordinary explanation eliminated common sense."[43] Against the "clear and definitive victory" of mythical thought, however, Cassirer sought to recuperate occidental rationalism by returning to "the struggle against myth" in ancient Greek philosophy. In direct opposition to the mythic and frightening god whose powers exceed and defy human understanding, Plato introduced the idea of *logos* to displace primitive myth with a rationally conceived model of human agency. To banish the dissolute power of extravagant myth, as Peter Gordon notes, Cassirer eventually returned to the Socratic ideal of self-direction and extolled the human capacity to "choose our fate and thereby remain authors of our political future."[44]

Just as Cassirer was impelled to retrieve the Greek *logos* against divine illumination, Li also aimed chiefly to show how Confucian philosophers in the Eastern Zhou Dynasty (770–256 BCE) developed rational conceptions of "ritual propriety" that could supplant the mythos of shamanistic rituals. Whereas shamans and magicians invented religious rituals to communicate with the divine, it was with the Duke of Zhou and Confucian sages that "ritual" (*li* 禮) became a set of moral norms about the cultivation of human virtue. In contrast to the mythic and whimsical spirits, ghosts, and supernatural forces whose power frightened shamans into submission, Confucius regarded the cultivation of "humanness" (*ren* 仁) as the ultimate purpose of ritual learning. Rather than submitting to a whimsical, supernatural force through religious ritual, Confucius extolled the power of ritual to awaken our capacity for moral perfection and self-direction. By "transforming religious ritual into a ritualized affirmation of humanness" (*shili guiren* 釋禮歸仁), Confucian philosophers turned away from the question of

---

43. Finchelstein, *Fascist Mythologies*, 1.
44. Gordon, *Continental Divide*, 303.

transcendence and moved toward a pragmatic search for ideal ethical-kinship relations and secular political order.[45]

The question remains, however, of whether Confucian this-worldly aesthetics could reconcile emotional cultivation with the rationalist ideal of enlightenment. Despite his enormous influence, Li's rejection of other-worldly ethics left many critics discontented. Would the secular orientation of Confucian pragmatic rationality be sufficient to provide an ultimate ground for the postrevolutionary cultural renewal? And how could the Confucian pleasure principle help to address the crimes and traumas of the socialist past? As we shall see in the next section, the solace of other-worldly ethics remained attractive to a generation of humanist writers who strove to confess their sense of irredeemable guilt and shame in the age of apology.

Emotion and Other-Worldly Guilt

Notwithstanding its initial vigor, aesthetic fever was but one among many intellectual ferments that transformed the post-Mao cultural milieu. Whereas Li Zehou proclaimed the necessity of cultivating this-worldly pleasure, humanist writers and critics called out the biblical guilt that all participants of the Maoist violence consciously and unconsciously shared. The most renowned spokesman for a "repentance consciousness" (*chanhui yishi* 懺悔意識) was Ba Jin, the veteran socialist writer who, even under enormous pressure, boldly encouraged his generation to "speak the truth" and publicly called for establishing a "museum of the 'Cultural Revolution'"—a *lieu de mémoire* exhibiting "concrete and real objects, and reconstructing striking scenes" to engrave the traumatic upheavals of the Mao era into national memory.[46] As a seasoned political survivor who witnessed innumerable false trials, fabricated confessions, and cruel deaths of his colleagues, Ba Jin wrote an exhaustive memoir to confess his participation in the persecution of his friends and acquaintances. Such an expression of moral guilt spoke to the specific question of complicity and how the

---

45. See Li Zehou, *Youwu daoli, shili guiren*.
46. Ba, "Wenge bowuguan," 601–4.

perpetrators of mass violence could break their guilty silence, spread the word of contrition, and initiate a spiritual and moral renewal among the Chinese people.

Although Ba Jin's proposal for a repentance consciousness found widespread resonance among the post-Mao generation, there had been growing disagreement about how to come to terms with the consequences of mass violence and the complicity of the Red Guards. Against the humanists' wish for reconciliation through confession—a categorical negation of the Mao era—a new politics of silence quickly became the official stance on the controversies concerning remembrance of the past. In the 1981 "Resolution on Certain Questions in the History of Our Party since the Founding of the PRC," the party leadership avoided addressing the murky relation between the perpetrators of violence and their victims, and in turn used the equivocal rhetoric of "collective guilt" to exculpate the mass participation of political persecution in the Cultural Revolution.[47] With the exception of the Gang of Four trial, the resolution refrained from condemning any specific groups—Red Guards, rebel workers, or the accomplices of Mao's ultraleftist scheme—as the real culprits of revolutionary violence.[48] In other words, to move forward required not to remember but to forget.

47. While "collective guilt" is often used in Western scholarship to describe a group-based moral feeling toward the group's immoral actions, the CCP deployed the term to shield specific groups (e.g., Red Guards who howled abuse at their teachers) from moral anxiety or guilt by ascribing responsibility to the universal yet abstract category of the "people." According to this logic, because everybody had been duped by the Gang of Four to participate in the Cultural Revolution, no specific groups should bear single responsibility for the bloody outcome. For a definition of collective guilt, see Branscombe and Doosje, "International Perspectives on the Experience of Collective Guilt."

48. Susanne Weigelin-Schwiedrzik argues that the party advocated the idea of universal complicity to avoid provoking revenge syndrome. By refraining from naming specific perpetrators, the regime in transition hoped to reconcile conflicts and avoid continued factionalism. However, as Alexander C. Cook proposes, this instrumental approach failed to offer a credible transitional justice and hence seriously jeopardized the legitimacy of the post-Mao regime. See Weigelin-Schwiedrzik, "In Search of a Master Narrative for 20th-Century Chinese History"; Cook, *The Cultural Revolution on Trial*, 227–34.

Between political repression and cultural thaw, a wave of scar literature and "reportage literature" (*baogao wenxue* 報告文學) did emerge in the early 1980s to present graphic, tear-jerking depictions of the chaos and violence in the socialist years that destroyed the ethos of the Chinese intelligentsia. Much to Ba Jin's chagrin, however, personal and literary testimonies typically idolize the Chinese literati as "either hapless, innocent victims or, occasionally, defiant resisters"[49] of the tyranny of the masses, bypassing the fact that many also played the role of informers, declared their allegiance to the police state, and launched scathing attacks on their colleagues for self-preservation.[50] During the 1957 Anti-Rightist Campaign, for instance, the appalling ritual of mutual incrimination created an oppressive "chain-of-prey" syndrome that turned victims into perpetrators and perpetrators into victims.[51] For many critics, the excessive, narcissistic commemoration of the intellectual as the tragic hero and the sole victim of the revolution evaded the shameful memory of complicity and could rarely be counted as a paradigm of moral learning. Moreover, scholars were alarmed by the dubious affinities between the anguished voice of humanism and the Communist language of "speaking bitterness" (*suku* 訴苦), a political ritual in the 1950s land reform campaign that galvanized rural peasants into fierce struggles against the "exploiting classes."[52] If the humanistic expression of trauma and grievance bears a striking resemblance to the orchestrated revolutionary practice of speaking bitterness, how could such an interpellated emotive utterance facilitate transitional justice?

The limits of humanist reflection raised the poignant question as to whether the Chinese civilization lacked the "confessional awareness" integral to Western faith traditions. Whereas Li Zehou hailed Confucian pragmatic mentality as a superior form of humanist reason, his close ally Liu Zaifu (fig. 1) was more willing to venture into the realm of

---

49. Zha, "China: Surviving the Camps."
50. For a detailed study of the bystander morality in China's reeducation camps, see Ning Wang, *Banished to the Great Northern Wilderness*.
51. Ning Wang, "Victims and Perpetrators."
52. For speaking bitterness, see Hershatter, *The Gender of Memory*; Anagnost, *National Past-Times*, 17–44.

FIGURE 1. Li Zehou (left) and Liu Zaifu (right) in Boulder, Colorado, 2018. Photo courtesy of Liu Jianmei and Tu Xinshi.

Christian transcendence. Born in 1941 into a peasant family in southern Fujian, Liu studied Chinese literature at Xiamen University, served as an editor for the Beijing-based magazine *New Construction* (*Xin jianshe* 新建設), and joined the party in 1979 to assist several senior literary leaders and veteran writers with manuscripts and speech writing. During his appointment as the director of the Institute of Literature at the Chinese Academy of Social Sciences from 1985 to 1989, Liu eagerly sponsored academic discussions oriented toward cultural liberalization—a grave political error that eventually led to his downfall after the Tiananmen protest. His most acclaimed—but also fiercely contested—monograph appeared in 1986 under the title *On the Composition of Human Character* (*Xingge zuhe lun* 性格組合論). Its central message was that humanist literature must transcend the morbid modalities of Maoist aesthetics and reassert the multifarious facets of personhood—an immensely rich "inner universe" (*nei yuzhou* 內宇宙) characterized by the incessant metamorphosis of emotions, desires, and streams of (un)consciousness. The blasphemous book was bombarded with criticisms from orthodox Marxists, for whom the filthy term "individual" (*geren* 个人) was associated with selfishness, narrow-mindedness, and bourgeois hypocrisy. Yet Liu's vigorous insistence on the polyvalent composition of characters found widespread resonance among the younger generation of writers, who strove to replace the bloated and lifeless Maoist collective subjectivity with the individual self as the unique locus of reason and will.

When it came to the question of guilt, however, Liu seemed to have slackened his secular humanism in favor of a religious sensibility beyond the human domain. As Liu struggled to start a second phase of life in the United States after 1989, he began to reflect on how Chinese intellectuals bore a collective responsibility for their transgressions during the Cultural Revolution, a biblical sin above and beyond the jurisdiction of law and morality. Admittedly, Liu's effort to posit an existential guilt drew him much closer to the proponents of Sino-Christian theology who contended that only the transcendent God of the Bible could promise a form of purification beyond flimsy humanism. The thirst for God's salvation reflected an increasingly radical theological view—namely, that the secular vocabulary of "trauma," "reason," and "reconciliation" was insufficient to address the endless catalog of apocalyptic violence and terror that nullifies the very notion of humanity and progress. Echoing Adorno's statement that writing poetry after Auschwitz was impossible, the young Christian theologian Liu Xiaofeng—the protagonist of chapter 4—mourned that the totality of Chinese tradition from Confucianism to Maoism could not maintain its historical innocence after the excessive crimes perpetrated by the Red Guards. Such language of oppressive contamination resembles the abundant biblical metaphors flowing beneath the West German intellectual discussions about the Nazi past. As Ralf Dahrendorf pointed out, "'guilt' (*Schuld*) in German always has the undertone of the irredeemable, incapable of being canceled by metaphysical torment."[53] For

---

53. Dahrendorf, *Society and Democracy in Germany*, 288–89, quoted in Moses, *German Intellectuals and the Nazi Past*, 21; for other works that discuss the culture of guilt in postwar Germany, see Parkinson, *An Emotional State*, 25–66; Mitchell, *The Origins of Christian Democracy*; Berger, *War Guilt*, 35–82.

this reason, the German-Swiss philosopher Karl Jaspers (1883–1969) posited a "metaphysical guilt" in his famous 1947 book, *The Question of German Guilt*. Jaspers defined metaphysical guilt—in contrast to legal, political, and moral guilt—as each German citizen's innate responsibility for Nazism's criminal deeds regardless of their individual involvement. Humanist reason exhausts itself when confronting the ultimate evil—the final category of guilt is answerable solely before a transcendental God.[54]

For Liu Zaifu, however, biblical guilt served less as a sacred religious doctrine than as a cognitive hypothesis that could facilitate an intrinsic sense of moral conscience more effectively than external political indoctrination. In *Guilt and Literature* (*Zui yu wenxue* 罪與文學) (2002), Liu and his co-author, Lin Gang 林崗 (1957–), differentiated between two categories of individual responsibility in the wake of the Cultural Revolution: a "limited legal responsibility" that entails imposing judgment on an individual's deeds in terms of their legal and political consequences, and an "infinite moral responsibility" that describes how, regardless of external trials, one's actions are ultimately judged by their "inner conscience" (*liangzhi* 良知). From this perspective, the state-sanctioned idea of the "innocence of the deceived," which shielded the participants of Red Guard violence from punishment by ascribing all treasonous crimes to the Gang of Four, not only failed to pursue legal justice, but also completely sidestepped Ba Jin's urgent call for moral introspection. Many Chinese were thus either reluctant to admit—and in some occasions, denied outright—the fact that they had "cheered, glorified, and promoted Mao's catastrophic revolution," or "actively attacked, purged, and betrayed others" in the mass campaigns against the so-called counterrevolutionaries.[55] Echoing Jaspers's religiously tinged metaphysical guilt, Liu's coinage "a sin without sin" (*wuzui zhi zui* 無罪之罪) referred to the crimes committed by a person who unconsciously participates in a "structure of complicity" (*gongfan*

---

54. Jaspers, *The Question of German Guilt*; for an analysis of metaphysical guilt, see Norrie, "Justice on the Slaughter-Bench."
55. Liu and Lin, *Zui yu wenxue*, 132.

jiegou 共犯結構),⁵⁶ an implicit yet contagious situation that constitutes an indelible sense of guilt.

Meanwhile, Liu's eulogy for a quasi-religious original sin betrayed his conviction that the Chinese inability to mourn might be attributed to the absence of repentance awareness in Confucian secular reason. For the American anthropologist Ruth Benedict, the Judeo-Christian tradition cultivated a transcendent form of guilt that is answerable solely before God, and the absence of such a higher order in Asian religions promoted a secular culture of shame that emphasizes the social group as the primary source of ethical standards.⁵⁷ Whereas Asian shame cultures are characterized by an externally imposed situational ethic, Western guilt cultures are defined by an internally motivated (and therefore superior) moral conscience. Although such binarism has recently been challenged by philosophers and psychologists,⁵⁸ Liu felt that the lack of higher, transcendent morality in Chinese secular reason thwarted the self-critical process of moral introspection in the post-Mao Chinese public sphere. For instance, even though the writers of scar literature poured out their sociopolitical indictment of a corrupt system, their moral testimonies were less concerned with showing contrition and more concerned with demanding restitution and compensation from the state.⁵⁹ Such reluctance to engage in a soul-wrenching search for one's inner evil, Liu further proposed, might stem from the Confucian belief in the benevolence of human nature (*xingshan lun* 性善論). Confucius, who believed in a person's instinctual predisposition to goodness (*shan* 善), regarded wicked behaviors not as the manifestation of the ultimate evil, but rather as a temporary deviation from the ideal of moral perfection.⁶⁰ Whereas Jaspers's invocation of the Nazis' "satanic criminality" harked back to Christian thinking on

---

56. See Jianmei Liu, "Liu Zaifu's Three Voyages of Life," 190.

57. Benedict, *Chrysanthemum and the Sword*; for a critique of Benedict's culturalist paradigm, see Berger, *War Guilt*, 123–74.

58. For instance, see Berkson, "A Confucian Defense of Shame."

59. Liu and Lin, *Zui yu wenxue*, 157.

60. Liu's rather generalized discussion simplifies the sustained debate on the question of human nature in the Confucian tradition. For instance, in contrast to Mencius's belief in the benevolence of human nature, Xunzi developed a rich discourse on the question of natural evil. Meanwhile, late-Ming Neo-Confucianism also

the cosmic evil, Liu deplored that the absence of a religious dimension in Confucianism prevented further reflections on the metaphysical, ontological dimension of radical evil.[61] Even though Liu was not—and never became—a Christian, he nevertheless believed that something was deeply flawed in the secularist "national characters" of the Chinese people who avoided any direct confrontation with the problem of evil and could not feel the anguish of contrition.

Liu struggled to create a quasi-religious guilt that could provide the post-Mao generation with a spiritual dimension beyond the tutelage of secular humanism, but many scholars have nonetheless perceived a disturbing resemblance between the Christian culture of sin and the Maoist discourse of guilt. The American psychologist Robert J. Lifton views religious conversion as the essential ingredient in the Maoist thought reform. In Vincent Goossaert and David Palmer's reading, Lifton described the thought reform as a process punctuated by "an initial phase of togetherness and friendly bonding; a second phase of intense criticism and struggle . . . and a third phase of 'rebirth.'"[62] To become a "new socialist man," the suspect—capitalist, bourgeois intellectual, or class enemy—must confess every sinful conduct in his past life to purge the reactionary remnants in his mind. The goal of such ritualized conversion was not simply to manufacture subordination but to "thoroughly destroy his sense of autonomous individuality" so that the culprit "feels gratitude and love for the leader who restored him to the correct path."[63] As Yu Liu points out, the Maoist model of psychological engineering follows the Christian logic of "sin-salvation" to manufacture excessive feelings of inherited guilt.[64] In a striking

---

produced a systematic depiction of the sources of evil. See Chan Chi-keung, *Wanming wangxue yuanelun*.

61. In Sinophone scholarship, the critique of Confucian perfectionism was initially proposed by Chang Hao, who argues that the lack of "dark consciousness" in the Confucian tradition has led to political totalitarianism. See Chang Hao, *Youan yishi yu minzhu chuantong*, 23–43.

62. Goossaert and Palmer, *The Religious Question in Modern China*, 180; see Lifton, *Thought Reform and the Psychology of Totalism*.

63. Richard Bernstein, *China 1945*, 133.

64. Yu Liu, "Maoist Discourse and the Mobilization of Emotions in Revolutionary China."

similarity to Liu Zaifu's notion of structured complicity, the Maoist-Marxist lexicon defines guilt as one's active or passive complicity in sustaining the system of class exploitation against the proletariat. Whereas Liu Zaifu identifies biblical guilt as the deeper form of the individual's moral conscience, the Communist Thought Reform instrumentalized the indelible sense of class guilt to destabilize individual consciousness and encourage self-denial. In this regard, it is precisely the power of moral redemption—not the obsession with the mundane—that mobilized Chinese intellectuals to redeem their souls by completely submitting to the party.

Liu Zaifu's and others' theologically informed vision of moral responsibility was therefore fraught with tension. On the one hand, Liu's expression of guilt reveals his own disappointment at the inability of the post-Mao generation to practice mourning and contrition for past misdeeds.[65] Yet the appeal for a collective moral learning risks colluding with the Maoist rhetoric of guilt that reinforces the psychology of self-criticism and self-recrimination. For many intellectuals who were subject to interrogation at the hands of Red Guards, the quasi-religious discourse of guilt was replete with Maoist political connotations. If we widen our scope to consider a lineup of scholars and writers who reacted with cynicism and suspicion, we may be tempted to conclude that the post-Mao memory culture suffered from a surfeit of guilt rather than a lack of it. The most representative figure was arguably the eminent German-trained Indologist Ji Xianlin, who urged his generation to reckon with the imbrication between self-willed confession and forced conversion. Ji was the founding director of the Department of Eastern Languages at Peking University. As the number one "reactionary academic authority," he was subject to severe physical and mental abuse during the Beijing Red Guard movement. Although Ji remained silent in the early reform period, he published his memoir *The Cowshed* (*Niupeng zayi* 牛棚雜憶) in 1998, providing a revealing and sincere testimony of how intellectual communities endured violence and torture at the height of the Cultural Revolution. The term "cowshed" refers to the makeshift prisons constructed by the Red Guards to detain

---

65. See Lizhi Fang, "The Chinese Amnesia."

reactionary professors and fallen school officials on their own college campuses. Ji was denounced by Nie Yuanzi 聂元梓 (1921–2019), the militant leader of the Peking University Red Guard faction, as a "hidden counterrevolutionary" and sent to the cowshed for "reeducation" for nine months.[66] In the preface, Ji confessed that he had refrained from publishing this memoir because he did not want to take revenge on his persecutors, but he was deeply disturbed by the failure of his generation to express any feelings of guilt or remorse for their role in facilitating violence and destruction. He invoked the stereotypical image of a cynical, amnesic, and unfeeling Chinese who refuses to reflect on the question of what caused the breakdown of basic ethical norms in the Cultural Revolution. To avoid colluding with the Maoist mandate of self-denunciation, meanwhile, Ji offered a modest twist on Ba Jin's call for repentance by asking his peers to simply "offer an objective description of what happened" as historical records for posterity.[67]

Despite Ji's candor, his confession is infused with anguished feelings and moral anxieties and cannot be read as a simple record of "what really happened." As Paul de Man's reading of Rousseau's confession suggests, the recognition of guilt always "implies its exoneration" in the name of the transcendental principle of truth.[68] As a confessor who acknowledged his complicity in persecuting others, Ji did not hesitate to excuse himself by emphasizing his "minor" involvement in the rebel movement. Ji frequently described himself as a harmless, naïve political drifter who did not succumb to the infatuation and the thirst for apocalyptic violence that engulfed his leftist colleagues and activist students. He only reluctantly joined Jinggangshan (井冈山)—an underdog rebel faction—to avoid being accused as a bourgeois bystander. Indeed, Ji trivialized his thoughtless compliance by portraying himself as a gullible, apolitical man who was tragically pulled into the whirlwind of mass campaigns without harboring any deep ideological convictions himself: "Since we had been directed to oppose

---

66. Although Ji claims that he was persecuted by Nie and her vindictive followers, Nie denied such accusation in her memoir. See Nie, "Da Ji Xianlin jiaoshou"; Buckley, "Nie Yuanzi."

67. Ji, *The Cowshed*, xxvi.

68. De Man, *Allegories of Reading*, 279.

the rightists, we did. After more than a decade of continuous political struggle, the intellectuals knew the drill. We all took turns persecuting one another."[69] As a clueless and reluctant joiner, Ji thought that he merely half-heartedly performed persecution—the verbal criticism of his colleagues—like a "drill" without any evil intentions. The true radical evil, Ji insinuated, resides in those student activists who found sadistic, perverted pleasure in inflicting excruciating physical and psychological pains upon their prisoners. This comparison exculpates the "minor guilt" of joiners like Ji while inculpating those Red Guards who showed no signs of remorse after abusing and murdering countless prisoners in the cowsheds. To be sure, Ji did not shy away from expressing his overwhelming sense of guilt and shame for his "herd mentality." But confessing in the name of "sincerity" also serves to excuse the confessor, thereby redirecting moral guilt toward others.

If the murky boundary between apology and excuse reveals the therapeutic underpinning of confession, Ji's antipathy toward the Communist invocation of guilt further casts shadows on any hopes for redemption through the inculcation of moral conscience. Ji mentioned that the CCP created an "almost Christian feeling of guilt" among intellectuals to enforce endless "self-criticisms."[70] During the 1950s Thought Reform Campaign, for instance, intellectuals were expected to undergo a meticulous yet purifying public confession known as "taking a bath" (*xizao* 洗澡), a process that involved expunging impure thoughts and improper desires to enable a moral rebirth. As Elizabeth J. Perry points out, Ji likened the Maoist demand for confession to the suffocating strictures of Christian baptism. Ji would later recall his ordeal of "taking a bath" in front of a public assembly: "This was the first time in my life that I had undergone this sort of trial. Each word felt like a sharp arrow piercing my soul. It was as though I had become a Christian convert, filled with a conviction of 'original sin,' and the more intense the accusations grew the more relaxed I felt . . . When in the end those assembled agreed that I had passed muster, I was moved to the point of actually shedding tears. It seemed that my bourgeois

69. Ji, *The Cowshed*, 178.
70. Ji, *The Cowshed*, 174.

thoughts truly had been washed away."[71] But Ji's "bath" did not leave him spiritually cleansed. He began to feel ashamed of pursing his own scholarly learning abroad while his fellow countrymen sacrificed their lives to establish New China. Over the years, his self-hatred gradually developed into a disdain for the entire class of the intellectual—the parasitic, bourgeois, and pleasure-seeking literati who squandered the blood and sweat of the proletarians.[72] Pious confession did not lead to purifying catharsis, but instead brought an externally imposed stigma of social inferiority.

At first a passionate believer in the transformative power of the new socialist man, Ji willingly participated in the thought reform in order to seek redemption from the party, only to be disappointed by Mao's strategic manipulation of guilty consciences for the purpose of creating ideological fanaticism and legitimating violence. Thus Ji is confronted with a dilemma: if the quasi-religious notion of class guilt was wielded like a moral cudgel to sanitize the minds of intellectuals and promote unconditional subordination to the party's command, how would the humanist culture of contrition and apology be different? The theological language of guilt, in Ji's view, risks lapsing into the Communist discourse of confession that instrumentalizes religious sentiment for the purpose of ideological indoctrination. The troubling affinity—or contagion— between class guilt and biblical sin may ultimately lead many to cynically reject any possibility of future reconciliation. As Zha Jianying has pointed out, Ji's expression of remorse is intermittently accompanied by a "strange tone of sarcasm and self-mockery" that deflates the sincerity of the narrator's voice.[73] In the wake of the Cultural Revolution, as Ji sarcastically puts it, the conventional wisdom that "the scholar can be killed, but he cannot be humiliated" (*shi ke sha, bu ke ru* 士可殺, 不可辱) gave away to the solemn reality that "not only can the scholar be killed,

---

71. Quoted in Liang and Hu, *Ji Xianlin dazhuan*, 105–6; quoted in and translated by Perry, "Missionaries of the Party," 81.

72. For related studies of the political representation of the intellectual in the Maoist discourse, see Pang, *The Art of Cloning*, 216–38; U, *Creating the Intellectual*.

73. Zha, "China: Surviving the Camps."

he can also be humiliated."[74] This mixture of dark humor and bitterness, I suggest, betrays Ji's profound pessimism toward Liu Zaifu's scenario of reconciliation through confession.

The Convergence of Pleasure and Guilt

This chapter has reconstructed the enduring bond between Li Zehou's this-worldly pleasure and the humanist reflections on other-worldly guilt to reveal the emotive basis of the New Enlightenment. Li's notion of pleasure was grounded in the May Fourth aesthetic discourse that highlighted the inculcation of this-worldly affection as an alternative to the quasi-religious appeals of the Maoist sublime. Li stressed aesthetic cultivation of human sense and sensibilities, in opposition to the expressions of fervent emotions and apocalyptic visions that were characteristic of the ideological fanaticism of the Mao era. Meanwhile, Liu Zaifu and other humanist writers underscored the religious underpinning of guilt to stimulate an inner morality through which to expel all secular political commands. Whereas Li prioritized a realistic ethical and psychological noumenon in Confucian aesthetics to refute the romantic and sublime figure of the proletarian subject, the humanists' espousal of religious sin provided Chinese writers with a spiritual dimension to voice guilt and repentance for the collective crimes of the socialist past. Finally, their reflections on this-worldly pleasure and other-worldly guilt have merged in exorcising the myth of revolutionary utopia. Maoist revolution bespeaks a utopian impulse to provoke a violent rupture through which human emancipation will be actualized in an apocalyptic manner. By contrast, Li and Liu's "farewell to revolution," an attitude stemming from their antagonism toward ideological fanaticism, sought to dispel the powerful attractions of revolutionary utopianism and anticipate new emotive norms for postsocialist Chinese society. Whereas Li recommended that contemporary Chinese practice affective sensibilities and profane reason in a world without a messiah and redemption, Liu and other humanist writers underscored

---

74. Ji, *The Cowshed*, 140. Ji recalled that the comment was initially made by Zhou Yang in their first encounter after the end of the Cultural Revolution.

the culture of contrition to stimulate one's sense of moral guilt and interrogate the myth of revolutionary violence.

Notwithstanding their shared commitment to purging revolutionary fervor and unreflective hysteria, an unbridgeable gulf separates Li's this-worldly pleasure and Liu's other-worldly guilt. Li's excavation of secular reason represents the return of Confucian aesthetics that hails affection toward this world as the ultimate source of transcendence. Li reflected on the compatibility of sense and sensibility and strove to forge a syncretic aesthetic education that could realize Kantian enlightenment while also drawing nourishment from Confucian ethics of emotion. Against all forms of other-worldly sentiments, Li spoke of this-worldly pleasure as a salutary distancing from all messianic gods, be they Christian deities or socialist prophets. A postrevolutionary "new sensibility," as Li envisioned it, must "not be founded in speculation, faith, or divine grace," but only "in the fluid and changing emotions themselves."[75] Eventually, Li's sentimental education culminates in *le* (樂): the cultivation of virtue and benevolence, the willingness to ground one's self within the bounds of finitude, and the appreciation of a secular life free from religious hallucination and utopian passion. Liu Zaifu, however, could not plunge into the romantic world of Confucian humanity and shake off the indelible guilt that tormented his generation. That the secular vocabulary of Confucian ethics was inadequate, especially in the wake of the satanic criminality of the Maoist past, was evident in Liu's yearning for a biblical notion of guilt. What for Li is constitutive of enlightened sentiment—that is, pragmatic rationality—becomes for Liu the cardinal moral lacuna that has obstructed the inculcation of a guilty conscience. Thus, humanist writers embraced a quasi-religious guilt—a notion of irredeemable, existential original sin above and beyond all secular morality—to initiate a collective moral learning process. This other-worldly guilt involves a heart-wrenching search for one's inner evil and endless waiting for spiritual salvation that is always yet to come.

Pleasure and guilt may thus appear so diametrically opposed as to preclude any possible correlation. Why should we even speak of their

---

75. Li Zehou, *The Chinese Aesthetic Tradition*, 56.

convergence? Above all, the enduring affinity between Li's and Liu's distinctive views of emotional cultivation mirrors what Ludwig Wittgenstein calls "family resemblance": a sufficient number of similarities repeatedly underpin their shared concern, yet none of these could be reduced to a single trait. Although Li Zehou, Liu Zaifu, and Ji Xianlin each proposed a different set of emotions—from guilt and shame to pleasure and sarcasm—for mastering the past, they were bound by an overriding consensus about the normative role played by emotions in prescribing the moral rejuvenation of the Chinese people after the revolution. In other words, fundamental to the theory of pleasure and guilt is a heartfelt belief that the psychological, emotive dimensions of the inner self could be harnessed to engender a strong commitment to enlightenment rationality. For both Li and Liu, it would be impossible to construct a liberal and democratic public culture without a painstaking process of moral learning and sentimental education. Such a family resemblance between pleasure and guilt demonstrates that emotive norms carried a special urgency in the post-Mao cultural conversation about revolutionary violence, memory politics, and the fate of Chinese enlightenment. The intricate connection between reason and emotion reveals how the post-Mao generation harked back to not only the May Fourth sentimentalism, but also to the ancient poetics of *qing* 情 (emotion) that imbued *li* 理 (reason) with moral, affective, and aesthetic connotations.

Furthermore, my case studies have sought to restore the exciting and confusing, dynamic yet volatile intellectual sentiments of the early reform period. The irresolvable paradox between pleasure and guilt was in fact emblematic of the conflicts and crises of the New Enlightenment movement itself: the forward-looking dynamics of the cultural avant-garde went hand in hand with the backward gaze of the melancholic humanists. However much present-day revisionist historians have condemned the cultural politics of the 1980s as dangerous radicalism or depoliticized politics, intellectuals of the time were animated by something idealistic and genuine—the conviction that they could alter the trajectory of history and save the Chinese people from the tutelage of revolution. Between hope and tragedy, the window of opportunity for sentimental education was nonetheless narrow: the climax of the New Enlightenment lasted for only five years (1985 to 1989) before its abrupt demise in the wake of the June Fourth crackdown. In the end, both pleasure and guilt have irretrievably receded into what Stefan Zweig elegiacally calls "the world of yesterday," which contains the unrealized dreams of the past and anticipations of the future that has become obsolete.

The end of the 1980s enlightenment, however, should not color our assessment of the enduring legacies of Li and Liu. Indeed, the cult of enlightened sentiments has continued to generate new tensions and confrontations from the 1990s to this day. The following chapters will demonstrate how a broad spectrum of cultural critics, ranging from leftist writers and neo-Marxist intellectuals to conservative theologians and popular nationalists, voiced their suspicion toward and discontent with the emotive norms proposed by the enlightenment thinkers. First and foremost, however, the accusatory undertone that the Chinese had failed to exhibit certain moral feelings toward past atrocities led to an emotionally sanitized culture in which any revisionist attempts to defend socialist values were denounced as whitewashing the totalitarian past. As the next chapter will reveal, the adamant belief in contrition and apology has continued to invest post-Tiananmen liberals with a moral certainty and tough-mindedness about the catastrophic result of socialist revolution.

CHAPTER TWO

The Liberal Imagination

The Politics of Mourning in the "Chen Yinke Fever"

> Plenty of people, who have suffered directly or vicariously from the results of the Bolshevik victory, or still fear its remoter consequences, desire to register their protest against it; and this takes the form, when they read history, of letting their imagination run riot on all the more agreeable things that might have happened. . . . This is a purely emotional and unhistorical reaction.
> —E. H. Carr, What Is History?

In January 1983, the renowned Princeton intellectual historian Yu Ying-shih 余英時 (1930–2021) published a polemical essay titled "On the Scholarly Spirit and the Late State of Mind of Chen Yinke" (論陳寅恪的學術精神和晚年心境) in Hong Kong.[1] Born in 1890, Chen Yinke 陳寅恪 (1890–1969) came from a prestigious late Qing family of gifted poets and scholar-officials. He was trained as a linguist and orientalist, with wide-ranging research encompassing Sanskrit, Buddhism, and

---

The discussion of Chen Yinke's loyalism in this chapter appeared in a condensed form and under a different theme in an article titled "Between Conformity and Dissent: Two Chinese Thinkers in Search of Esotericism," published in *Critical Inquiry* 50, no. 4 (Summer 2024).

1. See Yu Ying-shih, "Lun Chen Yinke de xueshujingshen he wannian xinjing."

Sino-Indian cultural exchanges in the medieval period. The young Chen traveled extensively and studied at Harvard and in Berlin before returning to the Institute of National Learning at Tsinghua University to assume a professorship in 1925. By 1949, Chen had established his reputation as one of the preeminent Chinese historians of his generation. Due to his steadfast refusal to conform to Marxist historiography, however, Chen withdrew into inner exile after the PRC's founding and meditated on the question of loyalism. In the last twenty years of his life, Chen experienced a cultural nostalgia for the Ming-Qing literati world of poetry, friendship, and elegance, finding special inspiration in the female writer Chen Duansheng 陳端生 (1751–c. 1796), the author of the prosimetric fiction *Love in Two Lives* (*Zaisheng yuan* 再生緣), and the legendary courtesan-poetess Liu Rushi 柳如是 (1618–1664), who participated in the Ming loyalist opposition against the Manchu conquerors. His last work, *An Extended Biography of Liu Rushi* (*Liu Rushi biezhuan* 柳如是別傳), showed how Liu's poetic musings on the falls of dynasties were intermingled with the spirit of resistance.

Whereas Marxist scholars denounced Chen as an unrepentant "white expert" (*baizhuan* 白專)—a reactionary historian who indulged in loyalist sentiment—Yu Ying-shih contended that Chen's enigmatic turn from history (*shi* 史) to poetry (*shi* 詩) carried profound moral and political implications. In place of the pensive tone that had characterized Chen's earlier writing, later on his poetic mind appeared to be dominated by emotive utterances: anger, sarcasm, and profound pathos. Echoing Theodor Adorno's and Edward Said's meditations on Beethoven's late style, Yu argued that the seemingly erratic expressionism in Chen's late works did not represent the culmination of aesthetic harmony. Instead, Chen's eulogy for the loyalist heroine Liu Rushi and her ethical dilemmas during regime transitions was an allegorical expression of his intransigence against the imprisonment of thought under the Communist regime.[2] Thus Chen's heroic defiance embodied

---

2. Adorno argues that the "fissures and rifts" (*Risse und Sprünge*) in Beethoven's late music are the sign of aesthetic disunity that negates the seamless totality of Hegelian philosophy. Said further deploys the term to characterize "intransigence, difficulty, and unresolved contradiction" in artistic lateness. Although Yu does not explicitly invoke Adorno and Said, he shares a similar discomfort with the conventional

a most extraordinary show of "cultural loyalism" (*wenhua yimin* 文化遺民), an affective syndrome that applauds the continuity of Chinese cultural tradition against political ruptures.

Meanwhile, Yu's characterization of Chen as a cultural icon was accompanied by his persistent attempt to reveal Chen's profound dissatisfaction with Mao's socialist experiment. Many liberal intellectuals left mainland China in 1949 to escape the Communist reign, but Chen turned down several opportunities to go to Taiwan and the West. In the later telling and retelling, Chen's refusal to "leave the parental state" (*qu fumu zhi bang* 去父母之邦) was hailed by PRC propogandists as an exemplary moral tale of how patriotic intellectuals embraced New China with utmost sincerity and enthusiasm. Yet Yu contended that, based on his exhaustive examination of Chen's 1949 sojourn in Guangzhou, Chen's choice to stay was a contingent event overdetermined by accidents and mishandled decisions, and that his tragic fate could have been drastically different had Chen crossed the Taiwan Strait.[3] Yu painted Chen as a desperate man fleeing from Communist forces: burdened with family, drifting from place to place, and frequently making misguided choices that eventually sealed off his path to the "free world." Moreover, Chen, who came to regret staying in New China during the tumultuous years of socialist campaigns, stoked a cultural nostalgia for the bygone republican era. In Yu's judgment, Chen's admiration for the uncompromising political integrity of Ming loyalists was a coded expression of his "refusal to serve two dynasties" (*bushi erchao* 不仕二朝).

After the publication of Yu Ying-shih's polemical essay, a mainland critic writing under the pseudonym Feng Yibei 馮衣北 published a

---

understanding of late style as harmony and resolution, and argues for irascibility against serenity as the defining character of aesthetic lateness. See Adorno, "Late Style in Beethoven"; Said, *On Late Style*.

3. Although Yu did not explicitly speculate on the plausibility of the counterfactual fate of Chen in his 1983 essay, he was dedicated to exploring the radically contingent nature of Chen's 1949 decision to stay. See Yu Ying-shih, *Chen Yinke wannian shiwen shizheng*, 45, 97–98, 268; for scholarly discussions concerning Chen's 1949 decision, see Yu Ying-shih, *Chen Yinke yanjiu*.

series of rebuttals against Yu's argument.[4] In Feng's view, the moral poignancy in Chen's late poems was not political dissent, but in fact "mild criticism" of Mao-era policy mistakes. Chen's so-called loyalist sentiment, Feng suggested, was inextricably bound up with his unwavering support for New China. While Yu explored the contingency of Chen's decision through the 1949 crisis, Feng retorted that Chen's refusal to commit to those more "promising" choices was precisely the act of a patriot whose moral integrity forbade him from seeking shelters in "colonial" Hong Kong or Taiwan.[5] Moreover, Feng questioned the emotional excess that fueled Yu's ideologically informed commemoration of Chen in the first place. Yu, who suffered from his political exile, projected his resentment by fantasizing about the alternative possibilities of Chen's fate supposedly closed off by the Communist ascendance. Thus, Yu's reading illustrates the dynamics of an intense anti-Communist affective syndrome that shaped his understanding of Chen as an alienated loyalist. As a result, Yu's preoccupation with the what-if speculations says less about Chen's late state of mind than it does about Yu's own emotional and unhistorical reaction to the 1949 divide.

This political-cum-academic debate anticipated the post-Mao rise of Chen's posthumous fame. "Chen Yinke fever" (*Chen Yinke re* 陳寅恪熱)—the upsurge of passion and pathos surrounding his life and scholarship—has exploded beyond the domain of academia and into a cultural fashion sweeping across the Chinese and Sinophone world since the early 1980s and into the 2000s. Public discussions, biographical narratives, dramas, and documentary projects have emerged to mourn Chen as "the last intellectual," "the master of national learning," and "the one to whom Chinese culture entrusted its fate" (*Zhongguo wenhua tuoming zhi ren* 中國文化托命之人). Both the intellectual and popular discourse have been preoccupied with the last twenty years of

---

4. Yu claimed that this "ideologically motivated attack" was masterminded by Hu Qiaomu (1912–1992), a member of the Central Politburo of the CCP, to address the accumulating debates surrounding Chen's case. It was only later revealed that the true identity of Feng Yibei is the Guangdong-based novelist and painter Liu Sifen 劉斯奮 (1944–). See Yu Ying-shih, *Chen Yinke wannian shiwen shizheng*, 243–57; Lu Jiandong, *Chen Yinke de zuihou ershinian*, 501.

5. See Feng, "Yetan Chen Yinke xiansheng de wannianxinjing," 8.

Chen's life under the era of high socialism, the period underpinned by a succession of political campaigns to educate, remold, and reform liberal intellectuals under the aegis of Marxism. Chen's death came to be regarded as a symbol of the wholesale destruction of republican China's intellectual legacy wrought by Mao's socialist revolution. Through heightened dramatizations, this liberal pathos transformed Chen's image from that of an apolitical thinker into a scholar against politics, a cultural loyalist resisting modernity, and an incarnation of Chinese liberalism in defiance of Mao's revolutionary mandate. The expression of feelings that stretch from empathy and melancholy to guilt and resentment created a volatile public space torn between violent suppression and the anguished remembrances of the Mao era.

The Pathos of Chinese Liberalism

This chapter analyzes how liberal-minded literary critics, popular historians, and public intellectuals debated the ethical and political implications of Chen Yinke's fate under socialism. More specifically, I am interested in how liberal pathos transformed Chen's tragedy into a moral tale of liberalism's hopes and survival in China's tumultuous twentieth-century experience. Here, a brief overview of modern Chinese liberalism can helpfully problematize this fusion of moral emotion and political vision. Both Benjamin Schwartz and Max Ko-wu Huang have traced the origin of Chinese liberalism to the late Qing thinker Yan Fu 嚴復 (1854–1921), who introduced John Stuart Mill's "On Liberty" (1859) to his Confucian contemporaries.[6] But although Yan bequeathed to his liberal heirs a set of preoccupations with the nationalistic pursuit of wealth and power, it was not until the breakout of the May Fourth Movement (1919) that classical liberalism—understood as the affirmation of individual liberty and the pursuit of political democracy—became a visible intellectual and cultural force in the nascent republic.[7] Scholars have paid particular attention to the group of reformist

---

6. See Schwartz, *In Search of Wealth and Power*; Max Huang, *The Meaning of Freedom*.

7. See Xu Jilin, "Xiandai Zhongguo de ziyouzhuyi chuantong," 27.

professors, editors, and writers that formed around the leading liberal intellectual Hu Shih 胡適 (1891–1962), who tirelessly promoted liberal values and campaigned for constitutional democracy as an independent critic.[8] Yet, as Jerome B. Grieder points out, Hu understood liberalism not as a political doctrine but rather as a particular set of dispositions or habits of the mind characterized by a profound aversion to party politics and ideological indoctrination.[9] The task of liberal intellectuals, in Hu's view, was to illuminate the social and political "problems" (*wenti* 問題) of China through fair-minded, dispassionate research, and to encourage incremental and moderate reforms to ease—rather than resolve—political conflicts among contending parties.[10] Throughout his career, Hu Shih deployed the concepts of freedom and independence to dissuade his leftist and rightist colleagues from allowing their political passion to affect their empirical assessment of China's social reality. Nevertheless, the liberals' fastidious penchant for political detachment has been condemned as a "temperamental aloofness" to practical politics, a moral blindness to the suffering of the masses, and ultimately a naïve fantasy to promote moderation in a chaotic society shaped by brutal violence and radical revolution.[11]

Although Hu Shih's tepid liberal stance failed to provide a clear "intellectual spectrum" (*sixiang guangpu* 思想光譜)[12] for his generation, post-Mao liberals celebrated Hu's gradualist and moderate reform program as a powerful retort to Mao's revolutionary politics. Beginning in the late 1970s, liberalism crystalized again in mainland China as a loose intellectual faction following the perceived failure of the Cultural Revolution and the subsequent rise of the New Enlightenment. Including outspoken critics, humanist writers, and proponents of humanist Marxism, these "enlightenment intellectuals" (*qimeng zhishifenzi* 啟蒙知識分子) sought to revitalize the liberal,

8. See Zhang Qing, *Hu Shi pai xuerenqun yu xiandai Zhongguo ziyouzhuyi*; Fung, *The Intellectual Foundations of Chinese Modernity*, 128–58.
9. Grieder, *Hu Shih and the Chinese Renaissance*, 314–50.
10. Hu Shih, *Wenti yu zhuyi*; for an analysis on the debate between problems and "isms," see Wang Fan-sen, "Anti-Ism Thinkers."
11. Grieder, *Hu Shih and the Chinese Renaissance*, 338.
12. Zhang Qing, *Hu Shi pai xuerenqun yu xiandai Zhongguo ziyouzhuyi*, 3–4.

cosmopolitan strain of the May Fourth legacy in support of Deng Xiaoping's reform.[13] Following the 1989 Tiananmen crackdown, however, paranoid liberals, guided by a nearly phobic reaction to the Leviathan state, embraced the neoliberal market as the guardian of political liberty. Unlike the aggressive and forward-looking dynamics of Western liberals, persecution and defeat nourished a grim, nostalgic, and dystopian historical vision at the heart of the post-Tiananmen liberal discourse. Indeed, for Chinese liberals, freedom is not associated with the general enlargement of positive political rights; rather, the proponents of liberalism have been consistently propelled by a dyspeptic yearning for a retreat into the "inner citadel" of negative liberty from all political malice.[14]

In view of the highly contested political motivations inherent in the post-Mao liberal renaissance, extant scholarly critiques have focused on how and why modern Chinese liberalism suffers a fatal deficit in normative values and cannot be expected to serve as an ideal moral-political design for Chinese society. More than half a century ago, the acclaimed thinker Yin Haiguang 殷海光 (1919–1969) described Chinese liberals as marked by "a premature birth followed by postnatal disorders" (*xiantian buzu, houtian shitiao* 先天不足，後天失調).[15] Yin held that liberalism failed in China not only because Chinese liberals themselves had misunderstood the multiple strains of Western liberalism, but also because liberalism provided no solutions to the Chinese life steeped in violence and disorder.[16] Yin's view that Chinese liberalism was "inauthentic" and offered no normative substance is widely shared by many PRC scholars, who in turn faulted post-Mao liberals for their blind faith in an alien ideology, their willful distortion of the liberal creed, and their failure to provide a muscular moral-political instruction in the realm of practical politics.[17]

---

13. See Xu Jilin, *Dangdai Zhongguo de qimeng yu fanqimeng*, 3–27.
14. Berlin, "Two Concepts of Liberty," 216.
15. Quoted in Fung, *The Intellectual Foundations of Chinese Modernity*, 138.
16. See Fung, *The Intellectual Foundations of Chinese Modernity*, 138.
17. See Xudong Zhang, *Postsocialism and Cultural Politics*, 52–62; Wang Hui, *The End of the Revolution*, 19–68.

Yet these critics are shying away from the profound moral and emotional appeal of liberalism in the post-Mao context. The forces driving the liberals' attachment to freedom were never purely intellectual, but were instead intertwined with complex emotions, memories, and political desires. As I will demonstrate, the controversy surrounding Chen Yinke's case was not so much about invoking normative values from Chen's scholarship as about creating a larger memory project that could vindicate the intellectual pluralism of the republican cultural milieu from which Chen emerged. The mutations in the postsocialist cultural landscape, from the "high-culture craze" of the 1980s, to the revival of political liberalism following the June Fourth crackdown, gave rise to a cultural nostalgia for republican China (1911–1949), a regime supposedly more liberal than its Communist successor. Thus revisionist historians painted a rosy picture of republican higher education as a golden era of academic freedom and intellectual deliberation. Victims of Mao's political campaigns lamented the disappearance of "republican-period intellectuals" (*minguo zhishifenzi* 民國知識分子), whose liberal political values and erudite learning were devoured by the ascendance of dogmatic Marxism in the Mao era.[18] Most importantly, this historical narrative was intermingled with a willful yearning for alternative ways out of China's otherwise catastrophic revolutionary twentieth century. By excavating the repressed liberal legacies of the republican era, it sought to undergird and valorize the search for a postrevolutionary liberal order.

This chapter does not attempt to provide a normative answer to the broader debates about the ideational or ideological implications of Chinese liberalism. I am more interested in the dynamics of intense affective syndromes and political emotions aroused by various liberal imaginations, inasmuch as the moral-psychological dimensions of liberal thinking have largely framed how Chen's tragedy has been read and narrated in the post-Mao context. Hence this chapter emphasizes the interrelations between the discursive constructions of Chen's images on the one hand, and the underlying political emotions on the other. As Benjamin Wurgaft noted, telling stories about heroic or tragic

---

18. See Zhang and Weatherley, "The Rise of 'Republican Fever' in the PRC."

intellectual figures always reveals "*our* political hopes and fears."[19] Similarly, the changing political narratives surrounding Chen serve as a guide to the manifold affective and emotional investments of inquiring critics and intellectuals in the post-Mao era. By analyzing how the debates over Chen stirred up a constellation of feelings and moral sentiments from melancholy and guilt to anger and resentment, I attempt to show that Chinese liberal thinking cannot be separated from the political emotions of the post-Mao intelligentsia. Although emotions do not cause ideologies, they add fuel to the fires.

With this goal in mind, I read the blooming of the Chen Yinke memory industry as an exemplary case of the memorial mania that informed the liberal politics of memory in the post-Mao era. Contrasting the Habermasian proviso of a rational-communicative public sphere, Erika Doss coined the term "memorial mania" to describe the explosion of affective responses and emotional attitudes that permeated public deliberation of the national past in contemporary America.[20] Similarly, Chinese liberals' obsession with commemoration produced excessive, frenzied, and passionate identification with tragic heroes, hapless victims, and defiant martyrs who survived, perished, resisted, and rebelled against Mao's revolutionary mandate. But whereas Doss highlights the visibly public contexts—geographical places, historical monuments, and public memorials—as the sites of American collective memory, Chen Yinke's readers have created allusive and sometimes obscure literary forms to disseminate heterodox thoughts and evade censorship. Furthermore, the amplified emotional tenor of liberalism has led to a willful tendency to yoke together disparate figures, from the indignant economist Gu Zhun 顧准 (1915–1974) to the fiery dissident Lin Zhao 林昭 (1932–1968), to discredit Mao's revolution as a series of moral catastrophes and totalitarian crimes.[21] As I will demonstrate, the emotional rather than purely intellectual fascination with Chen Yinke risks a lapse into moralism when the revolutionary past is viewed as nothing more than absolute evil.

---

19. Wurgaft, *Thinking in Public*, 13 (emphasis added).
20. Doss, *Memorial Mania*, 14–15.
21. For a refined study of Lin Zhao's martyrdom, see Jie Li, *Utopian Ruins*, 25–67.

In the following section, I typologize three distinctive liberal political imaginaries of Chen across time: a cultural loyalist in despair, an apolitical academician, and a martyr of liberalism. Following a chronological sequence, I first trace the ascent of Chen's posthumous fame to Yu Ying-shih's widely publicized polemics regarding Chen's cultural loyalism in the early 1980s. I then examine how mainland intellectuals grappled with the political implications of Chen's scholasticism in the immediate aftermath of the June Fourth crackdown. Last, I delineate how the liberals' reading of Chen was further transformed in the rancorous arena of ideological contestations in the post-Tiananmen era. Throughout my reading, I pay close attention to the dialectic between the affective structure of political imaginaries and the political tonality of emotions. Each section reveals how various searches for liberal political alternatives were intermingled with feelings and affects, and how these psychic energies in turn underlined and framed various expressions of competing political visions.

A Cultural Loyalist in Despair

In the fall of 1958, Yu Ying-shih accidentally came across Chen Yinke's draft piece "On *Love in Two Lives*" ("Lun *Zaishengyuan*" 論再生緣) at the Harvard-Yenching Library. The twenty-eight-year-old Yu, by then a stateless person, was in the midst of a profound political and emotional transformation as a result of his emigration from China to the United States.[22] In 1949, Yu enrolled at Yenching University but soon fled to reunite with his family in Hong Kong. He then studied with Qian Mu 錢穆 (1895–1990), the founder of New Asia College, before moving to Harvard to pursue his PhD degree in Chinese history. In the 1958 postscript that Yu wrote for Chen's draft piece, the emigrant scholar argued that Chen's seemingly quaint fascination with *Love in Two Lives*—an eighteenth-century "prosimetric fiction" (*tanci xiaoshuo* 彈詞小說)—carried esoteric moral and political messages. The "scholar-beauty fiction" (*caizi jiaren xiaoshuo* 才子佳人小說) features

---

22. See Yu Ying-shih, *Yu Ying-shih huiyilu*, 92–161.

the legendary heroine Meng Lijun 孟麗君, who dons a male disguise to make her way into courtly life and ultimately becomes prime minister. Yet Chen Yinke deliberately elevates the cultural significance of *Love in Two Lives* beyond hackneyed themes about courtly love and romantic reunion, arguing that Meng Lijun's playful and defiant attitude toward the Confucian "three fundamental bonds" (*sangang* 三綱)—the absolute authority of the emperor, the father, and the husband—brings into view the extraordinary expression of "freedom and independence" at its most intense.[23] Drawing a connection between Chen's elegiac tone and the ongoing political havoc in mainland China, Yu further contended that the historian's nostalgic reconstruction of the lost elite world of "literate gentlewomen" (*guixiu* 閨秀) not only was an allegorical expression of his loyalist pathos, but also conveyed "an extreme repugnance toward the current totalitarian regime."[24]

To illustrate how the changing foci of Chen's post-1949 research inspired Yu to develop the ideal of cultural loyalism, it is necessary to briefly recount the succession of political storms that devastated China's cultural elite in the early Maoist years. Beginning in 1957, Chen's life was plunged into chaos amid nationwide anti-rightist struggles. Just one year earlier, party leaders pushed forward the Hundred Flowers Movement (*Baihua yundong* 百花運動) to encourage intellectuals to speak out against socialist bureaucracy. Mao, the chief architect, brandishing the slogan "let a hundred flowers bloom and a hundred schools of thought contend" (*baihua qifang, baijia zhengming* 百花齊放，百家爭鳴), intended to mobilize all external "positive elements" to shake up the increasingly conservative and dogmatic nature of the party establishment. But when disgruntled students, professors, writers, and leaders of the democratic parties unleashed a flood of fierce criticism, Mao changed track and launched a ferocious counterattack against "bourgeois rightists," which resulted in the mass incarceration of nonparty intellectuals as well as lower-level party officials.

Even though Chen Yinke had not participated in the "blooming and contending" session, he was still branded as a "bourgeois historian" who indulged in a "reactionary sentiment." As the Anti-Rightist

23. Chen Yinke, "Lun *Zaishengyuan*," 59.
24. Yu Ying-shih, "Chen Yinke 'Lun *Zaishengyuan*' shuhou," 228.

Campaign merged with the Great Leap Forward, Chen Boda 陳伯達 (1904–1989), the vice director of the propaganda department, urged historians to launch a "historiographical revolution" (*shixue geming* 史學革命) by "emphasizing the present and denigrating the past" (*houjin bogu* 厚今薄古), that is, to prioritize Marxist vision of class struggles in their study of China's "feudal history."[25] Guo Moruo 郭沫若 (1892–1978), a high-ranking cultural cadre, targeted Chen for having "elevated the past over the present" (*hougu bojin* 厚古薄今). Inspired by Mao's pledge that "China would surpass Britain in iron and steel production within fifteen years," Guo urged young radicals to "overtake Chen's possession of historical knowledge" in a short amount of time and thereby demonstrate the superiority of Marxist historiography.[26] At Sun Yat-Sen University, junior colleagues and radical students were also mobilized to hold criticism sessions, draw big-character posters, and write critiques to vilify Chen's study of Tang aristocratic women as a "chronicle of whores."[27]

When news of the two massive campaigns reached Hong Kong and North America, it provoked mixed feelings of fear and indignation among overseas Chinese scholars. Haunted by apocalyptic fears of Communist totalitarianism, the prominent neo-Confucianist Tang Junyi 唐君毅 (1909–1978) lamented that Chinese culture was "falling apart like blown flowers and withered fruit" (*huaguo piaoling* 花果飄零). Meanwhile, Tang also called on overseas Chinese communities to preserve Confucian learning in dark times, or, in his prophecy, "the scattered spiritual roots will be self-planted somewhere on their own terms" (*linggen zizhi* 靈根自植).[28] Thus Yu Ying-shih experienced a profound sense of disillusionment after reading Chen's sentimental piece: "I have already lost my country, and now I am about to lose my culture."[29] From this moment on, Yu sought to transform Chen into a cultural hero around whom exiled liberals and conservative loyalists—those who found their beloved homeland destroyed by wars

25. See Huaiyin Li, *Reinventing Modern China*, 132–40.
26. Guo Moruo, "Guanyu houjin bogu wenti."
27. Lu Jiandong, *Chen Yinke de zuihou ershinian*, 233–69.
28. Tang, *Lun Zhonghuaminzu zhi huaguo piaoling*, 30.
29. Yu Ying-shih, *Chen Yinke wannian shiwen shizheng*, 2.

and revolutions—could rally. Thus Yu's reading did not aim at a faithful exegesis of Chen's scholarship. Rather, he claimed to project an "empathic understanding" (*liaojie zhi tongqing* 了解之同情) into Chen's inner world. The term "empathy" derives from Chen's Herderian approach to historical studies, which emphasized that every era could be appreciated only in light of its immediate values and systems. Chen added that to "stand in the same realm as thinkers of the past," the historian must "cultivate empathy [for their subject of study]."[30] In connection with this, Yu asserted that empathy enabled him to understand Chen's elusive and indirect modes of expression exactly as Chen might have understood them himself. He suggested that a cluster of strong affective states, from self-pity (*zishang* 自傷) to anger (*nu* 怒) and regret (*hui* 悔), manifest through indirect allegories and obscure references in Chen's writings under socialism. To feel the emotional torrents beneath the textual surface, however, the reader must exercise empathy and enter the internal realm of Chen's literary world.

Through his "empathetic interpretation," Yu cast Chen in the role of a loyalist (*yimin* 遺民), a notable moral and political identity throughout Chinese history. A compound of *yi* 遺 (to leave behind) and *min* 民 (subject), the term *yimin* originally referred to the Confucian literatus who, after surviving dynasty transitions, refused to serve the new ruler to demonstrate their unwavering loyalty to the bygone regime.[31] According to the ancient legend, Bo Yi 伯夷 and Shu Qi 叔齊, the two "remnant subjects of the Shang dynasty," refused to "eat the grains of the Zhou dynasty" and eventually died of starvation to show their political chastity. As the moral tale of ascetic nonparticipation shows, loyalism implies "unappeased longing for a lost world, as well as irrevocable alienation from the new order and inevitable tension with it."[32] Yet although the two sages retreated into inner exile to "leave the world and stand alone" (*yishi duli* 遺世獨立), the loyalist

---

30. See Chen Yinke, "Feng Youlan *Zhongguo zhexueshi* shangce shencha baogao," 279; for a comparison between Chen's "emphatic understanding" and Johann Gottfried Herder's *einfühlung*, see Chen Huaiyu, "Chen Yinke yu Heerde."

31. For related discussions, see David Wang, *Hou yimin xiezuo*, 6; Wai-yee Li, *Women and National Trauma in Late Imperial Chinese Literature*, 2.

32. Wai-yee Li, "Introduction," 8.

is to be distinguished from the "eremitic subject" (*yimin* 逸民) who completely withdraws from the whirlwind of politics and lives a reclusive life. As Wai-yee Li observes, the loyalists of the Ming were actively engaged in "resistance, commented on social ills, debated moral and philosophical questions . . . [and were] deeply concerned with the . . . transmission of tradition."[33] In other words, loyalist pathos—the irrevocable feeling of bereavement, loss, and displacement—can be transformed into an active preservation of cultural traditions and political integrity against all odds.

Invoking a cumulative tradition of loyalist resistance, Yu Ying-shih nevertheless understood Chen Yinke as a "cultural loyalist" rather than a "political loyalist," thereby skirting the question of political allegiance and framing Chen's position within a universal conception of China's cultural tradition.[34] Against the Maoist command for a "thought reform" (i.e., laying down past burdens and expunging reactionary thoughts), Chen deliberately identified himself with the late-Qing conservative cultural milieu to make clear his oppositional stance. Chen's cultural loyalism, as Yu suggested, was already manifested in the 1927 elegy he wrote for the Qing loyalist Wang Guowei 王國維 (1877–1927), a renowned scholar and a stubborn *yilao* 遺老 (remnant subject) who drowned himself in Kunming Lake at the Imperial Summer Palace shortly before the National Revolutionary Army entered Beijing. Much has been written about the mood of loyalist literary societies in the years following the collapse of the Manchu-led Qing dynasty. For desperate Qing loyalists, the Xinhai Revolution (1911) marked the end of a glorious civilization, not the beginning of one. Wang had recounted, often fatalistically, how centuries of Confucian-imperial order had been reduced to a magnificent shipwreck. When the Northern Expedition concluded, the violence of revolution, war, and warlordism further bequeathed the new republic a dark legacy of bitter division. In Chen's perspective, the magnitude of the tumult compelled Wang to commit suicide as a martyr dying for the splintered traditional Chinese learning:

---

33. Wai-yee Li, "Introduction," 8.
34. Yu Ying-shih, "Chen Yinke de xueshujingshen he wannian xinjing," 12.

Whenever a culture is in decline, the individual who is raised in this cultural milieu is destined to suffer anguish. The deeper he immerses into this culture, the more profoundly he feels the pain . . . China now confronts the greatest calamity and most unprecedented change in its millennia-long history, and our old culture seems to have been brought to an end. How can those whose very being represents a condensation and realization of the spirit of Chinese culture fail to follow its fate and perish along with it? This is the reason why Mr. Wang had to die, and his suicide will be deeply mourned by us and posterity.

凡一種文化值衰弱之時，為此文化所化之人，必感苦痛，其表現此文化之程量愈宏，則其所受之苦痛亦愈甚，迨既達極深之度，殆非出於自殺無求一己之心安而義盡也⋯蓋今日赤縣神州值數千年未有之鉅劫奇變；劫盡變窮，則此文化精神所凝聚之人，安得不與之共命而同盡，此觀堂先生所以不得不死，遂為天下後世所極哀而深惜者也！[35]

Whereas others dismissed Wang's martyrdom as ideologically reactionary—an expression of strong personal identification with the fallen Qing dynasty—Chen contended that Wang's self-willed death reached beyond "personal grievances" and "the rise or fall of one ruling house" to "manifest his will to independence and freedom" (先生以一死見其獨立自由之意志，非所論於一人之恩怨，一姓之興亡).[36] Even though Wang's conservative cultural vision was deeply intertwined with his loyalty toward the last Qing emperor, Puyi, Chen was determined to interpret Wang's loyalist stance through the prism of intellectual reasoning and moral conviction.

Whereas PRC critics condemned Yu's thesis of cultural loyalism as an ideologically motivated attack on the socialist intelligentsia, Yu insisted that his reading amounted to nothing other than "unraveling [Chen's] inner heart through faithful annotation" (*daixia zhujiao, fahuang xinqu* 代下注腳，發皇心曲).[37] Indeed, at the center of Yu's renewed engagement in the 1980s was the question of the "late state of mind" (*wannian xinjing* 晚年心境), which referred to Chen's

---

35. Chen Yinke, "Wang Guantang xiansheng wanci bingxu," 12, quoted in and translated by Shengqing Wu, *Modern Archaics*, 115–16.

36. Chen Yinke, "Qinghua daxue Wang Guantang xiansheng jinianbeiming," 247, quoted in and translated by Wai-yee Li, "Nostalgia and Resistance," 1.

37. Yu Ying-shih, *Chen Yinke wannian shiwen shizheng*, 35.

idiosyncratic efforts to "praise fair ladies" (*song hongzhuang* 頌紅妝) in the last twenty years of his life. In contrast to his earlier, rigorously philological approach to Sui-Tang political history, Chen's study of Chen Duansheng and Liu Rushi appeared to be fragmented, full of literary imaginaries, replete with autobiographical intentions, and punctuated by outbursts of emotion. Yu suggested that this willful literary imagination involved a transformation of conventional historiography into a *xinshi* 心史 (inner history from the heart).[38] The term *xinshi* harked back to the writings of Song loyalist Zheng Sixiao 鄭思肖 (1241–1318), whose manuscript *The Inner History from a Loyal Heart* was sealed inside an iron casket and hidden in a well at a Buddhist monastery at Suzhou for three and a half centuries before its accidental discovery.[39] In a manner reminiscent of Ming loyalists who excavated Zheng's untimely mediations for their tenacious resistance, Yu emphasized the moral obligation to retrieve Chen's "buried loyalist heart" from oblivion, violence, and devastation.

Yu's exemplary case was Chen's magnum opus, *An Extended Biography of Liu Rushi*, which recorded Liu's involvement in the anti-Manchu resistance movement (fig. 2). Historians have long described the Ming-Qing dynastic transition as a traumatic and protracted process punctuated by violent episodes such as the fall of Beijing (1644), the Yangzhou Massacre (1645), and the crackdown on the Jiangnan resistance movement.[40] In addition to political tumult and social disintegration, the imposition of Manchu customs and practices—especially the Tonsure Decree, which mandated changes of costumes and hairstyle—fueled the moral indignation of the Han people, who invoked the cultural and ethnic distinction between "Chinese" (*hua* 華) and "barbarians" (*yi* 夷) to express the extreme anguish of "being turned from a Chinese into a barbarian."[41] In sharp contrast to the turncoats who collaborated with the Qing regime, Liu Rushi was remembered for her uncompromising political integrity throughout the anti-Manchu resistance movement. After the collapse of the refugee southern Ming court (1645), Liu tried

38. See Yu Ying-shih, "Chen Yinke de shixue sanbian."
39. Haw, "The *History of a Loyal Heart (Xin shi)*."
40. For a comprehensive account, see Wakeman, *The Great Enterprise*.
41. Wai-yee Li, "Introduction," 2.

FIGURE 2. The first edition of *An Extended Biography of Liu Rushi* (1980) displayed at the former residence of Chen Yinke. Photo courtesy of Huang Jiaqi.

to drown herself in the pond to "perish with the [fallen] country" (*xunguo* 殉國) and avoid shameful survival. When her husband, Qian Qianyi 錢謙益 (1582–1664), a Ming court minister and leader of the Revival Society, was imprisoned for organizing a coup d'état, Liu allegedly "went to the seas to raise the morale of the [Ming loyalist] navy" (*zhi haishang kaoshi* 至海上犒師).[42] After the death of Qian, a decade into the new dynasty, Liu entered a Buddhist lay order and eventually committed suicide in bitter protest.

For Chen Yinke, nostalgic for a lost Confucian world torn apart by socialist revolution, revisiting the fall of the Ming through Liu's writing became an allegorical expression of loss and recovery. Between 1954 and 1964, Chen devoted almost all his energy to the writing of her biography. Having completely lost his sight, and suffering from prolonged illnesses, the historian would spend the night searching for

42. Quoted in Wai-yee Li, *Women and National Trauma in Late Imperial Chinese Literature*, 362.

sources in his memory and outlining the argument in his mind, after which he would ask his assistant to transcribe his words verbatim during the day.[43] In this manner, without ever leaving his studio, he reconstructed a late-Ming literati world of poetry, friendship, and elegance amid historical rupture and military violence. Through daring imagination and patient elucidation, Chen excavated the controversial yet epic life of a courtesan across time: Liu's humble beginning as a bondmaid sold into the household of a high official, her amorous encounters with southern China's most talented men of letters, and—inevitably—the crushing of the resistance and Liu's subsequent suicide in the wake of the Manchu ascendance. Recalling Liu's melancholic reflection that "the brilliance of spring has given way to the bitter rain of autumn" (春日釀成秋日雨),[44] Chen mourned that despite Liu's valor and resolve, the "propensity of the times" (*shishi* 時勢) did not side with the Ming loyalists.

For Yu, however, Chen's empathy for Liu was not simply a nostalgic look at a lost world destroyed by war and revolution. Rather, his sentimentality was tinged with a vexing web of uneasy feelings: shock mixed with disillusionment, melancholy indistinguishable from despair, and a hidden anger toward the Manchurian (and Communist) conquerors who persecuted literati and silenced dissent. Thus Chen turned the Ming loyalist into a transcendental idealist who embodies the spirit of opposition and independence. Above all, Chen took a Herderian approach to project his "lingering pathos for the fall of dynasties" (*xingwang yihen* 興亡遺恨) into Liu's interior realm, a poetic world in which an extravagant *fengliu* 風流 (lifestyle of aesthetic refinement and sensual indulgence) coexisted with covert political resistance. As Wai-yee Li notes, the "romantic loyalists of Jiangnan" (*Jiangnan fengliu yimin* 江南風流遺民) immersed themselves in the lost world of late-Ming courtesan culture to express their moral stance of nonparticipation in the new regime.[45] Similarly, Chen's affective attachment to the late-Ming literati world of poetry, friendship, and elegance was no less intermingled with political lament: "from Ming to Qing: a painful history both old and new"

---

43. Yeh, "Historian and Courtesan."
44. Liu Rushi, "Jinming chi yong hanliu," 221.
45. Wai-yee Li, "Introduction," 16.

(明清痛史新兼舊).⁴⁶ Having lived through tumultuous regime transitions, from the fall of the Qing dynasty to the fledging republican years and from the Sino-Japanese War to the Communist takeover, Chen read Liu's tragic life as a template and a cultural script for traditional Chinese literati moldering in the graveyard of socialism.

Most important for Yu, the moral indications of Chen's "praise of fair ladies" are visible only to those familiar with the classical literary analogy between female chastity and political integrity. As Wai-yee Li observes, Ming loyalists described service in the new regime as being equally disgraceful as a widow's remarriage.⁴⁷ Chen invoked this gendered allegory to satirize Chinese male scholars who "practice the way of the concubine" (*qiefu zhi dao* 妾婦之道) and "twist their scholarship to please the powerful" (*quxue eshi* 曲學阿世) throughout the 1950s. In a poem titled "The Female Impersonator" ("Nandan" 男旦), Chen referred to the theatrical tradition of female impersonation to describe the Communist Thought Reform as a gendered process of "transforming men into women" (*gainan zaonü taiquanxin* 改男造女態全新).⁴⁸ Just as female impersonators in Peking operas were trained to dress, behave, and sing like women, Chinese (male) scholars, in Chen's analogy, willingly castrated themselves and performed effeminate obeisance to the Maoist regime. And whereas socialist intellectuals, ironically, had become the true heirs of the female impersonator legacy, Liu Rushi was portrayed by Chen as a defiant male impersonator: the courtesan dressed as a Confucian scholar, styled herself "your younger brother" (*di* 弟) in her correspondence with male literati, and deployed abundant martial and military imagery to convey her determination to defend the crumbling Ming dynasty.⁴⁹ Against those "in modish attire who were not equal to ladies' virtue" (今日衣冠愧女兒),⁵⁰ Chen

---

46. Hu Wenhui, *Chen Yinke shi jianshi*, 1149, quoted in and translated by Wai-yee Li, "Nostalgia and Resistance," 12.

47. Wai-yee Li, *Women and National Trauma in Late Imperial Chinese Literature*, 8–9.

48. Hu Wenhui, *Chen Yinke shi jianshi*, 662–65, quoted in and translated by Wai-yee Li, "Nostalgia and Resistance," 5.

49. Wai-yee Li, *Women and National Trauma in Late Imperial Chinese Literature*, 132.

50. Yu Ying-shih, *Chen Yinke wannian shiwen shizheng*, 353.

argued that the courtesan Liu Rushi exemplified "the independence of spirit and freedom of thought of our people" (我民族獨立之精神，自由之思想) at its most intense.[51]

With the completion of *An Extended Biography* in 1964, Chen poured out the pathos and the passions of writing history from his heart, "unabashedly weeping for the departed; leaving this as a bequest for those yet to come" (痛哭古人，留贈來者).[52] For Yu, the political inference behind Chen's attachment to the courtesan loyalist was obvious: although the historian chose to remain in mainland China in 1949, Chen's self-willed inner exile into the world of Ming loyalists betrayed his profound sense of alienation from the socialist regime. Drawing a connection between Zheng Chenggong's 鄭成功 (1624–1662) navy forces and Chiang Kai-shek's (1887–1975) truncated island regime, Yu further proposed that Chen's sympathy for Liu was an allegorical expression of his lingering attachment to the Republic of China on Taiwan. After all, Liu and his comrades had feverishly supported Zheng's expedition and fantasized about Taiwan as the last bastion of the Ming loyalist cause. Yet, just as Zheng's military adventure to recapture the Lower Yangzi River area turned out to be a fiasco, Chiang's promise to retake the mainland proved to be illusory as well. In the end, Chen's "late state of mind" led Yu to a landscape of exile and homelessness: "For the place of escape, I cannot hope for a Mayflower" (避地難希五月花).[53] Finding no "peach blossom land" that could shelter his family from the whirlwind of politics, Chen withdrew into the elusive dreamworld of the courtesan and kept his distance from the "northern regime": he not only named his collected essays *The Collection from the Hall of Icy Willow* (*Hanliu tang ji* 寒柳堂集)—a coded reference to Liu's family name—but also called his own residence in Guangzhou (fig. 3) the "Hall of Golden Illumination" (*jinming guan* 金明館), after the studio in which the courtesan Liu wrote her poetry. In this respect, Chen's "history from the heart" embodied his "heartfelt longing for

---

51. Chen Yinke, *Liu Rushi biezhuan*, 1:4.

52. Chen Yinke, *Liu Rushi biezhuan*, 3:1224, quoted in and translated by Wai-yee Li, "Nostalgia and Resistance," 13.

53. Hu Wenhui, *Chen Yinke shi jianshi*, 475, quoted in and translated by Wai-yee Li, "Nostalgia and Resistance," 9.

FIGURE 3. The former residence of Chen Yinke, a two-story villa on the southern campus of Sun Yat-Sen University, Guangzhou. Photo courtesy of Huang Jiaqi.

returning to the southern dreamworld" (*suonan xinshi* 所南心史).[54] For the cultural loyalist, Liu's garden at Changshu brought back the "world of yesterday": Chen's childhood home of Nanjing, the gentle breeze and soft landscape of Jiangnan, and the fin-de-siècle splendor of the Guangxu-Xuantong era, all of which were torn apart by the ruthless storm of modern revolution.

To be sure, one can debate whether it is legitimate for Yu to infer Chen's secret sympathy for Taiwan from the seemingly arbitrary link between Zheng Chenggong's Kingdom of Tungning and Chiang's island state. Admittedly, Yu's praise for Chen's preservation of political integrity in his late years may have inadvertently reinforced the Cold War liberal narrative of "betrayal versus loyalty,"[55] a sentimental framework that dramatized Chinese intellectuals' confrontational stance against the socialist regime. Throughout his reading, Yu (in)voluntarily

---

54. Hu Wenhui, *Chen Yinke shi jianshi*, 720.
55. Xiaojue Wang, *Modernity with a Cold War Face*, 7.

bounced back to the dichotomy of resistance versus conformity as a linchpin for understanding Chen's political choice. As a result, a compassionate, sentimental, and sometimes moralistic tone consistently underpins Yu's poignant account of Chen's suffering under the Communist reign. Still, Yu's daring exploration of Chen's real and imagined resistance helped animate multiple types of liberal thinking in the post-Tiananmen era, as we shall see.

An Apolitical Academician

"One of the most notable scholarly fashions of the early nineties," the exiled Kantian philosopher Li Zehou remarked in 1993, "is the symbolic meanings invested in academicians such as Chen Yinke and Wang Guowei, and the waning halos of thinkers like Chen Duxiu and Lu Xun" (*sixiangjia danchu, xuewenjia tuxian* 思想家淡出，學問家凸顯).[56] The term "thinker" (*sixiang jia* 思想家) was used by Li to describe the prototypical May Fourth iconoclast who seized upon knowledge as a powerful way of inculcating radical values, inspiring revolutionary actions, and legitimating subversive beliefs. By contrast, the phrase "academician" (*xuewen jia* 學問家) carries the flavor of the Weberian scholar who ascertains neutral facts through accumulative learning. To be an academician in the Weberian sense is, first and foremost, to engage in empirical learning for the sake of self-clarification without providing immediate guidance for political action. Although Li argued that the 1980s New Enlightenment saw the fusion of radical thinking and cumulative learning, in the early 1990s, he bemoaned the parting of the two ways. The 1989 Tiananmen crackdown had shocked the liberal intelligentsia out of the dream of enlightenment that had set in since the early reform era. This shock prompted them to abandon the quixotic hope of democratization and retreat into scholasticism. Predictably, the aloof, eccentric, and apolitical character of Chen Yinke became attractive to those who wished to rehabilitate a hermit to juxtapose against the whirlwind of politics.

---

56. See Li Zehou, "Sixiang xueshu wenda," 270.

This melancholic identification with Chen the academician, however, reveals the disorientation of liberal thinking in the immediate post-Tiananmen era. After a decade of radically questioning Mao's socialism, deconstructing the power of the old Left, and promoting an enlightenment agenda, liberal-minded scholars sheltered in academic quarters stood still, shocked into silence by the resurgence of authoritarian politics. With the suppression of the student protest and the ousting of the reformist party leader Zhao Ziyang 趙紫陽 (1919–2005), conservatives moved to criticize Deng Xiaoping's reform program and reimposed draconian ideological indoctrination and heavy-handed political campaigns. As Joseph Fewsmith observes, in contrast to the liberal consensus of the 1980s, advocates of neoconservatism began to play a significant role in post-Tiananmen intellectual and political circles.[57] The authoritarian turn, as Els van Dongen suggests, thus compelled disheartened liberals into a series of debates on the intertwined relationship between revolution and radicalism in Chinese modernity.[58] In the midst of great uncertainties and anxieties, many scholars attributed the failure of the 1980s enlightenment project to the underlying creed of radicalism that had dominated twentieth-century Chinese political thought. From the May Fourth to the June Fourth movements, Chinese intellectuals embraced a succession of totalistic and monistic "isms" that favored historical ruptures, political actions, and moments of existential decisions.[59] The penchant for extreme thinking not only led to constant political polarization, but also marginalized moderate voices while stifling gradualist and reformist alternatives.[60]

For those who had become disillusioned with radical politics, Chen Yinke's lukewarm reformism suddenly appeared prescient. As early as 1933, Chen had self-consciously aligned himself with the late-Qing Confucian reformists Zeng Guofan 曾國藩 (1811–1872) and Zhang Zhidong 張之洞 (1837–1909), both of whom had proposed a reconciliation

---

57. Fewsmith, *China since Tiananmen*, 83–112.
58. See Van Dongen, *Realistic Revolution*.
59. See Yu Ying-shih, "Zhongguo jindai sixiangshi shang de jijin yu baoshou."
60. See Yu Ying-shih, "Chen Yinke de xueshujingshen he wannian xinjing," 26–27.

between "substantive Chinese learning" and "pragmatic Western knowledge" (*zhongxue wei ti, xixue wei yong* 中學為體,西學為用). Chen's empathy with the conservative literati was not merely a nostalgic paean to the bygone era of late-Qing reformism; rather, it was infused with his eclectic cultural stance. As he so succinctly stated, "I am devoted to a learning neither of the classical nor of the contemporary, with my thought originating from the Xianfeng-Tongzhi period" (寅恪平生為不古不今之學,思想囿於咸豐同治之世).[61] Here, Chen was referring to his scholarly expertise in Sui-Tang history (581–907), a period punctuated by vibrant cultural and intellectual exchanges between the Han Chinese and foreign races. Chen noted that Tang literati were beset by a creative tension between the commitment to preserve their identity (as anchored in Confucian antiquity) and the quest for more heterogenous cultural values to assimilate different racial and ethnic groups into the Han community. Above all, Chen stressed the idea that Confucian tradition thrives on its cultural inclusiveness, which was best manifested in the Tang rulers' cosmopolitan visions and practices.[62]

Needless to say, Chen's cultural syncretism did not always lead to a liberal agenda. For a new generation of Chinese conservatives, Chen's passionate conviction of China's unchanging national spirit (*guocui* 國粹) provided a theoretical stimulus for a nativist alternative. In the post-Mao landscape, cultural conservatism emerged as a broad spectrum of loosely connected intellectual quests in search of indigenous sources of modernization. Thus Yue Daiyun 樂黛雲 (1931–2024), a professor of comparative literature based at Peking University, sought to reevaluate the suppressed legacies of the Xueheng School in the 1920s. Yue lumped together a group of neo-humanist scholars such as Mei Guangdi 梅光迪 (1890–1945) and Wu Mi 吳宓 (1894–1978). In opposition to the older generation of Confucian revivalists who held a dichotomous view of "modern" versus "ancient," the Xueheng group were compelled to initiate a modernist transvaluation of Chinese antiquity

---

61. Chen Yinke, "Feng Youlan *Zhongguo zhexueshi* xiace shencha baogao," 285.
62. See Chen Yinke, "Li-tang shizu zhi tuice houji," 344; Chen Yinke, *Tangdai zhengzhishi shulungao*, 177–235.

in the time of national crisis. For Yue, their attempt to reconcile Confucian values with cosmopolitan humanism created a progressive cultural conservatism that could provide an alternative path for the post-Mao cultural renewal.[63]

Notwithstanding Chen Yinke's peripheral role in the Xueheng group,[64] Axel Schneider notes Chen's abiding affinity with the neohumanist ideal at the core of the Xueheng School's conservative stance.[65] Stressing "the universality of abstract ideas" (*chouxiang lixiang zhi tongxing* 抽象理想之通性), Chen argued that the cardinal principles of Confucianism, known as the "three fundamental bonds and five relations" (*sangang wuchang* 三綱五常), must be understood as malleable Platonic ideals rather than concrete institutions and frozen cultural forms.[66] As Chen expressed in his praise for Wang Guowei's martyrdom and Liu Rushi's loyalism, even the most "hackneyed" and "feudalistic" moral ideals could be transformed to resonate with the progressive spirit of "independence" and "freedom." Thus Chen shared the Xueheng group's dissatisfaction with the anti-traditionalist spirit of the May Fourth generation. As Chen himself put it, "creative thought must absorb and learn from foreign scholarship on the one hand, and maintain its national heritage on the other" (有所創獲者，必須一方面吸收輸入外來之學說，一方面不忘本來民族之地位).[67] Far from being a recalcitrant cultural fundamentalist, Chen held that a modern Chinese culture must simultaneously incorporate national tradition and universal humanism.

Yet Yue Daiyun's avowed desire to erect a conservative guru soon came into conflict with the movement to reclaim Chen's liberal legacy. In the early 1990s debate over "academic norms" (*xueshu guifan* 學術規範), for example, the liberals hailed Chen Yinke's reclusiveness

63. Yue, "Chonggu Xueheng: jianlun xiandai baoshouzhuyi."
64. Chen only published a few essays in *Critical Review*—a key journal of the Xueheng School—and his association with the group was largely because of a close friendship with its intellectual leader, Wu Mi. See Wu Xuezhao, *Wu Mi yu Chen Yinke*.
65. Schneider, "Bridging the Gap."
66. Chen Yinke, "Wang Guantang xiansheng wanci bingxu," 12.
67. Chen Yinke, "Feng Youlan *Zhongguo zhexueshi* xiace shencha baogao," 284–85.

as a model of neutral learning. Participants in the discussion shared the concern that scholarly pursuits during the 1980s New Enlightenment suffered from a surfeit of political activism and ideological "big talks," resulting in the decline of academic standards. In the aftermath of Tiananmen, liberal-minded scholars insisted that academic inquiry lacked the capacity to forge worldviews and guide practical action. Following the Weberian ideal of a "value-free" scholarship and Isaiah Berlin's seminal discussion of the "foxlike intellectual," several participants emphasized that only a professionalized and specialized academia could secure intellectual autonomy against the advance of authoritarianism.[68] They further argued that scholarship, if it were to remain a critical posture in the state-directed public sphere, must cleave to certain norms—a self-clarification of its own methods, boundaries, and limits—to facilitate the incremental progression of knowledge.

At this critical juncture, Chen's lifelong antipathy toward ideological doctrines resonated with an audience deeply averse to any political precepts. For historians in particular, Chen's philological method, which was rooted in Qian(long)-Jia(qing) evidential learning, provided a neutral historical approach that, in turn, offered an alternative to both the Maoist historiography and the 1980s modernization narrative.[69] For Chen, historical records of the past were so scattered and diffused that any attempts to organize them into an "all-embracing system of thought" were doomed to "drift further away from truth" (其言論愈有條理統系，則去古人學說之真相愈遠).[70] Chen's rigorous historicism, by contrast, prioritized the meticulous verification of historical data: names, birthplaces, and lineages of certain historical figures. The larger hypothesis was always based on the careful authentication of minute details. Thus, Chen's rigorous textualism quickly became a new norm for Chinese historians to reclaim objectivity in historical

---

68. See Zha Jianying, *Bashiniandai fangtanlu*, 116–47; Wang Hui, *Diandao*, 151.
69. See Huaiyin Li, *Reinventing Modern China*, 132–203.
70. Chen Yinke, "Feng Youlan *Zhongguo zhexueshi* shangce shencha baogao," 280.

studies.⁷¹ In opposition to the Maoist historiography that "prioritized (political) argumentation over fact" (*yilun daishi* 以論帶史), the advocates of Chen's evidential learning sought to restore the fragmented and disjointed nature of history against politically motivated approaches.

Nevertheless, the excavation of a scholastic, apolitical Chen struck some as ironic. After all, Chen was brought up in a prestigious literati family with a strong sense of political responsibility.⁷² In an essay titled "The Unfreedom of Literati" (最是文人不自由), Beijing-based intellectual historian Ge Zhaoguang 葛兆光 (1950–) pointed out that Chen was torn between two identities: the traditional Chinese "scholar-official" (*shidafu* 士大夫) with the self-assigned mission of "saving the nation" and the modern scholar who adheres to neutral academic norms.⁷³ Chen found it difficult to reconcile the unworldly character of the academician with the Confucian ideal of public and political engagement. Hence Chen had imbued his scholarly treatises with political concerns that far exceeded the Weberian academic quest. By eulogizing Liu Rushi as an icon of freedom and independence, for instance, Chen participated in the time-honored Confucian tradition of allegorical criticism—"entrusting [unexpressed] meanings to the words" (*jituo* 寄託)—to express his intransigent opposition to the politicization of learning under Mao's thought reforms.⁷⁴ The employment of encrypted images, archaic references, and an elliptical style allowed Chen to circumvent the Maoist censor and address an imaginary interlocutor, the "one who knows my melody" (*zhiyin* 知音)—that is, any person who could understand his anger and despair in these tumultuous times. In contrast to the Weberian academician, Chen sought to expose the scandal of censorship and reserve as a gift for posterity his hidden perception of the crisis of Chinese culture.

71. For a discussion of the implications of Chen's textualism for historical study, see Hu Shouwei, *Chen Yinke yu ershishiji Zhongguo xueshu*.
72. See Zhang Qiuhui, *Chen Yinke de jiazushi*.
73. Ge, "Zuishi wenren buziyou," 3.
74. Yu Ying-shih, *Chen Yinke wannian shiwen shizheng*, 175.

Notwithstanding Chen's seminal attempt to establish a middle realm between politics and scholarship through esotericism, Ge lamented that his search for the larger social and political significance of learning was doomed to fail in China's tumultuous twentieth century. Ge invoked the aesthetic imaginary of "crying out blood" (*tixue* 啼血) to convey Chen's profound grief and loss induced by his ill-fated esoteric "political intervention." The sense of alienation was conveyed through Chen's poetic images, such as "sightless and lame" (*shiming binzu* 失明臏足), "feeble and deformed [body]" (*shuaican* 衰殘), "buried bones" (*maigu* 埋骨), and "loneliness and resentment" (*guhuai yihen* 孤懷遺恨). For Ge, this self-pitying posture was an intense emotional expression of frustration and indignation toward Chen's own chaotic political age that had failed to realize his talents and ambitions. In this light, Chen's seclusion was only a reluctant retreat, or an imaginary escape, from being caught up in the tide of politics.

The quintessential dilemma between politics and scholarship was also keenly felt by Ge's generation. Ge brought his feeling of disarray in the post-Tiananmen era into his interpretation of Chen's paradoxical sense of "scholarly freedom": hermeticism enabled Chen to engage in pensive learning, but also restricted his purview to the ivory tower. Likewise, liberal intellectuals in the early 1990s were also trapped between the call for academic norms and a deep-rooted desire for political engagement. Yet whereas Ge used Chen's case to voice his ambivalence toward the Weberian academician, other scholars responded in more optimistic tones. In a rebuttal titled "The Freedom of Literati," Lü Peng 呂澎 argued that Chen's "literati mentality"—a compassionate yet somewhat impressionistic view of politics—was the main cause of his tragedy. Upholding a positivistic understanding of the political, Lü suggested that neither moral outrage nor outright resistance would prove sufficient to understand Chinese politics.[75] Meanwhile, literary scholar Chen Pingyuan 陳平原 (1954-) used the moderate term "this-worldly temperament" to mitigate the perceived chasm between politics and learning.[76] For Chen, it was no longer acceptable for a modern

---

75. Lü Peng, "Zuishi wenren you ziyou."
76. Chen Pingyuan, "Xuezhe de renjian qinghuai."

academician to allow moral compassion to play a predominant role in his learning. In this regard, Chen suggested that one should maintain moral compassion for political issues while acknowledging one's inability to understand the complex mechanisms of the political field. In the end, "humanistic sentiment"—a feeble, lukewarm temperament—became the last means by which liberal scholars could connect themselves to the lost literati tradition.

A Martyr of Liberalism

In 1995, Sanlian Joint Publishing House (三聯書店) released a book that instantly provoked fervent debate in the Chinese public space: Lu Jiandong's *The Last Twenty Years of Chen Yinke* (陳寅恪的最後二十年). At mid-decade, China's intelligentsia remained mired in disarray. Deng Xiaoping's Southern Tour in 1992 had initiated another round of radical marketization, leading to the explosive rise of mass entertainment in the public life. The increasing visibility of commercialism spawned a series of conservative laments for the decline of the "humanist spirit," from scathing attacks on Wang Shuo 王朔 (1958–)—the literary world's most unabashed dandy novelist—to angry outcries against the waning of "ultimate values" under the nascent culture industry. The chorus of moral indignation was driven by the assumption that certain prominent intellectuals had betrayed their noble cause to collaborate with the entertainment industry, run side business, or even engage in stock market speculation. But humanist scholars frequently deployed vague and metaphysical terms such as "ultimate concerns," "spiritual value," and "cultural crisis" without any adequate definition.[77] As a result, the intellectual community was desperate to seize upon a concrete case—a towering figure who embodied the heroic "humanist spirit"—to resist the rising tide of commercialization.

At this critical historical juncture, Chen Yinke appeared as something like a godsend to an audience primed to hail him as the bearer of Chinese humanism. "Because of the sensational appeal of Chen's

---

77. See McGrath, *Postsocialist Modernity*, 25–58.

legendary life," Classical scholar Zhang Qiuhui remembered, "the originally vague, pale, and feeble 'humanist spirit' finally became concrete, vivid, and touching."[78] At the time, many learned readers were just starting to take an interest in Chen's turbulent life under socialism. Tales of Chen's heroic resistance began to circulate in intellectual communities, provoking heated emotional responses to the anguished memories of political persecution. Whereas the conciliatory tone of humanism in the 1980s had construed intellectuals as the victims of Mao's political campaigns, more and more scholars and writers began to tackle the thorny issue of intellectuals' complicity in the collective crimes of the revolution. As mentioned in chapter 1, prominent public figures, such as Ba Jin, Ji Xianlin, and Liu Zaifu, offered compelling reflections on how intellectuals themselves bore moral responsibility for their shameful roles in the Cultural Revolution. But Chen Yinke stood out because of his fierce nonconformist stance throughout his life. Just as the eminent liberal economist Gu Zhun defiantly declared "my hands have not been tainted by blood" during the Cultural Revolution, Chen's refusal to participate in any political campaigns turned him into a moral paragon in the eyes of the post-Mao generation.[79]

However, the public desire to paint Chen as a courageous political figure had to confront the extant official narrative, which projected an eccentric, aloof, and even timid man of letters. Throughout the Mao era, Marxist historians criticized Chen's nonchalance toward political matters and claimed that Chen's historicism led to an empty, dry, and formulaic obsession with the archive, the quintessence of bourgeois antiquarianism. During the Cultural Revolution, Chen was harshly denounced as a "vicious remnant of the Qian(long)-Jia(qing) evidential learning" who squandered the blood and sweat of the laboring class to satisfy his luxurious lifestyle and arcane interests.[80] Even Chen's colleagues remembered him as a hermit who turned a blind eye to all

---

78. Zhang Qiuhui, *Chen Yinke congkao*, 91.
79. For example, Xu Jilin argues that "Gu Zhun and Chen Yinke are the two greatest moral icons in twentieth-century China." See Xu Jilin, "Gu Zhun de daode shijian," 121. It is worth noting that the posthumous cult of Gu Zhun went hand in hand with that of Chen in the mid-1990s.
80. Lu Jiandong, *Chen Yinke de zuihou ershinian*, 466.

political matters.⁸¹ Although Yu Ying-shih's reading had sparked interest within cultural circles since the 1980s regarding Chen's esoteric defiance, it was Lu Jiandong's touching biography that fundamentally transformed the public image of Chen from that of a self-pitying scholar into that of a liberal martyr. A scholar based in Guangzhou, Lu had spent years digging into archives and conducting interviews about Chen's sojourn in Sun Yat-Sen University, where he held a professorship in the history department until his death.⁸² At the time, mainland and Taiwanese scholars had already penned several biographies of Chen, but most avoided confronting the experience of political persecution that loomed large in Chen's last twenty years. Lu, meanwhile, provided a solemn account of Chen's political trials.

In the biography, Lu deploys backshadowing to dramatize Chen's tragic confrontation with the Communist state. "Backshadowing," as Michael André Bernstein and Gary Morson both define it, is a tendency to evaluate past historical events in light of their "eventual denouement."⁸³ Similarly, Lu described Chen's last twenty years as a succession of mounting disasters, a chain of ominous events backshadowed by his ultimate downfall at the hands of the Red Guards. In his final days, activists at Sun Yat-Sen University deliberately surrounded Chen's house with loudspeakers to "let the reactionary academic authority listen to the angry accusations of the revolutionary masses."⁸⁴ Just as Bernstein argues that "the tragic is a mode of comprehending, and giving form to events as a narrative,"⁸⁵ Chen's excruciating death compelled Lu to interpret his subject's last twenty years in terms of one foregone conclusion: that from 1949 onward, every historical event simply contributed to a later, more tragic confrontation between Chen and an increasingly militant and hostile state. The chapter titles chosen by Lu poignantly convey the precariousness of Chen's life through aesthetic images such as "Aftermath of a Cataclysm" (*jiehou yuxu* 劫後

---

81. Gan Shaosu, *Zongdai he wo*, 204.
82. See Wang Xiaohui, "Jiushiniandai de Chen Yinke xiangxiang."
83. Michael Bernstein, *Foregone Conclusions*; Morson, *Narrative and Freedom*, quoted in Wurgaft, "The Uses of Walter," 370.
84. Lu Jiandong, *Chen Yinke de zuihou ershinian*, 480.
85. Michael Bernstein, *Foregone Conclusions*, 10.

餘緒), "Bare Survival" (*caojian tousheng* 草間偷生), "Almost Nothing Remains" (*suosheng wuji* 所剩無幾), "Elegy" (*wange* 輓歌), and "Long Night" (*changye* 長夜). These emotionally charged expressions and analogies highlight Chen's sense of fear and despair as he passed through a succession of political storms, from the Thought Reform and the Anti-Rightist Campaign to the Cultural Revolution. Although Lu also detailed moments of joy and hope between catastrophes, they appear to be fleeting, rare, and illusory.

Lu also presents a moving picture of Chen's physical and mental distress in his last years. Chen suffered from a degenerative eye disease and completely lost his vision in the 1940s. In 1962, an accidental fall left him physically disabled at the age of seventy-two, after which his hearing began to deteriorate as well. In addition, Chen also relied heavily on imported medicines to treat a gastrointestinal ailment. Lu selects a number of images from Chen's poetry and other writing to illustrate an angry and disturbed spirit, a feeble and deformed man of letters whose chronic ill health and worsening bodily decay only reinforced his determination to assert his moral and political integrity. Such a contrast between corporeal suffering and spiritual strength, Lu notes, is manifested in the epilogue that Chen wrote for *An Extended Biography of Liu Rushi*. Knowing that his days were numbered, Chen used the metaphor of bodily decay to convey his anguish: "Sightless and lame I have become, but I am not yet deaf and dumb" (失明臏足，尚未聾啞).[86] Here, physical illness paradoxically endowed Chen with a critical insight into the enormous cultural devastation wrought by Mao's revolution.

In addition to the heart-wrenching description of Chen's physical suffering, Lu also highlights Chen's stubbornness, especially a willful tendency to turn down professional opportunities regardless of the dire political consequences that might follow. Lu portrays Chen as a fiery dissident who rowed against the tides of his time and resisted entirely the possibility of reconciling with political reality. Whereas Yu Yingshih had offered a forceful reading of Chen's esoteric nonconformism,

---

86. Chen Yinke, *Liu Rushi biezhuan*, 3:1224, quoted in and translated by Wai-yee Li, "Nostalgia and Resistance," 13.

Lu supports Yu's speculation with several critical historical episodes.⁸⁷ According to Lu, Chen not only refused to meet political luminaries such as Guo Moruo and Kang Sheng 康生 (1898–1975), but also turned down invitations to join the new establishment. The most famous case occurred in 1953, when Chen adamantly rejected an offer to lead the newly established Institute of History in Beijing. Lu's account dramatizes this event by describing Chen's tendency to stir up political confrontation and even showcases his anti-Marxist stance. When his disciple Wang Jian 汪籛 (1916–1966) paid a visit to Chen's home, hoping to persuade his teacher to accept this offer, Chen was reportedly greatly infuriated by Wang's "Marxist rhetoric and indoctrinating tone."⁸⁸ Chen angrily listed two conditions under which he would accept the offer: first, he explicitly demanded that the institute be exempt from Marxist studies; and second, he asked for a written dispensation from Chairman Mao or President Liu Shaoqi (1989–1969) that guaranteed academic freedom.⁸⁹ Chen also declared that all his disciples should abide by the principle of "free thinking and independent spirit," and that because Wang Jian had conformed to Marxism-Leninism, he was no longer Chen's student.

Throughout the biography, Lu's tone is melancholic, consumed by rage, and driven by a poignant sympathy toward Chen's sufferings; it might be read as an outward expression of Lu's disappointment at the inability of Maoist intellectuals to appreciate the profundity of Chen's nonconformist morality. Chen, the last of his kind, had to endure physical distress, suffer insults, and overcome fear and despair to assert his integrity. Chen's generational peers, by contrast, appeared conciliatory, sycophantic, and submissive. Thus, despite the lack of coherent political thinking in Chen's works, the pathos aroused by Chen's case made him a convenient object for frustrated liberals who could not find a clear path out of the shadows of Tiananmen. Indeed, dramatic accounts of Chen's heartrending tragedies struck a nerve with liberal intellectuals

---

87. For Yu's review of Lu's book, see Yu Ying-shih, "Chen Yinke yanjiu de fansi he zhanwang."
88. Lu Jiandong, *Chen Yinke de zuihou ershinian*, 103.
89. Lu Jiandong, *Chen Yinke de zuihou ershinian*, 111–13.

because they immediately identified with—or fancied themselves to be—the lonely, angry, and courageous Chen: resistant to Marxist "reeducation," betrayed by disciples, and burdened by the task of preserving the last remnant of Chinese culture against all odds. This morally driven narrative transformed Chen's hermetic stance into an act of martyrdom, and Chen himself into the towering moral icon long sought by the post-Mao generation.

This emotional attachment to Chen's life may help explain Lu's biography's popularity beyond the domain of academia. Inspired by Lu, similar melodramatic narratives of Chen began to appear in newspapers, magazines, and popular nonfiction works, followed by an explosion of conferences and cultural events devoted to ritualizing Chen as "the one to whom Chinese culture entrusted its fate." Scholars and cultural luminaries hailed Chen as a martyr who had died for academic freedom. Chen, fooled by the illusion that there were still freedom and independence to defend in Communist China, adhered to his liberal values against the storm of political persecutions that gradually crushed his faith and body—or so the story went. In the meantime, these sentimental accounts were scorned for their manic displays of mourning. Critics charged that Lu frequently deployed "flamboyant yet hollow rhetoric" and "exaggerating, melodramatic phrases" to amplify Chen's psychological trauma and cultural despair.[90] The excessive, self-pitying pathos was deemed too much, too morose, and too fetishistic, straining boundaries between resistance and passivity. Zhang Qiuhui described Lu's overwrought grief as "a cloud that is too thick to dissolve." Gu Lin remarked, "This book makes you cry yet offers no serious reflection."[91] Widespread among literary critics was the suspicion that the fevered pitch of grief aroused by Chen's misfortune reinforced the shared feeling of permanent frustration and hopeless resignation among Chinese intellectuals.

For disgruntled liberals, however, the extensive media coverage of Chen's physical and spiritual sufferings further valorized their moral repulsions against Mao's socialist revolution. Thus, liberal scholars

---

90. See Zhang Qiuhui, *Chen Yinke congkao*, 96.
91. See Zhang Qiuhui, *Chen Yinke congkao*, 95–96; Gu Lin, "Gu Lin zhi Zhi An han," 81.

actively participated in the dissemination of Chen's melodrama in the mass media. They believed that this tragedy could shock, educate, and ultimately transform public emotion, a frozen landscape characterized by apathy, forgetfulness, and the "inability to mourn."[92] For Chinese liberals, the political cultivation of a family of interrelated emotions—empathy, shame, and guilt—did not merely provide ways to come to terms with China's revolutionary past. Rather, the intense pathos and poignant feelings conjured by Chen's death animated perceptions, memories, and affirmative emotions to reclaim China's stillborn liberal mentality in the postrevolutionary era.

Yet despite the liberals' claim that they were bearing witness to truth, their moralistic undertone reflected a desire to intervene, repair, and even undo the unbearable past by proposing a normative set of criteria for evaluating moral and political conduct. In other words, the emotionally charged liberal discourse came very close to declaring that empathy, guilt, and mourning were the only appropriate emotional response to the case of Chen in particular and the demise of the republican-period intellectuals under Mao's revolution in general. The commemoration of Chen led to a series of public confessions among Chen's disciples and colleagues. For instance, Zhou Yiliang 周一良 (1913–2001), a former student of Chen, read a lengthy piece of self-criticism at an academic conference in 1999. In his "Confession to Mr. Chen," Zhou conveyed his remorse over his politically motivated attacks against his teacher in the 1950s. Calling himself a "turncoat" who "bent scholarship to please authority," Zhou sincerely pleaded that he should be "expelled" from among Chen's followers due to this ignoble betrayal.[93] In this regard, Zhou and many others took Chen's great refusal as a moral standard against which one must acknowledge one's active or passive complicity in the collective crimes of the Mao era.

---

92. Mitscherlich and Mitscherlich, *The Inability to Mourn*; Parkinson, *An Emotional State*, 113–46.

93. Zhou Yiliang, "Xiang Chen xiansheng qingzui." Zhou's confession was by all means sincere, and I do not mean to question his genuine willingness to confess. See chapter 1 for my analysis of the politics of confession.

Debating Chen Yinke's Legacy in Contemporary China

In 1998, the renowned Shanghai-based liberal scholar Zhu Xueqin 朱學勤 (1952–) published a manifesto titled "The Emergence of Liberalism in 1998" (一九九八：自由主義學理的言說).[94] Zhu contended that the complex matrix of China's liberal modernity—repeatedly interrupted by wars and revolutions—had finally made its return in the post-Tiananmen era. He traced the roots of contemporary Western liberalism to the eighteenth-century English and Scottish thinkers who defended personal rights and freedom against all forms of collective power. Parliamentary democracy and a market economy were organic outgrowths of the moderate, anti-utopian, and pluralistic vision of classical liberalism.[95] Zhu then moved on to discuss the parallels between China's modern experience and the European Enlightenment. In particular, he identified Chen Yinke's refusal to commit to any ideological doctrines as a perfect embodiment of classical liberalism—a practice and belief in the relative validity of each individual's convictions. In this light, Chen's suspicious hermeneutics—his eclectic, skeptical, and nonconformist stance—echoed Berlin's idea of negative liberty against the all-encompassing and intrusive revolutionary ideology of the Mao era. For Zhu, the widespread public admiration for Chen's liberal attitude in contemporary China signaled an opportunity for classical liberalism to reemerge in China after having been suppressed for nearly half a century (fig. 4).

Why is it so difficult to let Chen Yinke rest in peace? One can debate whether (neo)liberal ethics is at all plausible as a way to understand Chen's legacy. What seems beyond dispute, nonetheless, is that the "Chen Yinke fever" has significantly shaped the self-definition of the liberal intelligentsia in the post-Mao era. This chapter has described how liberal-minded intellectuals actively participated in mourning Chen as a poignant symbol of the aggregating cultural catastrophes of the Mao era. From the early 1980s to the 2000s, the legacy of this

---

94. Zhu Xueqin, "Yijiujiuba," 237–56.
95. Zhu Xueqin, "Yijiujiuba," 238.

FIGURE 4. The tomb of Chen Yinke and his wife Tang Yun at Mount Lu Botanical Garden in Jiujiang, with Chen's motto "the independence of spirit and freedom of thought" carved on the tombstone. Photo by the author.

once-obscure thinker—whose readership never extended beyond scholarly circles during his lifetime—became the center of mounting political contestations and public attention. From Yu Ying-shih's excavation of cultural loyalism through the lens of Cold War liberalism, to the multifarious imaginations of reformist alternatives in post-Tiananmen intellectual thinking, to Lu Jiandong's melodramatic portrait of a liberal martyr, to the extensive reproduction and consumption of a cult figure in the popular media, Chen's life and works have been consistently narrated through different formulas. These accounts created a participatory mode of reading and remembering both the immemorial and the unspeakable against a state-sponsored politics of amnesia. Above all, tales and stories about Chen have inspired Chinese readers to engage with the fin-de-siècle debate over the meaning of freedom in multiple senses—its dimensions, its power, and the price Chen paid to bring it into existence.

Moving away from polarized ideological debates, this chapter argues for the interconnectedness of Chinese liberalism and moral emotion. Post-Mao liberal imaginations were exemplified in a constellation of moral and emotional responses to Chen Yinke's tragic fate under socialism. A dedicated believer in Chen's esoteric resistance, Yu Ying-shih underscored the profound pathos and remorse in Chen's "late state of mind" after he "wasted" the opportunity of leaving for the "free world" in 1949. Clearly, Yu's impulse to unravel Chen's loyalist heart from oblivion betrayed his own dissatisfaction with Mao's socialist experiment. Meanwhile, frustrated liberals in mainland China, traumatized by the 1989 Tiananmen incident, held up Chen's lukewarm reformist stance as a talisman against political radicalism. Their emotional and political investment in the apolitical academician bespoke a yearning for an incremental path of Chinese learning that could promise intellectual autonomy against ideological fanaticism. Subsequently, Lu Jiandong recounted a heart-wrenching story about how a liberal martyr was betrayed, persecuted, and tortured to death by the murderous Maoist regime. The liberals' melancholic identification with Chen's martyrdom produced heightened accusations regarding the absence of guilt and mourning in the public memory of the Maoist past.

All three narratives of Chen begin with larger claims about the moral and political lessons to be learned from his tragedy. In the first, the construction of Chen's cultural loyalism consists in trying to expand the scope of Chinese culture beyond, and against, the patronage of the Communist state. In the second, the iconic academician represents a deliberate turn away from political radicalism and toward Weberian incrementalism. In the third, the work of mourning is intermingled with the quest for poetic justice and the desire to come to terms with China's revolutionary past. But while recounting Chen's tragedy, these intellectuals were irresistibly propelled by moral indignation and emotional excess. The urges to redress historical injustice and to retrieve political alternatives have determined how Chen's life and thought are narrated and interpreted in the post-Mao context. A strong emotional investment is evident in all three elegies about how Chen endured humiliations, accusations, and betrayal in the rising political storms of the Mao era. In this sense, reading for the latent and subtle moral-psychological undercurrents of the liberal temperament means understanding Chinese liberalism as a dynamic expression of the moral attitudes, dispositions, and affective structures that undergird political argument.

Furthermore, to reframe Chinese liberalism as an outward manifestation of psychic energies does not subject political attitudes and statements to "presubjective" and "nonsignifying" affective forces. Rather, the liberal disposition is connected to a complicated cognitive structure—indeed, to a philosophical conception about the role of human agency and historical progress. In the case of Chinese liberalism, its proponents' moral certainty and recalcitrance about the catastrophic result of the socialist experiment contributed to a fervent attempt to retrieve more promising historical possibilities supposedly closed by the ascendency of Mao's revolution. Yu Ying-shih's compassionate tone harbored a series of what-if fantasies regarding Chen's imagined emigration to the free world. Likewise, the quest for academic norms betrayed a self-conscious attempt to salvage the reformist and incremental path of Chinese modernity buried under a century of intellectual radicalism; Lu Jiandong's elegy for Chen's last twenty years is no less mingled with a genuine moral desire to mend historical injustices.

Nonetheless, the lacuna of the liberals' emotionally charged reasoning merits further attention. As Peter Gay puts it in his reflection on the European Enlightenment intellect, "they never wholly discarded that final, most stubborn illusion that bedevils realists—the illusion that they were free from illusions."[96] Underneath so much of the pathos and polemics surrounding the figure of Chen is the presupposition, in the words of Xiaojue Wang, that "there could be alternative ways out of the political predicament of that time."[97] The adamant belief in the better alternative beyond socialist revolution has decidedly structured the liberals' readings of Chen's tragedy. Still, one may doubt whether the 1950s "free world," characterized by escalating Cold War militancy, could have provided a cultural haven for Chen to realize his ideal vision of Chinese learning. On the other hand, the liberal call for moderation and restraint in the post-Tiananmen era appears to have been an almost instinctual response to fears aroused by the June Fourth debacle.

---

96. Gay, *The Enlightenment*, 13, quoted in Grieder, *Hu Shih and the Chinese Renaissance*, 315.

97. Xiaojue Wang, *Modernity with a Cold War Face*, 8.

The advocates of negative liberty apparently forgot how the apolitical and ill-conceived middle course proposed by the republican liberal elites proved to be profoundly irritating and alienating to both the Kuomintang (KMT) and the CCP in the 1920s and 1930s. Meanwhile, Lu Jiandong's meticulous accounts of Chen's interactions with the socialist state revealed how the party vacillated between "courteous respect" (*liyu* 禮遇) and political suppression when confronting Chen's nonconformism. This curiously undermines Lu's unidirectional persecution thesis.

Above all, although liberals claim to retrieve moderate political alternatives spurned by radical revolutionaries, their moral indignation enforces a stable and deterministic historical narrative leading to categorical negation of socialism as the absolute evil. By linking their alternate worlds to the republican liberal intelligentsia who were destroyed by Mao's revolution, the liberals of the post-Mao era attempted to cut themselves off from China's socialist past—and from much of their own history. The desire for the rebirth of liberalism fueled an excessive moral repulsion at the crimes and atrocities of socialist revolution. Alienation and *ressentiment*, nourished through the perilous years of revolution, festered in the liberals' revanchist call for China's stillborn liberal values. Nevertheless, just as Berlin observed, the liberals' "state of wounded consciousness" often leads to deeply illiberal precepts;[98] the intense physic energy at the core of the Chinese liberal imagination has endorsed their bitter and morally driven charges against the socialist Other.

Predictably, the pitfalls of the liberal alternative were picked up by leftist historians. Capitalizing on the mounting grievances arising from neoliberal market reforms, neoleftist intellectuals embarked on an ambitious project to refurbish the critical potential of Mao's revolutionary practice in the post-Tiananmen era. From the leftist perspective, the liberal desire for alternatives is motivated by a neoliberal schema to circumvent the socialist years through a "strategy of containment,"[99] leading to the legitimation of a market economy as the "end of history." Holding themselves up as the guardians of a working class betrayed by

---

98. See Müller, "Concepts, Character, and the Specter of New Cold Wars," 3.
99. See Jameson, *The Political Unconscious*, x.

China's capitalist turn, left-wing critics contended that the liberals' exclusive focus on elite memory has effectively wiped out the lived experience of the underprivileged masses for whom the socialist welfare state meant economic security and cultural dignity. The Left's take on the subaltern perspective is salient in the controversial work of Gao Mobo, *Gao Village*, which paints a rosy picture of rural life in Gao Village in Jiangxi Province during the Cultural Revolution.[100] A former "barefoot" doctor from Gao Village, Gao argued against those liberal historians who he felt had gone too far in their total negation of Maoism. In the case of Gao Village, for instance, instead of generating violence and destruction, Maoist mass campaigns brought great improvements in culture, education, and public health. Although Chen Yinke and other urban intellectuals perished miserably under Mao's political campaigns, the residents of Gao Village enjoyed a higher standard of living due to Mao's determination to bridge the rural-urban divide. The publication of Gao's piece in early 2001 was met with critical opprobrium from many liberals, who in turn launched a national media campaign to boycott and condemn the leftist historian for "reviving the poisonous legacy of the Cultural Revolution."[101] Ironically, both the liberals and the Left displayed the same type of militant rhetoric and ideological extremism that they so abhorred in the other.

Ideological battles aside, the multifarious uses of Chen Yinke's image in the age of mass media remain a puzzle. By the early 2000s, facile discussions, dubious anecdotes, and even myths about Chen were circulating in popular media and online forums: inevitably, the cultural industry had turned Chen into kitsch. The reaction among scholars and intellectuals spanned the rather narrow range from disappointment to disgust. In a 2002 satirical essay titled "Rationales for Not Talking about Chen Yinke," the historian Yi Zhongtian 易中天 (1947–) commented on the genre of "fanciful accounts" (*xishuo* 戲說) that underlined the popular narrative of Chen. The rhetoric of dramatization that was characteristic of this genre was inextricably bound up with popular entertainment. As Yi noted, a kind of cheap artifice to the rise of public enthusiasm toward Chen belonged less to political

100. Gao, "Shuxie lishi: *Gaojiacun*."
101. Xu, Dang, and Jiao, "Zhiyi *Gaojiacun*."

commitment and more to the attraction of hackneyed tales of "talented scholars and beauties" (*caizi jiaren* 才子佳人). Sentimental appeal displaced meaning, and the desire to consume the rare and extravagant overrode the need to comprehend. Moreover, Yi observed that consumerism completely distorted the Chen cult toward different ends. The myth of Chen's learning and morality served as spiritual solace to the middle-class audience who had to endure the moral ambiguities of everyday life. Ironically, admiration for an other-worldly saint revealed a subtle acknowledgment of the current generation's inability to reach the heights of Chen's political engagement. As Yi put it cynically, the mythos of Chen's "independence" and "freedom" must be recognized as the profound "dependence" and "unfreedom" of the entire Chinese intelligentsia.[102] The displacement of serious opinions by theatricalized "fanciful accounts" in popular media make Chen's pursuit of freedom increasingly unreal. Ultimately, Chen's tale provides a phantasmagoric imaginary for contemporary Chinese to momentarily escape from the authoritarian regime they are stuck within.

The continued reappearance of Chen Yinke in contemporary Chinese cultural and political debates is a vivid reminder of the divided memories of China's socialist past. As this chapter shows, Chen has become a barometer with which to gauge various forms of liberal political imaginaries, from counterfactual speculation on China's stillborn liberal alternative to melancholic remembrances of the republican intelligentsia—forms that manifest divergent yet invariably powerful emotions and moral sentiments encompassing despair, guilt, and anger. Through heightened dramatizations, Chen's image was transformed by contending political formulas into a signifier of heroic dissent. To this day, Chen stands at the center of the emotionally charged accusations of violence and brutality that liberals hurl against Mao's revolutions, lending his moral aspiration to their idealistic search for China's postrevolutionary political order in the new millennium.

---

102. Yi Zhongtian, "Quanjun motan Chen Yinke."

PART II

The Fusion of Emotion and Political Vision

CHAPTER THREE

Left Melancholy

A Dialogue between Chen Yingzhen and Wang Anyi

> It's all in vain. We've tried in various ways to change the world; the point is now to interpret it.
> —Jacques Rancière, *Althusser's Lesson*

> Here we are, condemned to live in the world as it is.
> —François Furet, *The Passing of an Illusion*

> Philosophy, which once seemed obsolete, lives on because the moment to realize it was missed.
> —Theodor W. Adorno, *Negative Dialectics*

The protagonist of Theo Angelopoulos's 1995 film *Ulysses' Gaze* takes a Homeric journey to the Balkan nations, a land rife with civil wars, ethnic hatred, and the ruins of a socialist utopia. In a story that emulates the epic narrative of *The Odyssey*, the traveler mournfully moves through Albania, Bulgaria, and finally into the former Yugoslavia. In the middle of his journey, the kaleidoscopic images of spectral

---

An earlier version of parts of this chapter appeared in "Left Melancholy: Chen Yingzhen, Wang Anyi, and the Desire for Utopia in the Post-Revolutionary Era," *Modern Chinese Literature and Culture* 33, no. 1 (Spring 2021): 122–60, published by the Ohio State University. Reprinted with permission.

figures, broken dreams, and destruction converge on a barge drifting down a river; it carries a dismembered statue of Lenin, whose huge arm still points firmly toward the sky. Lenin's disembodied head stares out to a distant horizon beyond the diegetic world. The gaze offscreen once belonged to great socialist leaders who inspired grand revolutions and projected heroic futures. As a trope of narration, this socialist-realist gaze visualizes progress as a moral-political imperative, a firm reminder that the socialist utopia is visible to those who believe in it.[1] In this scene, however, the gaze is not shared by the people watching from the riverbank as the statue of Lenin glides down the river; instead, the crowds stare at Lenin's broken body in a cryptic silence. There is a lingering melancholy but no enthusiasm. Their gazes, devoid of utopian passions, are empty and mournful.

With his visual eloquence, Angelopoulos captures the profound melancholy permeating global left-wing culture after 1989. With the breakdown of Communist regimes, left-wing thinking suffered from a disillusionment with a constellation of theories, emotions, and memories oriented toward a socialist utopia. The possibility of unifying theory and praxis was undermined by both the loss of a coherent analysis of class struggle and the disappearance of mass political movements. The socialist moral-political vision of historical progress was shattered by a postmodern distrust of grand narratives, and the analytical dissection of capitalism was invalidated by the emergence of the post-Fordist mode of production. Unable to overcome this theoretical impasse, the Left embraced a "culture of defeat"[2] with an elegiac acknowledgment that the chance for socialist revolution has "now irrevocably passed."[3]

Yet to declare the "end of history" simplifies the dynamic of an indefinite turn toward the realm of memory, for fin-de-siècle left-wing culture casts a sentimental gaze toward the bygone socialist era. For

---

1. Donald defines the socialist-realist gaze as a singular spectatorial position that reinforces the party's version of history through sublime images. See Donald, "National Publicness."

2. Enzo Traverso describes the history of socialism as a "constellation of defeats" that spanned across two centuries, from the French Revolution to 1989. See Traverso, *Left-Wing Melancholia*, 22; Perry Anderson, *Considerations on Western Marxism*, 24–48.

3. Jay, *The Dialectical Imagination*, xvii.

many, the lived experience of socialism was saturated with personal memories, ideals, and pursuits. The peculiar experience of its collapse entailed a profoundly painful feeling of loss and self-denial.[4] Here, Sigmund Freud's distinction between mourning and melancholia is relevant: although both mourning and melancholia arise in response to bereavement and loss, the mourner quickly recognizes the reality and lets go of the lost object through mourning. By contrast, melancholia indicates a pathological state; with an excessive devotion to the lost object, the melancholic remains immersed in "self-reproaches and self-reviling," threatening the ego's fundamental well-being.[5] Hence, the psychoanalytical perspective considers Left melancholy as a passive disposition synonymous with a pathological reaction to loss.

However, the refusal to sever the link with an unsettling past may signify more than political passivity. For leftist intellectuals in particular, a melancholy syndrome produced not only the pathos of defeat, but also efforts to excavate the emancipatory promises of socialist ideals. In this perspective, a melancholic Marxism may still imagine utopian political alternatives, even though this power to arouse fantasies, hopes, and expectations has been repeatedly betrayed by actual Communist regimes that deployed them. In expressing political disillusionment, melancholy at the same time nourished a determinate, if not self-destructive, loyalty to leftist political struggles against disarray and resignation.

Fin-de-Siècle Socialism

To illustrate my point, in this chapter I shift the focus from Western Marxism to the Asian context. For the Euro-American Left, socialist revolution has always been a distant mirage, an alien but alluring dream, and an imagined utopia constructed vis-à-vis the materialistic and philistine capitalist reality. For the Chinese and Sinophone writers who lived through decades of turbulent revolution, however, socialism

---

4. For instance, Wendy Brown asserts that leftist intellectuals after 1989 suffered "a lost way of life and a lost course of pursuits." See Brown, "Resisting Left Melancholia," 460.

5. Freud, "Mourning and Melancholia," 244.

appears simultaneously imagined and real, emancipatory and oppressive, promising and full of betrayal. Why did these writers continue to tarry with leftist melancholy at the moment when state socialism was failing worldwide? Is the dystopian turn of their literary narrative animated by an emancipatory purpose? More pertinently, how does the category of melancholy extend and modify our understanding of fin-de-siècle (post)socialism in the Chinese context?

Informed by these questions, I trace the pathos of failure and defeat that have pervaded left-wing literary imaginations in Chinese and Sinophone literature following the end of the Cultural Revolution. Whereas the dystopian turn of Western Marxism was informed by the collapse of socialist regimes in 1989, the emergence of Left melancholy in the post-Mao era was inextricably shaped by the exhaustion of Mao's Cultural Revolution. In the 1960s, the inauguration of Mao's most radical political experiment offered an inspiring political alternative for the Left all over the world, with its rhetorical commitment to mass politics, humane economy, and anticolonial struggles.[6] Since the late 1970s, however, Mao's utopian vision and the historical practice of revolution were "placed on trial" by the reformist leadership.[7] In mainland China, humanist literature began to address the anguished memories of collective violence and political persecution conducted in the glorious name of revolution. The younger generation was no longer certain about the positive image of socialist utopia, or even whether it was possible. From the search-for-roots movement to modernist literature, from "high-culture fever" to postmodern fad, the socialist sublime was repeatedly criticized as a type of feudal backwardness, as a bureaucratic form of domination, and as political tyranny. The new literary discourse reversed the utopian narrative of Communist literature, with youthful activism replaced by sad contemplation, idealist yearnings curbed by traumas, and the enthusiastic support of socialism yielding

---

6. For an analysis of the emancipatory potential of Maoist mass politics, see Wang Hui, *The End of the Revolution*, 3–18; for a case study of the intersection of politics and science in Mao's effort to build a more humane agricultural economy, see Schmalzer, *Red Revolution, Green Revolution*; for the global reception of the anticolonial and anti-racial dimensions of Maoism, see Cook, *Mao's Little Red Book*.

7. See Cook, *The Cultural Revolution on Trial*, 35–135.

to a solemn realization of its inevitable collapse. Simultaneously, the total negation of the Maoist experiment not only shook many Sinophone activists' faith in the revolutionary mandate, but also raised serious questions about the legitimacy of their own anti-authoritarian struggles. Their elegiac tone, signaled by a reluctance to impose a historical verdict on the Maoist political alternative, further complicates the different interpretations, contested memories, and divergent literary representations of Mao's utopianism.

Exploring this major historical transition, this chapter focuses on the literary exchange between the Taiwanese leftist writer Chen Yingzhen 陳映真 (1937–2016) and the Shanghai-based novelist Wang Anyi 王安憶 (1954–) to illustrate how writers across the Taiwan Strait came to terms with the ruins of Maoist utopia. Chen was one of those veteran Sinophone Marxists whose socialist faith was thwarted by the exposure of the human costs of Mao's Cultural Revolution, and whose melancholic reflections on the failure of radical politics were underpinned by a persistent, one might say outdated, belief in the utopian promise of revolution. By contrast, nascent consumer capitalism fundamentally altered Wang Anyi's perception of China's socialist past. In her 1990s literary productions, Wang projected a mournful gaze toward the intertwining of her own family lineage with the revolutionary history of Shanghai. Whereas Chen's utopian socialism was driven by despair over the forgetting of the leftist cause in post–Chiang Kai-shek Taiwan, Wang's literary chronicle explores the complex and continuous negotiations between the quotidian and the heroic dimensions of Mao's revolution against the consumerist valorization of Shanghai's bourgeois modernity. Admittedly, Wang and Chen remained deeply divided about the meaning of this revolutionary legacy—its transformative power, its moral and ethical implications, and the price Chinese people have paid to bring it into existence. However, I seek to demonstrate how Chen's and Wang's narratives converge on an impossible mourning for socialist culture in a radically shifting present.

To be sure, the invocation of Left melancholy did not happen merely in the Chen-Wang encounter. Contemporary Chinese left-wing intellectuals with different theoretical orientation and ideological beliefs, ranging from orthodox Marxists to the New Left and from the former Red Guards to the radical proponents of Neo-Maoism, all took up pro-Mao nostalgia as a powerful way to mourn the passing of the socialist utopia and criticize widespread corruption, nepotism, and wealth inequality in the market era. Yet in these debates, the defenders of Mao have rushed to reestablish an untroubled image of the socialist past, with a deliberate political agenda to revitalize Mao's legacy against the neoliberal present. Whereas the stalwarts on the Left have utilized red nostalgia as a strategy of resistance, I demonstrate how Chen and Wang have treated melancholy aesthetics not as an incubator for ideological conviction but rather a paradoxical stance between faith and irony, loyalty and doubt, and action and reflection.

Here my inquiry builds on a growing scholarly engagement with the "melancholic turn" of global Marxism. Twentieth-century Marxist theoreticians consider melancholy to be a pathology underpinned by hesitation, despair, and self-hatred, with reactionary political consequences: from Walter Benjamin's indictment of the "conservative and backward-looking" gaze of the Weimar leftists to Wendy Brown's criticism of the political paralysis of the New Left in the wake of the Thatcher-Reagan offensive,[8] and from the student radicals' denouncement of bourgeois sentimentalism as political acquiescence and submission in May 1968 to Georg Lukács's caricature of the Frankfurt School as emanating from the "Grand Hotel Abyss."[9] For them, melancholy infects the leftist cause not because it is inherently reactionary; instead, its excessive pathos immobilizes decisive action and encourages political resignation, thereby collaborating with the reactionary forces it seeks to dispel. Moreover, contemporary Marxist scholars contend that the employment of psychoanalytical categories in Marxist analysis inevitably offers a therapeutic answer to sociopolitical questions of class and hegemony, reducing political quests to the ultimately liberal-individualistic horizon of ego psychology.[10]

Nevertheless, although melancholy does produce psychological distress and political passivity, it also provides insight into the structure

---

8. Benjamin, "Left-Wing Melancholy," 28–32.

9. Lukács, *The Theory of the Novel*, 22.

10. For a critical debate on Marxism and psychoanalysis, see Butler, Laclau, and Žižek, *Contingency, Hegemony, Universality*; Breckman, *Adventures of the Symbolic*, 183–261.

of the real. In other words, the melancholic's refusal to mourn harbors a rebellion that reorients the repressed possibilities of the past into an ambiguous future. Therefore, the paradoxical nature of melancholic reflection is not easily subject to such pejorative appellations. For instance, Benjamin's antipathy toward melancholy is intermingled with his musings on German *Trauerspiel* (tragic drama), through which he gradually came to realize the weak messianic promise of Marxism.[11] Needless to say, Adorno's (in)famous "resignation" unveiled the oppressive mechanism of the "pseudo-activity" that underlies the radicals' obsession with political praxis.[12] Žižek's seeming retreat into psychoanalytical categories betrays a wounded attachment to the Marcusian approach that locates political emancipation in the interior structure of the psyche.[13] Even Mao's uncompromising visions of the revolutionary saga are complicated, if not weakened, by his mournful writing on sacrifice, death, and historical vicissitude.

In connection with this, the Confucian literary tradition also persistently emphasizes the positive moral outcomes of melancholy. The Chinese equivalent *youyu* 憂鬱 is composed of two independent characters: whereas *yu* 鬱 functions as an adjective indicating abundant, *you* 憂 refers to an emotional state of distress and sorrow.[14] But in contrast to the Greco-Roman notion of melancholy as a medical disease of humoral imbalance, Confucius stresses that *you* facilitates moral introspection and prevents humanity from falling into vileness.[15] As the one who possesses the "legitimate transmission of the Way" (*daotong* 道統), the Confucian scholar-official must constantly "feel concern for the concerns of the world" and "defer pleasure until

---

11. Benjamin, *The Origin of German Tragic Drama*; for an analysis, see Pensky, *Melancholy Dialectics*.
12. Adorno, "Resignation."
13. Marcuse, *Eros and Civilization*.
14. Xu Shen, *Shuowen jiezi zhu*, 514.
15. Although Sinologists like Wolfgang Kubin declared that classical Chinese literature lacks an expression equivalent to melancholy, this essentialist stance ignores an expansive array of meanings in the Chinese discourse of *you* that deviate significantly from the Christian tradition. See Yue, "Youyu: Zhongguo shiye"; Kubin, "Introduction."

the world can take pleasure" (先天下之憂而憂，後天下之樂而樂).[16] However, conscientious meditations on a wide range of thorny political issues usually become a depressing burden, as the literati's dogmatic pursuit of moral purity in political matters leads to self-reproach and self-reviling. Such time-honored "crisis consciousness" (*youhuan yishi* 憂患意識), or, as Gloria Davies renders it, "patriotic worrying,"[17] has exerted a powerful normative hold over modern Chinese intellectuals and writers in the age of national cataclysm. Even though the introduction of Western psychology has complicated the Confucian ethical vision of *you* with a clinical assessment of the morbid "melancholia," a lineup of May Fourth writers such as Yu Dafu 郁達夫 (1896–1945) and Mao Dun 茅盾 (1896–1981) displayed the moral burden of what C. T. Hsia calls "obsession with China" as they ruminated on how to combat the squalor, corruption, and malaise of their own country.[18]

With this critical genealogy in mind, this chapter explores the aesthetic, affective, and political dimensions of Left melancholy as it has manifested in the literary narratives of Chen Yingzhen and Wang Anyi. Admittedly, the divergence in life paths and political convictions between these two writers is so profound as to foreclose, at first glance, any association. Born into a devout Christian minister's family in northern Taiwan, Chen grew up searching for radical leftist beliefs against Chiang's autocratic rule, finding a special appeal in Mao's utopian vision of revolution. Although the revelation of the atrocities of the Cultural Revolution led to the final disappointment for many Taiwanese leftists, Chen had earned his reputation as the "last Marxist" who never quite managed to break his cathexis with revolution. Wang, however, belongs to the Red Guard generation, the first generation born after the founding of the PRC and coming of age in the heat of Mao's Cultural Revolution. Revisiting her adolescent years through the lens of melancholy, Wang displayed in her literary creation a postrevolutionary ennui that resisted any political idealism. Yet despite these differences, Chen and Wang engaged in a series of

---

16. Fan, "The Pavilion of Yüeh-yang," 158–59.
17. See Davies, *Worrying about China*, 15–57.
18. For an excellent study of the Chinese reception of psychoanalysis, see Larson, *From Ah Q to Lei Feng*; for obsession with China, see Hsia, "Obsession with China."

heated debates concerning the meaning of the Chinese revolution throughout the 1980s and early 1990s, which has profoundly influenced their literary engagement with fin-de-siècle socialism in the years to come. Hence the fact that both a believer in utopian socialism and a skeptic of revolution displayed a shared leftist sentiment deserves further explanation.

In view of the ambivalent political emotion and diverse literary practices inherent in the Chen-Wang dialogue, I do not try to situate these two writers squarely in the ideological spectrum of the political Left. Rather, I use the term "Left melancholy" to mediate the tension between Chen's leftist political conviction and Wang's reflection on the lived experience of socialism. On the one hand, it designates Chen's political identification with the millenarian vision of proletarian revolution, and, on the other hand, incorporates Wang's ambivalent memories and complex feelings of growing up under socialism. By stressing the intersections and contrasts between the utopian ideal and the everyday reality of socialism, I therefore look beyond leftist melancholy to understand the complex and fluid articulations of stressing emotions, experiences, and literary manifestations that contributed to the dynamic expressions of Left melancholy across the Taiwan Strait. To the critics who might point out that Chen's and Wang's profoundly rich literary outputs go beyond the category of "left-wing literature" (*zuoyi wenxue* 左翼文學), I propose that we understand their socialist sentiment not as an expression of political affinity but as a critical dialogue with the utopian vision of Chinese leftist fiction to the extent of parody, mockery, and, not infrequently, radical disavowal. Above all, by highlighting their dystopian thinking about the Chinese revolution, I am not treating Left melancholy as the mere expression of despair and defeat. I am more concerned with illustrating the dualistic nature of the melancholic: the eternal contestations between thinking and acting, politics and aesthetics, and backward gaze and messianic futurity.[19] As I demonstrate later, this "paradoxical

---

19. Scholarly discussions of the double bind of melancholy have been shaped by Adorno's negative dialectics. The contradiction between Adorno's epistemological despair and his search for a radical aesthetics of hope provides a dialectical method to reconceive the positive connotations of melancholy. For Gillian Rose, Adorno's

simultaneity"—of an aporetic mood and a radical openness to hope—has exerted a profound impact on Chen and Wang as they reckon with the ethical and political implications of Mao's failed utopian experiment.

The inner dynamics of melancholy show that the haunting presence of the socialist past is more complicated than the answer provided by the extant paradigm of post-Communist nostalgia, a critical concept that has been widely used to analyze the surge of socialist memories and emotions in postsocialist regimes. My understanding of left-wing literature is in many ways congruent with the paradigm of nostalgia. However, although both melancholia and nostalgia lead to the realm of memory, the underlying emotions are drastically different. Restorative nostalgia, as Svetlana Boym defines it, fantasizes about a "transhistorical reconstruction of the lost home."[20] It sometimes slides into a romantic idealization of the past as the source of truth and tradition. Commenting on the post-Mao reinvention of the socialist past, Geremie Barmé contends that nostalgia mythologizes the Maoist years into a golden era of cultural confidence and political unity. This formula further contributes to a sloppy "totalitarian mentality" that offers a single and reductive political solution to the complex socioeconomic problems of the present.[21] By contrast, melancholy infuses the past with a desolate emptiness that nullifies any (ab)uses of memory as the source of political legitimacy. Psychologically, it leads to a retreat to bourgeois interiority rather than an active engagement with reality; philosophically, it views history as characterized by catastrophes without any impulses for restoration; politically, it might produce permanent inaction

---

"melancholy science" represents a "sociology of illusion" that reveals the paradoxical outcome of reason beyond simple resigned pessimism; Robyn Marasco deploys Adorno's dialectical rethinking of aporia to tease out a genealogy of critical theory driven by the "disquietude of despair"; Peter E. Gordon uses "paradoxical simultaneity" to characterize Adorno's rejection of and reliance on the philosophy of bourgeois interiority. See Rose, *The Melancholy Science*; Marasco, *The Highway of Despair*; Gordon, *Adorno and Existence*, 6.

20. Boym, *The Future of Nostalgia*, xviii. Boym also offers a distinction between restorative nostalgia and reflexive nostalgia.

21. See Barmé, *In the Red*, 321.

but not totalitarian passion. Thus I see melancholy and nostalgia as almost diametrically opposed. Above all, the employment of the term "nostalgia" threatens to obscure the dialectical passion of Left melancholy that sustains the possibility of what it simultaneously negates.

To substantiate my argument, I examine the contribution of Chinese and Sinophone writers to the polemical dimension of Left melancholy. In post-Mao China and post-Chiang Taiwan, mournful musings on the failed revolutionary promise became an anchoring point for leftist writers to rearticulate a Marxian commitment no longer bound up with Marxist ontology. I first give a brief overview of the discourse of melancholy in modern China. Then I move to examine Chen Yingzhen's literary testimonies to the repressed memory of Taiwanese leftism during the Martial Law era (1949–1987). In the last section, I read Wang Anyi's 1990s literary productions as an ambiguous response to Chen's utopian socialism. Each section shows how melancholy implies political choices, and more importantly, how the melancholic narration of politics arouses excessive sentiments, moral claims, and political controversies regarding the value and the cost of revolution.

The Melancholic Intellectual

The melancholic intellectual, characterized by vacillation and estrangement, is a predominant literary prototype in twentieth-century China. The protagonist is usually a jaded youth emerging from a petty-bourgeois background with obscure origins, who receives a modest education in the art of letters and experiences abject poverty as a result of the declining family fortunes. They cultivate their interior realm with art, literature, and refined idleness, and their passion for politics—if there is a passion at all—is almost indistinguishable from an aestheticized experience of radical freedom in chaotic times. He is good at contemplative reflection but lacks a decisive commitment to action. His flamboyant call for politics betrays only an obsession with the magic of literary style. When he accidentally "falls" into a revolution, his sentimentalism increases his distance from politics and evokes suspicions in his comrades. Plagued by defeat and disillusionment, he ultimately confesses that his political (mis)adventure remains under the spell of that very ideal of melancholic criticism he seeks to abandon.[22] Thus, for Lu Xun 鲁迅 (1881–1936), who supported a stringent "call to arms" (*nahan* 呐喊), the persistent reluctance to forfeit his meditative stance produced a profound "hesitation" (*panghuang* 彷徨) that underlined his maladjusted pilgrimage to revolution; Qu Qiubai 瞿秋白 (1899–1935), who was irresistibly propelled by the storm of Communism toward militant uprisings, was always haunted by "superfluous words"—mournful confessions that described his political career as a "farce" caused by "historical misunderstandings."[23] Mirrors and mediums of their time, these intellectuals and writers produced a string of literary protagonists who share their authors' dispositions, sentiments, and fates. In their attempt to overcome the ailment of melancholia, they presented the dilemma between acting and thinking through a melancholic narrative that turned out to be more creative, more sophisticated, and more illuminating than their putative political beliefs.

The tragicomedy of melancholy and its overcoming is a recurring drama in the life of Chen Yingzhen. He was born into a rural Christian family in north Taiwan in 1937, and his formative years were shaped by the most tumultuous period of mid-twentieth century China: the Civil War and the 1949 national split, when Chiang Kai-shek's Nationalist government was driven by Mao's Communist army to the offshore province of Taiwan. The defeated Generalissimo soon placed the island state under martial law and instituted a series of bloody purges to consolidate his rule. Chen experienced the national cataclysms through a succession of personal traumas: the sudden death of his young brother, the passing away of his beloved stepfather, and the endless violence, arrests, and executions that pervaded his social circles. The permeating terror made an indelible imprint on his personality. But Chen was also the child of explosive leftist movements in postwar Taiwan. During the Martial Law period, Chen confronted first the violent suppression of Communist uprisings in the 1950s White Terror, then the escalating

---

22. The original literary prototype has an obvious masculine bias that I have represented in my choice of the pronoun "he."

23. Qu, *Duoyu de hua*.

social protests of the 1960s, and finally the relaxation policy under Chiang Ching-kuo's presidency that led to the awakening of native Taiwanese identity. Although Chen remained a devout Marxist throughout his lifetime, he possessed a melancholic, if sometimes pessimistic, temper. Hence his eschatological vision of revolution was frequently tinged with a strange, dystopian tone.

Chen established himself in the 1960s as a leftist writer versed in modernist aesthetics.[24] His early fictions always portray a pure idealist afflicted by the traumas of war and terror. A strong existentialist theme accompanies his realistic depictions of the bleak political atmosphere of the White Terror. His protagonists experience a constellation of defeats and losses that gradually destroy their political aspirations and passions. The failure to confront the crude reality in turn produces long-lasting psychological agonies and nourishes a nihilistic vision of history. In "My Kid Brother Kangxiong" ("Wo de didi Kangxiong" 我的弟弟康雄) (1959), for instance, Chen illustrates Kangxiong's vain pursuit of socialist utopia through the confessional tone of his sister. Both Kangxiong and his sister rebelled against bourgeois hypocrisy only to confront their powerlessness against the reactionary social hierarchy. Kangxiong turns to fantasizing about his imaginary egalitarian kingdoms, whereas his sister conforms to the bourgeois norm by marrying into a rich Christian family. After an illicit affair with his landlady, the brother eventually commits suicide out of shame. In delineating Taiwan's socioeconomic exploitation and spiritual degradation, Chen's story unveils at the same time the profound sense of defeat and the despair that incapacitated progressive intellectuals in the postwar era.

For Chen's disillusioned protagonists, melancholy offers an imaginary escape from the oppressive political regime. Although the melancholic resorts to a contemplative posture to alleviate painful feelings of loss, that self-healing glides into a desperate withdrawal from the public world, gesturing toward a half-willing collaboration with the social reality. Melancholy's double bind is manifested in the sister's conversion from a leftist sympathizer to a bourgeois hypocrite after

---

24. For an analysis of the modernist aesthetics in Chen's early works, see Sung-sheng Chang, *Modernism and the Nativist Resistance*, 148–76.

Kangxiong's sudden death. The sister possesses a sensorial, if not morbid, attachment to grief and remorse. To her, Kangxiong's suicide appears overwhelming and unbearable, and escape thus becomes an inevitable means to maintain the ego's well-being. The sister's marriage to an "earnestly polite, straitlaced, upper-crust type"[25] signifies her willingness to trade her rebel conscience for a materialistic living. Meanwhile, her ruminations on Kangxiong's political ideals do not animate any decisive actions, only a feeble guilty conscience to "rebuild his [Kangxiong's] gravesite and make it luxurious."[26] Melancholy valorizes her Faustian bargain and leads to a return to the bourgeois norm.

Yet to conclude the melancholic embodies a reactionary mentality simplifies the dynamics of Chen's literary aesthetics. Above all, his melancholy writing expresses a dilemma between the desire for narration and the urge for action. Chen employed a sorrowful and compassionate tone to explore the psychological wound inflicted on the individual. However, excessive pathos achieves a sensational effect and threatens to nullify any visions of political progress. This tension underpins Chen's criticism of the complicity of the melancholic intellectual in the repressive political order. Another short piece, "The Village Teacher" ("Xiangcun jiaoshi" 鄉村教師) (1960), narrates the tragedy of a petty-bourgeois intellectual whose every effort to bring progressive politics to a suffocating rural town is forestalled by his own vacillation and pessimism. Wu Jinxiang, who served in the Imperial Japanese Army during the Pacific War, returns to his hometown in rural Taiwan. The Wertherian youth's eager pursuit of social enlightenment soon comes into conflict with his inability to become an active, practical fighter. After a series of failures, Wu confesses that his passion for politics rests merely on a melodramatic imagination, a feeble and passive gesture that involuntarily "turns knowledge into art, thinking into aesthetics, and socialism into literature."[27] Wu's repentance suggests that the melancholic intellectual is acutely aware of the necessity to transform his bourgeois sentimentalism into politically engaged forms of writing and thinking. However, he remains immersed in his pathos,

25. Chen Yingzhen, "My Kid Brother Kangxiong," 205.
26. Chen Yingzhen, "My Kid Brother Kangxiong," 209.
27. Chen Yingzhen, *Chen Yingzhen zuopinji*, 1:30.

unable to overcome his political pessimism. Moreover, Wu's inaction increases his sense of guilt, leading to a self-denunciation of his collaboration with the Japanese imperial war machine. The story ends with Wu's open acknowledgment of his participation in cannibalistic acts during the war, a striking metaphor that highlights his complicity.

Chen's meditations on political quietism hark backs to the dilemma of literary realism in the May Fourth era.[28] Although realist writers such as Mao Dun hailed fiction as the agent of political empowerment, their desire for narration involuntarily encouraged an aesthetic withdrawal from the degradation of the social. Writing became a form of ideological distraction that displaced the call for action with endless self-reproach. Such a pensive tone, as Marston Anderson and David Wang point out, demonstrates a propensity to defer and deter revolution in the face of bleak political reality.[29] Lu Xun, for example, reviewing the flourishing of "revolutionary literature" following the 1927 Shanghai massacre, was struck by the peculiar dissonance between rhetorical militancy and political passivity in the leftist literary arena. Against the facile expectations about literature "begetting" revolution, Lu Xun poignantly stated that the creation of "revolutionary literature" merely serves as an aesthetic ornament in the absence of real revolution. By writing down "kill, kill, kill" and "blood, blood, blood," armchair activists proffer fantastical notions of resistance on a piece of paper. In Lu Xun's perspective, leftist literature is a form of distraction, a mode of consumption, and a way of procrastination, all of which defer and dilute a serious commitment to radical politics.[30] Continuing Lu Xun's polemics, Chen contends that the flimsy investment of intellectuals like Wu in progressive politics is informed only by intuitive flashes and literary imagery, with a penchant for decadent aesthetics that frequently maimed their capacity to transform narration into action. In this regard, Wu's sadness is intermingled with a masochistic intoxication with war, disaster, and

---

28. For a detailed discussion of Chen's relationship to the May Fourth leftist tradition, see Chen Sihe, "Shilun Chen Yingzhen de chuangzuo yu wusi xinwenxue chuantong."

29. See Marston Anderson, *The Limits of Realism*; David Wang, *The Monster That Is History*, 80.

30. Lu Xun, "Geming wenxue," 3:567–70.

oppression, all of which compel him to strive for revolution only in fantasy or daydreams. Thus, melancholy offers a sentimental account, an imaginary solution, and even a narrative pleasure as one comes to terms with the impossibility of change.

Chen's attempt to overcome the passivity of bourgeois melancholy culminated in his famous 1975 preface titled "On Chen Yingzhen" (試論陳映真). Over the course of the 1960s, Chen had devoted himself to the escalating student protests and the thriving leftist intellectual discourse, but his political activism came to an abrupt halt in 1968, when he was arrested by the secret police for organizing Marxist reading groups and sentenced to jail. Almost a decade later, he was released following the special amnesty after Chiang Kai-shek's death in 1975, only to find that the Taiwanese cultural arena had been fundamentally reshaped by a cluster of economic and political metamorphoses, particularly the exponential growth of the market economy and the outburst of the nativist sentiment. Above all, the waning of leftist activism compelled Chen to reflect on his earlier romantic and melancholic approach to literature, which, from the "scientific" standpoint of Leninist-Maoist reflection theory, reveals the progressive-reactionary double bind of the "petit urbanite intellectual":

> In the modern social hierarchy, a petit urbanite intellectual occupies a middle position. During the time of economic prosperity, it's easy for these intellectuals to climb upward to gain quite an amount of interest from the upper stratum. However, during times of economic depression, they usually slide down into subaltern status. Thus, when the opportunities are abundant, they appear high-spirited and optimistic; and when they fall into a lower rank, they appear frustrated, sorrowful, and hesitant.
>
> 在現代社會層級結構中，一個市鎮小知識分子是處於一種中間的地位。當景氣良好，出路很多的時候，這些小知識分子很容易向上爬升，從社會的上層得到不薄的利益。但當社會的景氣阻滯，出路很少的時候，他們不得不向著社會的下層淪落。於是當其升進之路順暢，則意氣昂揚，神采飛舞；而當其向下淪落，則又顯得沮喪、悲憤和彷徨。[31]

---

31. Chen Yingzhen, "Shilun Chen Yingzhen," 3.

Indeed, Chen's "confession" reads like a political manifesto calling for the replacement of his earlier "Chekhovian melancholy" with a "cold and realistic analysis" under the aegis of Marxist class politics.[32] However, closer scrutiny of the essay reveals a cluster of ambiguities that defy Chen's overt Marxist rhetoric. Two contradictory concerns can be detected: a desire to articulate a rigid class analysis that implies the effacement of subjective emotions, and an affectionate identification with the downtrodden, those whose tragedies could not be narrated without a sentimental mood. Just as Chen demands a political praxis to do away with "boredom, self-reproach, and profound feelings of powerlessness"[33]—those pessimistic moods that incapacitate ill-fated youths and lonesome revolutionaries—his lukewarm tone betrays a lingering sympathy toward their frustrations, narrow-mindedness, and naïve visions. At one moment, Chen declares, "None of those small-town intellectuals in Chen Yingzhen's literary world dare to stand up for action."[34] Elsewhere, Chen indulges himself in a succession of desolate imaginaries: impoverished towns, numb crowds, rotten corpses, wasted hopes, and, on top of all this, perpetual repetitions of defeat. This obsession with bourgeois decadence conveys a fragile humanistic voice: after all, for those whose lives are engulfed in economic poverty and vicious oppression, emancipation is illusory, and withdrawal seems to be the only viable path toward salvation.

This unresolved tension between an activist imperative and a meditative mood underlines Chen's self-criticism of his sentimental style. As a result, the essay's "hard" Marxist position is always softened by a melancholic dimension, a hidden contemplative stance that rejects crude class analysis. Chen aspired to transform himself into a Maoist ideologue, but he could never formulate a satisfying literary style that conformed to Maoist dogma. Whereas Mao saw nothing in humanistic sentiments but a desperate holding on to bourgeois self-interest, Chen's insight into the progressive-reactionary double bind reveals how the bourgeois intellectual's failure to act bears within itself a hidden insight, transforming a sentiment of hopelessness into a contemplative

32. Chen Yingzhen, "Shilun Chen Yingzhen," 8.
33. Chen Yingzhen, "Shilun Chen Yingzhen," 8.
34. Chen Yingzhen, "Shilun Chen Yingzhen," 7.

critique of his own limitations. Whereas Mao's fundamentalist belief in revolution prescribes a didactic role for leftist literature to promote socialist ideology, Chen's mournful tone always points beyond ideological fanaticism and carries nuanced feelings, experiences, and passions aroused by leftist utopian visions. This discrepancy, as we shall see, indicates the persistence of melancholy despite Chen's tireless efforts to adopt a more militant perspective.

The Vanquished Left

Viewed retrospectively, Chen's cry against leftist melancholy reflected the crisis of Taiwanese Marxism in the post-Chiang era. Beginning in the 1970s, the Nationalist government suffered a succession of political setbacks, starting with the expulsion from the United Nations in 1971, followed by Richard Nixon's rapprochement with China in 1972, and culminating in the surge of dissident movements against the authoritarian regime. In the cultural arena, the rhetoric of liberal-versus-leftist battles was marginalized by the growing tensions between mainlanders and native Taiwanese. The awakening of an islander identity produced heated exchanges on the cultural politics of nativist literature, on the erosion of Sinocentric orthodoxy, and on the waning halo of high literary culture.[35] The advent of the postmodern further valorized the expansion of the consumerist literary market and the quest for a new Taiwanese national identity. These new conditions—commodification, political relaxation, and the search for Taiwanese culture—posed serious challenges not only to Chen's literary stylistics in particular, but also to his apparently outdated belief in the Sinocentric socialist revolution in general. Like the dislocated Rip Van Winkle, Chen-like Marxists have become "exiles in their own land."[36] Chen, whose incarceration hardened his faith in the traumatic, bloody, but eventually triumphant path leading to the realization of socialism in Taiwan, found it difficult to adjust to the temporal dislocation caused the waning of leftist movement under market capitalism.

35. See Sung-sheng Chang, *Literary Culture in Taiwan*, 90–140.
36. See Braester, "Taiwanese Identity and the Crisis of Memory," 216.

Simultaneously, the identity crisis of the Taiwanese Left coincided with China's revisionist turn in the late 1970s, a dramatic reorientation that proclaimed the bankruptcy of the Maoist alternative to Western capitalist modernity. Maoist China, in Fabio Lanza's terms, stood "as the signifier of global equality in regard to issues of development, ideology, and political power."[37] Against this backdrop, Deng Xiaoping's determined turn away from Mao's socialist utopianism aroused poignant feelings among the Sinophone Left, from confusion and anger to disillusionment and resignation. Moreover, rumors and testimonies of the great atrocities conducted by the Red Guards found their way to the Taiwanese public, producing an outburst of shock and disbelief among leftist activists, many of whom had sacrificed themselves for Mao's noble ideals. Chen Yingzhen expressed his frustration with the flood of memoirs, photos, and exposé writings, which, despite their "anti-Communist propagandistic rhetoric," revealed the disturbing reality of conformity and persecution beneath the surface of Mao's utopian promise.[38] For Chen's comrades, it wasn't simply a question of visiting Mao's promised land and finding it to be no more than a carefully staged Potemkin village. Rather, the revelation of the revolution's ugly face was unbearable for those adhering to the emancipatory promise of radical politics. The Sinophone activist Liu Daren's 劉大任 (1939–) acclaimed novel *Azaleas Cry Out Blood* (*Dujuan tixue* 杜鵑啼血), for instance, described how a diasporic writer's pilgrimage to China during the Cultural Revolution becomes a voyage into the heart of madness and terror. The touching political allegory of falsehood and betrayal indicated that these veterans of socialism were rapidly shedding not only their mainlander identity, but also the ideals, theories, and utopian visions that defined the ontological dimension of the Left.

As a result, Chen's literary creations from the 1980s illustrate the predicament of the vanquished Left in the post-Chiang period. "The vanquished" conveys a twofold meaning in Chen's thinking. The Marxist vision of political struggle implied an empathic identification with the oppressed, but this moral indignation was inextricably

---

37. Lanza, *The End of Concern*, 6.
38. Chen Yingzhen, *Chen Yingzhen zuopinji*, 8:34.

intertwined with a solemn awareness that Marxists themselves were now disappearing from the post-Chiang Taiwanese scene. In this regard, Chen's deep empathy with the muted voices of political victims of the Chiang era was intermingled with his own tragic sense of belonging to a vanishing political generation whose identities, ideas, and passions were being eclipsed by the irreversible process of historical change. Here Chen's elegiac undertone should not necessarily be understood as an acknowledgment of defeat. In fact, the dialectic vision of Marxism persistently portrays setbacks to socialist struggles as the midwife of historical progress. Instead of destroying its political ideals, historical defeats create an epistemological potential for the proletarian class to rethink its strategies and tactics with critical insight. By contrast, the victor preaches "an apologetic vision of the past based on a providential scheme" whose "self-satisfied historical reconstruction" eventually destroys its political wisdom.[39] This dialectical imagination conjures a messianic vision that a socialist utopia would begin anew on the ruins of time in defiance of all earlier setbacks. Thus, the defeated Left is always animated by a pessimistic identification with the vanquished on the one hand, and an optimistic claim to the poetry of the future on the other.

Chen certainly borrowed this dialectics to overcome the pervasive defeatism among his comrades. Without openly denouncing Mao's Cultural Revolution, Chen formulated a strategic diagnostic, contending that the "corrupted and fallen" nature of the Chinese revolution did not nullify the dignity and the honor of those leftist writers who confronted violence and persecution with protest and resistance.[40] From this perspective, defeats invariably nourish hope, for progressive visions are attainable only by confronting the burden of one's own failure. But simply subscribing to the emancipatory potentials of leftism raised a poignant problem: if resignation ultimately valorizes an apologetic vision of history authorized by the victor, outright resistance is undermined by a reluctance to address the human costs of revolution. In what sense, then, could Chen retrieve the utopian promise of

---

39. See Traverso, *Left-Wing Melancholia*, 25.
40. Chen Yingzhen, *Chen Yingzhen zuopinji*, 9:27.

the revolution in the face of the miseries, losses, and privations produced by actual socialism in practice?

In this regard, Chen's 1983 novella "Mountain Path" exemplifies an effort to come to terms with the thorny question of idealism and its betrayal. The story starts with Cai Qianhui, a middle-aged woman who has endured hardships for thirty years to bring the Li family from utter poverty to a comfortable bourgeois life, when she suddenly collapses from a mysterious disease. The family immediately assembles first-class doctors and medical supplies to treat her, only to be told that Cai has simply lost the desire to live. The reader is informed of the cause of Cai's "illness" only after her death. It turns out that Cai's enigmatic disease was triggered by the recent release of her friend Huang Zhenbo, a socialist imprisoned by the KMT regime for more than thirty years. It awakens her to the painful memories of losing her fiancé Li Guokun, who was arrested along with Huang for a similar reason but was summarily executed in 1950. However, the subsequent discovery of Cai's posthumous letter to Huang Zhenbo completely alters the previous narrative. In the letter, Cai confesses that she was originally betrothed to Zhenbo and only knew Guokun as Zhenbo's close comrade. Moreover, the traitor who sold the two to the KMT police was none other than Cai's brother. Out of a guilty conscience and to atone for her brother's betrayal, Cai claimed to be Guokun's fiancée after his execution to help Guokun's family make their way out of destitution.

In Cai Qianhui's self-willed death, one finds a dialectic between hopeless withdrawal and its apparent opposite, the most extreme expression of faith through self-purgation. Above all, the defeat suffered by Qianhui appears to be overwhelming. As she painstakingly asks in the letter, "If the revolution fails on the mainland, does that mean [Guokun's] death and [Zhenbo's] long-term imprisonment have turned into meaningless punishments more cruel than death or life in prison?"[41] For Cai, the Maoist ideal of revolution transcends the exigencies of political strategy to sustain her existence. A failure of faith not only threatens to nullify all past struggles but also devastates Qianhui's psychological well-being. Despite its seemingly defeatist appearance, the

---

41. Chen Yingzhen, "Mountain Path," 20.

melancholic reaction to loss brings into view extraordinary expressions of ideological devotion: the profound pains inflicted on the ego by loss serve to sustain her revolutionary passions. The disintegration of her ego is therefore a necessary condition for the preservation of her political integrity. For Qianhui, a masochistic identification with the lost cause provides the only means to continue her revolution in a world devoid of hope.

Qianhui's unwillingness to detach herself from loss inevitably leads to self-reproach, culminating in a delusional expectation of punishment. In her confession, her physical well-being causes moral guilt, because she is able to move on and even thrive in the face of her comrades' tragic death and imprisonment. Furthermore, the fact that she receives the finest medical care, that she brings the Huang family into the upper middle class, that the family now enjoys a consumeristic life in a capitalist heaven—all these expose her implicit conformity to bourgeois comforts. Qianhui realizes that the deeper tragedy lies in the ironic outcome of her devotion: she came to the Huang family with a determination to "eat bitterness," a Communist ethic that regards self-abnegation as a necessary route to proletarian consciousness; but her sacrifice has served as a Weberian Protestant ethic that rationalizes the accumulation of wealth, eventually transforming her and her family into "tamed animals" of capitalism. Frustrated by this most unlikely result of her saintly devotion, Qianhui could only ease her sense of guilt through self-annihilation. As David Wang comments, her self-willed hunger is motivated by an "anorexic logic," a physical ordeal that attempts to reclaim the moral rectitude of Communism in recognition of her sinful complicity.[42] Qianhui's pathological reaction to loss ultimately contributes to her death, but only through death could she retrieve the meaning of revolution in the wake of its fall.

"Mountain Paths" points to how melancholia could be transformed into a poetics of resistance. But such feverish ideological fanaticism certainly raises eyebrows. After all, Qianhui's persistence remains tethered to a deep faith in the emancipatory promise of Mao's utopian project even after its collapse. But does not this utopianism rely on a

---

42. David Wang, *The Monster That Is History*, 138–42.

romanticization of Maoist politics in its reluctance to interrogate revolution's human costs? Wu Jinxiang, Chen's earlier fictional character, takes pains to admit how his naïve idealism rests on flimsy aesthetic imaginaries rather than serious political analysis. How would Qianhui's idealism be different? Could we even say that Qianhui's self-destructive loyalty merely expresses a blind faith in Maoist politics, resulting in meaningless sacrifice? This is precisely the rejoinder proposed by Wang Anyi, the subject of the next section.

Utopian Verses

In 1983, Wang Anyi met Chen Yingzhen for the first time in the American Midwest. The daughter of the renowned Shanghai-based writer Ru Zhijuan 茹志鹃 (1925–1998), Wang had just published several short stories that won her national recognition. The biographical stories meticulously described a young girl's emotionally charged experiences of coming of age: political frustrations, youthful yearnings, and the fashioning of a private self against the backdrop of socialist revolution. As the first generation born after the founding of New China, Wang and her peers feverishly embraced Mao's Cultural Revolution only to be disillusioned by the rampant violence and factional warfare that spread across major cities from 1966 to 1968. Following Mao's instruction to rusticate educated youth, Wang then volunteered to be "sent down" to work in a rural commune in northern Anhui Province, but was disappointed by the poverty and hardship of peasant living. Soon, she left for a local art performance troupe in Jiangsu, and eventually returned to Shanghai in 1978, where she began her writing career and participated in the post-Mao cultural renaissance.

Before Wang encountered Chen, her work was underpinned by a self-conscious individualism. For the nascent humanist writers in the 1980s, bourgeois privacy was endowed with an emancipatory potential to break away from Mao's revolutionary mandate. From Liu Zaifu's affirmation of the inner universe of selfhood to Zhang Xianliang's magnified sexual hedonism, the vindication of individuality fractured and undermined the collective ethics of the socialist norm. Wang's early novels, which include an autobiographical dimension, offer a distinctively female perspective on the literary representations of postsocialist individualism. However, Wang's journey to the United States fundamentally redefined her identity in the post-Mao literary landscape, transforming her pale sentimentalism into more serious reflections on the socialist legacy.

Both Wang and Chen were invited to participate in the International Writing Program at the University of Iowa (fig. 5). Chen had long aspired to converse with writers from his "socialist homeland." Against his expectation, Wang, who had lived through the tumultuous years of revolution, could not hide her nonchalance toward Maoist rhetoric. Despite their mutual affection, the brief sojourn soon brought Wang into a series of confrontations with Chen.[43] Whereas Wang enjoyed walking "beneath shelves full of commodities" in the supermarket, spilling out unapologetic admiration for the enticing glamour of materialism, Chen for his part considered Wang's passion for American capitalism a sort of naïve Oedipal rebellion against her mother's socialist asceticism.[44] By contrast, Chen's open endorsement of socialist values struck Wang as hypocritical in the sense that he "enjoyed the benefits of the very individualism that he was now criticizing."[45] Bemused by the all-too-familiar cliché of sacrifices in Chen's novella "Mountain Path," Wang sarcastically pointed out that Cai Qianhui's blind faith in socialist utopianism merely "contributed to history's having gone awry."[46] Meanwhile, what Chen had called "the false appearance" of individualism provided restless energy for Wang's cohort.

The tension-ridden overture mirrors the drastically different historical experience and political sentiments that divided Wang's and Chen's assessments of the Maoist utopia. But the divergence might not have to be approached through the dichotomous rhetoric of bourgeois sentiment versus socialist fantasy. Wang soon discovered that Chen's passion for socialism was not impressionistic. Instead, it was motivated by a deep-seated religious piety, a messianic vision of human

---

43. For an excellent historical reconstruction of this encounter, see Po-hsi Chen, "Wang Anyi, Taiwan, and the World."
44. Wang Anyi, "Utopian Verses," 22.
45. Wang Anyi, "Utopian Verses," 27.
46. Wang Anyi, "Utopian Verses," 27.

FIGURE 5. Chen Yingzhen (back, left) and Wang Anyi (front, right) at the 1983 Iowa Writing Program. Photo courtesy of Wang Anyi.

emancipation. In a biographical reflection on her American journey titled "Utopian Verses" (1993), Wang contemplates with sadness and admiration a Christian eschatology that deeply shaped Chen's utopian socialism. Hearing about Mao's revolution through shortwave radio, Chen connected the "grandiose scenes of the heroic mass revolution on the land across the straits" to the construction of the Tower of Babel, whose sky-piercing top symbolizes a genuine desire for transcendence.[47] Such an imaginary served less as a political dogma than as a messianic religious faith. This conviction generated a "divine emotion" that moved Chen to pursue his Promethean dreams in the realm of the secular and the profane.[48] Hence Wang became deeply attracted to Chen's perseverance, whose foreseeable tragic end provoked in her a mixed sense of "extreme sadness and solemnity."[49]

47. Wang Anyi, "Utopian Verses," 14.
48. Wang Anyi, "Utopian Verses," 16.
49. Wang Anyi, "Utopian Verses," 41.

At the same time, Chen's theologically informed socialism engendered a peculiar form of melancholia for Wang. On the one hand, Chen's selfless devotion made Wang realize that her own literary passion was driven by the pragmatic purpose to gain fame and status, demanding "excessive retribution in this life."[50] Her obsession with her personal experience narrowed her literary vision to her own sentiments, without deeper reflections on collective history. In Wang's judgment, the post-Mao generation had failed to envision a clear, robust, and enchanting alternative to Chen's messianic faith. On the other hand, to transcend the individualist horizon demanded messianic aspirations. But Wang could not articulate a new vision of history from the ruins of the socialist utopia. In Žižek's radical twist of the Freudian paradigm, melancholy occurs when "we get the desired object, but are disappointed in it."[51] Similarly, Wang's incurable sense of lack stands for a disappointment with the lived experience of socialism. Having lost her desire for revolution, Wang suffered from a spiritual lethargy—indeed a postrevolutionary ennui that paralyzed her capacity to imagine any forms of human emancipation. Because neither socialist faith nor sentimental individualism could furnish a clear path for Wang, Chen's defiant gesture provided a spiritual resource for her to come to terms with her accentuated sense of lack in the postsocialist reality.

A Chronicle of Revolutionary Shanghai

Returning from the Iowa trip, Wang went on to have an illustrious career with a ceaseless stream of writings that gradually carried her to a prestigious place in the Chinese literary canon. An often-overlooked fact is that her extraordinary encounter with Chen left an indelible mark on her subsequent literary path. Chen's utopian socialism transformed her pale sentimentalism into more serious reflections on the collective experience of the post-Mao generation. As Wang bluntly puts it, she "would have already become a materialist" had she not

---

50. Wang Anyi, "Utopian Verses," 22.
51. Žižek, "Melancholy and the Act," 662.

encountered Chen.⁵² Indeed, Wang's autobiographic writings composed in the early 1990s portray a succession of spiritual crises prompted by the increasing visibility of commercialism in the literary field. While the scholarly elite expressed moral indignation and advocated spiritual resistance against crass materialism, Wang traced the emerging crisis of literary humanism to the lacuna of the 1980s enlightenment project. Her novella "The Story of My Uncle" features Shushu, a former rightist writer whose incarceration and exile in the Maoist years have unexpectedly won him immense popularity in the reform era. By way of contrast with the hapless victims portrayed in scar literature, Wang depicts a savvy literary star who is as politically defiant as he is egotistical and entrepreneurial, quarreling over status and money and indulging in sexual liaisons whenever possible. Most strikingly, Wang calls Shushu nothing but a cultural merchant and a sexual predator who "turns his traumatic past into cultural capital, providing him with an extraordinary novelistic imagination to attract female fans; indeed, every girl dreams of becoming the female protagonist in his tragic romance."⁵³ In sharp contrast to the deadly gravity of Chen Yingzhen's thinking, Shushu's flirtation with history reveals not the moral courage to confront the dark side of revolution but only a frivolous and harmless eroticism that celebrates male libido and induces cynical laughter. Above all, hedonism is the dominant emotional register that underpins Shushu's pursuit of enlightenment.

The question of materialism became more perplexing as Wang Anyi also engaged in a sustained dialogue with the growing public enthusiasm toward Shanghai-style literature. After decades of stagnation, the city's economic renaissance in the 1990s gave rise to a cultural nostalgia for Shanghai's prerevolutionary past, a period of laissez-faire capitalism and cultural cosmopolitanism defined by Xudong Zhang as the "classic moment of Chinese bourgeois modernity."⁵⁴ In the cultural milieu, the fascination with the sensuous and the quotidian, the excavation of a Shanghai-style literature that championed modernist aesthetics, and the resurgence of free-market ideology, intermingled with

---

52. Wang Anyi, "Yingte naxiong naier," 83.
53. Wang Anyi, "Shushu de gushi," 3:42.
54. Xudong Zhang, *Postsocialism and Cultural Politics*, 186.

a cosmopolitan desire, all worked to fetishize prerevolutionary Shanghai as the epitome of a cultural fashion and ideological dogma long repressed by Mao's successive political campaigns. Literary critics hailed Wang as "the legitimate heir of Shanghai literary style," and her 1990s literary creations were said to embrace this trendy nostalgia by projecting a sentimental gaze toward the bourgeois life of old Shanghai.[55] Despite Wang's own reservations, popular media further constructed a willful genealogy that linked her aesthetics to the self-pitying tone of Eileen Chang, whose writings epitomized the phantasmagoric facades of wartime Shanghai.

However, Wang distanced herself from the consumerist embrace of Shanghai's bourgeois modernity. As Xudong Zhang observes, Wang's literary narrations of Shanghai middle-class ethics are intertwined with mourning "the loss of the immediate past."[56] As the flow of bourgeois symbols and fashions effaced and replaced socialist norms and experience, memories of the failed revolution persisted in Wang's political unconscious. As a result, Wang could never get rid of her deep sense of irony toward the revanchist undertone of the Shanghai bourgeoisie, whose hubristic proclamation to bring an end to history once and for all echoed the equally triumphant rhetoric of Mao's proletarian fighters barely forty years earlier. In *The Song of Everlasting Sorrow*, Wang ruthlessly mocks a postrevolutionary dandy named Old Class (*Lao kela* 老克拉), whose poor imitation of bourgeois delicacy betrays his modest proletarian origin. Likewise, "A Tale from the Cultural Revolution" ("Wenge yishi" 文革轶事) features a caricatured interclass marriage between the daughter of a former capitalist family and a working-class young man in 1960s Shanghai. The need for survival overcomes the Maoist call for class struggle.

In these writings, the persisting quotidian affairs of class, envy, and stoic survival do not just defy the Marxist script of class struggle

---

55. Many critics focus on Wang's most celebrated novel, *The Song of Everlasting Sorrow*, which eulogizes Shanghai as a cultural icon and haven for the petty bourgeoisie who resisted and survived Mao's successive campaigns in the socialist era. See David Wang, "Haipai zuojia, youjian chuanren."

56. Xudong Zhang, *Postsocialism and Cultural Politics*, 211.

but also turn socialist heroic drama into a Benjaminian *Trauerspiel*. In Walter Benjamin's perspective, whereas Greek tragedy hails the agency of the hero by revealing the cosmic and divine significance of his tragic fate, the king of the *Trauerspiel* is traumatized by the lack of higher metaphysical purpose in a world of cosmic disorder. The sovereign feels melancholic because his hold on power only contributes to the reproduction of rampant violence. He eventually responds to this baroque drama with a mad, self-destructive lamentation and indecision, which culminates in his suicide.[57] Likewise, Wang's mournful subjects are repeatedly thrown into confusion because of the absence of a higher moral order. The proletarian and the bourgeoisie resemble each other in their obsession with the frivolous and intricate facade of urban modernity, in their ruthless and desperate struggles to survive, and in their aversion to the grand narrative of revolution and enlightenment. The immutable character of egoistic humanity evokes a cyclical regression of victory into defeat, revolution into farce, and hope into disillusionment.

In this sense, Wang's 1993 novel *Documentation and Fabrication* (*Jishi yu xugou* 紀實與虛構) represents her ambitious attempt to re-create the drama of Shanghai's 1949 "liberation" with a playful melancholy. Alternating between autobiography and fiction, Wang's voice transgresses conventional genres to connect her autobiographical narrative with two forms of collective history. The first narrative traces Wang's maternal lineage to the Ru family, a Mongolian nomadic tribe in ancient times, while the second one recounts how she spent her adolescence in socialist-era Shanghai, with her ideas and beliefs shaped not only by the revolutionary mandate but also by the specters of old bourgeois values. Wang's constant searching for a real or imaginary identity is manifested in her attempt to juxtapose family episodes with socialist history. As Ban Wang suggests, the fabrication of an ancestral origin is "a melancholy attempt to mourn the decline of history by reawakening myth,"[58] a gesture practiced by the search-for-roots literary movement in the 1980s. But the mythic dimension of Wang's

57. See Pensky, *Melancholy Dialectics*, 60–107.
58. Ban Wang, *Illuminations from the Past*, 135.

root-searching tale is complicated by the other documentary mode that records her formative experiences in revolutionary Shanghai. The juxtaposition of the two narratives indicates that mythology and history are not opposed to each other. Natural history and human history are intertwined on an eternal stage on which catastrophes repeatedly unfold.

The modern part of the novella features Wang's traumatic experience as an outsider in socialist Shanghai. Growing up in a family of Communist cadres, Wang constantly feels rejected by her peers, most of whom come from former capitalist families. The elite status of revolutionary cadres is seriously compromised by their uncultivated tastes and rural habits. Wang is embarrassed because, unlike most of her classmates, who were born into the upper echelon of the city, her parents entered Shanghai only in 1949, singing and dancing the "rice-sprout song," a northwestern folk art known for its gaudy costumes, raspy music, and exaggerated bodily movements. Whereas her playmate appreciates Western musicals, Wang's taste tends toward images of army uniforms and troop parades. Ironically, although the Communist victors in the civil war take over the city, defeat adds to the symbolic capital of the Shanghai bourgeoisie, who embody a bygone cultural sophistication and aesthetic taste unseen in the Communists' rusticated lifestyle.

Moreover, the Shanghai bourgeoise, their political status amputated, continued to flout the new regime's egalitarian ideology. Their prestige was not simply secured by the governmental policy of appeasement, which granted former national bourgeoise comfortable lives under the socialist economy. Instead, their symbolic power was magnified by the open demonstration of their ritualistic mannerisms. Wang describes how her playmate's mother remained deeply wrapped up in a middle-class aristocratic lifeworld after liberation:

> Her mother was that kind of Miss Shanghai who grew up drinking American milk, went to a salon to style her hair either in Hepburn's or in Taylor's fashion. On Sunday, she went out in a fancy dress with her daughter. This family was especially noticeable on the streets of Shanghai, where people stared at them with a sense of envy. Proud of themselves, they swaggered as if they were masters of this city.

她母親是那種將好萊塢明星當做偶像，到理髮店不是做個「赫本」式，就是做個「泰勒」式的喝美國牛奶長大的上海小姐。星期天出門，她穿的炫人眼目，女孩也光艷照人。阿太總是在陽台上目送他們遠去，滿心的歡喜。在上海的馬路上，他們這一家尤其引人注意，人們看他們的目光充滿羨嫉。而他們態度傲然，昂首闊步，儼然是這城市的主人。[59]

For Wang, the haughtiness of the girl's family is mingled with an elegant spirit, a cultivated lifestyle, and an outpouring of bourgeois refinement, all of which overshadow the moral rectitude and the perfunctory courtesy of Communist ethics. After all, human nature is vulgar, and it needs embellishments to satisfy its vanity, to showcase its charm, and to accommodate its ambition to rule. Superficial as it is, the bourgeois obsession with style relies on a pragmatic foundation to naturalize its cultural hegemony; the public display of exquisite style legitimates bourgeois social privilege. At this point, a nearly comic inversion of the victor and the vanquished confuses Wang. The Communists, who exercise de facto power over Shanghai, have to emulate the dominant bourgeois aesthetics to acquire a place in the city; the bourgeoisie, who supposedly need to be rectified, continue to exercise their flamboyant style as an object of appreciation and envy. Wang's melancholy arises from this paradox: Did the Communists take over the city, or did the bourgeoisie retake the city by co-opting Communist ethics?

Wang's anxiety to anchor herself in the city's bourgeois past is soon to be swept away by the coming of the Cultural Revolution. The Red Guards' avowal to reaffirm the cultural leadership of the proletarians not only ignites Wang's political ambition but also satisfies her desire to finally join the ruling class. Yet Mao's redemptive call to "strike down all capitalist roaders" eventually fails to provide her with sublime feelings. Aside from grandiose ideological slogans and fervent political passions, the Cultural Revolution begins in her neighborhood an explosion of voyeuristic desire. Red Guards raid the homes of great families and search for souvenirs, treasures, and properties in the name of

---

59. Wang Anyi, *Jishi yu xugou*, 216.

purging "reactionary elements," which also satisfies their scopophilic pleasure. Wang witnesses one such house raid. Red Guards storm a wealthy capitalist's home and then open it up for public exhibition, with the intention to expose all the damp and moldy secrets of the bourgeois way of life so as to educate the masses. However, the spectators are drawn to the quaint and treasured objects on display, including a ceramic of the Ming-Qing era, the silk underwear of the lady of the house, and a silver dinner set. In the sublime name of revolution, Red Guards create a theatrical show to satisfy the erotic gaze of the masses. Moreover, after finding out that the capitalist had two mistresses living elsewhere, the Red Guards force his mistresses to live with his wife under the same roof. The endless fighting among his many women offers a malicious pleasure to the gathering crowd.

Unfortunately, the Red Guards, who take pride in their self-appointed heroism, are soon traumatized by the purging of their fathers when Mao suddenly turns against the so-called capitalist roaders within the party. The sudden downfall of these Red Guards resonates with Benjamin's depiction of the tyrant who tends to lose power at a moment of emergency. In contrast to Greek heroes, whose decisive actions restore the divine order, the tyrant, who "displays nearly comic indecision"[60] in the absence of a theological postulate, contributes to the continuum of catastrophic violence. Similarly, these frustrated Red Guards desperately try to cleave to their tyrannical power as masters of this city in the face of their declining political privilege. They seek to strike up a revolution again, this time by patrolling the streets wearing shining military uniforms and promoting Mandarin to disgruntled Shanghai citizens. Dialect and dress, once the great weapons of the bourgeoisie, become embellishments for the Red Guards' soulless revolution. As for their bourgeois antagonists, sophisticated codes of dress and language standards serve as social distinctions that separate these red heirs from the masses. Ironically, this outward turn of the revolution reduces Communist ideology to ornaments and fashion. As Wang confesses, she exuberantly embraces the new dressing code not because of her belief in revolution, but out of a cynical desire to "follow the trendy

---

60. Pensky, *Melancholy Dialectics*, 79.

fashion of the city." Wang and her comrades' obsession with fashion signify a revolution that is exhausted, marooned, and devoid of higher moral meaning.

In the end, Wang finds herself to be an outsider to both bourgeois Shanghai and the socialist revolution. Whereas her effort to emulate bourgeois aesthetics is hampered by her mother's ideological Puritanism, her hope for a redemptive revolution is shattered by its degeneration into a bourgeois obsession with style and fame. When the documentary narrative reaches its end, it is accompanied by the completion of the other narrative—the Ru family's emergence into modern times through the coming of age of Zhijuan. Intertwining these two plots produces a circular structure: the primordial experience of exile and exclusion that characterizes Wang's maternal family does not end with Zhijuan's entry into Shanghai; instead, the sense of spiritual rootlessness returns and pervades the political and emotional torrents she is about to encounter in socialist Shanghai. Family saga and revolutionary chronicle together produce a perpetual repetition of exile and exclusion. This cyclical reproduction of barbarism is the ultimate cause of Wang's melancholy.

Toward a Melancholic Marxism

This chapter marks out the contours of Left melancholia through the literary journeys of Chen Yingzhen and Wang Anyi. Throughout his life, Chen constantly wrestled with the melancholic bent of Taiwanese leftism: his remembrances of historical traumas, his critique of bourgeois passivity, and his call for decisive actions were all tinged with an incurable sadness, transforming his dogmatic Marxism into an empathetic identification with the vanquished and the downtrodden. By contrast, Wang's melancholy was not driven by an outburst of thwarted revolutionary passions. Full of sorrowful imagery and an ironic tone, her autobiographical works reveal conscious and continuous negotiations with the waning experiences of socialism, a ghostly memory repressed by the resurgence of bourgeois cultural fashions in the postrevolutionary era. Disagreement over the value and the meaning of the Maoist revolution remains in the intellectual exchange between

Chen and Wang. Chen's indomitable belief in the redemptive mission of the Maoist regime looks outlandish and antiquarian to Wang's generation, whose experience was shaped by the catastrophic outcomes of state socialism. For Chen, Wang's attempt to blend the sublime with the comic, to find the egoistic desires beneath the revolution's noble claims turns serious politics into an object of amusement. Yet they are still deeply attracted to each other's personalities, thoughts, and literary styles. Chen's religious devotion to an inextricably lost cause helps Wang overcome her postrevolutionary ennui. Meanwhile, Wang's concern for the fate of the nation beyond the personal dimension arouses Chen's expectations and hopes in his lonely battle against the neoliberal valorization of individual desire. These rifts and affinities that both created tensions and nourished friendship are faithful testimony to the divergent political interpretations and contested literary representations of Mao's revolution across the Chinese and Sinophone world.

The paradoxical outcomes of melancholy underpin the multiple layers of Chen's and Wang's literary narrations of politics. I read their melancholy not as a pathology but in connection with the pathos and the passions of thinking and writing in the absence of revolutionary hope. Admittedly, the forms and tonalities of melancholic literature might signify despair and encourage political quietism. But just as Benjamin "exploited his own melancholia in order to overcome it,"[61] so the two Chinese writers share a dialectical passion for retrieving revolution's unrealized promises at the moment of its fall. For Wang and Chen, melancholy was always implicated in a sustained reflection on the ambiguous relationship between thinking and acting, politics and aesthetics, and backward gaze and messianic futurity. Their Sisyphean efforts to overcome these tensions help to bring out the emancipatory potential of melancholy at its most intense. For Chen, the elegiac tone of the "petit-urbanite intellectual" frustrates his utopian passions with the pathos of defeat at the same time that it empowers him with insight into the structural causality of social misery. Wang's playful melancholy, meanwhile, questions the Maoist narrative of progress by unveiling the political trauma and drama caused by the incongruities between

---

61. Pensky, *Melancholy Dialectics*, 19.

the revolution's heroic calls and its nearly comic realizations. Their writings are thus best read not as attempts to reconcile the duality of Left melancholy, but as critical projects to seize hold of the melancholic in a "paradoxical simultaneity," between an aporetic mood and a radical openness to hope.

Wang's and Chen's melancholic musings on revolution occurred at a time when the global leftist movement confronted the collapse of socialist regimes with fear, confusion, and resignation. The crisis of the Left was further accompanied by a global intellectual transition from revolutionary Jacobinism to democratic reformism. Since the early 1980s, the dissidents of Eastern Europe propagated the social and political ideal of civil society against the oppressive regimes of bureaucratic socialism. In post–May 1968 France, ethics became the predominant norm for grappling with the problems of democracy. The New Philosophers rejected the antinomian revolution of May 1968 and embraced a moralistic eulogizing of human rights and reformist politics.[62] In the Anglo-American world, the market-oriented reform of Thatcher and Reagan enchanted massive privatization in the noble name of political liberty. As a result, the polycentric shift toward neoliberalism now projected the past romance with Marxism as an "irresponsible attachment to Communism," "the opium of the intellectuals," and "infantile liberalism," and celebrated the collapse of socialism as "the passing of an illusion" and "the end of history."[63] Admittedly, these "strategies of containment"[64] provide an ideological deciphering of socialism from the reductive and singular standpoint of the victor. The demonization of left-wing politics is bound up with a narcissistic self-congratulation that skirts the complex relations of capitalist domination. Nevertheless, this intellectual offensive has raised a number of critical issues in regard to both Marxism in particular and the legitimacy of radical politics in general: How did a conglomerate of an authoritarian party, a new

---

62. See Bourg, *From Revolution to Ethics*.

63. The quoted phrases come, in the order of their appearance, from Judt, *The Burden of Responsibility*; Aron, *The Opium of the Intellectuals*; Wolin, *The Wind from the East*; Furet, *The Passing of an Illusion*; Fukuyama, *The End of History and the Last Man*.

64. See Jameson, *The Political Unconscious*, x.

privileged class, and political persecution rise at the very heart of the utopian aspirations for new forms of humanity? How has Marxism provided justifications—both theoretically and practically—for political tyrannies during the twentieth century?

To address these questions, melancholy has become a crucial rallying point in end-of-the-century Marxist discourse. Post-Marxism, as Warren Breckman defines it, represents a melancholic response to "the specific loss of Marxism as a privileged object, intellectual investment, and emotional cathexis."[65] To rescue radical politics from its misadventures in Stalinism, post-Marxist thinkers responded to the loss of the socialist project with a conception of radical democracy no longer tethered to hegemonic politics. In this regard, Jacques Derrida's intervention is a timely illustration of a melancholic grasp of the Marxian spirit.[66] For Derrida, the disarticulation between Marxism and emancipatory politics generated a spectral Marx devoid of messianic hope, a hauntology infused with visions of the future that have become obsolete. Derrida further argues that this irreversible collapse of the political alternative envisioned by the Left might not be regarded as the end of Marxist criticism. Rather, it was only when Marxism was displaced from its teleological commitment to political dogma—only when it became spectral—that the cultural Left could regain insight into the contradictions of capitalism. Derrida's embrace of the spectrality of Marxism endows him with "a weak hold" on certain spirits of Marxism,[67] simultaneously affirming the Marxian pursuit of justice *and* negating Marxist ontology. In other words, a melancholic hold on revolution's emancipatory promise must always be an *empty* promise that forever defers and contests the authoritarian impulse of messianism.

The stories of Chen and Wang provide a striking parallel to the melancholic turn of global Marxism. Confronting the collapse of Maoist utopia, the vanquished Taiwanese leftists have abstained from any messianic impulses that anticipate revolution's actualization in the

---

65. Breckman, *Adventures of the Symbolic*, 192.
66. See Derrida, *Specters of Marx*; for a heated discussion on Derrida's spectral Marxism, see Sprinker, *Ghostly Demarcations*.
67. Breckman, *Adventures of the Symbolic*, 192.

present. Devoid of any specific names, parties, and concrete political agendas, Chen's faith in Chinese socialism involves an endless waiting for a revolution that has never occurred and will perhaps never come. Likewise, Wang's effort to reclaim her memories of socialism is not an attempt to resurrect the Maoist sublime. Rather, it inscribes the revolutionary past into the emotional and psychic formation of her personal identity, a structure of feeling shaped by but not necessarily tethered to, Mao's socialist project. The blurry nature of the melancholic loss invokes an amorphous hauntology of a revolutionary past, thereby transforming loss into a traumatic kernel, an unknowable lack without which a postrevolutionary identity cannot endure. Ultimately, melancholy provides ample aesthetic means to linger over the Maoist utopia while maintaining a critical awareness of its irrevocable wrongdoings. Echoing Derrida's call for a "New International . . . without status, without title, and without name," Chen's and Wang's mournful gestures are no less intermingled with a paradoxical remembrance of a Chinese revolution without a revolutionary mandate.[68]

Together, the unlikely resonance between post-Marxism and Chinese left-wing writings in the postrevolutionary era sheds light on the emancipatory potential of Left melancholy. It illustrates how melancholy revitalizes the Left with a deliberately weak hold on the Marxian pursuit of justice. Haunted by the dangerous memory of oppression, post-1989 leftism could never dissociate itself from the dark inheritance of revolutionary violence. A spectral lingering on Marxism thus avoids dangerous liaisons between radical democracy and authoritarianism. Melancholic Marxism serves not as a messianic doctrine with a concrete and realizable historical telos. Rather, through endless deferral and waiting, melancholy transforms a certain spirit of Marxism into a weak promise of "messianicity without messianism."[69] Because a Derridian messianicity "precedes and exceeds all specific religious beliefs as such," the indefiniteness of the melancholic's loss appears as an ascesis that refrains from returning to a historical messianic vision of revolution on the one hand, and a radical openness to what is yet to

68. Derrida, *Specters of Marx*, 85.
69. Derrida, *Specters of Marx*, 211.

come on the other.⁷⁰ Instead of causing political paralysis, melancholy ultimately liberates the Left from its putative and normative commitment to the totalizing agenda of socialist modernity.

On the other side, numerous criticisms from the Marxist camp have also emerged to complain that the "melancholic turn" of post-Marxism has dragged the Left toward a "highway of despair." For the stalwarts on the Left who never quite managed to break with the ontology of revolution, the mournful tone of critical theory is said to be "too morose, too destructive, or too slow in speaking to the urgent political demands of our time."⁷¹ Mired in aporia, the Left gets caught up in a masochistic self-negation, frustration, and political resignation. It was not surprising, then, that the preeminent PRC scholar Wang Hui called on his neoleftist fellows to rediscover the emancipatory potential of class politics. Wang vehemently denounced the neoliberal "depoliticized politics" that had affected the Chinese public consciousness, where entire dimensions of the revolutionary past—anti-colonialism, mass democracy, the warfare state, and class struggle—were buried under the hypocritical rhetoric of "market transition."⁷² In the age of "great reversal" (*diandao* 顛倒), the legacy of revolutionary struggle had taken a ghostly form—almost invisible yet still persistent—that haunted our recollections of a supposedly dead, exhausted, and repudiated political past. Sketching a ghostly genealogy of antimodernist thinkers from Zhang Taiyan 章太炎 (1869–1936) to Mao, Wang proposed to rethink the utopian promise of the Chinese revolution through the prism of "downward transcendence" (*xiangxia chaoyue* 向下超越)—that is, seeking inspiration not from the telos of human emancipation but from the phantom domain haunted by ruptures, setbacks, graves, executions, and demons. Here, Wang Hui is indebted to Lu Xun, who once likened his penchant for the dark side of reason to discovering "the abyss in the heaven, the void in the all-encompassing, and salvation in despair" (...於天上看見深淵。於一切眼中看見無所有；於無所希望中

---

70. For a detailed discussion of Derrida's distinction between messianism and messianicity, see Kearney, "Derrida and Messianic Atheism," 203.
71. Marasco, *The Highway of Despair*, 7
72. Wang Hui, *The End of the Revolution*, 3–18.

得救).⁷³ Thus, in his seminal rereading of Lu Xun's satirical novella *The True Story of Ah Q*, Wang Hui described Ah Q—the tragic fool who is arrested and eventually beheaded for his participation in a revolutionary uprising—as driven by an instinctual, almost biological, desire for a violent proletarian revolution. Most strikingly, Wang Hui's attempt to rekindle the weak yet demonic power of the Ah Q–like subalterns bespoke a messianic impulse to provoke a sense of rupture through which lost meanings, suppressed desires, and failed battles of socialism will be fulfilled in an apocalyptic manner.

But for Lu Xun the pessimist, Ah Q's political zealotry generates as much revolutionary momentum as "involutionary" desire for "spiritual victory" (*jingshen shenglifa* 精神勝利法)—a delusionary sense of self-affirmation. In Lu Xun's literary world, revolution incites not the coming of the messiah but only laughter, mockery, bloody spectacles, and, in Giorgio Agamben's phrase, "larval specters" whose presence reveals not "poetry of the future" but only traces of a disfigured revolutionary past.⁷⁴ To be sure, the revolutionary spirit Wang wants to retrieve is not a source of Maoist dogmatism, but a "hidden revolutionary ethos that exists only in the fleeting, amorphous, biological instinct [of Ah Q]."⁷⁵ Even though the pretentious fool, because of his physical impotence, has to make do with an imaginary revenge rather than decisive political action, there is a utopian spark that can start a prairie fire. In Ah Q and his comrades' instinctual thirst for a radical change, Wang Hui discovers not political melancholy but the aspirational significance of China's revolution that retains certain validity even after monstrous failures. Wang Hui's radical twist yields a provocative and at times deeply disturbing conviction: revolution is never completed, which is why we must maintain "fidelity" to the utopian aspiration of leftist radicalism, apart from its restricted historical application.

Ironically, beneath Wang's passionate campaign against postrevolutionary amnesia, something amnesic has ever loomed over the neoleftist

73. Lu Xun, "Mujiewen," 2:207, quoted in and translated by David Wang, "Utopian Dream and Dark Consciousness," 147.
74. Agamben, "On the Uses and Disadvantages of Living among Specters," 39–40.
75. Wang Hui, *Ah Q shengming zhong de liuge shunjian*, 88.

undertaking. The Chinese New Left spoke so much about how to revitalize the utopian ideal of mass democracy and the awesome power of the "superpolitical party" against the dispossession of the working class under neoliberal statecraft.[76] Never, ever, did they explain why Mao's party with a supposed "self-correction mechanism"[77] had steered the country into a succession of human catastrophes. Above all, the need to recover the alternative political imagination even at the cost of self-reflexivity was the driving force behind the utopianism of the New Left. Yet these grand theorists remain vague about what the return of Maoist politics would entail—a radical "delinking" from the world capitalist system, a total negation of liberal democracy, a (re)installment of class struggle, or even a national and global war? The explosion of militant imaginations seems to be undermined by a sloppy dismissal of the intertwinement of revolution and authoritarianism throughout the twentieth century.

The melancholic Left, by contrast, cautions us from rushing to reestablish an untroubled bond with Mao's revolutionary legacy. The pathos of the Sinophone Left is manifested in Chen Yingzhen's last novella, *Homecoming* (*Gui xiang* 歸鄉) (1999), where the jaded Taiwanese veteran soldier, after being stranded in Communist China for more than four decades, returns to his homeland only to find out that the place once so familiar to him now appears utterly strange. Just like his protagonist whose homecoming has become a voyage into transcendental homelessness, Chen might have taken himself as a wandering ghost harboring memories of the homeland yet finding nowhere—be it socialist motherland or Taiwanese homeland—to return. Yet for the "last Marxist" doubly alienated by the failure of the revolution across the Taiwan Strait, the desire for homecoming does not lead to a vehement passion to repeat Maoism but instead to a reluctant retreat into a phantom dimension, a space where memory has failed and socialism has been derailed. Wang Anyi, meanwhile, was perhaps never obsessed with Maoist political ideals in the first place. In her novel *The Age of Enlightenment* (*Qimeng shidai* 啟蒙時代) (2007), Wang nevertheless narrates the experience of growing up under the heat of the Cultural Revolution

---

76. For superpolitical party, see Wang Hui, *China's Twentieth Century*.
77. Wang Hui, "Zhongguo jueqi de jingyan jiqi mianlin de tiaozhan."

as a journey of political enlightenment. She describes how Mao's children entered the carnival of revolution in a blissful daze, searched for the meaning of life, encountered friendship, love, and betrayal, and, above all, confronted the hard and ruthless political realities of the day that eventually shattered their revolutionary romanticism. By "enlightenment" Wang doesn't mean man's release from his "self-incurred tutelage" but a wounded consciousness: the revolution, no matter how inspiring, carries with it a feeling of sadness or a profound disappointment at how far Mao's world falls short of its utopian promise. Above all, the dynamic interactions between the poetry of revolution and the prosaic reality shows that Left melancholy must not be read simply as the political manifesto of the defeated leftists. Rather than succumb to either the lure of messianism or the pathos of defeatism, melancholy provides emotional cultivation, aesthetic expression, and philosophical intervention to dwell on, rather than return to, the specter of Marxist revolution.

In the end, we return to the image of Lenin in *Ulysses' Gaze*. The broken statue of the Soviet leader might not necessarily signify the disintegration of the Marxian pursuit of justice. Instead, Lenin's disembodied statue speaks to a radical "disincorporation of power"[78] that subverts and decentralizes authoritarian impulses. As the symbol of a unitary subject, Lenin must be dethroned from the power center so that Marxism may be carried on in the postrevolutionary era. The leftist tradition survives as long as the center of radical politics is no longer occupied by any messiah. What remains is a melancholic subject who meditates on the empty place at the center of radical politics, waiting for the weak promise of redemption in the dystopian world.

---

78. Laclau and Mouffe, *Hegemony and Socialist Strategy*.

CHAPTER FOUR

A Passion for God

Liu Xiaofeng and the Conservative Revolt against Modernity

> It is nothing but a prejudice to assume that revolutionaries think while reactionaries only react.
> —Mark Lilla, *The Shipwrecked Mind*

> There is no reason to crawl to the cross . . . of liberalism. And even then: rather than any cross, I'll take the ghetto.
> —Leo Strauss, "Letters to Karl Löwith"

Beginning in the 1990s, intellectuals in mainland China were drawn increasingly away from the ideal of liberal democracy and toward conservative cultural politics. In the wake of the 1989 Tiananmen protests, party leaders shied away from political reforms and installed the

---

This chapter is a substantially revised version of the article "From Christian Transcendence to the Maoist Sublime: Liu Xiaofeng, the Chinese Straussians, and the Conservative Revolt against Modernity," *Modern Intellectual History* 20, no. 1 (March 2023): 323–44, published by Cambridge University Press. Reprinted with permission. The discussion of Leo Strauss and the Gongyang School (公羊學派) in this chapter also appeared in my article "Between Conformity and Dissent: Two Chinese Thinkers in Search of Esotericism," published in *Critical Inquiry* 50, no. 4 (Summer 2024).

tools of authoritarian governance to speed up economic growth. With the waning of Marxist orthodoxy and the suppression of the 1980s New Enlightenment, intellectual discourse underwent a thorough transformation from the consensus politics of the liberal reform to a renewed emphasis on the indigenous sources of modernization. Within the orbit of elite politics, neoconservatism emerged as a loose right-wing faction to advocate a state-centered "realistic response" to the perceived failure of socialist utopianism and the advance of Western hegemony. The authoritarian turn in politics inspired waves of conservative cultural practices that sought to rejuvenate Chinese tradition as a system of normative value in the post-Marxist public sphere. Governmental elites, academicians, and public intellectuals adhering to this faction dismissed liberal democracy as a nihilistic, technocratic, and Eurocentric model incompatible with the Chinese cultural and political tradition. Moreover, the conservatives' suspicion of reason and progress led to bourgeoning discussions on the role of "religion" (*zongjiao* 宗教) in the postsecular world, including both New Confucianism and the Sino-Christian theology movement. They called for a new religious consciousness to embrace the transcendent, the mystical, and the sacred against the secular order envisioned by enlightenment intellectuals of the 1980s.

In this context, Liu Xiaofeng 劉小楓 (1956–), whose work encompasses aesthetics, theology, and political philosophy, emerged as a key figure in the conservative revolution of the post-Mao era. After studying German philosophy at Peking University in the early 1980s, Liu made his intellectual debut with a series of essays on German Romanticism. Liu was particularly well known for his scathing critique of the this-worldly orientation of Confucian ethics, which he derided as inferior to the other-worldly virtue of the Judeo-Christian tradition. Moreover, the young iconoclast was convinced that only an utterly transcendent God could save the Chinese from their misguided pursuit of Mao's atheistic revolution. Whereas liberal critics mobilized the May Fourth quest for science and democracy to uphold a normative program of secularization, Liu's promulgation of Christian transcendence revealed the insufficiency of secular humanism to provide an "ultimate value" (*zhongji jiazhi* 終極價值) for the postrevolutionary era. Subsequently, Liu's interpretation and translation of Christian theology played a decisive role in the formation of the Sino-Christian theology movement, a collective scholarly endeavor to promote a contextual-historicist approach to Christianity in mainland China and Hong Kong. Hence, Liu was widely considered as one of the most prominent "cultural Christians" (*wenhua jidutu* 文化基督徒)—those intellectuals who actively participated in the scholastic discussions of Christian culture but refrained from church associations. A theological passion for ultimacy beyond secular reason, as Liu believed, would provide a robust moral grounding in the post-Marxist public sphere.

By the end of the 1990s, however, Liu gradually came to a radical conclusion that his quest for Christian transcendence beyond politics risked collapsing into secular liberalism, cordoning off religion within the sphere of private experience. He eventually discarded his earlier liberal-Christian stance and turned to the conservative political theology of the German American classicist Leo Strauss (1899–1973) and the Weimar anti-liberal legal theorist Carl Schmitt (1888–1985). The Schmitt-Strauss exchange on the theological basis of political authority provided the intellectual ammunition for Liu to reassert a "Confucian religion" (*rujiao* 儒教) against the secular enlightenment of the West. The restoration of "Confucian antiquity," Liu declared, could provide a "sacred canopy" to guide moral conducts and national politics in the postsecular era. During the first decade of the new millennium, partisans and devotees gravitated toward the circles of the "Chinese Straussians" then forming around Liu in Guangzhou and Beijing. The Straussian acolytes promoted classical learning, created elitist liberal arts educational institutions, and waged cultural wars to eradicate the presumed corrosive influence of Western liberal values lurking in the Chinese academia and beyond. This conservative backlash assumed an authoritarian form in 2013, as Liu made a bold proposal to identify the Confucian root of the modern Chinese revolution and celebrated Mao as a "sage-king" and a "founding father" of the socialist republic.

Revolution and Religion

This chapter explores how Liu's passion for ultimate values animated his intellectual transition from a devout cultural Christian to a neo-conservative guru. It also aims to make sense of the post-Mao intellectual debates on reason and religion as reflected in Liu's zigzagging journey. How to explain Liu's conservative turn after decades of devotion to Western and Chinese faith traditions? How to understand his fascination with the specters of revolution he had once repudiated? Most importantly, given that the core aim of cultural conservatism is to restore a traditionalistic social order based on authority, hierarchy, elitism, and heritage, why would Liu-like conservatives seek inspiration from their nemesis—Mao's iconoclastic revolution? Extant scholarship, most of which focuses on Liu's Straussian conservative undertaking, describes Liu's turn as a "regression," "break," or "intellectual betrayal."[1] One of the most crucial questions that has confronted Liu's critics is the catastrophic failure of the post-Mao liberalization trend as manifested in Liu's transition. Liberal critics poignantly asked: What could possibly have induced Liu to abandon the unfinished project of enlightenment and justify ancient and modern tyranny? Indeed, whereas the 1980s New Enlightenment was associated with a self-conscious break from the sublime myth of Mao's revolution, the rightward turn of Liu and his many acolytes seemed to have confirmed the disheartening return of authoritarian politics.

Nonetheless, this narrative has reduced Liu's complex intellectual saga into a single melodrama about the post-Mao enlightenment and its collapse. The dichotomous reading has obscured the dynamic and conflictual movement of Liu's life and writing across three periods of contemporary China: his coming-of-age as an educated youth in the Cultural Revolution, his search for ultimacy in the 1980s humanist trend, and the crystallization of his conservative thinking after the 1989 Tiananmen incident. Above all, it fails to see the profound and troubling affinity between Liu's earlier religious sentiment and his later fascination with political authoritarianism. By contrast, I contend that

---

1. For an analysis of how Chinese Straussians deployed Greek classics for the nationalist cause, see Bartsch, *Plato Goes to China*, 127–45; for a critical rejoinder against Chinese Straussians, see Marchal and Shaw, *Carl Schmitt and Leo Strauss in the Chinese-Speaking World*; for a defense of Liu's Straussian position, see Xu Jian, *Gujin zhizheng yu wenming zijue*; see also Tao Wang, "Leo Strauss in China"; Zhang Xu, "Shitelaosi zai Zhongguo"; Jiang Dongxian, "Searching for the Chinese Autonomy."

the entanglement between revolution and religion has been a sustained theme throughout Liu's lifelong search for ultimate values, from his youthful yearnings for Christian transcendence to the utter profanation of the sacred in his recent espousal of the Mao cult. From this view, Liu's earlier search for an other-worldly religious sentiment is continuous with his later obsession with this-worldly political theology. By stressing his sustained passion for God, I do not mean to deny all the radical twists and turns in Liu's thinking. Rather, tracing the commonalities linking the seemingly incompatible phases of Liu's journey reveals how his thirst for transcendence beyond politics paradoxically aroused the desire for an absolute ground for politics.

Liu's dramatic transition, I further propose, must be regarded as part and parcel of a generational endeavor to come to terms with the theologico-political legacies of Mao's revolution. Working within the Judeo-Christian tradition, Claude Lefort, Eric Santner, and others have proposed the "permanence of the theologico-political," the persistent haunting of the modern state by something outside of secular reason, an exception that compels political authority to invoke the tropes of transcendence (messiah, miracle, redemption) in the register of immanence (leader, party, socialism).[2] My application of Western political theology is indebted to Haiyan Lee's innovative engagement with the quasi-religious dimensions of Mao's image magic. Whereas political scientists have largely focused on the rational-functionalist dimensions of the Mao cult, Lee draws on Ernst Kantorowicz's discussion of medieval political theology and demonstrates how "the political-theological idea of Mao's two bodies lives on" in the posthumous cult of the Great Helmsman.[3] Together, Lee and other scholars show how Mao's supposedly secular revolutionary legacy continues to evoke powerful religious resonances in contemporary China, from fantasies of resurrection to yearnings of redemption. This brings profound ambiguity to the narrative about the post-Mao "secularization" that prevents us from seeing the spectral persistence of Mao's holy power in contemporary China.[4]

---

2. See Lefort, "The Permanence of the Theologico-Political?"; Santner, *The Royal Remains*.
3. Haiyan Lee, "Mao's Two Bodies," 264.
4. See Barmé, "The Irresistible Fall and Rise of Chairman Mao."

This chapter discusses the crucial role of passion—the spontaneous quasi-religious sentiment—that underpinned Liu and his cohort's enduring fascination with the revolutionary sublime. While the English word "passion" commonly refers to "strong states of any emotion," it is etymologically related to "the sufferings of Jesus on the cross," imbuing the term with rich Christian connotations.[5] Although scholars have cautioned against deploying theological categories to explain the quasi-religious lure of Mao's revolution, Liu and his followers were still obsessed with the abiding affinity between Christological worldviews and socialist utopianism.[6] From this perspective, although the post-Mao generation cognitively identified themselves with the rationalized discourse of modernization, their political emotions remained haunted by a profound loss of touch with what Sigmund Freud and Romain Rolland call an "oceanic feeling"—a quasi-religious passion that energized their earlier fascination with Mao's secular utopia. Rolland further contended that religious *sensation*—the "simple and direct fact of the feeling of the 'eternal'"—is independent of all religious dogma and formed the vital emotional drive for his pursuit of socialism.[7] Likewise, for many post-Mao thinkers, the quasi-religious lure of the Maoist sublime—the inscription of religious symbols, rituals, and values onto revolutionary politics—was one of the most troubling and yet enticing legacies of this revolution.[8] "That holy word, 'revolution,'" even the defiant political dissident Liu Xiaobo 劉曉波 (1955–2017) admitted, possesses "a not-to-be doubted quality of righteousness and a not-to-be-blasphemed sacredness," conjures up "devotion, sacrifice...

---

5. Fisher, *The Vehement Passions*, 4–5.
6. See Leese, *Mao Cult*; Perry, *Anyuan*, 5.
7. See Parsons, "The Letters of Sigmund Freud and Romain Rolland," 173. Although Rolland and Freud differ significantly over the interpretation of religious mysticism, they both use "oceanic feeling" to describe a vitalistic, quasi-religious passion for the sublime that is completely independent of institutionalized religion (e.g., dogma, credo, and Church organization). Thus I qualify my use of the term to describe the quasi-religious passion aroused by Mao's utopian revolution, and do not seek to confuse secular revolution with religion. See Freud, *The Future of an Illusion*, 11–13.
8. For a definition of political religiosity, see Gentile, *Politics as Religion*; for an analysis of the quasi-religious aspects of Mao's revolutionary politics, see Goossaert and Palmer, *The Religious Question in Modern China*, 187–90.

idealism, and romantic feelings," and indicates "a willingness to 'die nine deaths without regret.'"[9] Even though this religious devotion generated class hatred and caused violent bloodshed at the height of the Cultural Revolution, the abandonment of Mao's revolutionary legacy in the market triggered a willful totalitarian nostalgia among many children of Mao, who in turn embraced an idealized account of the socialist past as a golden era of grand prosperity.

This chapter therefore explores how Liu's vehement passion for God—be it Christian God or Maoist messiah—informed his intellectual transformation from a cultural Christian to a Chinese Straussian. Throughout this dynamic journey, Liu was convinced that Mao's quasi-religious utopianism was an appeal for sustained social cohesion and political legitimacy, and in his eyes the waning of socialism in the post-Mao era entailed disenchantment. Therefore, Liu struggled to carve out a space for religion—first Christianity and then Confucianism—as an alternative to the Maoist sublime. As one of those "educated youth" who emerged in the 1980s with idealistic passions only to be thwarted—or tempted—by the powerful attraction of political religiosity, Liu's dramatic (de)conversion serves as an excellent guide for exploring the dilemma between modern rationalism and its theological discontents that confronted the post-Mao generation.

Admittedly, my proposition about the continuity of Liu's passionate thinking will certainly incur objections. Not for nothing was Liu frequently criticized for propagating the thoughts of the most extreme minds—from Schmitt, known as the "Crown Jurist of the Third Reich,"[10] to Strauss, who refused to "crawl to the cross of liberalism";[11] from Kang Youwei 康有為 (1858–1927), who invested Confucianism with mystical foundations, to Mao, whose poetic imageries and political visions entailed enormous human suffering. The metamorphosis of Liu's tension-ridden oeuvre produced endless polemics. He was admired, denounced, and vilified as an anti-traditionalist in the 1980s, an

---

9. Liu Xiaobo, "That Holy Word 'Revolution,'" 310.

10. Schmitt was termed the "Crown Jurist of the Third Reich" (*Kronjurist des Dritten Reiches*) by Waldemar Gurian.

11. Strauss, "Letters to Karl Löwith," 84.

unorthodox Christian in the 1990s, a Straussian acolyte in the 2000s, and an unrepentant neofascist in the contemporary scene.[12] Ironically, these accusations, most of which tend to measure the value of ideas according to certain political standpoints, reflect the characteristic ideological-cum-academic scandal making of PRC intellectual life. We must recall that Jürgen Habermas, who was outraged by Heidegger's eulogy for the "inner truth and greatness" of National Socialism, nevertheless proposed to "think with Heidegger against Heidegger."[13] Hence Liu's political undertaking should not inhibit us from analyzing the development of his thought from within its own categories and systems. To the critics who might fault my approach for depoliticizing Liu's thinking, I propose that criticism benefits from "reading the idea against itself."[14] A careful reconstruction of Liu's lifelong search for religious passion will shed light on the incongruities of his thinking.

Meanwhile, the symbolism of Liu's "political collusion" raises important questions about the political responsibility of intellectuals in contemporary China. Notwithstanding the trademark Straussian animosity toward the public, Liu was intensely preoccupied with the manifold interactions between his philosophical claims and China's changing political dynamics, to the point of neurosis. Liu, after all, was not just an exegete, but also a supreme manipulator of intellectual politics, mixing aesthetic provocations and political metaphors with abstract philosophical treatises. To be sure, those who value Liu's intellectual sincerity could compare his naïve political romanticism to Thales of Miletus, the Greek mathematician who "grew so absorbed in contemplating the heavens that he stumbled into the well at his feet."[15] Yet to his critics, the facts of Liu's tyrannophilia were rarely in dispute: his efforts to portray liberal democracy in diabolical terms—the tyranny of the masses, of capital, and of modern nihilism—went hand in hand with his glorification of Confucian-cum-revolutionary totalitarian

---

12. See Marchal, "Modernity, Tyranny, and Crisis"; Møllgaard, *The Confucian Political Imagination*, 3.
13. Gordon, "A Lion in Winter."
14. See McCormick, *Carl Schmitt's Critique of Liberalism*, 7–8.
15. Gordon, "Heidegger in Black."

politics. Hence my purpose is not to produce a dichotomy of high-minded ideals versus their ideological contamination. Rather, by tracing the inner movements of Liu's ideas *and* restoring his zigzagging course to the horizon of its original articulation, I seek to elucidate the deeply contradictory nature of his thinking as a combination of metaphysical rumination and opportunistic intent, philosophical insight and political dogmatism, sincerity and hypocrisy.

Because Liu's two major interventions concerned Christianity and Confucianism, their place in contemporary Chinese intellectual discourse merits a preliminary review. The revival of multiple religions in the post-Mao era has created heated debates among Western scholars regarding modern China's "religious questions"—the "mutual adaption of religion and the modern political and social framework of Chinese societies."[16] Deng Xiaoping's policy of reform and opening-up that began in 1978 loosened state regulation on the Protestant church, which led to a surge in Christian adherents in the countryside during the 1980s and in urban centers from the 1990s onward. The Christian resurgence was accompanied by increased attention to Western theology from official church leaders, independent pastors, religious scholars, and public intellectuals.[17] Extant scholarship identifies the writings of Liu Xiaofeng and his fellow cultural Christians (e.g., Yang Huilin and He Guanghu) as a secular academic discourse fundamentally different from Church theology.[18] Instead of adhering to Christian rituals and doctrines, proponents of Sino-Christian theology focus on the moral and cultural value of Christianity for contemporary Chinese society.[19] In particular, Liu's unorthodox aversion to doctrinal theology stands out in the scope of religious studies. Liu's iconic status as the most representative cultural Christian has in fact obscured the underlying disagreements between him and the major motifs of Sino-Christian theology.

---

16. Goossaert and Palmer, *The Religious Question in Modern China*, 2.

17. Chloë Starr and Zhuo Xinping divide contemporary Chinese theological writings into three major clusters: official church theologies, academic theology, and house-church writings. See Starr, *Chinese Theology*, 224–39; Zhuo, *Christianity*.

18. See Lai and Lam, *Sino-Christian Theology*; Yang and Yeung, *Sino-Christian Studies in China*; Starr, *Chinese Theology*, 240–62.

19. For representative works, see He Guanghu, *He Guanghu zixuanji*; Yang Huilin, *Zai wenxue yu shenxue de bianjie*.

Liu's thirst for transcendence beyond historical reasoning, which was rooted in his training in German Romanticism, was fundamentally incompatible with the contextual-historicist underpinning of the Sino-Christian theology movement.

Meanwhile, Liu's turn to "Confucian religion" went hand in hand with the nationalistic assertion of "Mainland New Confucianism" (*dalu xinrujia* 大陸新儒家) from the 2000s onward.[20] The Confucian revival since the early 1990s was a complex phenomenon overdetermined by many factors, including the castigation of the May Fourth iconoclasm among Chinese intellectuals, the resurgence of "national learning," and the anti-Western mood sponsored by the party-state.[21] In contrast to the reformist stance of overseas Confucian scholars, mainland Confucians projected an aggressive vision of Confucianism as a "national religion" (*guojiao* 國教) underpinned by exclusive doctrinal, spiritual, and political systems. Although many scholars attribute this trend to a xenophobic and authoritarian mentality, the proliferation of competing discourses on the role of Confucianism in the public and political spheres—from civil religion to constitutional political design—went beyond reactionary sentiments.[22] In this context, Liu Xiaofeng's Straussian interpretation of Confucianism has been described as "speculative," lacking a clearly expressed theoretical basis in Confucian canon and practice. My study aims to situate Liu and mainland Confucians within a shared agenda to rejuvenate a muscular form of religious piety toward "Chinese antiquity"—a coherent system of Confucian scriptures, rituals, and mythologies. They both reserved particular ire for the secularist myopia of the May Fourth generation, which transformed Confucian literature from sacred "scripture" (*jing* 經) to "history" (*shi* 史) and "historical data" (*shiliao* 史料), sowing the seeds of "nihilism and relativism." Above all, this concerted assault on the ideal of a wholly secularized society urges us to acknowledge that

---

20. See Angle, "The Adolescence of Mainland New Confucianism."

21. For a comprehensive overview of contemporary Chinese Confucianism, see Makeham, *Lost Soul*; for a critical analysis, see Dirlik, "Confucius in the Borderlands"; for the question of national learning, see Schneider, "Bridging the Gap."

22. See Jiang Qing, *A Confucian Constitutional Order*; Ming Chen, "On Confucianism as a Civil Religion."

China's conservative trends are not simply an atavistic revolt against the West. Instead, the minds of the Liu-like intellectuals have been consistently shaped by Western academic discourses, from the postcolonial decentering of the West to the postmodern "suspicious hermeneutic"[23] toward reason and progress.

Finally, Liu Xiaofeng's Straussian undertaking was informed by the powerful resurgence of authoritarian political theology in the postsecular West. Here, Liu deployed the term "political theology" in a generic sense to describe the quasi-religious dimension of secular political authority. Secularization for political theologians was a double movement punctuated by the occupation of religion by politics as the fundamental form of modern collective identity on the one hand, and the persistent haunting of the secular political order by theological values and concepts on the other.[24] In the political sphere, the "normative deficit of modernity" has prompted Carl Schmitt to repudiate Weberian rationalization for reducing the modern state to a hollow machine. For the anti-liberal jurist who believed that a mystic-auratic leadership was indispensable to the fundamental existence of the Weimar Republic, the decisionistic intrusion of a charismatic sovereign outperforms quantitative and technical electoral politics in the midst of war and revolution.[25] A century after Schmitt first coined the notorious term "political theology," discussions of political theology have metamorphosed beyond the dark legacy of vitalist-spiritual leadership and moved toward a generalized skepticism about the Whiggish narrative of modern rationalism. In response to the upsurge of religious fundamentalism in the postsecular world, critics frequently castigated the secularist myopia of liberal pluralism: "deontological liberalism," which prioritizes right over good, is nourished by presuppositions that it cannot itself secure.[26] To compensate for the liberal state's failure to offer a robust defense of its norms, champions

---

23. See Felski, "Suspicious Minds."
24. See Santner, *The Royal Remains*, xii; Kahn, *The Future of Illusion*, 1–22.
25. Schmitt, *Political Theology*; for elaborations on the question of modernity's normative deficit, see Gordon, "Critical Theory between the Sacred and the Profane," 469.
26. See Sandel, *Liberalism and the Limits of Justice*, 1.

of enlightenment therefore proposed to reintroduce religious sources of authority, affiliation, and community as a moral-political remedy for our postsecular age.[27]

As an avid reader of Western political theology, Liu Xiaofeng mobilized these discourses to develop powerful new visions of a Chinese politico-religious state. Whereas scholars of European thought use "shared horizons"[28] to illuminate the manifold interactions and affinities among these German thinkers, I use "transformed horizons" to describe Liu's cross-cultural engagement with religion. Sharing the Western concern with the question of divine nexus, Liu nevertheless reoriented these theological discussions toward causes that were not endorsed by their authors. Liu repeatedly emphasized that his reading was irresistibly marked by a particular "problematic"—a Chinese consciousness was always already inscribed in his exposition of Western theology.[29] This creative appropriation goes beyond the mere "reception" and "globalization" of ideas, into the recontextualization of political theology into post-Mao Chinese intellectual debates.[30] It requires examining both the inner coherence of the concepts and the Chinese context that transforms theological passions toward different ends.

In the following, I focus on the three main stages of Liu's intellectual development: early Romanticism in the 1980s, transitional Straussian conversions in the post-Tiananmen era, and finally Maoism at the millennium turn. At first, Liu prioritized Christian transcendence to refute the sublime myth of revolution. But he was soon caught up in the radical gulf that separates Chinese culture from the Judeo-Christian tradition. In the second stage, Strauss's thesis on the quarrels between the ancients and the moderns liberated Liu and his conservative acolytes from their schizophrenic stance between Chinese cultural tradition and Western values. It further enabled Liu to undermine the

---

27. See Habermas, *An Awareness of What Is Missing*, 15–23.
28. See Gordon, *Rosenzweig and Heidegger*, xix.
29. See Liu Xiaofeng, *Xiandaixing shehuililun xulun*, 3.
30. For a critique of the reception paradigm, see Derman, *Max Weber in Politics and Social Thought*, 4–8; for a study of the globalization of Schmitt, see Müller, *A Dangerous Mind*, 219–44.

cognitive achievement of enlightenment in the name of a return to antiquity. This reversal further led to the rise of a neoconservative agenda to revive China's Confucian heritage against "nihilistic" May Fourth values. In the final stage, Liu proposed to refurbish a "Confucian Mao"—a conservative transvaluation of Maoist ideals—as a mythic-muscular form of political leadership to provide spiritual solidarity for the divided Chinese nation. Each episode reveals how Liu's vehement thirst for transcendence fueled his searches for ancient, medieval, and modern forms of divine nexus, and how these politico-theological doctrines in turn framed his changing visions of the Chinese political order in the post-Mao era.

Early Romanticism

Most post-Mao conservatives had been ardent revolutionaries. Liu Xiaofeng was no exception. He was born in 1956 into a petty-bourgeois family outside Chongqing, a southwest hinterland remote from coastal metropolitan centers. There he experienced the heightened revolutionary passions, factional infighting, and rampant violence of the Cultural Revolution. The Red Guard movement was particularly violent in this cultural backwater, with over twelve hundred deaths in the vicious factional warfare in Chongqing alone.[31] The spiraling cycle of bloodshed was masterminded by none other than Mao and his leftist acolytes, whose radical policy of arming the Left led to the widespread use of rifles, grenades, and even heavy artillery and tanks in the clashes between conservatives and rebel fighters. Although Liu was too young to participate in the Red Guard organizations, the magnitude of the tumult left a deep mark. With his own eyes, the boy witnessed prolonged and deadly armed battles in his neighborhood, usually with heavy casualties.[32] From then on, Liu was haunted by a vexing web of uneasy feelings toward Mao's apocalyptic revolution: passion mixed with fear, freedom tainted by violence, and a messianic yearning for a sublime cause beyond all flimsy matters.

31. Guobin Yang, *The Red Guard Generation*, 18.
32. Liu Xiaofeng, "Jilian Dongniya," 43.

The Red Guard rebellion came to a dramatic halt after two years in 1968, when Mao waged a new national campaign known as Up to the Mountains, Down to the Countryside (*Shangshan xiaxiang* 上山下鄉) to dispatch urban students to settle in China's vast rural areas. Under the Chairman's instruction to rusticate urban youths, Liu was sent to labor in a nearby village after graduating from high school. He and his cohort were able to return to the city to resume their education in 1977, one year after Mao's death. In 1978, Liu enrolled as a German literature major at Sichuan Foreign Language University in Chongqing. Upon graduation, he entered Peking University in 1982 to study German Romanticism with prominent aestheticians such as Zong Baihua, Yue Daiyun, and Hong Qian. In the early 1980s, intellectual circles in Beijing were marked by boisterous crazes for a new enlightenment to rebuild China's cultural and spiritual values. Political uncertainties unleashed a burst of intellectual synergism, a mode of inquiry that imported divergent theories of modernity for the postsocialist cultural renewal. In conjunction with the efforts of the reformist leadership to contain the excessive cult of Mao, Chinese intellectuals inaugurated a series of "cultural reflections" to address the human abuses, mass violence, and other forms of severe social injustice conducted in the frenzy of Maoism. From the surge of scar literature to the debate on Marxist humanism and the "high-culture fever," the multivalent liberal assaults on Mao's legacy—the cult of personality, ultraleftist violence, and ideological fanaticism—sought to dethrone the omnipresent revolutionary leader from the cultural arena. Advocates of secular humanism fulminated against the religious aura of Mao as a remnant of "feudalistic superstition." The attitude of "great refusal" was manifested in the motto of the acclaimed poet Bei Dao 北島 (1949-)—"I—do—not—believe"—which deplored the dehumanizing dogmas of Maoism that exploited sacred sentiments toward vicious ends.

Motivated by the humanists' call for a return to bourgeois normalcy, Liu penned elegant essays on Schelling and Schlegel, alongside humanistic critiques of revolutionary violence. Notably, the German Romantics' search for a "beautiful soul" inspired Liu to reclaim a refined bourgeois interiority. Liu conceived of the interior as the locus of authentic selfhood, a realm that nourishes transcendental beauty against the degraded exteriority characterized by torture, deceit, and enmity. For Liu's cohort, bourgeois privacy was endowed with an emancipatory promise to break away from the tyranny of Maoist collectivism. Thus, in his bold rereading of Nikolai Ostrovsky's (1904–1936) red classic *How the Steel Was Tempered*, Liu described the protagonist Pavel Korchagin as driven not only by revolutionary passion but also by an instinctual, almost erotic desire, toward Tonia Toumanova, an elegant girl from the old Ukrainian aristocracy. After Pavel's conversion into a "socialist new man," however, he is determined to break up with Tonia. Liu was shocked by how Pavel deploys rude revolutionary language to humiliate his former lover: for the Bolshevik fighter, Tonia's beauty and glamor, her gentle and magnanimous temper, are now nothing but morbid "bourgeois mannerisms." For Liu, Pavel's revolutionary zeal generates as much iconoclastic momentum as malicious pleasure in destruction. By contrast, Liu saw in Tonia's fall an archetype of classical tragedy, a pure heart and rare beauty devoured by the demonic revolution.[33]

To be sure, the expression of bourgeois sentimentalism was one of the major motifs of the New Enlightenment. From Dai Houying's 戴厚英 (1938–1996) bestseller "Humanity, Ah Humanity" ("Ren a ren" 人啊，人！) (1980) to Liu Binyan's 劉賓雁 (1925–2006) reportage "Between Man and Monster" ("Ren yao zhijian" 人妖之間) (1979), the indictment that "all revolutions devour their own children" was characteristic of the soul-searching mood poignantly presented in the humanist literature at the turn of the 1980s. But what distinguished Liu's tone from the optimism of the humanist writers was his gloomy vision of human finitude. For instance, he frequently invoked the term "the fragility of existence" to describe the dependency and venerability of human existence that rest on groundless conditions after the collapse of religion.[34] Here, Heidegger's evident influence was accompanied by a shocked awareness of the insufficiency of secular vocabularies to describe the violent apocalypse conjured by Mao's revolution.[35] In Liu's perspective, the mass atrocities of the Mao era nullify any possibilities

---

33. Liu Xiaofeng, "Jilian Dongniya," 40–52.
34. Liu Xiaofeng, "Xushi yu lunli," 1–11.
35. For an account of the reception of Heidegger's philosophy in the 1980s, see Zha Jianying, *Bashiniandai fangtanlu*, 166–245.

of humanity, progress, and liberation. By declaring that idealism could no longer be redeemed, Liu articulated an apocalyptic sensibility, indeed a yearning for a redemption that would only come through a divine being beyond human reason.

The split between Liu and the advocates of humanism began to take more concrete shape in the subsequent debate over the question of aesthetic transcendence. By the middle of the decade, an aesthetic fever was sweeping across Chinese universities, creating tensions between orthodox Marxists and the young generation. As discussed in chapter 1, the Kantian-Marxist aesthetician Li Zehou coined the term "cultures of pleasure" to highlight the cultivation of natural and secular emotions at the origin of Confucian aesthetics. Liu, however, was dissatisfied with Li's penchant for this-worldly pleasure. He wished to clear the fog of secular reasoning that tethered aesthetics to certain material, sensuous bases. In contrast to Li's Marxist emphasis on the ontology of social beings, Liu developed an "ontology of poetry" (*shi de bentilun* 詩的本體論) to define a transcendental aesthetic realm.[36] Once again, Liu's notion of the "poetic self" betrayed his fascination with German Romantic poets. The poetic capacity for moral meaning and aesthetic judgment could overcome Kantian rigorism. For Liu, the whole purpose of aesthetic cultivation was to uplift oneself onto the transcendental realm of art and beauty.

Liu's thirst for transcendence beyond historical reasoning gradually drove him to embrace the transcendent God of the Bible as the true source of the sacred. Following the path of the German Romantics, he came to realize that the poetic self was, after all, predicated on the archetypal divine person, a theological linkage between the infinite God and its incarnation in finite humanity. Christian transcendence points to an ultimate ground for human existence far beyond flimsy humanism. At this moment, Liu's engagement with Western faith traditions was motivated by the absence of a transcendental deity in Confucianism. Etymologically speaking, the Confucian term "religion" (*jiao* 教) connotes the teaching of rituals (*lijiao* 禮教) that edifies the political

---

36. Liu Xiaofeng, *Shihua zhexue*.

regime through moral education.³⁷ As chapter 1 shows, the Confucian preoccupation with the politics and ethics of this world led to a distinctive emphasis on the aesthetic inculcation of secular humanity in the May Fourth discourse on aesthetics. But Liu's yearning for religious transcendence ran decidedly against the May Fourth aesthetician Cai Yuanpei's call to replace religion with aesthetic education. The young iconoclast believed that the rationalist ideal of aesthetic cultivation risked losing sight of religious transcendence beyond the secular world.

In 1988 Liu published his second monograph, *Salvation and Easiness* (*Zhengjiu yu xiaoyao* 拯救與逍遙), a bold call to cast off Sino-Western cultural differences in order to confront the more fundamental question of ultimate values. In a prefatory remark, Liu refuted the predominant assumption shared by Chinese aestheticians since the May Fourth era that Confucian-Daoist aesthetics provide a unique spiritual ontology to overcome Western industrial modernity.³⁸ In Liu's judgment, the May Fourth generation was naïve to assume that a combination of Daoist naturalism and Confucian ethics could resolve the spiritual crisis of modernity. To mistake scientific rationality for Western modernity, Liu contended, was the cardinal error of this cultural nationalism that completely bypassed the Judeo-Christian tradition of the West. Most importantly, Liu believed that if transcendence were tethered to a specific cultural form, then ultimate value ceased to be ultimate. On this view, fundamental values would seem to acquire a universal appeal beyond specific cultural forms. Liu suggested that if all human beings by their very nature thirst for ultimate meaning above culture, then the Confucian-Daoist tradition must emulate Christianity to point beyond secular moral cultivation and political ethics.

To explain the spiritual lacuna of the Confucian-Daoist tradition, Liu offered a seminal reading of the lyrics composed by Qu Yuan 屈原 (c. 340–278 BCE)—the high minister of the southern kingdom Chu. After being deposed from his official post, Qu wrote sober and melancholic essays to reflect on his tortured partnership with the ill-fated Chu regime. Liu puzzled over Qu's enigmatic *Heavenly Questions* (*Tianwen*

---

37. See Chen Xiyuan, "Zongjiao."
38. Liu Xiaofeng, *Zhengjiu yu xiaoyao*, 1–39.

天問), which comprises ontological questions concerning the origin of the cosmos and the mysteries of Heaven and Earth. He argued that Qu's quest for cosmological questions represented his utter despair over the Confucian ideal of benevolent rule. Ideally, literati gain moral edification by serving under a virtuous and competent regime. Higher morality is attainable only if they provide political service to the sage-king, who is the incarnation of the heavenly way. Hence, Qu's despair derives from his loss of touch with Heaven after his political banishment. Wandering through mountains, marshes, and rivers, Qu turns to nature and cosmos to look for alternative ways to communicate with the divine. Tragically, the Confucian emphasis on the sage-king as the sole transmitter of the divine prevented Qu from finding salvation beyond political service. His eventual suicide revealed the inability of Confucian literati to secure transcendence outside of secular politics.

If Confucianism fails to provide answers for salvation, a Daoist withdrawal into nature seems to be an important, though less exhilarating, alternative. Liu proceeded to examine the critical term "easiness" (*xiaoyao* 逍遙) in Daoist aesthetics, which has provided ultimate values for the disillusioned literatus-turned-hermit in Chinese history. According to Liu, easiness has its origin in the Daoist "pleasure principle": the desire to secure this-worldly pleasure as the sole purpose of life. Relative to the Confucian rectification of pleasure into moral-political ends, Daoist pleasure is more of an entity in itself, one that is transhistorical and transmoral. In Daoism, the self's sensorial, emotional, and spiritual autonomy harmonizes with cosmological movements. In this regard, hermitism provides a spiritual haven. However, Liu noted that the Daoist assurance of "easiness," which locates transcendence within the mundane world, is almost diametrically opposed to the Christian notion of salvation through Christ. In the end, when salvation is attainable through the appreciation of the secular, the quest for transcendence dissolves into the moral affirmation of this-worldly existence.

The lacuna of Daoist aesthetics remained clear for Liu: when the rebellion against moral-political cultivation is transformed into an appreciation of the state of nature, Daoism completes, rather than negates, the Confucian quest for human perfection in the profane realm.

Furthermore, Liu chastised the perfectionist underpinning of Confucian-Daoist aesthetics as an ossified tradition devoid of transcendence. Since humanity has the capacity to reach perfection through moral cultivation and political governance, human beings can acquire that knowledge of the good without divine guidance. By contrast, Liu eulogized the Christian notion of sin, which for him promised salvation in most extraordinary ways: "Sinfulness is the primary linkage through which humanity is related to God. It makes men realize the insufficiency as well as the depravity of their natural state. Only through salvation can the sinner return to God" (罪感恰恰是把人與上帝重新聯繫起來的第一個環節，使人意識到自己的自然狀態實際上是不自足的，自然狀態就是淪落狀態。淪落要走向贖回，罪人只有回到上帝身邊才能重生).[39] In Protestantism, the existential phenomenon of guilt makes humanity realize that imperfection is the essential structure of the profane world. This ontological priority of sin in turn establishes Christian faith as the only source of transcendence. In this regard, Liu insists that Christian redemption dwarfs all forms of Confucian-Daoist perfections precisely because of its acknowledgment of human imperfection.

With a single metaphysical leap, Liu traversed the ground separating Confucian-Daoist tradition and Christianity and prioritized the latter's exclusive relationship to the divine. This iconoclastic reading betrayed his profound frustration with the lack of other-worldly ethics in Chinese cultural traditions. Notwithstanding his impressionistic understanding of Christian faith,[40] Liu's unbounded synergism carried iconoclastic messages. His passion for God—the unconditional truth of divine revelation, the insurmountable gulf between humanity and the divine, and the aversion to historical reasoning—sprang out of serious

---

39. Liu Xiaofeng, *Zhengjiu yu xiaoyao*, 158.

40. Critics have questioned Liu's Christian faith because Liu approached his topic primarily through the works of Max Scheler, Søren Kierkegaard, and Fyodor Dostoevsky, rather than a direct engagement with biblical scriptures. As Fredrik Fällman puts it, "for Liu and his generation the Bible is not primarily a daily source of spiritual comfort, but a foundation for their spiritual journey" (Fällman, "Hermeneutical Conflict?," 58). Liu's Christian belief could not be taken as an acceptance of biblical authority, but as an open-ended interpretation at the boundary of faith and reason.

reflections on the wrongdoings of Maoist political religiosity. Liu needed to completely abandon Confucian-Daoist tradition precisely because he was concerned about the trajectory from Chinese perfectionism to Mao's socialist utopia. In the face of a contaminated Chinese tradition, Liu nourished a longing for redemption through an utterly transcendent God. However, his fundamentalist thirst for ultimacy—that which alone redeems and salvages humanity—gradually reoriented him toward political theology.

From Cultural Christian to Chinese Straussian

In the years following the 1989 Tiananmen incident, the Chinese intellectual space was in the midst of a large-scale transition. The 1980s utopian passion for a humane socialism evaporated quickly in the wake of the conservative backlash against reform. The shock of the bloody crackdown, combined with a fear that the party was reviving Leninist ideological indoctrination, provoked anger among Beijing's cultural vanguard. From 1992 onward, Deng Xiaoping's Southern Tour reinvigorated the market reform and prompted many establishment intellectuals to "dive into the sea"—that is, engage in profit-driven, lowbrow cultural production. The disorienting tempos of market-Leninism compelled academic elites to search for a new normative value beyond the 1980s enlightenment project. At mid-decade, new currents of thought produced heated exchanges on the concept of civil society and incremental reforms, on the revival of Confucianism and national learning, on the waning halo of the humanist spirit, and on the return of the Mao cult. These debates illustrated how the question of fundamental values acquired new urgency in the face of surging consumerism and authoritarianism.

Liu left for Switzerland in 1989 to pursue a PhD in Christian theology at the University of Basel. He returned to Hong Kong in 1993 as a research fellow at the Chinese University of Hong Kong. Categorizing himself as a cultural Christian, Liu softened his earlier iconoclasm, and turned to advocating Christian ethics as moral instruction for the contemporary Chinese society. The term "cultural Christian" is moderate insofar as it enables Chinese intellectuals to study Christian theology without converting to Christianity.⁴¹ This ambivalence on Liu's part bespoke a desire for religious reasoning on the one hand and a caution against organized religion on the other. Liu's advocacy for a culturalist orientation of religion was usually associated with a larger intellectual trend known as Sino-Christian theology. Beginning in the early 1990s, scholars of Christian studies created theology journals, conferences, and study programs to discuss the normative potential of religion in the post-Marxist public sphere. This broad coalition attempted to resolve the crisis of humanistic value by invoking theological insights. Proponents argued that a theological passion for truth beyond secular reason provided a robust moral grounding to counter the disorienting tempo of globalization. Chinese humanities must remain open to a "nonreligious religion" because theological methodology points toward a path to secure the certainty of meaning against postmodern encroachment.⁴²

Yet Liu's relationship with the major motif of the cultural Christian movement was fraught with tensions. In Liu's judgment, the designation of Christianity as a culture adhered to a liberal rationalist theology whose historical reasoning nullified the absoluteness of faith. Chinese theologians since the republican era have sought to "indigenize" the divine personality of Jesus to bring biblical teachings closer to the Confucian tradition. This contextual theology often associates God with the Mandate of Heaven and reads Jesus as a Confucian saint, thus transforming divinity into morality, and turning redemption into sanctification. Liu criticized the contextual theology for reducing Christian faith to Confucian ethics. For him, Sino-Christian theology, which denotes the merely historicist reception of the divine, must "unlearn" its specific cultural forms in order to attain a transhistorical relationship with the self-unveiling God.⁴³ In a landmark essay titled "Sino-Christian Theology and the Philosophy of History," Liu took a radical departure from the cultural-historical approach in order to embrace the absolute, transcendental, and unconditional truth of revelation. In

---

41. See Liu Xiaofeng, "Wenhua jidutu xianxiang de shehuixue pingzhu"; Starr, *Chinese Theology*, 244.
42. See Starr, *Chinese Theology*, 240–62.
43. See Liu Xiaofeng, "Hanyushenxue yu lishizhexue," 102–4.

this passionate manifesto, Liu urged his fellow Chinese Christians to "abandon [their] obsession with 'indigenization' and 'Sinicization'" in order to "confront the Christ Event" (*zhimian jidu shijian* 直面基督事件)—the miraculous birth, death, and resurrection of the Savior. For Liu, who firmly believed that "divine revelation transcends all national-historical categories," any culturalist tendency to illustrate the Christ Event with Chinese examples would collapse the boundary between "the word of God" (*shenyan* 神言) and "the word of man" (*renyan* 人言).[44]

In many ways, Liu's critique was inspired by the crisis (*Krisis*) theology of the Weimar theologian Karl Barth (1886–1968), who contended that the liberal-historicist approach to religion risks closing the gulf between humanity and God. In his most iconic outcry, Barth argued that true faith rests on the conviction that "God is God."[45] As Peter Gordon forcefully argues, Barth made a critical distinction between two forms of revelation: revelation as an experience and revelation as an event. The theologian dismissed the experience as the "merely human reception of divine intelligence" and hailed the theological importance of the event as the "self-unveiling of god."[46] From this perspective, the liberal Protestant advocacy for an anthropological interpretation of Christian doctrine rested on a sacrilegious confusion between experience and event and sowed the seeds of relativism. To assert the primacy of divine self-revelation, Barth declared that one must embrace an utterly transcendent God above and beyond the realm of historical criticism.

Hailing Barth as the greatest Christian theologian since Martin Luther, Liu followed Barth's call to clear away historical reasoning and affirm the unconditional truth of the divine. Sino-Christian theology is relativistic not only because it anchors the eternal on a specific cultural form, but also due to its erroneous emphasis on the human interpretation of divine intelligence. Furthermore, Barth's qualitative distinction between God and man provided Liu with a powerful criticism of the quasi-religious lure of socialist utopianism that had sustained the sacred

---

44. Liu Xiaofeng, "Hanyushenxue yu lishizhexue," 99–100.
45. Barth, *The Epistle to the Romans*, 11.
46. Gordon, "Weimar Theology," 159.

appeals of Mao's secular revolution. In a critical introduction to the theology of Barth, Liu declared that the Barthian motto "God is God" could serve as a trenchant critique of the scandalous liaisons between other-worldly sentiments and this-worldly political authoritarianism throughout modern Chinese history:

> The twentieth century was characterized by endless waves of social movements. Taking certain "isms" as their ideological foundation, these social and political movements strove to arouse sentiments of sacredness by claiming to realize a perfect society in this world. Such a sacred cause enchanted secular politics with messianism and mobilized millions of people to devote their lives for these utopian projects. Yet from West to East, the sacralization of this-worldly causes and secular political authority led to a succession of catastrophes.
> 二十世紀是一個社會政治運動層出不窮的世紀。這些社會政治運動往往以某某「主義」為思想基礎，以追求真理、實現人和此世的理想為目的，並竭力把自身神聖化。被神聖化了的世俗理想和世俗運動誘發了千百萬人的生命激情，激勵起無數志士仁人為之奮鬥和獻身，發動無知的群眾為之所用。可以說，把此世的作為、此世的權威、此世的運動神聖化乃是二十世紀的一大特徵。然而，不管在西方還是東方，這些被神聖化了的、自詡擁有絕對真理的此世作為、此世權威、此世運動恰恰是人世災難的根源。47

To manipulate the divine for the purposes of secular political persuasion, as both Liu and his cultural Christians believed, was the cardinal error of the Cultural Revolution. Many had written about the quasi-religious halo of Mao at the height of revolutionary frenzy: his "thought" inspired spiritual salvation, his *Little Red Book* was treated as the "Chinese Bible," his portrait brought divine miracles, and his "traveling mangos" became a sacred relic of worship nationwide.[48] In his memoir, Liu recounted how zealous Red Guards in Chongqing, including thousands of teenagers filled with strong sentiments, rushed

---

47. Liu Xiaofeng, "Shangdi jiushi shangdi," 45; for an excellent interpretation of how the Cultural Revolution has decidedly influenced Liu's understanding of Barth, see Guan, "Ping Liu Xiaofeng de hanyu jidushenxue," 237–38.

48. See Landsberger, "Mao as the Kitchen God."

to the street to demonstrate their will to sacrifice themselves for Mao's sacred cause. Yet, as ideological hysteria spiraled into violence, Mao's revolution turned against its own children. Recalling a funeral that he had attended after a bloody factional warfare, Liu poignantly discovered that the "revolutionary martyr" was only a high school girl. "Her fragrant lip should have been expecting tender kisses," he wrote with agony, "but all ended as several bullets shot through her chest."[49] In Liu's judgment, the enormous human costs of revolution revealed Mao's promise of redemption to be an illusion if not a lie. Furthermore, it illustrated how the language of the sacred had become so corrupted by the Maoist ideological manipulation that any genuine passion for God risked collapsing into a dubious glorification of Mao as the savior of the people.

Whereas the experience of profound immersion in the sacred and rigid doctrine of Maoism compelled other cultural Christians to search for a rationalist exposition of the Bible rather than a religious devotion to it,[50] Liu became more convinced that only a "true God"—one who is not tainted by any secular, natural, and profane associations—would rescue the Chinese from their misguided pursuit of Maoist utopia.[51] Precisely because Maoist fanaticism drew its strength from "the sacralization of this-worldly political authority," Liu proposed that all this-worldly categories be discarded—including culture, language, history, and human reason—in favor of bowing before a true divine. Thus, Liu interpreted "God is God" as a warning that any attempts to transgress the boundary between the sacred and the mundane risk regressing into the political religion of Maoism.

However, the Barthian extremism of absolute transcendence came into conflict with Liu's desire to affirm the worldly manifestation of the

---

49. Liu Xiaofeng, "Jilian Dongniya," 46.

50. As Starr points out, Chinese cultural Christians saw a dubious affinity between Maoist ideological indoctrination and Christian liturgy. The residual distaste for organized worship turned them away from church theology and toward the academic study of religion. See Starr, *Chinese Theology*, 244.

51. Sun Yi typologizes two forms of Sino-Christian theology in the post-Mao era: while the majority of cultural Christians adopted a cultural-humanist interpretation of Christian theology, Liu Xiaofeng's approach was characterized by an ontological affirmation of the absoluteness of God. See Sun Yi, "Hanyu shenxue yu 'jidu shijian.'"

Christian divine in the Chinese-speaking world. In any case, God must encounter and forge a bond with man in a way man can recognize, experience, and cherish. If God does not reveal himself in secular history and his message is not perceptible to the Chinese people, how could salvation be possible at all? After all, the eventual unintelligibility of divine grace was incompatible with Liu's anxious attempt to recuperate a religious remedy for the disenchanted postrevolutionary world. Furthermore, just as Barth's disdain for secular-historical categories ironically led him toward a Manichean vision of history—a mechanistic, soulless world lacking any divine guidance[52]—Liu must have realized that his thirst for an utterly transcendent God risked falling into Gnostic occultism, thereby paradoxically acknowledging, rather than rebelling against, the nihilistic nature of the profane.

If a true divinity is too remote to provide any instructions for secular living, then the descent into political theology—the investment of secular politics with the charisma of sacred authority—becomes a viable, though dangerous, option. Whereas Barth, confronting the rising tide of the pro-Nazi German Christian movement in the 1930s, still cleaved to the "one Word of God" and rejected any allegiance to "events, powers [and] historical figures," Liu was unwilling to retreat into inner emigration and cordoned off religion within the private sphere.[53] At this moment, Leo Strauss provided new inspiration. Reading Strauss as early as 1993, Liu was instantly gripped by his "unremitting efforts to fight against nihilism and relativism."[54] It nevertheless took him more than a decade to spawn a Chinese Straussian school. Liu's radical turn is surprising in that he ceased to write about Christian faith after confronting Strauss. Moreover, Strauss not only dispelled Liu's illusions about re-enchanting the world through a transcendent God, but also led him back to affirm Maoist political religiosity.

The reasons for Liu's further shift from Christian faith remain unclear. I suggest that Strauss's preoccupation with the "theologico-political predicament" provided vital ammunition for Liu to reconsider

---

52. Gordon, "Weimar Theology," 158.
53. Quoted in Gordon, "Weimar Theology," 172.
54. Liu Xiaofeng, *Shitelaosi de lubiao*, 1–2.

the Barthian dilemma between God and man.⁵⁵ Although Strauss shared Barth's zeal for sustaining the radical otherness of God, he was more concerned with how to restore and live with the fragile balance between human knowledge and divine revelation. For the Weimar émigré, medieval thinkers were confronted with the powerful forces of orthodox religion unknown to the classical world. The irresolvable tension between Athens (philosophy) and Jerusalem (revelation) compelled Abu Nasr Muhammad al-Farabi (870–950) and Maimonides (1138–1204) to develop a double idiom that publicly conformed to religious law while still hinting at philosophical truths. In contrast to them, modern intellectuals taking their cues from Niccolo Machiavelli and Thomas Hobbes explicitly transgressed the boundary between philosophy and politics and installed their vision of mass democracy as a coercive social norm. The pursuit of immediate political goals eventually turned philosophy into a weapon and an instrument.⁵⁶ Through Strauss, Liu criticized the prototypical May Fourth iconoclast who, without realizing the fundamental difference between the truth claims of politics and philosophy, plunged into a succession of dangerous ideological doctrines and totalistic political beliefs ranging from revolution to enlightenment. As a former liberal humanist who had been traumatized by the powerlessness of the Chinese intelligentsia during the June Fourth crackdown, Liu praised the outward political docility of medieval thinkers as an art of balancing between the quest for wisdom and subordination under the law. Against the reckless demands of the modern, Liu held esotericism as a higher form of morality, a passion for timeless philosophical truth beyond political squabbles.⁵⁷

Hence, Strauss turned Liu's attention increasingly away from Barth's absolutist idea of religion and to the role of the philosopher in a world devoid of transcendence. Most importantly, how should Chinese thinkers negotiate the murky boundary between philosophy and politics under political authoritarianism? According to Strauss, heterodox thinkers of the Middle Ages had evaded political persecution by

---

55. Strauss, "Preface to the English Translation," 1.
56. Strauss, *On Tyranny*, 22–105; for an analysis, see Wurgaft, *Thinking in Public*, 65–88.
57. Liu Xiaofeng, *Shitelaosi de lubiao*, 11–85.

"writing between the lines," that is, by deliberately deploying rhetorical artifices including senseless repetitions, strange distractions, and misleading quotations, all of which served as "awakening stumbling blocks" that confused the censor while indicating to the "trustworthy and intelligent" pupils of philosophy the presence of secret messages. Strauss presupposes a vast gulf between a thoughtless and potentially hostile crowd and a secret, self-selective "republic of letters" tied together by the love of wisdom. Addressing both "the vulgar masses" and "the gentlemen," an esoteric thinker skillfully writes double-talk: a "popular teaching of an edifying character" that conforms to public decorum, and a "philosophical teaching concerning the most important subject" meant to guide the identification and formation of an intellectual elite.[58] In a word, resistance to the all-intrusive, ever-interfering rule of the polis is "the minoritarian affair of a few 'thoughtful men'" rather than the popular reaction of the downtrodden.[59]

Echoing Straussian hermeneutics, Liu contended that esotericism was deeply rooted in classical Chinese philosophical tradition before the advent of May Fourth nihilism. Strauss's minute scrutiny of old books inspired Liu to excavate the ancient Gongyang School (*Gongyang xuepai* 公羊學派), a heterodox Confucian theology that originated in the Western Han Dynasty (202 BCE–220 CE). To emphasize the mystical-prophetic aspect of Confucian teaching, Gongyang devotees argued that *Spring and Autumn Annals* (*Chunqiu* 春秋), one of the Five Classics and the earliest surviving Chinese chronicle, was compiled and written by Confucius himself and concealed under a drily factual exterior "subtle words with profound meaning" (*weiyan dayi* 微言大義). Although the *Annals* consist merely of short entries on events such as battles, astronomical phenomena, and diplomatic negotiations, Gongyang exegesis seeks to unveil the sage's moral judgment and political intention behind the eloquence of terse expression and articulate silences.[60] Similar to a Straussian "who reads secular books religiously,"[61] a Gongyang disciple

---

58. Strauss, *Persecution and the Art of Writing*, 36.
59. Abbeele, "The Persecution of Writing," 4.
60. See Wai-yee Li, *The Readability of the Past in Early Chinese Historiography*, 30–31.
61. Dannhauser, "Leo Strauss."

reads *Annals* not as a historical record (*shi* 史) but as a sacred canon (*jing* 經) central to Confucian values and practices. For Liu, the history/canon dichotomy fits neatly into Strauss's distinction between "popular teaching" and "philosophical teaching." Even though Gongyang sectarians held the conviction that Confucius the "uncrowned king" (*suwang* 素王) was destined to rule, they had to hide their advice, judgment, or remonstrance on statecraft beneath brief and cryptic accounts of historical events to avoid public attention. This esoteric literature, as Liu pointed out, harked back to Confucius's claim that the sage would dedicate himself to "transmission, not composition" (*shuer buzuo* 述而不作)—that is, that he would pass down his secret message to a chosen circle of talented men who had the proper dispositions and potential to become philosophical kings.[62]

Obviously, Liu's somewhat arbitrary reading suffers from many weaknesses. Confucius might have had significantly different reasons from Plato for employing indirect expressions. Although both offered pragmatic solutions to mitigate the tension between the thirst for truth and the necessity to comply with the law of the city, Strauss treated the philosopher's love for wisdom as a higher form of virtue. As Daniel Tanguay demonstrates, esoteric writing is for Strauss a tactical retreat designed to preserve the zetetic (inquiry-driven) character of philosophical inquiry against the intrusive law of the polis.[63] In Gongyang teachings, however, virtue is attained only when contemplative learning and political practice are brought together to formulate a "ritual-law" (*lifa* 禮法), an actualization of Confucius's political design. The ritual-law is not a defective imitation of philosophical virtue, but rather plays a decisive role in orienting Confucian literati's pursuit of knowledge. In sharp contrast to Strauss's Socratic-Platonic defense of philosophy as the best way of life, Gongyang scholars sought to restore the Confucian political ideal of the "kingly way" (*wangdao* 王道) through statecraft. Confucius wrote between the lines not because he regarded political conventions as inferior to his philosophical inquiry, but out of frustration at his lifelong failure to find a benevolent king to enact his vision of ideal political order.

62. See Legge, "Wei Ling Kung," 297; Liu Xiaofeng, "Liuyi shengren zan," 162–63.
63. Tanguay, *Leo Strauss*, 7.

Liu's negligence of Strauss's disquieting awareness of the tension between conviction and knowledge has profound consequences. Strauss gestures to religious convictions in exchange for his secret pursuit of eternal truth. Liu, on the other hand, read the subordination of reason under faith as the prerequisite for a stable polity. In this regard, theological values and rituals, regardless of their fictitious nature, could be utilized by philosophers to secure their place in the secular political regime. Liu therefore paid particular attention to Strauss's elucidation of the philosopher-king. In Strauss's reading of Maimonides, the precarious status of philosophy before the biblical law asks for a philosopher-turned-prophet who is a "teacher and governor in one."[64] By practicing prophetology, the prophet creates a divine law that safeguards the civil order and simultaneously justifies his pursuit of philosophy as private knowledge. While it remains unclear whether Strauss himself regards the prophet as capable of producing the perfect kingdom envisioned by Plato, Liu saw parallels between Maimonides's prophet and the Gongyang notion of the "uncrowned king." In support of their vision of a philosopher-king, disciples of the Gongyang School appropriated Daoist mythologies to formulate a theological underpinning for Confucius's divine personality. In particular, Daoist notions, including "Five Elements cosmology" (*wuxing shengke* 五行生剋), "prophetology" (*fuchen zaiyi* 符讖災異), and "divine retribution" (*da fuchou* 大復仇), were introduced to sanctify Confucius as the chosen sage-king. According to Liu, both Maimonides's prophet and the Confucian uncrowned king wielded political theology to justify their exclusive ties to governance.

Yet by returning to the Gongyang exegetic tradition, Liu in fact shifted the meaning of Strauss's esotericism from self-exile into self-empowerment. Following the Gongyang tradition, Liu understood the "esoteric writing" thesis not as the defense of philosophical eros but as the art of constructing myths around the philosopher's own politics and personality. He was fascinated by the late Qing scholar-reformer Kang Youwei, who manufactured diverse political theologies to support his mystical-political vision of a "Confucian religion" (*kongjiao*

---

64. Strauss, *Philosophy and Law*, 120.

孔教). In his radical thesis *Confucius as a Reformer* (*Kongzi gaizhi kao* 孔子改制考) (1897), Kang argued the Gongyang School had been right about Confucius's commitment to restoring the moral-political order of the ancient "three golden ages" (*sandai zhi zhi* 三代之治) at the origin of Chinese civilization. However, Kang contended, latter-day scholars associated with the rival Ancient Text School (*Guwen jingxue* 古文經學) distorted the Confucian canon to authorize a conformist political ideology no longer based on the utopian design of the ancient sage-kings but on the absolute moral authority of the imperial court. To liberate Confucianism from the shackles of the ancient régime and justify himself as the preacher of the master's "true" teaching, Kang adopted various Christian cultic practices in his Confucian Association (*Kongjiao hui* 孔教會) and installed himself as the "archbishop of Confucian religion" (*kongjiao jiaozhu* 孔教教主). The secret message behind Kang's self-mythologizing act, Liu believed, was that theological values and rituals could be utilized for purposes of political persuasion. Like Maimonides's idea of a philosopher-turned-prophet, Kang appropriated the auratic appeal of a Christlike Confucius to justify his exclusive right to speak for the "legitimate transmission of the Way." Rather than subordinating themselves to the imperial court, Kang and his disciples hoped to monopolize the power of "governing through religious cults and civilizing the realm through the gods" (*yi shendao shejiao* 以神道設教). Finally, these attempts at self-mythologization endowed the Confucian literati with a secret mission to "reformulate the political system under the mandate of heaven" (*shouming gaizhi* 受命改制).[65]

Strauss having taught Liu that philosophical life could not be in tune with the demands of politics, why would Liu mobilize esotericism, the art of pursuing eternal wisdom, toward political ends? As Robert Pippin suggests, Strauss "seems mostly concerned with the political problem of philosophy rather than a philosophy of politics."[66] By contrast, Liu responded to Strauss's dilemma precisely by developing a "philosophy of politics," or a political theology that hails the sage-king as able to overcome the insurmountable tension between polis and knowledge once and for all. As Strauss put it, a "sectarian is born" when

---

65. Liu Xiaofeng, "Weishu yu zuopai rujiaoshi," 2.
66. Pippin, "The Modern World of Strauss," 448.

"his 'subjective certitude' of the truth of a solution becomes stronger than the consciousness that he may have of the problematical character of his solution."⁶⁷ Likewise, Liu's dogmatic belief in the necessity of political theology replaced his erstwhile pursuit of transcendence. At this moment, a neoconservative guru was born.

A Conservative Revolution

During the time when Liu was decoding Strauss's teaching, China experienced a decade of sustained economic growth. Popular expectations for China's growing power exploded in a new prosperous era. Intellectual debates, which had been polarized by the neoleftist-versus-neoliberal confrontations in the early 2000s, evolved into complicated engagements with the dream of a world power. Advocates of liberalism introduced Habermas's constitutional patriotism to paint a cosmopolitan future for a pluralistic China. Neoleftists responded by theorizing the "China model" of state-controlled capitalism as a messianic alternative to American neoliberalism. Cultural conservatives, meanwhile, sought to reach beyond these artificial and alien ideologies by returning to China's "civilizational tradition" before the advent of the modern. Here it is important to note the abiding affinity between Liu's newly acquired Straussian classicism and the cultural politics of Chinese conservatives. Although post-Tiananmen conservatives had been supporters of the 1980s reformist consensus, they had grown increasingly uneasy with the atomized individualism of market liberals, which they chastised as vicious nihilism and crass materialism that diminished culture and community. To be sure, members of this group—Confucian revivalists, cultural nationalists, and advocates of political meritocracy—were not Burkean conservatives infatuated with the monarchical or pastoral past. The general tone was cheerful and aggressive, if not chauvinistic. Their cultural hero was Zeng Guofan 曾國藩 (1811–1872)—the quintessentially Chinese Confucian, not Chen Yinke the cosmopolitan.⁶⁸ These "forward-looking" conservatives called for the

---

67. Strauss, *On Tyranny*, 196.
68. See Guo and He, "Reimagining the Chinese Nation."

party-state's muscular intervention into the cultural sphere, restoring the absolute authority of the Confucian-traditionalist doctrine against liberal pluralism.

Overall, the conservative revolt owed its resilience and successes to the fact that it represented a powerful alternative to the radical anti-traditionalism of the liberals and the Left. In the conservative worldview, the May Fourth generation unleased the evil twins of revolution and enlightenment that plunged China into a new dark age. In particular, the anti–May Fourth sentiment animated Confucian revivalists to envision the return of Confucian-civilizational state. The eminent academician Chen Ming 陳明 (1962–) called on his mainland Confucian fellows to break with the liberal-democratic framework of overseas neo-Confucianism and resuscitate Kang Youwei's muscular vision of Confucian theocracy. A moderate variant was developed by Jiang Qing 蔣慶 (1953–), who passionately supported Marxist humanism until 1989, when political turmoil compelled him to search for indigenous sources of political legitimacy. Whereas the mainstream "heart-mind Confucianism" (*xinxing ruxue* 心性儒學) focused on the cultivation of "inner sagehood" (*neisheng* 內聖), Jiang celebrated an "external king-rule" (*waiwang* 外王) that imposed obligatory commandments on the people. Instead of relying on the cultivation of inner moral sensibility, the efficacy of the king-rule is assured by a "Confucian constitutional order" that evokes fear and obedience.[69]

Although the link between Confucian revivalism and Straussian classicism was tenuous at best, the nascent Chinese Straussians quickly jumped onto the bandwagon of cultural nationalism. In the early 2000s, Liu began to collaborate with Gan Yang 甘陽 (1952–), a returnee from Chicago's Committee on Social Thought, to mastermind a "Strauss fever" among the Chinese students of political philosophy. Yet, far from portraying Strauss as an exegete on Platonic philosophy, Chinese Straussians paid particular attention to the "political influence" of Strauss's neoconservative disciples in North America. Ever since the U.S. invasion of Iraq in 2003, a flood of journalistic articles had depicted Strauss, who passed away in 1973, as a Machiavellian mastermind who,

---

69. Jiang Qing, *Zhengzhi ruxue*.

over decades, had secretly built a consortium inside Washington and inspired his disciples to fabricate Platonic "noble lies" to assist imperialist foreign policies like those of George W. Bush. Although the connection between Strauss's immediate students and the White House was grossly exaggerated,[70] Gan Yang suggested that the use of weapons of mass deception deployed in the lead-up to the Iraq war emanated directly from the doctrines of the Straussian school. In Gan's perspective, American Straussians since the 1970s have consistently deployed esotericism to replace the liberal-egalitarian underpinning of the American creed with classical and aristocratic notions. Gan also spoke with special authority about the strictures of "political correctness" imposed by the "tenured radicals" in the humanities, the vulgarizing trend of hedonistic liberalism that contributed to the "closing of the American mind," and—of course—the heroism of the Straussians who defended the foundational principles of Western civilization against all odds.[71] Above all, the powerful rise of American neoconservatism from the cultural wars of the 1980s taught Chinese Straussians a cynical lesson: the ultimate victory belongs to the Straussian Right who stormed the White House rather than the postmodern Left who "marched on the English Department."[72] Echoing Marx's apt formulation that "the weapon of criticism cannot replace the criticism of the weapons,"[73] Gan was determined to look beyond the tempest in an (academic) teapot and resort to realist power politics to realize his civilizational mission. In a word, esotericism for Gan was subordinated to a Nietzschean "will to power."

Predictably, Liu and Gan's didactic Straussian tone dragged them into a succession of schisms with the liberals, but controversies bred attention, and attraction gave rise to an academic cult. Students who

---

70. The interconnectedness between Straussian political thought and neoconservatives in America has been a subject of intense debates. For a polemical interpretation that delineates Strauss's influence on neoconservatism, see Drury, *Leo Strauss and the American Right*; for a critical attempt to disassociate Strauss from the American Right, see Zuckert, *The Truth about Leo Strauss*, 197–227.

71. Gan Yang, *Zhengzhi zheren Shitelaosi*.

72. For a comparison proposed by Todd Gitlin, see Gitlin, *The Twilight of Common Dreams*, 126–65.

73. Marx, "A Contribution to the Critique of Hegel's 'Philosophy of Right,'" 251.

got tired of radical (mostly French) theories were mesmerized by the "prophet" who claimed to reveal esoteric messages to the chosen few. Devotees celebrated Strauss's intellectual supremacy that presumably surpassed those "high priests of democracy" who had fallen from wisdom to preach a compendium of mediocre knowledge. The expanding influence of Chinese Straussians eventually led to the creation of two liberal arts colleges to promote Greco-Roman and Confucian learning at China's flagship universities—Gan's Boya College at Sun Yat-Sen University (2009) and Liu's Center for Classic Studies (2009) at Renmin University. Soon, the Straussian habit of forming dogmatic cliques and indulging in pedagogical narcissism became the object of much criticism, if not ridicule. As critics pointed out, the imperative to enshrine Strauss's intellectual supremacy tended to fill students with contempt for outsiders who had not followed the curriculum of "Great Books" initiated by Chicago University president Robert M. Hutchins in the early 1930s. Yet just as Strauss was scornful of mass education, his self-identified Chinese disciples too were convinced that such an elite consciousness was the necessary step to build a cultural aristocracy within China's state educational system.[74]

Although Liu and Gan could not officially register themselves as Confucian revivalists, they were convinced that Strauss's classicism restored the noble quest for fundamental values against the cultural relativism of the liberals: the glories of the Confucian-imperial model, the importance of "becoming naïve again,"[75] and the basic need to tell right from wrong. Yet this atavistic philosophy could not avoid confronting Mao's legacy. Against the conservative wish to retain the image of an unchanging Chinese cultural heritage untainted by the ugliness of Western modernity, the doctrine of Maoism was ironically the legitimate heir of modern nihilism. The animosities of the earthly peasant Mao toward the Confucian gentry had fostered a populist ideology that pitted the silent majority against the cultural aristocrats throughout the Communist revolution. After 1949, decades of socialist campaigns have further decimated the Confucian meritocratic ideal

74. Gan Yang, *Wenming, guojia, daxue*, 323–37.
75. The term was coined by Werner Joseph Dannhauser. See Dannhauser, "Leo Strauss."

of the "four occupations" (*simin shehui* 四民社會) that privileged the scholar-official above peasants, artisans, and merchants. Even though Deng Xiaoping's reform abandoned Mao's ultraleftist adventure in favor of a developmentalist alternative, Mao's radical egalitarianism is still recognized as a centerpiece of PRC's official ideology. To include or exclude this revolutionary tradition therefore entails contamination on the one hand, and state suppression on the other.

Indeed, Chinese Straussians had no illusions about the modernist, egalitarian, and nihilistic features of Mao's mass democracy. But neither were they prepared simply to negate socialist history as a foreign anomaly. Gan Yang therefore proposed to resuscitate the political mythology of "three heritages" (*santong shuo* 三統說) created by the Gongyang thinker Dong Zhongshu 董仲舒 (179–104 BCE). In his effort to sanctify the ascendance of the Western Han dynasty (202 BCE–9 CE), Dong contended that "a new king must keep safe the heritage of the two [earlier] kings as a means of maintaining the connection of the *santong*" (蓋聞王者必存二王之後所以通三統也).[76] Likewise, according to Gan, Chinese conservatism should incorporate the zeitgeists of the two previous "dynasties"—Mao's socialist egalitarianism and Deng's market reformism—so as to "unify three heritages into a single strand" (*tong santong* 通三統).[77] Nonetheless, this crude appropriation, based on the fantasy that a sanitized Maoism could become the carrier of traditional morality, was utilitarian at best.

If Gan was an opportunist, then Liu proved to be a much more sophisticated intellectual adventurer with a determination to fundamentally alter the horizon for understanding Maoism. In fact, Liu resolved the conservative paradox with a stunning declaration that revolution is restoration. Against the scholarly consensus to associate Mao's egalitarian ethos with the French Revolution, Liu traced the genesis of Mao's radical project to what he called the "Confucian revolutionary spirit."[78] As Liu explained, the term *geming* 革命 (revolution) first appeared in the ancient Chinese classics *I Ching*. While *ge* 革 is deeply imbricated in the ancient ritual of sacrifice, *ming* 命 refers to the mythic

---

76. Quoted in Loewe, *Dong Zhongshu*, 296.
77. Gan Yang, *Tong santong*.
78. Liu Xiaofeng, "Rujia gemingjingshen yuanliukao."

act of transmitting the mandate of the heaven. With the two characters combined, *geming* connotes the symbiotic relationship between political legitimacy and Heaven's will. In Liu's judgment, whereas moderns viewed revolution as a violent break from tradition, Confucian literati believed that revolution, which was guided by cosmological movements, was meant to restore the benevolent rule at the origins of Chinese civilization.[79] With this radical twist in place, Liu further contended that Mao's quest for revolution was motivated by conservative considerations: his utopian socialism derived not from May Fourth antitraditionalism but from "the Confucian belief in human perfectibility, the call for a virtuous ruler, and the conservative defense of Chinese civilization against alien encroachment."[80] Dismissing Western influences as flimsy, Liu viewed Mao's revolution as something that erupted organically from the Confucian search for restoration.

Furthermore, Liu chose to express his commitment to Mao not via philosophical jargon, but as an act of religious conversion. Liu's moment of decision took place in April 2013, four months after the polarized debate on constitutionalism in China. Reformist intellectuals drew inspiration from President Xi Jinping's vision of the "Chinese Dream" and petitioned for the "dream of constitutional governance" in the liberal-leaning newspaper *Southern Weekly*. In response, state propaganda authorities purged top editors of *Southern Weekly* and engineered counterattacks against the liberals' wishful dream.[81] Whereas the crude intervention of the party censor ignited a storm of protests from liberal-minded journalists and activists, the Straussian philosopher, by then still held by many as the spiritual leader of a youth rebellion against Mao, delivered a stunning speech in Beijing to celebrate the socialist patriarch as a mystical and charismatic founding father of the Chinese nation. Liu attributed the "spiritual trauma" of China's twentieth century to the corrosive influence of republicanism—the enlightenment culture of popular sovereignty that diminished spiritual solidarity and led to incessant civil wars. To overcome the fragility of liberal pluralism, Liu proposed to reinstall a fearful and quasi-religious

79. Liu Xiaofeng, *Yimei weijian*, 249–65.
80. Liu Xiaofeng, "Rujia gemingjingshen yuanliukao," 116.
81. See Yuen, "Debating Constitutionalism in China."

sovereign who would bind his subjects into an organic national body. At last, Liu implied that Mao be the perfect candidate for such an earthly God: as the trinity of the uncrowned king, the national founding father, and the revolutionary leader, Mao personified China's centennial civilizational struggle toward a politico-theological "middle kingdom" in the most sublime ways.[82]

Liu's blatant Maoism ignited a storm of controversy. *The Beijing News* (*Xin Jingbao* 新京報) used the Nietzschean phrase "twilight of the idols" to describe the shock and disbelief among Liu's acquaintances, who read the Maoist turn of the iconoclast as a phyco-political drama of a failed Oedipal rebellion ending in the revenge of the [socialist] father.[83] In a widely circulated public letter, the veteran Kant scholar Deng Xiaomang 鄧曉芒 (1948–) rebuked his former friend for confusing politics with aesthetics. In Deng's judgment, Liu's tendency to invest tyranny with metaphysical-auratic appeals reflected a conformist mentality deeply rooted in the "feudalistic tradition" of China's imperial cult.[84] The transnational outreach of Chinese Straussians also attracted Western commentators. The Columbia professor Mark Lilla expressed his confusion toward China's "strange taste" in authoritarian political theology, which he took as an extravagant expression of "tyrannophilia"—the Platonic fantasy of being able to advise the tyrant and produce a perfect regime.[85] Seeing their oracle besieged by the priests of liberalism, Liu's loyal followers quickly defended the Maoist rhetoric as an esoteric form of "ethical" action. Invoking American neocons' defense of Bush's war, Chinese Straussians claimed that it is wise to "lie nobly" in order to conceal the unpleasant truth from the public. Liu's accusers had failed to read between the lines to appreciate the hidden meanings of his provocations.

But cases of the master's hidden insight were hardly the rule. As Tanguay suggests, the extreme artfulness of esoteric writing consists precisely in "making the reader believe that what is most important is always hidden, even though what is essential is very often found on the

---

82. Liu Xiaofeng, *Bainian gonghezhiyi*, 68–95.
83. Wu Yashun, "Ouxiang de huanghun."
84. Deng, "Ping Liu Xiaofeng de xueli."
85. See Lilla, "Reading Strauss in Beijing."

surface of the text."[86] On the surface, Liu's obsession with the question of the founding father certainly bears the imprint of American Straussians who sought to replace Lockean-liberal conceptions of the American founding with classical political virtues. Strauss had associated the Declaration of Independence with classical natural rights that posit a normative and obligatory commandment against the permissive tendency of modern rights.[87] His American disciples further reclaimed a conservative core of American founding, from the crafting of the Constitution as an "educational ascent" designed by virtuous founders,[88] to the embodiment of "ancient faith" in Lincolnian statesmanship.[89] In their reading, the foundational truth of America was said to be characterized by thirsts for political distinction and moral virtue in opposition to the vulgarizing intentions of hedonistic liberalism. Echoing the Straussian revolt against modern egalitarianism, Liu also sought to "excavate" the conservative core of Mao's founding act from the leftist doctrine of mass democracy and proletarian consciousness. Praising Harry Jaffa's bold reinterpretation of Lincoln's ancient political wisdom, Liu asked, how could Chinese scholars reclaim classical political virtues from Mao the founding father?[90]

At first glance, Liu's reconfiguration of Maoism from the conservative tenet was anachronistic at best: Where to locate Mao's so-called ancient political virtues? To answer this question, Liu engaged a lengthy dialogue with the preeminent New Confucian scholar Xiong Shili 熊十力 (1885–1968), who struggled to reconcile Confucian teaching with socialist ideology in the 1950s. Invoking the Confucian vision of "harmonious flows" (chonghe 冲和) as the ultimate condition for the world's disclosure, Xiong endorsed Mao's apocalyptic revolution for

---

86. See Tanguay, *Leo Strauss*, 4; Strauss, *Thoughts on Machiavelli*, 13.

87. Unlike many of his patriotic American disciples, Strauss's view of American politics remained equivocal and hesitant. Although he categorized the American regime as the classical and religious residues of the "first wave of modernity," he was pessimistic about Americans' diminishing political virtue in his reflections of the crisis of liberal education. See Strauss, "What Is Liberal Education?"

88. Berns, *Freedom, Virtue, and the First Amendment*; Diamond, "Democracy and 'The Federalist.'"

89. Jaffa, *Crisis of the House Divided*.

90. Liu Xiaofeng, *Yimei weijian*, 225.

annihilating all political conflicts and bringing greater peace to humanity.[91] Yet while Liu praised Xiong for his Heideggerian effort to "remold the Six Confucian Classics" (*taozhen liujing* 陶甄六經), he sought to refute Xiong's modernist vision of "Confucian socialism." In particular, Liu problematized Xiong's glorification of Mao as a "democratic saint." In Xiong's perspective, Mao the democratic saint is not a formidable sage-king who stands before and above the people, but an egalitarian model that everyone could emulate. The equal opportunity to imitate and become a sage-like Mao thus demonstrates the egalitarian promise of socialism. By contrast, Liu opposed Xiong's claim that "universal wisdom" (*puzhi* 普智) under a democratic ruler could become possible. He warned that the desire to enlist a saint's wisdom into the service of egalitarianism led to the breakdown of distinctions and hierarchies, resulting in an anarchistic state in which "the worthies and the sages disappear in obscurity."[92] The equalizing impulse of Xiong's design inevitably leads to the dissolution of the fundamental differences between the ruler and the ruled, the nobleman and the commoner—distinctions that marked salient features of ancient political virtues.[93] In the end, Liu credited Xiong for coming up with an ingenious design of treating Mao as a sage-king. But he rejected Xiong's socialist egalitarianism by emphasizing Mao's role as a miraculous tyrant who could never be imitated or challenged.

In this circuitous way, Liu's exegesis reveals his conservative reinterpretation of Mao's founding act. Liu was convinced that a fundamental break with China's revolutionary past required a conservative transvaluation of Maoist ideals: the replacement of modern, nihilistic, and egalitarian impulses of revolution with classical, culturalist, and meritocratic values. This project stretched from Liu's etymological investigation of revolution as restoration to his idiosyncratic attempt to identify Confucianism as the indispensable basis for Mao's socialist project. By "discovering" Mao's esoteric conservative impulse, Liu's radical hermeneutics salvaged the Chinese revolution from its dangerous

91. Xiong, *Lun Liujing*.
92. Zhuangzi, "All under Heaven," 425, quoted in Liu Xiaofeng, *Gonghe yu jinglun*, 280.
93. Liu Xiaofeng, *Gonghe yu jinglun*, 74–103.

liaisons with modern egalitarianism. Mao's (mis)adventure was, above all, intended to restore the rule of the sage-king, so one should not let its "occasional" anti-traditionalist elements obscure Mao's role as the carrier of Confucian tradition. The result was a conservative shrine erected around Mao that kept both the liberal and the Left out of reach. This conservative drama recounted how the centennial struggle to actualize a Confucian perfect regime was reduced to a shipwreck by the May Fourth movement of 1919, and sought to return to the primordial status of Chinese religious-political civilization by remolding Mao's revolution as an artificial placeholder for a continuous Confucian cultural tradition.

While American Straussians provided Liu with the means to refurbish the conservative spirit of Mao's founding, Schmitt's teaching injected this founding with a decisionist flavor, accompanied by irrational resentments against liberal values. As John P. McCormick contends, Schmitt endorses the Hobbesian understanding of fear as the primary source of political order: humanity's dangerousness requires the instillation of a fearsome sovereign who could frighten people into subordination.[94] Echoing Jiang Qing's notion of "political Confucianism," Liu also drew the muscular conclusion that only an absolutist "king-rule" (wangzhi 王制) could sustain social cohesion against internal and external threats. For the cynical realist, the painful bickering concerning Mao's rights and wrongs would never produce a decision, and the polarized reactions to a stigmatized national past nullified any substantive defense of the regime's virtue. The historicizing impulse of liberal historiographies on Mao led to sacrilegious acts against the foundational myth of the polis. Whereas liberal historians thought that the unveiling of Maoist catastrophes contributed to societal enlightenment, Liu believed that the less-gifted masses would only take this as a corruption of binding social mores and cultural traditions. In many cases, people need a moralized and sanitized account of the founding father to positively identify themselves with a sacred founding. Schmitt taught Liu that Chinese republicanism always requires a Sorelian myth that invokes "miraculous" decisions to guard

---

94. McCormick, "Fear, Technology, and the State."

the *nomos* of the Earth. Thus Mao could become a sovereign-ruler, a sage-king, and above all, a Chinese *nomos* of cultural confidence and political unity.

Yet Liu's eagerness to refurbish a Confucian Mao remains in many respects historically implausible and philosophically contradictory. Most importantly, the anti-traditionalist facade of Mao proved too difficult to fit into the conservative royal robe that Liu had knitted for him. Liu was forced to conclude that Mao's virtue was a mixture of Confucian political virtue and "modern radicalism,"[95] resulting in incessant "line struggles" (*luxian douzheng* 路線鬥爭) between these two poles. Liu noted that the clashes between the Confucian quest for the king-rule and the modernist search for socialist egalitarianism culminated in the Cultural Revolution. In his arbitrary judgment, Liu suggested that this radical anti-traditional revolution represented Mao's deviation from his pursuit of Confucian virtue into modern egalitarianism. Therefore, the atrocities of the Cultural Revolution were entirely the by-product of the French Enlightenment, and only a return to Mao's ancient political wisdom would do justice to these victims of Western violence.[96] Liu's shabby logic might be apprehended only from his Straussian esotericism: to retrieve Mao's ancient virtue from his nihilistic revolution, the wise must reformulate the tenet of Maoism from the classical perspective without exposing Mao's modern nihilism. Nevertheless, this also proved that Mao's socialist legacies were intertwined with modern nihilism throughout. The nihilistic kernel of Maoism eventually disrupted Liu's conservative revolution.

Leap of Faith

This chapter explores how Liu's passion for religion animated his transition from a cultural Christian into a neoconservative guru. The evolution of Liu's thought might be understood as occurring in three interrelated crises: an inaugural crisis caused by the waning of Maoist utopianism was temporarily resolved by Liu's search for Christian

---

95. Liu Xiaofeng, *Bainian gonghezhiyi*, 93.
96. Liu Xiaofeng, *Bainian gonghezhiyi*, 94.

transcendence; a second crisis, punctuated by the incompatibility between Chinese and Western faith traditions, forced Liu to abandon the Christian God and to return to the Confucian sage-king; and a third crisis, characterized by the antithesis between Confucian meritocracy and socialist egalitarianism, was reconciled through Liu's conservative transvaluation of Mao's revolution. Meanwhile, each new scenario emerged from and was responsive to the changing dynamics of China's cultural and intellectual landscape. Liu sought to overcome the crisis of socialist faith, to expose the lacuna of secular humanism, and to confront the uncertain conditions of the postsecular age. It is thus the complex and fluid articulations of divergent internal and external intellectual-political currents that unexpectedly, rather than inevitably, gave rise to Liu's authoritarian political theology.

While Liu's esoteric stance potentially nullifies any accusations that he is endorsing political tyranny, the authoritarian impulse of his conservative theology is unsettling. Despite the Straussian devotees' efforts to portray themselves as the guardians of a Confucian past betrayed by the May Fourth movement, their agenda often conjures up an anti-modernist resentment that is even more nihilistic than its liberal opponents. Liu does not seek to return to the pastoral origins of Confucian civilization. Rather, he uses an antiquarian nostalgia to beautify a highly aggressive doctrine of political hegemony. The so-called ancient political virtues are subordinated to a ferocious form of cultural chauvinism that is almost diametrically opposed to Confucian values such as benevolence and forbearance. Fueled by cultural frustrations and antipathy to Western liberalism, the Chinese Straussians resolutely reach beyond Burkean conservatism and strive to bring forward a new form of militant governance compatible with China's global power. At last, Liu's esoteric teaching recalls the image of a "Sphinx without a secret."[97]

In retrospect, Liu Xiaofeng struggled with the dialectic of the eternal and the temporal, immanence and transcendence, ground and nothingness in his effort to cope with the politico-theological predicament of Mao's revolution. His circuitous pilgrimage toward ultimate

---

97. Burnyeat, "Sphinx without a Secret."

values was characterized by ruptures, conversions, and creative (mis) appropriations. At the beginning, the young iconoclast deplored that the totality of Chinese tradition could not maintain its historical innocence after the dehumanizing practices of Mao's revolution. Thirty years later, Liu now cultivates a muscular yearning for the sovereign perpetuity of the party. Did Liu eventually overcome his fear of revolutionary violence by embracing Mao's foundational power? This Kierkegaardian leap of faith shocked liberals as a scandalous tale of political regressions. But to simply project a psychoanalytic frame that narrates Liu's Maoist turn into a tragedy of "perverted Oedipal rebellion"[98] underestimates the complexity of Liu's reflections. Across the sophisticated intellectual resources that Liu has tinkered with, one can only mark out the vague contour of his passionate search for God: the thirst for transcendence beyond politics aroused the desire for an absolute ground for politics; the remote God of Barth materialized into the fearful sovereign of Schmitt; repugnance against the revolutionary masses fueled a dogmatic defense of aristocratic virtues. Finally, excursions into ancient, medieval, and modern forms of divine nexus did not negate revolutionary sacrality. Instead, Mao was ostracized from the postrevolutionary order only to return as the incarnation of a Confucian sage that is still to come.

98. For a critique of this psychoanalytic frame, see Gordon and McCormick, "Weimar Thought," 3–4.

PART III

The Manufactured Affect

CHAPTER FIVE

China Can Say No

Popular Nationalism and the Spirit of *Ressentiment*

> Life itself is essentially appropriation, injury, overwhelming of the alien and the weaker, oppression, hardness, imposition of one's own form, incorporation, and at least, at its mildest, exploitation.
> —Friedrich Nietzsche, *Beyond Good and Evil*
>
> Patriotism is the last refuge of a scoundrel.
> —Samuel Johnson, quoted in Boswell, *The Life of Samuel Johnson*

In the summer of 1996, a Beijing-based publisher released a book that became an almost instant bestseller and sparked a nationalist fever in Chinese public discourse: *China Can Say No: Political and Emotional Choices in the Post–Cold War Era* (中國可以說不：冷戰後時代的政治與情感抉擇). Authored by five young patriots, the book comprised a collage of anti-American slogans, unhinged reviews, and conspiracy theories covering a broad assortment of topics, from the corrosive effect of Hollywood movies to the perils of U.S. interventionism.[1] The overall

---

1. The essays included were individually written by five authors: Song Qiang 宋強, Zhang Zangzang 張藏藏, Qiao Bian 喬邊, Gu Qingsheng 古清生, and Tang Zhengyu 湯正宇. Zhang Zangzang is the pen name of Zhang Xiaobo 張小波.

narrative was brimming with hate toward the United States' "China containment" policy in the post-Tiananmen era. Referring to the 1995–1996 Sino-American military standoff in the Taiwan Strait, the narrators derided the hypocrisy of the United States, represented in the authors' view as a sinister rogue state justifying its greedy, mendacious, and chauvinistic foreign policy under the banner of universal human rights. Far from offering a rational dissection of Sino-U.S. foreign relations, however, their rancorous tone conveyed a sweeping assertion that China was being victimized by barbaric foreign perpetrators. Claiming that the Chinese people must resolutely say no to unjust foreign demands, the writers called for the vengeful return of a robust, muscular, and militant national consciousness, drawing on the demagogic power of anger to heal the wounded national pride.[2]

China Can Say No was published at a time when the Beijing authorities, intellectuals, and general populace were becoming increasing irate about China's isolation in the U.S.-led post–Cold War international order. The sensationalist narrative immediately provoked public expressions of resentment against the growing hostility and "imperial haughtiness" of the democratic West toward the People's Republic of China in the early 1990s. Disputes between China and the United States since 1989, including trade frictions, human rights, and the continued U.S. support for Taiwan, created moral indignation among the Chinese public and gave rise to a desire for revenge for all these real and imagined slights. Even though most foreign commentators dismissed *Say No* as "propaganda tracts" and slammed its amateurish analysis as "naïve" and "shallow,"[3] the success of revanchist nationalism in the domestic book market was astonishing. The first fifty thousand copies sold out on the day of release, and another hundred thousand copies within one month. The estimated total sales would eventually reach two to five million, with some claiming that the number of local reprints and pirated versions were much higher.[4] The book was subsequently translated into eight languages, generated international headlines, and

---

2. Song Qiang et al., *Zhongguo keyi shuobu*, 61–92.

3. For an analysis of the Western media reception of the book, see Blanchette, *China's New Red Guards*, 90–91.

4. Wen, "*Zhongguo keyi shuobu* chuban yinqi hongdong."

ushered in a wave of *Say No* sequels, including *How China Can Say No* (中國何以說不), *Why China Can Say No* (中國為什麼說不), and *China Can Still Say No* (中國還是能說不) (fig. 6).⁵ Together, *Say No* and its numerous copycats vindicated an aggressive and aggrieved nationalist sentiment within Chinese society at large.

More pertinently, the outpouring of emotion by the naysayers—anger, frustration, sarcasm, zealousness, and even masochistic pleasure—requires us to recognize the power of negative affect in the making of popular nationalism. The most evident public feeling behind the torrent of say-no declarations was *ressentiment*. The French term *ressentiment*, which derives from the Latin intensive prefix *re-* and the root *sentire* (to feel), connotes a hateful and vindictive reaction to an unwarranted injury or slight.⁶ A resentful subject is immediately gripped by a sense of grievance in response to what they perceive to be unjust treatment. To relieve themselves of an abiding sense of inferiority, they unleash anger upon the real or imagined perpetrator of their suffering. Thus the Chinese naysayers depicted Western nations as obstructing China's rise by interfering in its domestic affairs and asserting a repugnant brand of moral superiority in universal values. The resentful narrative took pleasure in transforming this awareness of impotence (China's unpopularity in the new world order) into an unscrupulous thirst for revenge (standing up to the West), while residing comfortably in the conviction that vindictive desires facilitate the attainment of justice. The perception of civil resentment as a moral feeling was thus essential for understanding the Chinese public response to the U.S.-led international order in the post-Tiananmen era.

This chapter reads the virulent yet polemical declaration of Chinese nationalism in terms of the unruly and eruptive affective state of *ressentiment*. I argue that *ressentiment*—a constantly morphing assemblage of strong negative emotions—has been the principal psychological motor behind the explosive rise of popular nationalist sentiment

---

5. See Song Qiang et al., *Zhongguo haishi neng shuobu*; Peng Qian, *Zhongguo weishenme shuobu*; Zhang Xueli, *Zhongguo heyi shuobu*.

6. I choose the French *ressentiment* rather than the English "resentment" to emphasize a peculiar strong nuance of a lingering hate. See Scheler, *Ressentiment*, 5.

FIGURE 6. Front covers of the *Say No* series, including *China Can Say No* (Beijing: Zhonghua gongshanglianhe chubanshe, 1996), *How China Can Say No* (Beijing: Hualing chubanshe, 1996), *Why China Can Say No* (Beijing: Xinshijie chubanshe, 1996), and *China Can Still Say No* (Beijing: Zhongguo wenlian chubangongsi, 1996). Photo by the author.

since the 1990s.[7] My central aim is to explain how the moral psychology of *ressentiment*—the repression of shame, the impulse to detract, and the inversion of values—underwent a process of diffusion through the capillaries of Chinese nationalist discourse. Engaging the polemics surrounding the publication of *China Can Say No*, I suggest that nationalist expressions of hatred increased as an instinctual and immediate moral reaction to a series of Western affronts in the post-Tiananmen era. Yet the perceived injustices triggered complex affective constellations— from defensive disavowal to unbounded xenophobia, and from the masochistic desire for utter humiliation to the pompous expression of national superiority. The dynamic interaction between vengeance and vulnerability conjured up a schizophrenic Chinese identity vacillating between cultural frustration and national pride.

Whereas previous chapters focus on the cultural elite, the protagonists of this chapter are a group of populist writers and grassroots intellectuals who actively promoted the resentful narrative of Chinese nationalism. Although both establishment intellectuals and enlightened literati in the 1980s were exclusively affiliated with state-sponsored institutions, journals, and media, the pluralization of the public sphere in the 1990s created new intellectual identities, ranging from political dissidents and grassroots activists to technocratic elites

---

7. This chapter primarily engages the Nietzschean discourse of *ressentiment*, but I am also aware of the abundant literary and cultural expression of *yuan* 怨 in the Confucian tradition. The Chinese character *yuan* is etymologically related to *hui* 恚 (indignation), *dui* 懟 (anger), and *hen* 恨 (hatred). Yet in contrast to the negative connotation of *ressentiment*, early Confucian thought emphasizes the need to "release or redirect one's anger" (*fafen* 發憤) toward ethical ends. As Michael Ing and Eric Nelson point out, the Confucian *yuan* arises from a frustrated desire for affection and must be channeled toward promoting relationships of reciprocal recognition. For example, Confucius famously says in *The Analects* that "poetry shows how to regulate feelings of resentment" (*shi keyi yuan* 詩可以怨). The Neo-Confucian master Zhu Xi also recommends the state of "indignant but not resentful" (*yuan er bunu* 怨而不怒) as a positive moral emotion of self-restraint. Whereas Nietzsche argues that the failure to gain recognition leads to excessive hatred, Confucianism stipulates that a "gentleman" (*junzi* 君子) controls and transforms his anger into an ethics of alterity. Thus, the Confucian notion of self-cultivation might not be an appropriate framework to approach the resentful discourse of Chinese nationalism. For a detailed analysis of *yuan*, see Ing, "Born of Resentment"; Nelson, "Recognition and Resentment in the Confucian Analects."

and media intellectuals.⁸ In sharp contrast to the elitist discourse of academic circles, the advocates of popular nationalism quickly learned to wield the demagogic power of the emergent mass media created by the marketization of cultural production. They deployed an apodictic, sensationalistic, and impressionistic style and replaced abstract theories and definitions with metaphors and myths. Impatient with neutral analysis and rhizomic theorizing, they were motivated by a shared goal: to capture public grievance, explain the cause of the suffering of the nation in an aphoristic manner, and steer anger and frustration toward a real or imagined enemy. Admittedly, scholars and critics generally dismiss popular nationalism as an "emotional swamp" not worthy of serious attention. The say-no farce was thus taken as an outward manifestation of a xenophobic Boxer mentality rather than a movement of considered opinion.⁹ As one reviewer observes, the naysayers were "more intent upon ... venting their emotions than formulating a scholarly argument."¹⁰ After all, in contrast to the millenarian, utopian vision of human progress envisioned in the political discourse of the liberal and the Left, Chinese nationalists the 1990s were only guided by a pragmatic, knee-jerking effort to manufacture a new political myth in order to cope with the erosion of socialist ideology. Yet I suggest that popular nationalists were refreshing precisely for their lack of theoretical sophistication, for their hyperbole and ineloquence, and for their gesture to what sociologist Arlie Hochschild calls the "emotional truth" of the underprivileged people, that is, a "deep story" that is "not necessarily literally true but 'feels-as-if' it's true."¹¹ As Mark Lilla contests in his salient analysis of political reaction, it is "nothing but a prejudice to assume that revolutionaries think while reactionaries only react."¹² One cannot explain why the post-Tiananmen public were consumed by *ressentiment* without understanding the passions,

8. For an analysis of the changing intellectual field in the 1990s, see Veg, *Minjian*, 7–12.
9. For an analysis, see Barmé, *In the Red*, 255–80; Blanchette, *China's New Red Guards*, 83–103.
10. Quoted in Blanchette, *China's New Red Guards*, 90.
11. For a nice summary of Hochschild's argument, see McIntosh, "The Trump Era as a Linguistic Emergency," 22.
12. Lilla, *The Shipwrecked Mind*, 3.

the convictions, and—*yes*—the distorted insights of these unscrupulous figures.

This chapter therefore moves away from the earlier emphasis on how emotion shapes intellectual argumentation and turns to explore the manufactured nature of nationalist affect. *Ressentiment*, in other words, is not only understood as the Kantian "initial orientation" that informs political conviction but also perceived as the result of deliberate psychological engineering. To explain how negative affect was mobilized by the sorcerers of nationalism, it is useful to offer a critical investigation into the moral and political connotations of *ressentiment*. Whereas Aristotle and his followers condemn this bitter affective state as an "unqualifiedly negative" and "ungovernable" emotion incompatible with the nature of justice,[13] Friedrich Nietzsche's (1844–1900) genealogical criticism provides a more nuanced understanding of the moral psychology of *ressentiment*. In *The Genealogy of Morals*, Nietzsche traces the origin of this venomous passion to a "slave revolt in morality." The abject and impoverished slave, who cannot confront the almighty master by means of a violent uprising, retaliates through the inversion of values: slave mentality is hailed as good while the morality of the nobles is vilified as evil.[14] But while Nietzsche suggests that the slave revolt has fundamentally transformed the moral landscape of the West, he also criticizes the reactive, self-serving, and self-destructive nature of *ressentiment*. To assert himself over and against the paralyzing force of domination, the resentful subject falsifies an "illusory hierarchy of values" in accordance with his personal desire and interest, culminating in a delusionary sense of self-affirmation at any cost.[15] Ironically, aggressive feelings do not lead to subversive deeds. Rather than initiating immediate political action, *ressentiment* eventually "consummates and

---

13. See Engels, *The Politics of Resentment*, 4; for a discussion of Aristotle's pessimistic view of the destabilizing effect of resentment and envy in polis, see Saxonhouse, "Aristotle on the Corruption of Regimes"; for a theoretical diagnosis of the antithetical relationship between resentment and justice, see Nussbaum, *Anger and Forgiveness*, 1–13.

14. See Nietzsche, *On the Genealogy of Morals*, 14; Nietzsche, *Beyond Good and Evil*, 195.

15. Scheler, *Ressentiment*, 41; see also Elgat, *Nietzsche's Psychology of Ressentiment*, 13–23.

exhausts itself" in passivity.[16] In the end, the impulse to rebel against injustice issues merely in scowling, sarcasm, and slander.

Following Nietzsche's critique, Max Scheler (1874–1928) argues that *ressentiment* is structurally produced by modern egalitarian societies. The humanitarian search for the equality of all is in its essence a calculated expression of hatred, envy, and revenge against the ruling minority. Yet set against the humanist thirst for the "universal love of mankind," the discrepancy between the "political, constitutional, or traditional status of a group" and "its factual power" has paradoxically detonated the "psychological dynamite" of *ressentiment*.[17] In modern capitalist democracies, the fluidity of status hierarchies, the visibility of competition, and the disjuncture between the promise of equality and the experience of discrimination have created a fertile breeding ground for the rampant expression of jealousy and malice among all deprivileged groups.[18] Hence *ressentiment* threatens to undermine the rational-communicative elements of public discourse, leaving the political sphere ripe for exploitation by populist leaders and sensationalist media.

Whereas Scheler condemns the corrosive affect borne by *ressentiment*, political sociologists argue that modern governance from authoritarianism to liberal democracy has used popular *ressentiment* caused by lost entitlement to justify political violence and solidify existing power structures. In connection with Hochschild's claim that "feeling rules" in social relations,[19] David Ost has coined the term "anger regimes" to emphasize anger as "structurally intrinsic" to any existing economic and political arrangements.[20] As *ressentiment* is "something that the system inexorably produces," politics is less about eliminating disappointment and anger than about *managing* negative emotions by various means.[21] By encouraging the public expression of anger,

---

16. Nietzsche, *On the Genealogy of Morals*, 39.
17. Scheler, *Ressentiment*, 33.
18. For a sociological study of resentment, see Turner, "Max Weber and the Spirit of Resentment."
19. Hochschild, *The Managed Heart*, 56–75.
20. Ost, *The Defeat of Solidarity*, 21.
21. Ost, *The Defeat of Solidarity*, 26.

political leaders turn citizens against each other to reify neoliberal or authoritarian rule over participatory democracy.[22] The recent rise of right-wing populist movements in the Euro-Atlantic world exhibits a sharp turn away from the deliberative model of liberal democracy and toward the mobilization of violent hatred directed at immigrants and ethnic minorities.[23]

But the politics of *ressentiment* did not always produce a divided and distracted public. Scholars of China studies have elucidated how negative affect—anger, frustration, and humiliation—has been tamed and put in the service of an assertive nationalist agenda. For instance, Lucian Pye traces the massive outbursts of patriotic sentiment throughout modern China to a widespread sense of cultural and psychological frustration with the "crisis of Chinese authority" in the face of a powerful West.[24] Instead of turning citizens against each other, the shameful memories of China's subjugation and defeat in the nineteenth and twentieth centuries bind cultural and political elites to a common cause to rejuvenate the national spirit. Jing Tsu also holds that the "complex of failure" among the May Fourth generation stirred up passionate assertions of racial superiority and civilizational solidarity in dark times.[25] While the nationalist origin of Chinese Communism remains a thorny matter, Elizabeth J. Perry considers the management of negative affect to be the key ingredient of the CCP's "emotion work" (*yuqing gongzuo* 輿情工作)—a conscious strategy of psychological engineering that directs the anger of the masses against internal enemies and external threats.[26]

In connection with this, scholarship on contemporary Chinese nationalism focuses on how party leaders carefully managed antiforeign sentiments in the turbulent era following the extinction of the Leninist regimes after 1989. Suisheng Zhao argues that the rise of

---

22. Engels, *The Politics of Resentment*, 1–24.

23. For instance, see McVeigh and Estep, *The Politics of Losing*; Shoshan, *The Management of Hate*.

24. Pye, *The Spirit of Chinese Politics*, 1–11; Pye, *The Mandarin and the Cadre*, 36–74.

25. Tsu, *Failure, Nationalism, and Literature*, 1–31.

26. See Perry, "Moving the Masses."

"state-led pragmatic nationalism" in the 1990s was an instrumental response to the collapse of Communism in Eastern Europe and the Soviet Union. In Xudong Zhang's judgment, the entrenched Chinese state reacted to domestic popular protest and the international anti-Communist tide by adopting a "cynical pragmatism and opportunism" as "the sole source of its legitimacy." Jessica Chen Weiss also suggests that the orchestration of nationalist sentiments provided Chinese leaders with "a means of showcasing domestic pressure" as leverage in the diplomatic disputes with Japan and the United States.[27] Together, these observations demonstrate how the narrative construction of "China's victimization by predatory imperialist powers" fueled a patriotic fervor for national rejuvenation and bolstered the CCP's legitimacy as the guardian of national interests.[28] Above all, divisive hate could be transformed to prop up cultural confidence and sustain social cohesion in the midst of national cataclysms.

Most importantly, the proactive management of public affect connotes a new conception of *ressentiment* no longer bounded by its reactive and repressive features. Rather, the Chinese case illustrates how the expression of hate may be harnessed to empower subaltern subjects and solidify the "slave revolt in morality," albeit with serious compromises. As I demonstrate, the *Say No* authors' bitter rebellion against predatory foreign powers drew inspiration from the Maoist political ritual known as "speaking bitterness." In the case of a carefully rehearsed and publicly exhibited mass gathering, the subaltern subject is encouraged to vent their grievance against the "exploiting classes" and "evil remnants." Here, the resentful are not defined by their inferiority and their reactive character. Instead, the revolt of the subalterns amounts to a fateful moral revolution in tune with Mao's idiosyncratic declaration that "the downtrodden is the most intelligent and the noble is the most stupid" (卑賤者最聰明，高貴者最愚蠢).[29] Thus speaking

---

27. See Suisheng Zhao, *A Nation-State by Construction*, 209–47; Xudong Zhang, *Postsocialism and Cultural Politics*, 29; Weiss, *Powerful Patriots*, 5.

28. Garver, *China's Quest*, 476.

29. Mao Zedong, "Beijianzhe zui congming, gaoguizhe zui yuchun"; for a Nietzschean analysis of the Maoist inversion of values, see Horng-luen Wang, "Understanding Contemporary Chinese Nationalism."

bitterness represented not only the imposition of the party's ideological worldview, but also an act of empowerment that transformed the weak and the oppressed into the bold and aggressive vanguard of revolution. Far from the Nietzschean assessment of *ressentiment* as espousing poisonous and self-destructive tendencies, the engineering of righteous anger created powerful public emotions and sacred political identities for the launch of the CCP's nationalist-cum-revolutionary project.[30]

With the legacy of Maoist *ressentiment* in mind, I also challenge the extant scholarship that emphasizes an all-powerful Chinese state as the primal organizer of *ressentiment*. Much has been said about how the official memory of China's "century of humiliations" (*bainian guochi* 百年國恥) and the state-orchestrated Patriotic Education Campaign contributed to the remarkable resurgence of patriotic ardor in the 1990s.[31] For instance, studies of China's anti-foreign protests use the analogy of "red light, green light" to describe the state's proactive role in managing nationalist protest: "the government signals when to go, when to stop, and when to exercise caution."[32] Even though this perspective does not treat nationalists as mere puppets of the regime, it focuses almost exclusively on how the state agent deployed patriotic propaganda and inflammatory media to prop up popular anger. In contrast, I situate the artificial production of say-no sentiment within an ensemble of contending political agents, from the state apparatus and sensational media to elite and populist intellectuals in the post-Tiananmen era. The ascendancy of nationalism was never an orchestrated event under the singular direction of the state. Within the intellectual field, the sorcerers of Chinese nationalism—a group of right-wing intellectuals, hawkish politicians, and disgruntled populists—were initially guided only by a cynical, pragmatic, and often desperate effort to save the disgraced Chinese state from disintegration, to create a unifying mythology to cope with the erosion of socialist ideology, and to manufacture a political consensus to shore up the legitimacy

---

30. See Chan, *Children of Mao*; Su, *Collective Killings in Rural China*.
31. See Suisheng Zhao, *A Nation-State by Construction*, 209–47; Garver, *China's Quest*, 476–82.
32. Weiss, *Powerful Patriots*, 3.

of the besieged Leninist party. The emotional resolve of *nation*, in that sense, reflected a mix of strategic intent and utilitarian exploitation in the waning of the international Communist movement in the early 1990s.

By focusing on the complex interaction between the popular and the official nationalist discourse, I argue that the explosive rise of the say-no phenomenon represented an important shift from elite orchestrated patriotism to grassroots nationalism created by means of commercialization, mass-media culture, and populist revolt in the pluralized intellectual field of the 1990s. As I demonstrate, the emergence of spontaneous and vibrant national sentiment surrounding the say-no genre was not the result of the CCP's strategic emotional work. On the contrary, these populist authors made a genuine assertion that the indignation of the Chinese people, represented as a morally pure and ultimately imagined collective identity independent of the regime's will, deserved recognition. As a result, nationalism became a popular moral stance detached from state-orchestrated patriotism, which was dismissed as dubiously pragmatic. Hence I propose a hermeneutical approach that presumes neither cynical conformity nor perpetual resistance on the part of the nascent grassroots nationalism in the post-Tiananmen era. My purpose is not to produce a dichotomy between hegemony and spontaneity. Rather, I seek to elucidate a dynamic affective cartography in which state-sanctioned patriotic sentiment and the volatile popular expression of anger interact to constitute an aggressive yet convoluted emotional backlash against an imagined Western villain.[33]

Engaging the sociopolitical analysis of *ressentiment*, my study nonetheless focuses on the aesthetic, literary, and political manifestations of negative affect at the narratological level. Although anger is always systematically generated by the social structure and engineered

---

33. Although anti-Americanism was the predominant ethos of the say-no literature, popular nationalism in the post-Tiananmen era drew heavily from a long tradition of anti-Japanese sentiments in modern Chinese history. While this study does not discuss the commonalities between the say-no authors and anti-Japanism, my analysis benefits from a rich scholarship on the politics of Sino-Japanese conflict. See Ching, *Anti-Japan*, 36–56.

by contending political forces, it is the construction of a narrative sequence—or what Hayden White calls "emplotment"[34]—that mobilizes unbounded and mercurial public rage against a concrete political enemy. Insofar as the public often remains confused about the causes of social and economic grievance, they must be provided with a manufactured narrative that "identifies the cause of people's dissatisfaction" and "promise[s] to take action against that cause."[35] In this regard, the resentful narrative of the say-no genre provides a reductive yet provocative answer that purportedly explains the *causes* of Chinese people's suffering and attempts to hijack the state apparatus by demanding immediate political actions against those causes. By crafting a story that "answer[s] the question of whom to blame,"[36] diffuse and amorphous anger is mobilized toward concrete and designated enemies: liberal intellectuals; immoral, corrupt bureaucrats; and, above all, Western imperialism. In short, storytelling plays a pivotal role in the discursive politics of *ressentiment*.

In what follows, I contextualize the 1996 bestseller by tracing a series of contributions to the popular intellectual discourse that conveyed bitter, eruptive, and intense emotions against "foreign aggressions." I look at how a cluster of affective constellations—from repressed shame to defensive rage and unrestrained hatred—were cultivated and engineered via an ensemble of rhetorical strategies and memory practices to solidify the narrative of modern China as a victim of Western hegemony for the past hundred years. First, I scrutinize multiple historical conditions that gave rise to the say-no phenomenon in the early 1990s. Next, I delve into the stylistic and aesthetic features of the say-no genre to reveal the excessive and irrational *ressentiment* that undergirds its political claim. Last, I delineate how the book was received by national and international media, and how the subsequent say-no craze fueled patriotic ire in the Chinese public domain. Overall, I seek to expose and interrogate the affective charges

---

34. White, *Metahistory*, 1–44.
35. Ost, *The Defeat of Solidarity*, 25.
36. Javeline, "The Role of Blame in Collective Action," 119, quoted in Ost, *The Defeat of Solidarity*, 23.

of *ressentiment* that underlined this fervent nationalism in the post-Tiananmen era.

The Business of Nationalism

The momentous rise of Chinese nationalism in the 1990s must be understood in the context of domestic upheavals and evolving world politics. In the wake of the 1989 Tiananmen protest, Chinese citizens experienced first the shock and frustration caused by military violence, then the protracted struggles between the reformist program and the conservative backlash, and finally the explosion of economic frenzy following Deng Xiaoping's 1992 Southern Tour. By the middle of the decade, the liberalization process, punctuated by continued economic growth and the pluralization of the public sphere, gave rise to a heightened sense of national pride. Against this backdrop, the public became increasingly aware of China's unpopularity in the post–Cold War international system as the last bastion of Leninism. The thwarted desire for recognition in turn fueled a resentment toward what the Chinese saw as Western arrogance in world politics. The public mood toward the United States darkened further over the years. The international backlash following the June Fourth crackdown led to a succession of diplomatic skirmishes with the United States that disrupted China's strenuous effort to normalize its global image, from Beijing's failed bid to host the 2000 Olympic Games to the lengthy and bitter negotiations over China's membership of the World Trade Organization.[37] The extensive (and often one-sided) media coverage of these incidents stirred up a widespread moral indignation against Western hegemony.[38] Claims of injustice and expressions of outrage were underscored by a bitter feeling associated with slight and injury. Thus the confluence of complex domestic and international forces provided a breeding ground for the eruption of vengeful nationalism.

37. For an analysis of China-U.S. relations in the 1990s, see Jing Li, *China's America*, 191–226; Garver, *China's Quest*, 463–556.
38. Suisheng Zhao, *A Nation-State by Construction*, 120–64.

Out of the tumultuous historical changes in the post-Tiananmen era, *China Can Say No* emerged as the first of a great many items of popular literature in which certain self-claimed "standard-bearers of nationalism" tried to establish their reputation (or notoriety) by screaming that China was being victimized by Western imperialism, with attendant feelings of injury and humiliation. However, the five young authors had not predicted the force of the explosive emotion that would be unleashed by their strategic invocation of nationalism. Most of the authors came from modest backgrounds, with no connections to the governing elite or to their liberal opponents. The publisher, Zhang Xiaobo 張小波 (1964–), who later became a successful book dealer and the CEO of Phoenix Cultural Media (*Fenghuang chuanmei* 鳳凰傳媒), was an avant-garde poet famous for his artistic assertion of metropolitan aesthetics in the 1980s.[39] After graduating from East China Normal University in the early eighties, Zhang was assigned to work in the art propaganda department of Zhenjiang for half a year, before he quit and returned to Shanghai to live a bohemian life with his friends. But Zhang's love of bourgeois decadence and distain for the establishment did not prevent him from becoming a savvy businessman. As Zhang became a professional book dealer in the early 1990s, he was struck by the vehemence with which the Chinese expressed their nationalist emotion in the wake of the Sino-American diplomatic disputes. Most importantly, Zhang realized that a popular genre had yet to be created to appeal to angry readers. Because disappointment and frustration were pervasive, producing a narrative that addressed and captured that anger would instantly turn angry patriots into avid readers.

Zhang's market mentality was formed by the epochal shift in the Chinese publishing industry that started around Deng Xiaoping's Southern Tour. The commercialization of the culture industry, the rise of popular television series, and the marginalization of highbrow literature had dismantled the mutually constitutive partnership between the literati elite and the state-owned publication channels. As scholarly communities (such as the protagonists of the previous chapters)

---

39. Zhang Taozhou, *Zhongguo dalu xianfengshige jianshi*, 86–90.

retreated to overseas forums and independent funding sources to secure intellectual freedom, work in commercial publishing emerged as an attractive career choice for those who felt impatient with scholasticism and yearned for greater public influence. On the one hand, the great divergence between the inner exile of liberal intellectuals and the aggressive expansion of mass culture produced emotionally charged discussions surrounding the complicitous role of the intellectual elite in the cultural industry, from the polarized reactions to the upsurge of consumer-oriented literature like the popularity of Wang Shuo's "hooligan literature" (*liumang wenxue* 流氓文學) to the moralistic defense of high culture in the debate on humanist spirit. On the other hand, the commercial press provided new spaces for Chinese intellectuals to disseminate their ideas to an increasingly educated and affluent urban middle class. Although book publishing remained a contentious process, popular authors and media intellectuals quickly learned to harness the novel power of print capitalism to make a profit. As Robert Culp suggests, a book is a "material object with a market value that is circulated, sold, and bought."[40] "Publishing circles" (*chuban jie* 出版界) have to compete with other cultural commodities—from television dramas to soap operas—to secure the necessary income. As a result, commercial logic determines how ideas and culture are presented and packaged.

Moreover, commercialization not only produced a depoliticized entertainment culture but also, unexpectedly, created an audience craving sharp and self-styled commentaries on a wide range of political issues, from domestic social problems to international politics. As Joseph Fewsmith observes, the 1990s witnessed a steep rise in the number of popular books dealing with foreign policy, a forbidden topic in the 1980s.[41] The resulting proliferation of "political treatises" (*zhenglunxing duwu* 政論性讀物), such as *China through the Third Eye* (*Disanzhi yanjing kan Zhongguo* 第三隻眼睛看中國), garnered wide

---

40. Culp, *The Power of Print in Modern China*, 9.
41. Fewsmith, *China since Tiananmen*, 13.

public attention and earned significant profits for the publishers.[42] However, there was a cheap artifice behind this political enthusiasm that belonged less to the iconoclastic spirit of the 1980s cultural critique than to consumer capitalism. True, the public was still concerned about the country's reforms and its troubled relationship with the West, but they had become less tolerant of grand, tedious, and abstract treatises. Readers preferred a more casual, entertaining, and aphoristic writing style, one that rested on apocalyptic images, facile conjectures, and self-promoting fantasies—all-encompassing big talk that reduced international politics into melodramatic theatrics. For a general audience, reading cautious scholarly analysis, which tends to stress thorny problems rather than offer pragmatic solutions, causes frustration and intensifies unease. In contrast, the absurdly abbreviated narratives of these political treatises, with their pompous boasts of China's "grand strategy" or causal invocations of America's "crumbling and corrupted governing elite," offered readers an imaginary insight into international relations. Self-affirmation displaced neutrality, and storytelling displaced that which was told. The treatises nevertheless sold extremely well.

This commercial farce led to the rise of a distinct populist mentality. Zhang Xiaobo recruited four young co-authors in 1995 to write a book that could appeal to rising nationalist sentiment. These were Song Qiang, Zhang's college buddy who served as an advertising manager for a magazine in Chongqing; Qiao Bian, a gardener working at the Beijing Gardening and Greening Bureau; Gu Qingsheng, a freelance writer in Beijing; and Tang Zhengyu, a reporter from the *China Business Times*. The members of this group proudly proclaimed themselves "wild-grass intellectuals" (*caomang zhishifenzi* 草莽知識分子) who represented the suppressed, excluded, and forgotten voices of the "common people." They reserved a particular ire for professional academicians, in their minds the embodiment of arcane, trivial, and narrow-minded scholasticism, which they dismissed as an ultimately useless craft devoid of spiritual power. Even though they largely refrained

---

42. Written by the ghostwriter Wang Shan, the book was officially credited to a fictional German Sinologist to boost its sales. See Wang Shan, *Disanzhi yanjing kan Zhongguo*.

from criticizing governmental officials, they showcased their contempt for the "immoral, corrupt, and effeminate political elite." Ironically, this populist revolt was accompanied by an entrepreneurial spirit. As a professional book dealer, Zhang Xiaobo was especially concerned about how to make the foreign policy book more accessible in the realm of massified culture. In contradistinction to the "dead," "exquisite," and "exhaustive" monographs penned by the experts of international relations, Zhang emphasized that only "verbal brutality"—terse, pompous, and unscrupulous language—could appeal to a general readership.[43] Whereas the neutral and aristocratic overtones of the cultural elite may have been the preference of university professors, by Zhang's logic, only the unabashed, fanatic, and sentimental outpouring of hatred could move angry Chinese readers to tears—leading them to buy the book.

This business mindset was also reflected in the production of the book. The actual writing took no more than a month. Zhang Xiaobo asked each writer to work on their own material and simply assembled the five disjointed parts together to form a "collection of views" of about four hundred pages.[44] Its assembly-line production process resembled that of the notorious cheap genre fiction produced in American "fiction factories," resulting in inconsistencies in the narrative. The style was no less chaotic. As Lucy Xing Lu observes, it was "written in the format of refutation and argumentation and filled with anecdotes, sarcastic remarks, catchy words, Mao's quotations, threat of retaliation, and profane language."[45] Yet, despite the cavalier attitude toward writing and editing, the authors consciously deploy rhetorical aggression to appeal to an imagined patriot whose wounded sense of national pride must be cured by egotistical self-assertion. The first part, titled "The Death of Heaven's Mandate and the Coming of a New Order" (*Cangtian yisi, huangtian dangli* 蒼天已死，黃天當立), is Song Qiang's frank autobiographical account of how he underwent a profound transformation from a naïve pro-American student to a proud patriot over the years. The following part, "Be a Chinese: The Emotional and Political Choices

---

43. Wen, "*Zhongguo keyi shuobu* chuban yinqi hongdong."
44. Suisheng Zhao, *A Nation-State by Construction*, 142.
45. Lucy Xing Lu, "Rhetoric of Nationalism and Anti-Americanism," 163–75.

in the Post-Cold War Era," lashes out with open disdain for America's vicious plot against China, which includes carrying out "cultural invasion" and promoting "peaceful evolution"; this section culminates in a passionate espousal of a sublime Chinese identity. The remaining sections portray the wickedness, materialism, and mendacity of the American mentality, with its hedonistic lifestyle, greed-driven capitalism, and interventionist foreign policy. In sum, the expression of hate through wanton, sadistic, and inflammatory rhetoric acquires a singular salience throughout the narrative.

Besides the textual packaging, the conscious engineering of nationalist sentiment is also reflected in the graphic design of the front and back covers. On the lower left-hand side of the front cover stands an American soldier with his hands on his hips, elbows cocked—an unabashed display of masculinity and militancy. The soldier's head is replaced with the colossal head of the Statue of Liberty, which insinuates that freedom and democracy are but thinly disguised versions of American imperialism. Moreover, the GI is standing before the Great Wall, a paradigmatic symbol of China's glorious history, territorial integrity, and national identity.[46] The juxtaposition of these two images conveys an explicit message: hostile foreign forces are encroaching on Chinese territory under the guise of peaceful evolution. Needless to say, the graphic illustration of an impending American military invasion excited thoughts of the Chinese as victims of Western aggression. The staging of this shocking imagery might be read as a deliberate attempt to solicit moral outrage against U.S. imperialism in Chinese readers. Moreover, the imaginary offence invites a defensive response. The back cover deploys the following slogans to express the authors' defensive rage: "The United States can lead nobody but itself; Japan can lead nobody, sometimes not even itself; China does not want to lead anyone, it only wants to lead itself." To emphasize the contrast between a low-profile, self-restrained China and a malicious West, the authors add a quote from Deng Xiaoping regarding Beijing's desire to seek a diplomatic rapprochement with the United States: "keep a low profile and bide your time" (*taoguang yanghui* 韜光養晦). Thus the combination

---

46. For an excellent study of the symbolic meaning of the Great Wall, see Rojas, *The Great Wall*.

of iconic images and anecdotes argues for patriotism as the product of an innate sense of justice.

The Psychology of *Ressentiment*

In conjunction with the hyperbolic cover design, the overall narrative constantly searches for external stimuli that inflict injury on the Chinese people. *China Can Say No* insists upon the idea of a hostile international world, which provides an explanation for China's predicament in post–Cold War world politics. As Blanchette argues, the new cohort of Chinese patriots in the post-Tiananmen era was guided by a "paranoid worldview that saw global conspiracies of Western domination, the infiltration of China and the party by traitors and 'hostile forces,' and a belief in an inevitable and unavoidable conflict with the United States."[47] For the naysayers, the international order is dominated by social Darwinist principles: past wars and impending wars, the art of sabotage and infiltration, the omnipresence of traitors and spies, and the apocalyptic confrontation between East and West. Above all, the urge to hold a real or invented enemy responsible for the suffering of the Chinese people is the essential feature of this "reactive nationalism" proposed by the *Say No* authors.[48]

The construction of a powerful enemy fosters a feeling of vulnerability. The *Say No* authors portray a vulnerable China surrounded by "international hostile forces," from the American government's expanded partnerships in Asia developed to contain China's rise to the growing Japanese militarism that clamored for aggression. To tear China apart, the Western bloc created an elaborate scheme of fostering cultural and political "peaceful evolution," from *Voice of America* radio broadcasts to CIA infiltration. Meanwhile, warnings of foreign intervention are accompanied by an existential fear of the impending collapse of the Chinese central government. In the section titled "Abandon Fantasy and Prepare for Future Struggle" (*Diudiao huanxiang, zhunbei*

---

47. Blanchette, *China's New Red Guards*, 84.
48. For a discussion of reactive nationalism, see Forges and Xu, "China as a Non-Hegemonic Superpower?," 489.

kangzheng 丟掉幻想，準備抗爭), the authors conjure up a gloomy vision of future China in a state of disintegration:

> What will China's future look like? The Kingdom of Tibet stands in the West, which consists of the Tibetan Plateau, Qinghai, the Uyghur region, large chunks of Yunnan Province, Western Sichuan, and the Tibetan residence in Gansu. The northern neighbor of the Kingdom of Tibet is the East Turkestan State, with most of the former Xinjiang, Ningxia, and Gansu as its territory. Inner Mongolia merges with Mongolia to form the Greater Mongolian Nation. The once-discarded Manchukuo has been reinstalled... Taiwan naturally becomes an independent republic that also includes parts of Fujian Province and Zhejiang Province... Guangdong and Guangxi Province also declared independence and established a sovereign republic with Hong Kong as capital.
>
> 未來的中國是怎麼樣的呢？「西藏雪山王國」屹立在西部，它包括西藏、青海、新疆鄰近藏北的地區、雲南省的大部、四川西部原西康地區和成都市以及甘肅省的藏族居住地。而「雪山王國」的北鄰則是以原新疆及寧夏、甘肅大部分為主體的「東土耳其斯坦國」。內蒙古則納入了「大蒙古」範圍，它的疆界南抵居庸關。曾被人民唾棄的「滿洲國」在東北地區死灰復燃⋯臺灣自然地，是一個獨立的「共和國」，這個「共和國」還包括福建省和富庶的浙江省的一部分⋯兩廣也宣佈獨立，成立以香港為首都的「主權共和國」。[49]

The apocalyptic vision is driven by a masochistic desire for utter humiliation: this future China will be a pathetically weak state whose shrinking territory contains only central areas in Henan and Hebei Provinces, a truly "middle kingdom" surrounded by a group of independent reginal powers that will have stolen or embezzled the national wealth of old China. There will also remain no centralized authority, no enlightenment or reform, and no prospect for China as a major civilization in the international order dominated by the rule of the jungle.[50]

One should not believe, however, that the naysayers preach the China collapse thesis. Instead, the fantasy of the doomsday cultivates a

---

49. Song Qiang et al., *Zhongguo haishi neng shuobu*, 37.
50. Song Qiang et al., *Zhongguo haishi neng shuobu*, 37–38.

fervent desire for self-preservation at any cost. Hostile actions and discrimination against China justify the need for the outpouring of anger; the Chinese people must resolutely and defiantly say no to the absurd demands made by the West. In their analysis of the recent Sino-American diplomatic skirmishes, for instance, the authors list an avalanche of U.S. conspiracies against China, ranging from diplomatic quarrels—such as trade frictions, disagreements over human rights issues, and the U.S. Congress's decision to boycott Beijing's bid for the 2000 Olympic Games—to historically rooted disputes, such as the U.S. support for Taiwan and Tibet. The book casts China in the position of an innocent victim constantly harassed by foreign aggressors. For the *Say No* authors, the so-called human rights abuses were being perpetrated by the U.S. government to vilify China, even though the economic reform had significantly improved the living standard of the Chinese people. The continued U.S. support for Taiwanese independence, from arms sales to the hosting of Taiwan's president Lee Teng-Hui, exemplified its chauvinistic intervention in China's internal affairs without any respect for the territorial integrity of the Chinese nation. The threat of retaliation that underpinned the Sino-American trade negotiations revealed the U.S. government's efforts to thwart China's economic development. Overall, the authors assert that the anger of the Chinese people, which resulted from the unfair U.S. treatment of China, is a genuine moral feeling arising from a keen sense of injustice.

Why, then, did the authors target the United States as the sole villain responsible for the displeasure of the Chinese people? To some extent, anti-American sentiment arose from the dynamics of the Sino-American confrontations of the post-Tiananmen era. As scholars of international relations have pointed out, the CCP's use of military violence to quell the popular protest in Tiananmen in 1989, which was widely covered by the international media, had disastrous consequences for China's global image.[51] In the United States, public sympathy for the

---

51. For critiques of how the media coverage of the massacre in Beijing transformed the Western perception of China, see Longxi Zhang, "Western Theory and Chinese Reality"; Chow, "Violence in the Other Country"; for an analysis of the Western diplomatic responses to the June Fourth incident, see Jing Li, *China's America*, 191–226; Garver, *China's Quest*, 463–84.

student and civilian protestors combined with a deep disappointment with the CCP's resistance to democratic transition turned into popular anger, which materialized in economic sanctions against China.[52] Although Deng Xiaoping quickly resorted to a "diplomacy of damage control" to address the PRC's unpopularity,[53] the "China threat" dogma was reinforced by a triumphant liberal missionary mentality following the disintegration of the Soviet Union, which contributed to the increasingly hardened stance of the United States concerning China.[54] The discursive construction by the U.S. media and political elite of China as a mortal enemy, laced with verbal militancy and self-assertion, caused a considerable shock among Chinese intellectual communities. For instance, Samuel P. Huntington's 1993 influential thesis "The Clash of Civilizations," which was translated and published in *Reference News* (*Cankao xiaoxi* 参考消息), ignited heated debates and fueled the rise of a neoconservative vision of foreign policy among Chinese international-relations specialists.[55] The neoconservative rebuttal proposed a crusading style of foreign policy—one that resorted to realistic power politics—to confront the U.S.-dominated international order.[56]

In contrast to the theoretically oriented scholarly discussions, the *Say No* authors emphasize the need to "feel" foreign aggression on an everyday basis for the purpose of reader identification. In prefatory remarks, the naysayers declare that they do not intend to write a political manifesto for China's diplomatic strategy. As the title suggests, the book is rather the expression of an "emotional choice" (*qinggan xuanze* 情感選擇) regarding the growing U.S. hostility toward China. Ironically, this affective rather than intellectual choice manifests first and foremost as a feeling of impotence. In an expanded sequel, the naysayers paint a self-pitying profile of an impoverished Chinese college graduate who sees himself as ineluctably weak and inferior to a powerful Western man:

---

52. See Garver, *China's Quest*, 472.
53. Garver, *China's Quest*, 485–504.
54. See Bernstein and Munro, *The Coming Conflict with China*.
55. See Wang Xiaodong, "Weilai de chongtu."
56. See Fewsmith, *China since Tiananmen*, 83–112.

> We are poverty-stricken liberal arts majors, college students, teachers, advertising clerks, and freelance writers. At the age of twenty-eight, I am already enslaved by tedious chores: marriage, children, and everyday quarrels. I fantasized about traveling around the world, but I have no passport, only bedsheets. But you [were born with a silver spoon]: baptized in childhood, you glided on Rollerblade through city streets at nine; kissed a girl in the gentrified neighborhood; participated in political protests at Hyde Park; as a member of the Green Party, you went to save whales thousands of miles away ... This is the ubiquitous difference between you and me.
>
> 我的生活軌跡是飢腸轆轆的文科複習生、不可一世的大學生、成天唉聲歎氣的窮教師、滿臉晦氣的廣告業務員和報紙、期刊的投稿人，年過二十八歲便過早地成為生活的奴隸，結婚生孩子，慪氣吵架，喝點小酒，談點大事，很想周遊世界，但沒有護照，只有床罩。而你從懂事那天接受洗禮，九歲時就在大街溜旱冰，在花園跟鄰居小女孩接吻，到海德公園搞政治抗議；作為綠黨成員，你到千里之外的海域拯救鯨魚…這就是你和我每時每刻所無處不在的差別和——分歧。[57]

Here the source of the authors' frustration is a competitive urge to confront the Western other. The narrator casts himself in the position of a jaded youth emerging from a humble and obscure background who has received a modest liberal arts education, struggles to make ends meet, and lacks the resources to support his family. His Western peer, in contrast, displays a refined aesthetic taste, political ambition, and cultural confidence. The world of this imagined Western other, marked by bourgeois affluence, promising economic prospects, and perhaps colonial adventure, is colorful, dynamic, and, most importantly, a conspicuous display of power. It is worth pointing out that none of the *Say No* authors had been to the West. Suffering from deep-felt shame about China's material and cultural backwardness, those afflicted by self-loathing tacitly acknowledge the fact that beyond the Chinese border lies the "good life" of the West, a life of abundance, excitement, modernity, and cosmopolitan adventure, of neon lights and cocktail parties. This leads to the tendency to indulge in constant

---

57. Song Qiang et al., *Zhongguo haishi neng shuobu*, 4–5.

self-deprecation. The *Say No* authors see the world in Manichean terms: the miserable, powerless, and provincial Chinese man versus the superior, self-assertive, and cosmopolitan Western other. As Scheler suggests, the noble person displays a "naïve self-confidence" because he does not need a justification for his superior status. For the common man, by contrast, moral values are born out of comparison; he constantly pursues power, property, and honor to overcome the oppressive feeling of inferiority.[58] Similarly, in contrast to the naïve self-confidence of their Western peer, the Chinese youth has become hardly more than a laboring, trembling, feeble "slave" in the presence of a "master." For the naysayers, comparison is a way not only to hold on to one's pride but also to deliberately seize and preserve Chinese identity through self-deprecation.

Self-loathing is further reflected in the generational consciousness of the naysayers, who came of age in the late 1980s. In their 1997 autobiography *The Spirit of the Fourth Generation* (*Disidairen de jingshen* 第四代人的精神), Song Qiang and his nationalist compatriots proudly declare that the driving force behind their patriotic sentiment is a distinctive "salvation consciousness" (*jiushi qinghuai* 救世情懷). But perhaps these reckless advocates of salvation consciousness were so zealous only because they were tormented by self-contempt. In particular, Song elaborates on how his cohort was caught between the poetry of heroic ideals and the prosaic postsocialist reality. In contrast to the revolutionary experience of the founder generation and the rebellious ethos of the Red Guard generation, the fourth generation of PRC youth was thrown into the quotidian world of economic frenzy without a sense of mission.[59] As Karl Mannheim argues, a sociological cohort comes into being through shared historical experiences.[60] However, the fourth generation acquired its political identity precisely from a lack of any unified and coherent generational experience to speak of after the dissolution of Maoist ideals and the collapse of the 1980s New Enlightenment. Song Qiang recounts how he admired the PRC founding fathers who carried out an arduous mission of national salvation. The

---

58. Scheler, *Ressentiment*, 37.
59. Song Qiang et al., *Disidairen de jingshen*, 3–15.
60. Mannheim, *Ideology and Utopia*.

Red Guard generation was similarly characterized by youthful adventure; they entered the Cultural Revolution with a passionate sincerity, encountered hardships in the "sent-down" movement, and searched for enlightenment in the 1980s. Their lives embodied certain qualities of heroism: recklessness, dynamism, idealism. In contrast, the fourth generation suffered from a spiritual lethargy and an inability to articulate a robust and enchanting faith comparable to revolution and enlightenment. Song Qiang deplores how "we in our thirties are without a shadow or a sound . . . It seems that we will perish in silence."[61]

Ironically, the pronounced awareness of impotence triggers a strong impulse toward revenge. As Geremie Barmé argues, "shame, weakness, and aggrieved sentiments . . . are used regularly by propagandists and politicians to inculcate patriotic ire."[62] The naysayers transformed their self-loathing into a malicious desire to disparage the American other as morally and culturally inferior to the Chinese tradition. In their woefully simplified analysis, American culture, as displayed in "trashy" Hollywood movies, is rendered as "nihilistic," "degenerate," and "pornographic." American politics is run by corrupt demagogues and greedy capitalists. American society is torn by ethnic hatred, class division, and rampant crime. American people are egoistic, ignorant, and suffer from a lack of critical thinking.[63] The conviction that Americans are inherently evil provides an existential enemy diametrically opposed to the "good" Chinese. The fundamental difference between us and them recalls the Schmittian friend-and-foe dichotomy. Carl Schmitt argues that although the political enemy—"the other, the stranger"—might not be "morally evil or aesthetically ugly," they must be emotionally treated as evil and ugly to make a political distinction between friend and enemy.[64] Similarly, the naysayers deploy a dichotomous rhetoric to show the essentially alien and mendacious character of the American other to affirm the Chinese way of existence.

---

61. Song Qiang et al., *Disidairen de jingshen*, 206, quoted in and translated by Gries, *China's New Nationalism*, 5.
62. Barmé, *In the Red*, 268.
63. See Lucy Xing Lu, "Rhetoric of Nationalism and Anti-Americanism," 168.
64. Schmitt, *The Concept of the Political*, 27.

Unlike Schmitt, who stresses the public nature of the enemy, the naysayers are eager to identify private and concrete targets that must be repulsed or repudiated.[65] The so-called enemy, in other words, is a psychological expression of personal vindictiveness. The authors are convinced that the materialist and philistine American ideology has infiltrated the Chinese mind, producing a generation of "Americanophiles" who adore everything related to the Edenic America, a country of "fresh air, cowboys, flaneurs, and Ivy League schools," inhabited by people whose elegance emanates from within. In the section titled "Screw Those Chinese" ("Wo tuoqi nazhong Zhongguoren" 我唾棄那種中國人), Zhang Xiaobo lists those "slavish Chinese" who display a sycophant "slave morality" before their "foreign master." These include well-groomed Beijing college professors who speak with glibness about their "acquaintance[s] at Oxbridge"; transnational corporate employees who feel compelled to show off their knowledge of Western dining etiquette; and overseas returnees who have penned popular novels about "money, sexual fantasy, and bourgeois melancholy in New York."[66] For Zhang, these figures embody classic symptoms of an inferiority-superiority complex; they suffer from a feeling of inferiority or impotence before Western masters, yet they retain a false sense of pride before their fellow Chinese.

This virile contempt for the "spineless Americanophiles" is also manifested through self-denouncing confessions. In the section titled "How I Was Corrupted by 'Pro-American Sentiment'" ("Wo shi ruhe zoujin 'qinmei qingxu' de" 我是如何走進「親美情緒」的), Song Qiang offers a revealing account of his "erroneous" fascination with American culture in the 1980s:

> While I was a college student in Shanghai in the late 1980s, the ethos of intellectual discussion was decidedly pro-Western. It's hard to imagine that any liberty-pursuing Chinese youth would not have strong feelings

---

65. As Schmitt defines it, an enemy "exists only when, at least potentially, one fighting collectivity of people confronts a similar collectivity." Schmitt, *The Concept of the Political*, 28.

66. Song Qiang et al., *Zhongguo keyi shuobu*, 55–59.

for the United States. This deep-rooted emotional attachment, though not necessarily expressed in fanatic forms, is real, lasting, and charged with warm sentiment, which shaped our perception of America . . . young professors, handsome presidents, democratic elections, sensational movies, Hemingway, Fitzgerald, and so on . . . the impact of great power was enormous. Every part of our daily life was related to the United States.

八十年代末我在上海念大學,那個時候討論的空氣十分濃厚⋯很難想象許多和我一樣有著自由思想特徵的中國青年不會對美國產生濃厚的感情。這種感情上的根深蒂固是真實的,它不一定以一種十分狂熱的形式表現出來,而是以深沉的、持久的、甚至是溫馨的狀態,左右著我們認識現實的尺度⋯二十幾歲的教授、英俊的總統、熱烈的選舉、高超的電影、從海明威到菲茨傑拉德等等⋯大國的衝擊是不可估量的,我們日常生活的每一部分⋯無一不和美國有關。[67]

The rhetoric of this passage harks back to the Maoist discourse of self-criticism. As chapter 1 points out, the origin of this confession genre could be traced back to the CCP's highly systematic method of ideological reeducation directed at the intellectual elite in the 1942 Yan'an Rectification Movement.[68] Yet while the coercive measures of the thought reform sought to highlight the party as a messiah that purges feudal or bourgeois elements from people's souls, Song Qiang created a self-willed confession, beginning with the relentless self-exposure that he was poisoned by the "enlightenment ethos" of the 1980s and that such "genuflection before the West" had deeply shaped his formative years. For Song, the opening to the West produced a sense of rupture with the Maoist vision of world proletarian revolution, when the influx of American culture, characterized by presidential elections, *Reader's Digest*, Henry Kissinger, and low-budget B movies, had influenced all leisure activities and intellectual pursuits in China. Even more notable is Song's judgment that this American fever does not manifest itself as a fascination with a crushing and uplifting sublime. Instead, the corrosive influence of Americanism operates at the most

67. Song Qiang et al., *Zhongguo keyi shuobu*, 3–7.
68. Lifton, *Thought Reform and the Psychology of Totalism*.

covert and intimate level: it speaks to your heart, transforms your appetite, conjures up your sensuous desire, stirs up your political imagination, and, by doing so, purges you of your Chinese identity and represses your patriotic sentiment. The eventual result of this "peaceful evolution," as Song warns, is that "we easily become subservient and even fall in love with our servility" (我們極容易變成奴隸，變成以後，還很喜歡).[69]

In the end, Song's sensationalized account of his quasi-religious conversion to nationalism enables him to assert his moral rectitude over those "traitors, compradors, and Americanophiles." Yet this self-assertion could also be read symptomatically as intentional self-deception. As Scheler argues, the subjects of *ressentiment* construe "an illusory hierarchy of values in accordance with . . . [their] personal goals and wishes."[70] Their invention of a new morality always entails "the counterfeit and self-deception of impotence."[71] Similarly, Song's embrace of nationalism is precipitated by a negative, nihilistic, and detractive affect. Just as Nietzsche explains that "man seeks a principle through which he can despise man," so Song invents a morally superior patriotic identity to "slander and bespatter" his pro-American peers.[72] Moreover, one is surprised to find that the entire book remains silent about the fundamental assumptions and values of this mythic and essentialized Chinese identity. Ironically, Song's Chineseness is affirmed not directly and spontaneously, but indirectly and reactively, by negating the American other. This negative dialectic reveals the clandestine self-deceptive logic at work: Song strives to deceive himself that he is truly committed to a patriotic cause to avoid the embarrassing fact that his patriotism derives from xenophobic impulses. Insofar as the whole say-no farce was motivated by a burning hatred against the American other, the sacrament of Chinese identity proposed by these self-claimed patriotists had nothing to do with a genuine commitment to any positive values and feelings, as we shall see.

69. Song Qiang et al., *Zhongguo keyi shuobu*, 16.
70. Scheler, *Ressentiment*, 41.
71. Nietzsche, *On the Genealogy of Morals*, 13.
72. Nietzsche, *On the Genealogy of Morals*, 253.

Divided Reception

China Can Say No was published at a time when both the Chinese public and the intellectual elite were increasingly embroiled in a conflict of perspectives on America: an emerging resentment against what they regarded as American imperial haughtiness in Sino-U.S. relations on the one hand and a growing acceptance of the American lifestyle on the other.[73] These two forces helped shape the Chinese perception of the United States as a "beautiful imperialist," defined by its delicate balance between a sober admiration for America's gleaming skyscrapers, cultural cosmopolitanism, and military power and a moral indignation against its hegemonic "China containment" foreign policy.[74] The affective undercurrent of love-turned-hatred exploded in early 1996, when China and the United States engaged in a military confrontation over Taiwan's first presidential election. Thus the ingenious timing of *Say No*'s release (June 1996) was crucial to its commercial success. As the Xinhua News Agency journalist Han Song commented, "if it had not been for the sabre-rattling in Sino-American relations in the first half of the year, the publishing of this book would have been a most ordinary event."[75] Indeed, the public enthusiasm for the book was reflected in the torrent of conferences, lectures, and invitations to interviews that immediately followed. The five virtually unknown authors became national celebrities overnight.

International media gave extensive coverage to the *Say No* affair. The number of foreign news reports on and reviews of *China Can Say No* soon numbered in the hundreds.[76] The book represented the vengeful return of a vitriolic, chauvinistic, and xenophobic nationalism, indeed, an unscrupulous Boxer mentality characterized by an unruly, irrational, and destructive rage. Nationalist Japanese politician Shintaro Ishihara (1932–2022), whose 1989 essay "The Japan That Can Say No" inspired Zhang Xiaobo and his nationalistic fellows, dismissed the

---

73. Jing Li, *China's America*, 192.
74. Shambaugh, *Beautiful Imperialist*.
75. Han, "I and the Dispatches on the Book *China Can Say No*," 98.
76. Han, "I and the Dispatches on the Book *China Can Say No*," 96–99.

Chinese copycats as "naïve" and "infuriating."[77] Patrick Tyler, a *New York Times* columnist, identified the authors' outpouring of anger as a blind and ferocious "Yankee bashing," with the explicit intent to "popularize . . . a wave of anti-Western nationalism." However, due to a "certain lack of knowledge about the issues," Tyler concluded that "their book is not so much political analysis as a handbook for anti-American and anti-British slogans, conspiracy theories and satire."[78] Other outlets of Western media quickly assumed that this patriotic farce had been masterminded by the Chinese government to garner public support for a crusading style of foreign policy in the wake of the Taiwan Strait Crisis. The British *Sunday Times* claimed, "The book has sailed past the omnipresent Chinese government censors and sold more than 100,000 copies in the past month, a sure sign of official approval."[79] The *Washington Post*, too, criticized Xinhua News Agency, the official state-run press agency, for promoting a "rabidly anti-American book called 'China Can Say No.'"[80] For Western journalists, the wide circulation of the book in China's "directed public sphere"[81] could not have been achieved without the approval of the authoritarian state. Indeed, according to the Hong Kong *Asia Weekly* (*Yazhou zhoukan* 亞洲週刊), a senior official at the PRC's Ministry of Foreign Affairs who requested anonymity revealed that top leaders praised the book for "laying a theoretical foundation" for a more assertive foreign policy against the West.[82] Clearly, this instant bestseller aroused various emotions ranging across disgust, fear, and suspicion in its international readership.

However, simply to denounce the Chinese government for its manipulation of popular sentiment overlooks the disparate trajectories between the say-no phenomenon and the official program of patriotism. Admittedly, the management of anti-foreign sentiment has played an increasingly prominent role in China's foreign policymaking since

77. "Breaking a Spell," Asiaweek.com, September 27, 1996, http://www.cnn.com/ASIANOW/asiaweek/96/0927/feat10.html.
78. Tyler, "Rebel's New Cause."
79. Sheridan, "Chinese Feed Their Fear of Foreigners."
80. Mufson, "China Puts Forth Persistent, Caustic Anti-U.S. Themes."
81. Cheek, *The Intellectual in Modern Chinese History*, 272–76.
82. Quoted in Song Qiang et al., *Zhongguo haishi neng shuobu*, 378.

the 1990s. The official endorsement was showcased in *Say No*'s afterward, written by Yu Quanyu, a senior journalist in the PRC's Publicity Department.[83] Yet the CCP was also keenly aware of the threat posed by grassroots nationalism. Within the orbit of foreign policy, as the confrontational approach to the United States was gradually replaced by the efforts of renormalization after the Taiwan Strait Crisis, Beijing swiftly moved to constrain public anti-foreign sentiment. Chinese officials reportedly banned the publication of *Say No*'s sequel in the mainland. From May through July 1996, Chinese and American officials worked together to create conditions for an exchange of summit visits between President Jiang Zemin and President Bill Clinton. With the shift in the political winds, the "emotional choice" propagated by the naysayers became a hindrance to the new norms of "PRC-US comity."[84] Against the naysayers' hysteric call to "burn Hollywood," for example, President Jiang Zemin publicly praised the Hollywood blockbuster *Titanic* in a speech to the National People's Congress in 1998 to signal his endorsement for Western cultural imports.[85]

The state's attempt to dampen public enthusiasm for the say-no fever was also reflected in a chorus of criticism in official media. On June 30, an article entitled "Dialogue Is Better Than Confrontation" ("Duihua bi duikang hao" 對話比對抗好) appeared on the front page of *Beijing Legal News* (*Beijing fazhi bao* 北京法制報). The author quoted Jiang Zemin extensively to advocate rational and peaceful dialogue against the militant and confrontational rhetoric of the say-no phenomenon. In the following year, Shen Jiru 沈驥如 (1942–), a research fellow affiliated with the Chinese Academy of Social Science, published a book-length critique of popular nationalism. Entitled *China Doesn't Want to Be "Mr. No"* (*Zhongguo budang "buxiansheng"* 中國不當「不先生」), Shen attributed the *Say No* authors' rash and irrational "rejectionism" to a deep-rooted "Red Guard mentality." In Shen's judgment, the rebels' call for ferocious mortal combat with the West drew inspiration from the Maoist motto "We should support whatever the enemy

83. Yu Quanyu, "Fangmei guilai, geng you xinxin," 427–35.
84. Garver, *China's Quest*, 638.
85. Parker, "Titanic Takes Chinese by Storm Following President-Led Ballyhoo."

opposes and oppose whatever the enemy supports" (凡是敵人反對的我們就擁護,凡是敵人擁護的我們就反對). Shen concluded that the cultivation of aggression, discrimination, and xenophobia went decidedly against the new emotional norm of mutual understanding and strategic cooperation in the age of multilateralism.[86]

Nonetheless, several domestic media outlets hailed the remarkable success of the *Say No* book as the triumph of the people. The term *minjian* (民間) was repeatedly invoked to designate the naysayers as antiestablishment insurgents motivated by genuine patriotic sentiment. As Sebastian Veg suggests, *minjian*, which is often translated as "among the people," "folk," or "unofficial," derives its grassroots connotation from the "historical dichotomy of *min* (people) and *guan* (officials)."[87] In this light, the anger of the grassroots patriots deserves respect because it signifies an innate sense of justice. Guangzhou's *New Weekly* (*Xin zhoukan* 新週刊) used a sensationalized headline to describe the populist passion of the *Say No* authors: "Petty Literati Challenged the Superpower, Folk Wisdom Shocked the Western World" (文弱書生挑戰強權老大,民間奇書震動西方世界). According to the report, the popularity of the book was due to the superiority of "folk politics" over "expert opinion," or the moral feeling of the silent majority superseding abstract and pompous policy analysis. Song Qiang allegedly said to the reporter that "the fact that we are not foreign affairs analysts makes our opinion more genuine and more representative."[88] Needless to say, the claim to exclusive representation implies a populist logic.[89] Put simply, the naysayers were waging a titanic battle against the hypocritical establishment to preserve a righteous and morally pure Chinese identity. Whereas Nietzsche regarded *ressentiment* as a sign of impotence, the *Say No* authors have proudly claimed that weakness is a moral virtue and a political asset that enables them to speak directly to the people and for the people. Therefore, even though the

---

86. Shen, *Zhongguo budang "bu xiansheng,"* 55–74.
87. Veg, *Minjian*, 17.
88. Zhang Liang and E Fan, "Wenruo shusheng tiaozhan qiangquanlaoda," quoted in Song Qiang et al., *Zhongguo haishi neng shuobu*, 417.
89. See Müller, *What Is Populism?*, 1–6.

book stirred up "rancor, primitive impulse, and xenophobia," as the article concluded, "it was meant to tell the world frankly ... this is what we are thinking."[90] The outpouring of hate was lauded as the expression of a morally justified emotion grounded in the authenticity of one's innate feelings.

However, for liberal Chinese intellectuals, the whole say-no farce was scandalous. The iconoclastic liberal essayist Wang Xiaobo 王小波 (1952–1997) penned a satirical review of the book titled "Common People, Foreigners, and Chinese Officials" ("Baixing, yangren, guan" 百姓·洋人·官). In a sarcastic tone, Wang suggested that the rhetoric was propelled by a cynical mentality deeply rooted in history. According to Wang, during the late Qing and early republican era, the Chinese lived in a hierarchical social structure, a "great chain of being," with "foreign devils" at the top, above Chinese officials, and the common people at the bottom. Instead of valorizing the permanent state of inequality, however, this tripartite hierarchy ran like a game of rock, paper, scissors: the almighty foreigners were afraid of the unruly Chinese masses, while Chinese officials, who could easily intimidate the common people, were afraid of foreign powers. This loophole in the hierarchy was used by the Boxers, who believed that killing foreigners would provide them with significant leverage to bargain with the oppressive Qing government. Similarly, the *Say No* authors' outpouring of xenophobia is driven by a strategic intent; given that the Chinese authority deeply fears the United States because of its superpower status, and the American government does not dare to mess with the Chinese people, attacking the Americans circuitously empowers the Chinese people in the presence of an authoritarian government.[91] This reveals that the naysayers' cynical performance of patriotism is driven by a pathetic survivor mentality. The acclaimed triumph of grassroots nationalism thus amounts to no more than the act of self-deception—an Ah Q–style "spiritual victory" that provides a delusionary emancipation from the oppressive authoritarian regime.

---

90. Zhang Liang and E Fan, "Wenruo shusheng tiaozhan qiangquanlaoda," quoted in Song Qiang et al., *Zhongguo haishi neng shuobu*, 419.

91. Wang Xiaobo, *Chenmo de daduoshu*, 72–74.

While most scholars treated the book with contempt, there is nonetheless a disturbing parallel between the resentful narrative of the populist revolt and the broader nationalist turn of Chinese academia. A few opportunists, tired of the daily chore of participation in esoteric academia, took advantage of their Western training to empower the popular discourse of *ressentiment*. In December 1996, the Chinese Social Science Academy Press published a sensational book that was widely conceived as a sequel to *China Can Say No*. Titled *Behind the Demonization of China* (*Yaomohua Zhongguo de beihou* 妖魔化中國的背後), the book was composed by several Chinese scholars and journalists who had studied at or visited U.S. universities. Unlike the *Say No* authors of the grassroots revolt, members of this group spoke with special authority about their encounters with Sinophobia in the United States. Again, an emotional and hateful rhetoric underlined their protestations against what was considered to be the unjust, racist, and ideologically informed representation of China in Western media and academia. One of the authors, Li Xiguang, a Xinhua News Agency reporter who served as a visiting journalist to the *Washington Post*, lashed out with hatred against the dark and abominable secrets of the American media establishment. Without a single word about repressive censorship in China, Li implied that the American mainstream media had double standards when it came to China. The so-called freedom of the press was merely the secret weapon in the post–Cold War ideological struggle, a propaganda scheme to inculcate anti-Chinese sentiment in Americans.[92] Meanwhile, one of Li's co-authors, Liu Kang, reserved particular ire for American China studies, in his mind a consortium built up by anti-Communist scholars and right-wing intellectuals with the ideological agenda to vilify China as the "illiberal," "inhuman," and "totalitarian" other.[93] To many Chinese readers, the fact that even those "cultural insiders" had joined the anti-Western concerto seemed to offer irrefutable evidence for the inherently imperialistic nature of the West.

Admittedly, the powerful resurgence of patriotic passion among those returnees and overseas intellectuals was not without reason. After

---

92. Li and Liu, *Yaomohua Zhongguo de beihou*, 1–77.
93. Li and Liu, *Yaomohua Zhongguo de beihou*, 142–73.

experiencing the collapse of socialist utopia, a generation of Chinese intellectuals had pledged their faith in the ideal of Western academia as the beacon of cosmopolitan reason, intellectual freedom, and cultural dignity. It was thus the profound emotional power of an imagined liberal West—an image constructed by translated literature, intellectual discourse, and cinematic fantasies—that drove the best and the brightest to study in Western countries since the institution of Deng Xiaoping's Open Door Policy. But when they finally arrived in New York, Berkeley, and Chicago, dragging large suitcases that contained bedsheets and their beloved books of the Western canon, they found themselves strangers to an academic culture of competition, individualism, and professionalism. Bit by bit, the perilous years of emigration, punctuated by culture shock, social alienation, and economic poverty, generated a deep sense of frustration among the diasporic PRC elites. Back home, they had been cultural heroes with grand visions of political reform and social enlightenment. In the United States, even their success was banal and tingled with an excruciating sense of self-betrayal: switch to law school, learn financial planning, and finally move into a gentrified middle-class neighborhood with a spacious lawn and a pet—a "bourgeois quagmire," in the words of Eleonory Gilburd.[94] The philistine American dream was preposterous to the children of Mao who searched for a an "oceanic feeling" generated by enlightenment, revolution, and national rejuvenation. Perhaps Mao's warning against the "sugarcoated bullets" of the bourgeoisie had been right all along. No wonder many disillusioned returnees from the United States spoke with resentment about the "imperialism" of academy, the "sensual and greedy" nature of capitalism, and the "cultural racism" of Western society.[95] One furthermore has to admit that their seemingly hypocritical conversion was

---

94. Gilburd, *To See Paris and Die*, 321.

95. In his analysis of the patriotism of overseas returnees, Garver argues that "greater familiarity with U.S. society not infrequently contributed to stronger Chinese nationalism." He points out that during the 1990s, Chinese visiting scholars often faced challenges when adapting to American academic culture. As a result, some returnees "inclined people to believe the worst about the United States." See Garver, *China's Quest*, 768–69.

tinged with humiliation and loss; having been cheated by quixotic enlightenment universalism, returnees took up nationalism as the last utopia for their intellectual odyssey.

As a result, the cohort of liberal intellectuals who dominated the earlier cultural debates were either silenced or marginalized in the great patriotic parade sweeping the public domain. As I have argued in chapter 4, Chinese intellectuals were drawn increasingly away from the enlightenment ideal of the 1980s and toward Chinese indigenous cultural and political tradition in the 1990s. The conservative cultural backlash drew on a variety of terms in the Western theoretical lexicon—from the postcolonial "decentering" of the West to the postmodern "deconstructive hermeneutics"—to affirm "Chineseness" over and against universal principles of enlightenment. Buzzwords such as "resistance," "indigeneity," "relativism," and "difference" acquired a singular salience for many cultural critics, who used them to create new values and moral schemes that stood in competition with the hegemonic discourse of liberal democracy. Although most academic intellectuals refused to participate in either the CCP's patriotic campaign or the popular discourse of xenophobia, they recognized that there was no way to reckon with the pervasive Orientalism in the Western political unconscious without invoking the myth of the Chinese nation. The dramatic shakeup in world politics, including Russia's abysmal economic regression, the exponential rise of the East Asian Tigers, and the Sino-U.S. diplomatic clashes, have compelled intellectuals to leave the dream of cosmopolitanism behind and adopt cynical, realistic, and nationalist tactics.

For many, the confluence of popular and intellectual expressions of *ressentiment* in the wake of the say-no phenomenon was deeply disturbing. In the eyes of foreign critics, the concerted attempt to find an external cause to blame might be read symptomatically as the unconscious display of repressed shame. As Anna Parkinson points out, the resentful subject finds "relief from its own guilt by making someone else the source of—and thus responsible for—its own 'bleeding' from 'long-healed scars.'"[96] The indelible scar left on the minds of the *Say No*

---

96. Parkinson, *An Emotional State*, 72.

authors and their intellectual compatriots was, of course, the June Fourth incident. Margaret Hillenbrand and Chloë Starr suggest that the fervent expression of national pride in Chinese public discourse in the 1990s was driven precisely by a "repressed shame at China's inhospitality to democratic ideas"[97] after the failure of the 1980s enlightenment. Similarly, John Fitzgerald observes that "the 'say no' authors appear to resent the twist of fate which delivered them into the world as citizens of a state that cannot afford the liberties that citizens of other states take for granted."[98] By blaming the United States for causing China's political predicament in the post-Tiananmen era, they dispensed with shame in favor of a defensive rage. As my analysis reveals, these intemperate advocates of patriotism were so vehement often because they had something to hide: a provincial upbringing, a superiority-inferiority complex, or a feeling of helplessness in a world shaped by perpetual globalization, social transformation, and cultural interactions.

This chapter has explored the politics of *ressentiment* against the backdrop of surging Chinese nationalism in the 1990s. Throughout my exposition, I seek to identify the revenge-seeking psychological state of *ressentiment* in the virulent debates surrounding the 1996 bestselling book *China Can Say No*. I suggest that the explosive effect of the say-no phenomenon reveals the emergence in the post-Tiananmen public sphere of a grassroots nationalism created by a populist mentality, commercialization, and the changing post–Cold War international order. My analysis is not confined to the singular case of the say-no affair. Rather, the case serves as a barometer of the changing emotional trajectory of the PRC's public discourse in the post-Tiananmen era. With China's monumental economic success and rising political influence, the rhetoric of *ressentiment* ushered in by the naysayers began to slowly but steadily course through government pronouncements, intellectual debates, state media, and bilateral forums at home and abroad from the 1990s onward. As China emerges as a world power that has repeatedly challenged the U.S.-led international order, the legacy of

97. Hillenbrand and Starr, "Chinese Neo-Nationalism," 134.
98. Fitzgerald, "China and the Quest for Dignity," 55, quoted in Hillenbrand and Starr, "Chinese Neo-Nationalism," 134–35.

ressentiment continues to exert enormous influence over Chinese public sentiment and intellectual discourse. As we shall see in the epilogue, the say-no farce aids our understanding not only of the resurgence of Chinese nationalism in the 1990s but also of the demonic power of *ressentiment* that continues to shape cultural and intellectual ferments in the age of Xi Jinping's Chinese Dream.

Epilogue

Searching for the Chinese Dream

> All men dream: but not equally. Those who dream by night in the dusty recesses of their minds wake in the day to find that it was vanity; but the dreamers of the day are dangerous men, for they may act their dream with open eyes, to make it possible.
> —T. E. Lawrence, *Seven Pillars of Wisdom*

> Dreaming is free, but speaking these dreams is not free. When we have dreams, we have real dreams; but when we speak those dreams, it is hard to avoid speaking lies.
> —Lu Xun, "On Dreams"

In 1969, a fifteen-year-old sent-down youth arrived at Liangjia River, a bleak and hardscrabble village in the northeast of the desolate Shaanxi Province. At that moment, the skinny teenager was in the midst of profound emotional and political transformation. When the Beijing Red Guard movement spiraled into chaos in the summer of 1966, his family became the target of intense abuse and violence. As the "child of a black gang," he was repeatedly singled out and beaten by the radicals. The boy was perhaps spared misfortune only because he volunteered for rural labor in late 1968, following Mao's call to rusticate urban youths in the countryside. For the next seven years, the poverty-stricken village provided shelter and brought an earthly politician out of the schoolboy.

In the later folklore retelling and political mythology, the young man's bildungsroman was enchanted with a mystic-religious charm, like "that of a monk who finds enlightenment through his wanderings."[1] China's future president was ready to "eat bitterness" (*chiku* 吃苦): he "lived in a cave dwelling with villagers, slept on a *kang*, a traditional Chinese bed made of bricks and clay, endured flea bites, carried manure, built dams and repaired roads."[2] Whereas other sent-down youths suffered egregiously from physical hardships, the boy not only endured but actually thrived from this harsh and down-to-earth lifestyle. Indeed, his trial embodied the Maoist ideal that enshrined corporeal suffering as a "physical testimony to ideological strength."[3] Day by day, the rough-and-tumble of Liangjia River taught him how the Chinese revolution was deeply rooted in the barren, ocher-colored hillsides of the Loess Plateau, in the primitive passions of the rural masses, and in the close ties forged between party cadres and the common people. Eventually, the seasoned statesman did not turn against the Maoist mythology of revolution. Instead, he learned—through purges and retribution—the fragility of political stability, the fickleness of human relations in vicious power struggles, and the need to resolutely assert oneself against all enemies. For the future leader of China, the tragedy of the Cultural Revolution was not that it ended with politics of the wrong kind—ultraleftist violence. Rather, the ultimate lesson was that the outcome of politics is always decided by the whims of the strong.

On November 15, 2012, the fifty-nine-year-old Xi Jinping assumed the position of the general secretary of the Chinese Communist Party, the first paramount leader to be born after the founding of the PRC. A new cycle of Chinese dreams and passions had just begun. Unlike his cautious predecessors who excelled in the "virtue of dullness,"[4] Xi the idealist possessed the freshness and audacity of youth. Soon the new

1. Khan, *Haunted by Chaos*, 209.
2. Osnos, "Born Red."
3. David Wang, *The Monster That Is History*, 140.
4. Khan, *Haunted by Chaos*, 170–208.

leader waged a ruthless anti-corruption campaign, taking down powerful "tigers" and "hegemons." The nationwide crackdown on official corruption won unprecedented popularity and further consolidated the legitimacy of his reform. President Xi also charted a new course for China in international affairs, including the launch of the Belt and Road Initiative, an ambitious geopolitical undertaking aiming to revive the Silk Road—the ancient trade routes between China and Europe, massive investments in Africa to help spur local infrastructure development and economic growth, and tenacious efforts to establish a "new type of major-power relationship" with the United States.[5] As the leader of a capitalist-driven country with socialist legacies, Xi the realist deliberately embraced contradictions and maintained a delicate balance between neoliberal economic policy and political conservatism. Eventually, that remarkable combination of realism and idealism, and that youthful spirit of strategy and conviction are what endowed the new leader with élan and esprit de corps.

President Xi also invited writers and intellectuals to participate in his design of the Chinese Dream, a utopian political vision that portrayed the mirage of a rejuvenated Chinese nation.[6] To assist in Beijing's exercise of soft power, liberals, leftists, Confucians, and nationalists must abandon their frivolous squabbles and contribute to the recovery of China's five-thousand-year-old civilizational past, the refashioning of cultural confidence, and the promotion of Chinese meritocracy against Western liberal democracy. In a manner reminiscent of Mao, President Xi portrayed himself as not only a benevolent patron friendly to intellectuals, but also a man of high culture. In his 2014 "Speech on Literature and Art," which again echoed Mao's landmark Yan'an talks on revolutionary culture in 1942, Xi littered his remarks with references to Confucius, Lu Xun, Jaspers, Balzac, and Tagore, along with nods to Dostoevsky. Party media boasted of Xi's close affinity with prominent "people's writers" such as Lu Yao 路遙 (1949–1992) and Jia Pingwa 賈平凹 (1952–). Mo Yan 莫言 (1955–), the Nobel Prize laureate in literature, accompanied President Xi on his foreign trips. Yet the president also warned against the corrosive

---

5. See Li and McCarron, "A New Type of Major Power Relationship?," 156–62.
6. Xi, *The Governance of China*, 38–41.

influence of commercialism that produced vulgar, plagiaristic, and nihilistic "cultural trash." Writers should not "lose themselves in the tide of market economy nor go astray while answering the question of 'whom to serve.'" He made it crystal clear that Chinese artists must "follow party leadership," "serve socialism," and "let people see the good, feel hope, [and] have dreams."[7]

Seasoned intellectuals were at first skeptical about whether dramatic policy changes could come from the high-flown ideological talk. For the past three decades, writers had learned to navigate the rhizomic space between the state-sponsored party literature and the growing force of the market, surviving and thriving by practicing the art of brinkmanship. They were wrong this time. Since President Xi's speech, substantial recourses have been channeled to realize the new leadership's vision of a socialist cultural renaissance, ranging across the fashioning of red classics, the promotion of patriotic art, and the assertion of China's geopolitical power through a massive culture export and a lavish propaganda charm offensive in the international arena. The cultural tsar also had little tolerance for those who turned down his invitation to the socialist utopia. New strictures on textbooks and classroom conduct sought to eradicate the corrosive influence of Western values in Chinese universities. The propaganda machine closed off the margins and tightened its grip on print and digital media, flooding the public sphere with ideological indoctrination and patriotic education. Dissent was not loyal opposition. It was high treason.

The Problem of Ideological Polarization in the Post-Mao Era

From this moment on, the Chinese Dream took on a momentum of its own. At this point, it may be useful to revisit the dynamic sentiments and intellectual ferment explored in the previous chapters. This book tries to make sense of the volatile emotions and affective intensities that underpinned political debates about the Maoist past from the late 1970s

---

7. Murong, "The Art of Xi Jinping."

to the twentieth-first century. It chronicles the rise of polarized reactions to the question of a derailed socialist revolution at the center of the post-Mao intellectual life. The post-Mao era saw the emergence of liberal intellectuals, conservative revivalists, nostalgic leftists, and grassroots nationalists, who arguably ranked amongst the most provocative thinkers and supreme political manipulators of twentieth-century China. In the wake of Mao's crumbling socialist utopia, liberal-minded intellectuals advocated a palette of scenarios for a "sentimental education" to address and undo historical trauma, from the anguished remembrances of persecution and exile to the humanistic confessions of guilt and shame. For the melancholic Left, however, the paradoxical nature of revolutionary utopianism was not easily subjected to such total negation. Instead, the lived experience of socialism was saturated with personal memories, ideals, and pursuits, all of which compelled the Left to retrieve the revolution's unrealized promise at the moment of its fall. Meanwhile, cultural conservatives took up the mythos of China's vanished civilizational heritage to critique the Left and the liberals' perverted embrace of secular modernity. Conservative acolytes called for a new religious passion that embraced the sublime and the irrational against enlightenment rationality. In conjunction with the conservative revolt against the liberal consensus, popular nationalists drew on the demagogic power of *ressentiment* to heal the wounded national pride and forge a muscular national identity against a real or imagined Western villain. In retrospect, these divergent attempts to express a diverse array of emotions, from the passions of belief to the pathos of defeat, from idyllic yearning for the religious sublime to the patriotic invocation of *ressentiment*, contributed to the vibrant, though no less virulent, cultural and intellectual ferment in the post-Mao era.

The intellectual rivals discussed in this book held clashing views on how to reconstruct a usable national past behind a new, postrevolutionary Chinese national identity. While liberal scholars regarded the work of mourning as the most appropriate moral-emotional response to honor the victims of revolution, leftist writers nourished a lingering melancholy for the emancipatory potentials of socialist utopianism against resignation and defeat. The conservative backlash cultivated a religious passion for a mythic narrative to invest postsocialist Chinese society with a scared cultural tradition. Angry nationalists, meanwhile, invoked the shameful memory of cultural humiliations and political defeats to fuel a patriotic fervor for national rejuvenation and an irrational desire for revenge. All four stances presented selective memories of the national past to legitimize their ideological agendas: liberals issued a revanchist call to finish the incomplete project of modernity; leftists attempted to fulfill the redemptive promise of revolution; conservatives sought China's ancestral roots beyond the horizon of modernity; and nationalists quested for China's awakening from "a hundred years of humiliations." Thus disputes over the significance of the revolution were interconnected with broader reflections on the multiple trajectories of China's modern experience.

Methodologically, this book offers an alternative way of thinking about the contemporary Chinese mindscape through the prism of affect and emotion. Such an approach allows us to see post-Mao intellectual debates as a combination of ideas and feelings, theories and experiences, emotive utterance and rational deliberation. The dialogic of emotion and intellect took three distinct forms throughout our journey. First, emotion itself is a system of ethical reasoning. For the enthusiastic readers of Chen Yinke, the act of mourning is a conscious political judgment about the moral catastrophes of Mao's revolution. Second, emotion serves as the initial orientation at the root of intellectual reflection. For Taiwan's "last Marxist" Chen Yingzhen, it was the pathos and agony of defeat that stimulated his lifelong search for a messianic socialism; likewise, Liu Xiaofeng's profound intellectual transformation from a cultural Christian to a dedicated Maoist has been consistently guided by his passion for the sublime and the eternal. Third, emotion can be deliberately manufactured for the purposes of political persuasion. Nationalist *ressentiment* was by no means a natural emotion shared by the masses; to the contrary, it was engineered by populist intellectuals and amplified by sensationalist media to conjure the powerful narrative of China's past humiliation and future glory. Above all, this tripartite framework strikes a balance between the affective underpinning of political imaginaries and the political tonality of emotions, between the role of human sentiment and affect in orienting intellectual thinking and the power of reason in reflecting the ethical and political connotations of emotion.

A Passion for God

President Xi Jinping's new political vision did not dissolve the polarized responses to China's revolutionary past. Rather, the return of the sublime galvanized the rival factions of intellectuals into action. In the midst of cynical conformity and blind chauvinism, cultural luminaries, national celebrities, and media charlatans pledged their faith in the Chinese Dream. Ironically, cultural conservatives—not the Left—mobilized quickly to ride the crest of Xi's cultural politics. Prominent Confucian scholars came out of the ivory tower to celebrate President Xi as a Confucian sage-king. Since the era of high socialism, the relationship between Confucianism and the CCP has been fraught with tensions, occasionally intimate but more often estranged. Mao was drawn to the study of Confucian classics and even modeled his ceaseless rectification campaigns after the Confucian notion of moral edification. But in general, his iconoclastic revolution was the most extreme expression of anti-traditionalism. On the most profound level, Mao's radical egalitarianism—characterized by land redistribution, class struggle, and mass democracy—has deeply shaken the Confucian social hierarchy that ranked the scholar-official above the peasant. President Xi, by contrast, envisioned an ideological fusion of Confucianism and socialism to fill the spiritual void in Chinese society. He publicly celebrated the 2,565th anniversary of Confucius's birth, visited the Kong Family Mansion in the city of Qufu, spearheaded a monumental project at Peking University aiming at a complete compilation of all Confucian classics, and urged governmental officials to learn from the neo-Confucian master Wang Yangming's 王陽明 (1472–1529) credo "the unity of thought and action" (*zhixing heyi* 知行合一).[8]

Needless to say, Confucian scholars were electrified by Xi's providential design. The *agape* aroused by the alluring Chinese Dream emboldened mainland Confucians to cast a mystic-political vision of Confucian religion, with a deliberate turn away from the reformist-democratic approach of overseas Confucians. The revival of Confucian

---

8. See Cui, "Yinian sanci qinjin rujia"; Johnson, "Forget Marx and Mao."

learning in mainland China was partly indebted to the efforts of the diasporic Confucian communities in Hong Kong, Taiwan, and Singapore. During the decades of fanatic anti-Confucian campaigns, overseas neo-Confucianists such as Qian Mu 錢穆 (1895–1990), Mou Zongsan 牟宗三 (1909–1995), Tang Junyi 唐君毅 (1909–1978), and Xu Fuguan 徐復觀 (1904–1982) fought desperately to preserve the scattered "spirited roots" of Chinese culture against geopolitical ruptures. In the 1980s, their vision of "cultural China" invigorated the minds of the Marxist-oriented mainland intellectuals almost like adult education. From the 1990s onward, the sustained resurgence of academic and popular interest in *ruxue* 儒學 (Confucian learning) has encouraged scholars across the Taiwan Strait to rejuvenate Confucianism as a "vital cultural and psycho-spiritual resource" in the post-Marxist public sphere.[9] That alliance, however, soon began to break in the age of cultural nationalism. Bit by bit, the mood of brittle triumphalism prompted several leading Chinese Confucians to declare the "adolescence of Mainland New Confucianism."[10] Whereas the forerunners of overseas Confucianism struggled to reconcile the moral ideal of sagehood with the liberal political model of limited government, mainland Confucians moved to resuscitate Confucianism as an authoritarian political theology. In their perspective, the clash of civilizations simply cannot be expunged from the world, and the moral imperative of overseas Confucian inquiry surrenders the civilizational aspiration of Chinese values to Judo-Christian liberal democracy.

To be sure, mainland Confucians were driven by passions and convictions no less genuine than those of progressive thinkers. Yet whereas overseas Confucians were haunted by apocalyptic fears of Communist totalitarianism, mainland Confucians felt themselves in a stronger position. Standing on the "right side of history," they believed themselves to be the guardians of much loftier ideals: about the return of the "golden age," the restoration of the "kingly way" and the crowning of the "philosophical king." In this context, the late Qing religious thinker Kang Youwei was summoned by the mainland Confucians to legitimize a

---

9. Makeham, *Lost Soul*, 2.
10. Angle, "The Adolescence of Mainland New Confucianism," 83–99.

postsecular Chinese Dream. In 2014, devotees and acolytes gathered in Nanhai—Kang's birthplace—to declare their allegiance to Kang's vision of the Chinese politico-religious state, not in the form of philosophical deliberation, but in the form of an orchestrated inauguration, an act of religious conversion. A consensus was reached: Kang's scenario of an institutionalized Confucian religion, punctuated by religious infrastructures and unified orthodoxies, offered more powerful ways of grounding politics, guiding moral conducts, and formulating national identities than enlightenment rationality.

While overseas Confucians submitted to the modern fate of Confucianism as a "wandering and disembodied soul" (*youhun* 遊魂), the new devotees of Kang Youwei decidedly jumped into the whirlwind of political theology, hoping to "borrow a corpse to enable the soul to return" (*jieshi huanhun* 借屍還魂).[11] Thus, Jiang Qing, who advocated the "political Confucianism" of the Gongyang School since the 1990s, presented a "Confucian constitutional order." From Jiang's perspective, parliamentary democracy, constrained by legal formalism, vulgar populism, and moral relativism, resulted in a fatal deficit in substantive morality. Drawing on Kang Youwei's idea of constitutional monarchy, Jiang articulated a tricameral legislature that incorporated the will of heaven, earth, and the human into a single sovereign body.[12] Meanwhile, Chen Ming criticized the secularist myopia of both the liberals and the Left, whose iconoclasm contributed to the destruction of Confucian sacred holism. In Chen's scenario, returning to Kang's vision of Confucian sacrality transcended the secular narrative of "revolution" and "enlightenment." Tang Wenming further contended that the Confucian notion of "religion" (*jiao* 教) is broader than its Western equivalent, for it refers to a comprehensive "edifying tradition" (*jiaohua* 教化) that encompasses Confucian scriptures, learning, and institutions. Chen Bisheng spoke about the need to resuscitate the learning of "Confucian scripture" (*jingxue* 經學). He condemned the May Fourth generation for historicizing Confucian literature, turning sacred scriptures to modern historiography.[13] Together, the participants aimed to

11. Yu Ying-shih, *Xiandai ruxue lun*, 32.
12. See Jiang Qing, *A Confucian Constitutional Order*.
13. See Gan et al., "Kang Youwei yu zhiduhua ruxue," 12–41.

rejuvenate a muscular form of religious piety toward Confucian civilization under the banner of Kang Youwei.

For good and for ill, these Confucian dreamers carried on the pilgrimage of Liu Xiaofeng and his Straussian disciples analyzed in chapter 4. The restoration of a divine Confucian worldview, as both the Straussians and the Confucians believe, provides a promising way of not just guiding moral conducts and national politics, but also elevating these norms above the secular ground. As deontological liberalism suffers from a normative deficit, Confucian sacred holism provides substantive support for China's civilizational struggles to revive the splendor of its origin. Furthermore, the surge of oceanic feelings coincided with a succession of fanatic speeches and sensational publications that hailed the quasi-religious underpinning of the Chinese Dream. Anthropologists and sociologists scrambled for intellectual ammunition, from the Confucian "all-under-heaven" to Durkheimian "organic solidarity." For them, China was never a secular nation-state; it must be regarded as a "microcosm," a "world-pattern state," and a "hyper-social civilization"—a transhistorical unity with sacred coherence.[14] Even the very term "China" was endowed with a miraculous "ontology of becoming": the all-inclusive tendency of Chinese civilization (*tianxia wuwai* 天下無外) manifests as a mystical "vortex" that constantly attracts and converts exterior "barbarians."[15]

But the Confucian fever soon turned out to be less monumental than ornamental. Against the ostentatious fantasy of mainland Confucians to "Confucianize the Chinese Communist Party,"[16] the Chinese government acted swiftly to curb the wild speculations prompted by Xi's public veneration of Confucius. Party media clarified that the CCP would not "dismiss the hundred schools and restore Confucianism as a state ideology" (*bachu baijia, duzun rushu* 罷黜百家，獨尊儒術). Confucianism would remain as a "learning," a "school of thought," rather than a "state religion." Xi had made nods to this ancestral legacy merely because it supplied China's malfunctioning propaganda machine with ideological grease and gasoline. This instrumental approach,

14. Wang Mingming, *Chaoshehui tixi*; Zhao Tingyang, *Tianxia tixi*.
15. Zhao Tingyang, *Huici Zhongguo*.
16. See Jiang Qing et al., *Zhongguo bixu zairuhua*.

as Elizabeth J. Perry has pointed out, harked back to CCP's strategic appropriation of religious symbols for the purpose of political persuasion.[17] Ironically enough, the zealotry of mainland Confucians was mingled with cynical utilitarianism. "The history of Confucianism has taught us," as Jiang Qing bluntly put it, "Confucian learning thrives from taking advantage of state-co-optations."[18] Without a tacit recognition of complicity, we would not have the time-honored political realism that has so thoroughly shaped Confucian learning for centuries. In the end, this drama does not condemn the naivete of Confucian dreamers. Rather, it shows us that, in the age of the Chinese Dream, religious passion is only an ephemeral moment of faith—and an eternality of thinly disguised complicities.

Between Melancholy and Nostalgia

On December 6, 2017, Feng Xiaogang's 馮小剛 (1958–) romantic epic *Fragrant Youth* (*Fanghua* 芳華) premiered in Beijing, after a release delay. The film was originally set to debut on October 1, China's National Day, but was abruptly withdrawn from the schedule just days prior. Rumors circulated about Feng's reckless attempt to test the limit of censorship by wandering into the forbidden zones of history: art troupes in Mao's revolutionary army, the Cultural Revolution, and the 1979 Sino-Vietnamese War. Indeed, Feng's nostalgic paean to the bygone era of "revolution plus romance" might have unnerved censors. But the tearjerker soon won the hearts of older viewers who had lived through the drama and trauma of Mao's last revolution. Despite initial anxiety over its commercial performance, the film beat Pixar's animated film *Coco* and took $48 million at the box office in the opening week, the highest earnings of any art movie in the history of the People's Republic.

Based on the semi-autobiographical story *You Touched Me* (*Ni chumo le wo* 你觸摸了我) by novelist Yan Geling 嚴歌苓 (1958–), the 146-minute movie tracks the tempestuous fate of a group of People's

---

17. See Perry, *Anyuan*, 5.
18. Jiang Qing et al., *Zhongguo bixu zairuhua*, 52.

Liberation Army dancers from the Cultural Revolution to the reform era: the coming of age under the heat of revolutionary heroism; the bucolic, sensuous, and occasionally poignant romance between young soldiers; and finally, the unfolding of cruel reality punctuated by war, violence, and the forgetting of the revolution in the age of crony capitalism. The plot revolves around two political pariahs of the time: the troupe's new recruit He Xiaoping, the hopeless daughter of a rightist intellectual, and the model soldier Liu Feng, the humble son of a carpenter. He Xiaoping entered the army compound in search of friendship and love, only to be humiliated by her comrades—the sons and daughters of powerful generals and party cadres. Liu Feng, whose altruism earned him the nickname "the living Lei Feng"—Mao's celebrated national hero—was falsely accused of sexual harassment after he expressed affection for the arrogant daughter of a high-ranked cadre. Eventually, both were dismissed from the idyllic bubble of the art troupe and reassigned to fight a bloody war on the Sino-Vietnamese frontline.

Nostalgia for the lived experience of socialism permeates the mise-en-scène of the movie. "Living socialism," as Alexei Yurchak argues, was quite different from the "official interpretations provided by state rhetoric." In the eyes of the last Soviet generation, socialism "had been indivisibly linked with a very real optimism and warmth," with "comforts and well-being" in a "well-furnished common space of living."[19] Similarly, Feng romanticizes the youthful years of socialist revolution as a time of passion, dynamism, and sincerity. With political upheavals—Maoist parades and struggle sessions—downplayed, Feng deploys images, sound, and texts to retrieve the collective lifeworld of the revolutionary art troupe: the self-contained military courtyard, the 1970s propaganda music, and Maoist slogans and dances. However, the physical, linguistic, and sonic details serve not merely as a Barthian "reality effect." Rather, Feng's obsession with the sensuous, innocent, and amorous aspects of youthful adventure defies and depoliticizes the revolutionary undertone of the socialist bildungsroman. The everyday military life, having once been saturated with ideological fanaticism,

---

19. Yurchak, *Everything Was Forever, Until It Was No More*, 8.

FIGURE 7. A poster for *Fragrant Youth* featuring the ballet dancers of Mao's revolutionary art troupe. From Feng Xiaogang, dir., *Fragrant Youth* (Huayi Brothers Media Corporation, Zhejiang Dongyang Mela Media, Beijing Culture Media, iQiyi, Yaolai Films and Television, Beijing Jingxi Culture and Tourism, August First Film Studio, Dongyang Shangshang Film, 2017). https://www.imdb.com/title/tt6654316/mediaviewer/rm4132461568/.

now reappears only as the symbol of adolescent effervescence devoid of political meaning. Indeed, feminist critics denounce Feng's unabashed celebration of sexualized female bodies: the elegant performance of the ballet dancers, the frequent display of slender, half-nude women soldiers in the locker room, and girls' lingerie glistening with water droplets (fig. 7). In this regard, Feng's socialist nostalgia is much more trivial than the "totalitarian temptation" that plagued post-Mao cultural life. It is simply voyeuristic.

Despite its shallow and playful aspects, the movie faintly echoes the solemn political melancholy that pervaded Wang Anyi's and Chen Yingzhen's elegies for Chinese socialism. As argued in chapter 3, melancholy is a form of resistance charged by an emancipatory political desire. The pathos of the defeat empowers the melancholic Left with a prescient insight to reflect on the dark inheritance of revolutionary authoritarianism. To be sure, Feng is not a committed Marxist in the tradition of Chen Yingzhen. Still, in response to Chen's thorny question about the "corrupted and fallen" nature of the Chinese revolution, Feng's film provides a visual critique of the remarkably tenacious power of the bureaucratic hierarchy in Mao's egalitarian kingdom. *Fragrant Youth* chronicles how a class of "red aristocrats" emerged at the very heart of the Communist Party. Notwithstanding Mao's radical call to root out the party power holders, the Cultural Revolution paradoxically provided a haven for the children of the bureaucratic elite to develop a collective identity and consolidate their privilege. Well protected by a self-contained courtyard, military power, and political network, these red heirs maintained a sense of superiority. They openly humiliated He Xiaoping, the daughter of an intellectual— "stinking old ninth" (*chou laojiu* 臭老九), whose "rancid sweat" smelled like "she's taken a dip in a swill bucket." Liu Feng, meanwhile, was punished for transgressing the invisible boundary of class: the carpenter exists only to labor tirelessly for the ruling elite, yet he was so deluded by the sweet promise of egalitarianism as to touch the daughter of a powerful party cadre. In this regard, their eventual banishment from the art troupe affirms the famous "bloodline couplet" that proclaimed the "hereditary permanence" of political status in Mao's socialist utopia: "If the father is a [revolutionary] hero, the son is also a hero; if the father is a reactionary, the son is a bastard" (老子英雄兒好漢，老子反動兒混蛋).[20]

Hence, *Fragrant Youth* is not simply a nostalgic look at the time of youthful innocence that has irrevocably passed. Instead, Left melancholy is tinged with a vexing web of uneasy feelings: shock mixed with disillusionment, conviction tainted by doubt, and a hidden anger toward a socialist regime that was socialist only in name. That melancholy-turned-anger culminates in the epilogue of the movie. In 1991, the children of Mao gathered for a reunion in the tropical Hainan Island—a capitalist heaven for tourists, smugglers and the nouveaux riches. All red aristocrats succeeded in joining the middle-class world of entrepreneurs, writers, and governmental officials. Yet Liu Feng the war hero had to eke out a living as a rickshaw driver. His unkempt beard, worker's

---

20. Quoted in and translated by Yiching Wu, *The Cultural Revolution at the Margins*, 61.

clothes, and military manner made him look anachronistic in the eyes of his comrades. Even though the episode offers a comforting reunion between Liu Feng and He Xiaoping, a deep sense of having been cheated by revolutionary heroism lingers until the very end. Alienated by Mao's class politics, the two have arrived in the postsocialist world and yet again find themselves to be outcasts and strangers. Their tragedy is a template, a cultural script, and an elegy for the melancholic Left languishing in the paradise of capitalism.

Robert Burton wrote in *The Anatomy of Melancholy* that "what cannot be cured must be endured,"[21] and similarly the Chinese Dream failed to cure Feng Xiaogang's melancholy. Indeed, Feng's generation was still haunted by a feeling of sadness about how far the post-Mao world fell short of the egalitarian promise of socialism. That disappointment and frustration had gathered momentum beyond cultural circles since the early reform era. Anger and grief have been pervasive among those veteran state workers who had their jobs, homes, and social networks taken away in the privatization process. From Wang Bing's 王兵 (1967–) documentary *West of the Tracks* (2003) to Zhang Meng's 張猛 (1975–) drama *The Piano in a Factory* (2010), the images of a crumbling socialist industrial utopia appeared as poignant symbols of alienation and oppression in the age of neoliberal capitalism. Under Xi's reign, the leftist turn of official propaganda first aroused considerable enthusiasm from radical Marxists and student activists, who decided to "take the state at its words"[22] and pressed for workers' equal rights. Yet the naïve proponents of leftist egalitarianism failed to heed the Burkean advice that "what equality ultimately means is a rotation in the seat of power."[23] Of course, the Communist regime in power behaved no differently than its capitalist nemesis in cracking down on labor strikes and social protests. This glaring disparity between words and deeds generated a schizophrenic, perhaps no less dystopian, topology for the Chinese Left. Between resignation and conformity, melancholy was nothing but a painful awareness of idealism and its betrayal.

21. Burton, *The Anatomy of Melancholy*, 297.
22. See Straughn, "'Taking the State at Its Word.'"
23. Robin, *The Reactionary Mind*, 9.

The Pathos of Liberalism

In August 2016, Fang Fang's novel *Soft Burial* (*Ruanmai* 軟埋) came out from People's Literature Publishing House in Beijing. The protagonist, Ding Zitao, lost her family in the 1950s Communist land reform—a brutal Maoist campaign that involved the mass killings of landlords by peasants and party cadres. A series of mysterious events and fortune helped Ding overcome all adversity under the socialist regime, bringing her from the brink of death to the status of a comfortable bourgeois living in the reform period. But Ding suddenly collapsed when her son, a successful entrepreneur, proudly showed her a mountain villa and the luxurious life he now lived. The woman had endured all the hardships throughout the revolutionary years, but now, surrounded by doctors and servants, she lost her desire to live and simply withered away. By the end of the story, one learns that the mountain villa originally belonged to Ding's family before 1949. In that landlord household, Ding had witnessed the torture and suicide of her entire family during the land reform campaign. Even though Ding survived the bloody event and moved on, the atrocious violence sowed the seed for her eventual collapse.

The treacherous, often senseless, and dehumanizing aspects of the land reform are reflected in the gruesome ritual of "soft burial"—a corpse buried in the earth without the protection of a coffin. In the novel, Ding was ordered by her father-in-law to bury the whole family without coffins. In Chinese funeral rites, a coffin keeps body and soul together in the transitional stage from the living world to the underworld, in hopes of future transmigration. But the fear of reentering the world of atrocities in the next life haunted the superstitious landlord. In a most cynical conformity to the Communist extermination of the landlord class, he demanded a soft burial so that his soul would not return to the world of savage violence. Furthermore, Fang Fang invests this macabre ritual with an allegorical implication about collective forgetting: "when they [the living] seal off their past, cut off their roots, reject their memories . . . their lives are soft-buried in time."[24]

---

24. Fang Fang, *Ruanmai*, 297.

She deplores the state-sponsored amnesia that softly and ruthlessly buried the painful memories of persecution and death during the land reform. Hence the "dispersed souls" (*hunfei posan* 魂飛魄散) of the landlords symbolize the unbearable burden of the past that haunts the living. With the ghosts of victims, perpetuators, and bystanders still hovering between life and death, the demand for poetic justice becomes an endless waiting without any hope of future vindication.

Fang Fang epitomizes a type of liberal intelligentsia that is now vanishing from the Chinese public life. Born in the 1950s, Fang Fang's political generation participated in the initial days of the Cultural Revolution but was soon disillusioned by the rampant violence of the Red Guard movement. Beginning in the late 1970s, the most talented and courageous men and women from this cohort sought to express their confusion, shock, and anger toward the dehumanizing dogma of Maoism that had unleashed savage hatred and caused meaningless deaths. Despite the spectacular power of the censoring apparatus, writers, poets, and philosophers in the 1980s sought to create a language of humanism—a framework of social and moral responsibility defined by Václav Havel as "living in truth"—to expose the labyrinth of repression, terror, and ideological lies fabricated by the Leninist state.[25] As chronicled in chapter 1, enlightenment thinkers condemned the Maoist class politics for cultivating extreme emotions—hatred and fear—for ideological purposes, which resulted in the breakdown of basic ethical norms. They sought to install a sentimental education that could transform the moral and emotional terrain of a paralyzed society steeped for decades in ideological fanaticism.

In this regard, *Soft Burial* belonged to the spiritual milieu of the 1980s New Enlightenment. In conjunction with Liu Zaifu's and Ba Jin's calls for "repentance consciousness," Fang Fang's moralistic undertone reflects her disappointment with the Chinese inability to mourn the atrocious crimes committed by peasants, intellectuals, and party cadres in the land reform campaign. Meanwhile, Fang Fang moves beyond the whiggish narrative of reconciliation and asks how even a sincere confession could not dispel the inherited guilt that passed from one

---

25. Havel, "The Power of the Powerless," 55.

generation to the next. Just as Karl Jaspers pointed out that "language fails" when the German people's "metaphysical guilt" brings them "face to face with nothingness," Fang Fang reveals that moral and legal paradigms are inadequate to address the monstrous, irreparable crime of "soft burial" that haunted the perpetrators and their offspring for decades.[26] The liberal pathos was a defiant challenge to the culture of amnesia under the new orthodoxy. For the indignant liberal, the tacit agreement of "not arguing" (*bu zhenglun* 不爭論) about political taboo not only displayed the lack of empathy with the victims of revolution but also failed to undo or at least acknowledge past traumas. As chapter 2 shows, the liberals' excessive moral indignation against the crimes and the atrocities of socialist revolution led to a categorical negation of the Maoist past as absolute evil. In many ways, this radical self-purgation resembles the "non-German German" approach proposed by the "redemptive republicans" in the West German discussion of the Nazi past: divorcing from corrupted national traditions was deemed as the only way for liberalism to take root in an authoritarian country.[27] Similarly, the shame of belonging to a contaminated political tradition compelled Chinese liberals to distance themselves from their lived experience of socialism. In the liberal scenario, a postrevolutionary Chinese identity should rely less on the continuities of a sacred national past than on a set of abstract universal principles of human rights. Only a Habermasian "constitutional patriotism" could ensure a democratic form of citizenship that is both binding and inclusive.[28]

However, whereas the German memory disputes were framed by an underlying consensus that condemned the Nazi past as a "perversion, a plague, a catastrophe, and finally a tragedy,"[29] no such consensus has informed Chinese public discussions about the Maoist past. The publication of *Soft Burial* provoked fanatic reactions from orthodox Marxists. A chain of ideological attacks against Fang Fang soon

---

26. Jaspers, *The Question of German Guilt*, 81, quoted in Moses, *German Intellectuals and the Nazi Past*, 21.

27. Moses, *German Intellectuals and the Nazi Past*, 105–30.

28. See Liu Qing, "Zhongguo yujing xia de ziyouzhuyi."

29. Meinecke, *The German Catastrophe*, 101–3, quoted in Olick, *The Sins of the Fathers*, 98.

proliferated on the internet. Hawkish reviewers branded the book as a "poisonous weed" containing harmful "historical nihilism," and denounced Fang Fang for "resurrecting the evil spirits of the landlord class." The propaganda department assessed the book as a sinister Western scheme of "peaceful evolution" and ordered to ban the novel. Several party-affiliated critics further declared that the founding legitimacy of Mao's proletarian regime rested precisely on eliminating landlords, warlords, and bandits through the land reform campaign. They growled that the novel denigrated the emancipatory aspect of class struggle and blamed Fang Fang for deviating from President Xi's literary policy. After all, the land reform was not Auschwitz. German republicans struggled to forfeit their national tradition in the wake of the Nazi genocide. Mao's classicide, by contrast, has been viewed by many neo-Maoist thinkers as an appealing alternative. Didn't Mao say that revolution was not a dinner party? For Fang Fang's opponents, insurrection, violence, valor, and martyrdom were more powerful than the liberals' feeble humanism when it came to forging a muscular national identity drenched in blood and sacrifice.

The story of Fang Fang's generation has no happy ending. In the fight against the COVID-19 pandemic, liberal intellectuals and writers became an easy target of online abuse. Fang Fang's *Wuhan Diary*, which chronicled life and death in her home city and exposed local officials' fumbling reaction to the outbreak of the pandemic, sparked backlash from Chinese patriots, who mounted a trolling campaign to vilify her as a "traitor to the Han nation." Although Wuhan officials' initial mishaps caused public outrage in early 2020, the central government responded aggressively, if not excessively, through a raft of draconian countermeasures, including imposing heavy-handed quarantine restrictions, building temporary hospitals, and setting up a national system of contact tracing to fight the silent killer. More revealing was the CCP's determination to reverse the coronavirus narrative in the global propaganda struggle over the political implications of the public health emergency. In line with President Xi's call to "tell the good China story" and his prophecy that "the East is rising, and the West is declining," writers, journalists, and filmmakers were mobilized to celebrate the country's success in extinguishing the deadly infection. Thus, COVID-19 was taken by Chinese nationalists as a stress test for global governance, exposing laissez-faire institutions as fragile and the "China model" as decisive and responsible.[30] In this context, nationalist critics fiercely denounced Fang Fang and her traitorous followers for "stabbing the nation in the back"—that is—fabricating negative information to undermine China's reputation in the intensifying Sino-American rivalry. Increasingly allied with the state propaganda, extremist-patriots began to portray those "public intellectuals" as a thoroughly Westernized group who succumbed to the temptations of fame and the lust for money. The entire liberal intelligentsia, as the accusation went, must be blamed for the erosion of faith in socialism and the sellout to the West.

However, it was not the virulence of ideological critique but the increasing irrelevance of the liberal prescription for China that had broken the back of many veteran liberals. Resounding is Yin Haiguang's remark that the program of liberal reform offered no solution to a society steeped in war and disorder. Likewise, what divided Fang Fang and her critics was an irreconcilable disagreement about how to best ensure national survival in the (post)pandemic world. With the residual faith in liberal cosmopolitanism shattered by the resurgence of authoritarian populism in the heartland of the West, even the staunchest Chinese believers in liberal democracy began, one by one, to abandon their political beliefs and look back on the optimism of the 1980s as naïve at best. In this environment, it was the popular sci-fi writer Liu Cixin 劉慈欣 (1963-)—rather than the Westernphilic Fang Fang—who captured public attention with a social Darwinist vision of a future global order. In his sci-fi trilogy *The Three-Body Problem* (*Santi* 三體), Liu describes the entire universe as a dark forest ruled by survival of the fittest and has no place for humanitarianism: "Every civilization is an armed hunter stalking through the trees like a ghost. . . . The hunter has to be careful, because everywhere in the forest are stealthy hunters like him. If he finds other life. . . there's only one thing he can do: open fire and eliminate them. In this forest, hell is other people."[31] As I argue

---

30. Perry, "China's (R)evolutionary Governance and the COVID-19 Crisis," 387–96.

31. Cixin Liu, *The Dark Forest*, 484.

elsewhere, Liu's gloomy tale reminded Chinese readers of their nation's precarious place in the postpandemic international order—a "world full of enmity, struggle, violence, conspiracy, espionage, and of course, human extinction."[32] Unlike Fang Fang's liberal-humanist call for transparency and disclosure in China's disaster management, Liu in his trilogy envisions a series of extreme and unthinkable measures, ranging across the exercise of emergency power, implanting ideological conformity, and curbing pacifism and escapism, to ensure (or impose) human solidarity in the wake of a total war against the technologically superior aliens. During the pandemic, Liu's obsession with the survival of the species found an unlikely echo when the CCP deployed social Darwinist rhetoric to showcase the resolve, sacrifice, and heroism of the party and the people to combat the rising foreign enmity toward China. Fang Fang was not defeated in spirit. Beyond the private domain, however, her liberal voice has become hardly more than a "trembling in the presence of illiberalism."[33]

From *Ressentiment* to Righteous Anger

In 2017, *Wolf Warrior 2* (戰狼2), a Ramboesque action movie became the first Chinese film ever to enter Box Office Mojo's global all-time top 100, with a stunning $874 million at the box office. Directed by action star Wu Jing 吳京 (1974–), the military adventure features Leng Feng, a former Chinese special forces operative with a troubled personality, who travels to a fictitious African state in search of his missing fiancée but becomes entangled in a brutal civil war between government troops, insurgents, and white mercenaries. A highly skilled soldier, Leng helps the Chinese navy rescue Chinese citizens and African civilians and finally defeats "Big Daddy," the villainous leader of the Anglo-American mercenaries. The movie's poster also displayed hawkish patriotism with the tagline: "Whoever offends the Chinese shall be wiped out no matter how far away" (*fanwo zhonghua zhe, suiyuan bizhu* 犯我中華者，雖遠必誅). The catchphrase captured the powerful rise

---

32. Hang Tu, "Long Live Chairman Mao!," 520.
33. Mansfield, *The Spirit of Liberalism*, vii.

of nationalistic sentiment in the age of the Chinese Dream. As chapter 5 shows, the chanting and raving of patriots in the 1990s took a milder form, amounting to little more than a defensive disavowal, a self-pity on account of Beijing's besieged status as the last bastion of dysfunctional socialism in the U.S.-led international order. But two decades later, China's emergence as a global economic superpower has imbued reactive nationalism with enmity and aggression. Now, buttressed by China's mighty economic power, zealous advocates of "wolf warrior diplomacy" favor a crusading style of foreign policy, combining cultural revivalism with a realistic strategy of geopolitical expansions. They dismiss the rational-communicative ideal of cosmopolitan cultural exchange and deploy populist rhetoric and sensational media to mobilize popular anger against concrete and existential enemies: arrogant liberals, foreign suspects, U.S.-backed international organizations, and, above all, "fraudulent" Western democracy.[34]

The explosion of *ressentiment* in Chinese public discourse was also an emotional, hateful response to the rightward turn of the West. In the age of Trumpism, the rise of right-wing populist movements in the Euro-American world was a sharp turn away from the deliberative model of liberal democracy and toward violent expressions of hatred directed at immigrants and foreigners. When racist and chauvinistic tweets by Western populist leaders reached Chinese public media, they further provoked mixed feelings of shock and rage among Chinese citizens. In return, unchecked expressions of anti-Americanism began to course through intellectual polemics, government propaganda, and public media at home and abroad. In the midst of the Sino-American trade war, international relations experts spoke with grim authority about the closing of the Thucydides's Trap—the destined war between the United States and China. An army of "little pinks"—a new generation of patriotic youth—waged virulent online attacks against all "Americanophiles," including liberal professors, Taiwanese separatists, and Hong Kong protestors. Returnees from the West lashed out with their contempt toward the Orientalism of Western academy, the materialistic and greedy nature of financial capitalism, and the cultural

---

34. For an analysis of wolf warrior diplomacy, see Martin, *China's Civilian Army*.

racism of Anglo-American society. Leftists and rightists, populists and elitists, chauvinists and cultural pessimists, fringe historians, literary critics, aestheticians, and poets all found violent delight in celebrating China's bid for world power. *Ressentiment* was no longer the assertion of the weak against the paralyzing force of the strong. It was hailed as a righteous anger, an "ode to joy," a hymn of moral regeneration, and a messianic calling for the eventual arrival of the Chinese Century.

Yet while *Wolf Warrior 2* incited patriotic ardor and enhanced President Xi's vision of China as the new guardian of global order, it also borrowed aggressively from Hollywood, radically reconfiguring the visual language of the "mainstream melody" to meld state-orchestrated patriotism and grassroots nationalism. The movie is replete with Hollywood formulas: a melodramatic plot, unbridled masculinity, military prowess, and the Orientalist conception of a failing African state. However, the image of a reckless warrior adds an individualistic flavor to the hackneyed Communist hero. Whereas the specter of the party-state looms all too large in the moral ideal of the flawless party soldier, Leng Feng frequents bars and taverns, has a penchant for alcohol and drugs, and follows his own instinct for justice and revenge. Meanwhile, in conjunction with the official rhetoric of China's peaceful rise, Leng's bohemian adventure takes place in Africa, a perilous but lucrative land, which endows him with a civilizing mission to end chaos and restore peace. But beyond colonial fantasy, *Wolf Warrior* also idealizes Chinese solidarity with the colonized and the downtrodden against Western imperialists. Chinese audiences were thrilled by the iconic yellow-race warrior who dares to say no to the swaggering American villain. In the film's climax, the venomous Big Daddy declares in front of Leng Feng that "people like you [the yellow race] will always be inferior to people like me [the white race]; get fucking used to it," to which Leng replies: "That's fucking past tense" (fig. 8). This graphic scene of a life-and-death struggle between the Chinese warrior and the evil American mercenary, as Chris Berry reads it, resonates with "the idea of China's humiliation and the need to overcome it."[35] The demonic power of anger heals the wounded national pride and binds the Chinese and

---

35. Chris Berry, "*Wolf Warrior 2*," 40.

FIGURE 8. The final duel between "Big Daddy" (Frank Grillo, left) and Leng Feng (Wu Jing, right). From Wu Jing, dir., *Wolf Warrior 2* (Deng Feng International Media, China Film Group, Bona Films, and Beijing Culture, 2017). https://www.imdb.com/title/tt7131870/.

Africans together in their shared struggle against Western racism and imperialism.

As argued in chapter 5, *ressentiment* has been the principal psychological motor behind the remarkable resurgence of popular nationalism in the post-Tiananmen era. Yet while the polemical declaration of *China Can Say No* in 1996 was driven by a "repressed shame at China's inhospitality to democratic ideas,"[36] the prevalent mood in *Wolf Warrior 2* is a righteous anger directed at the hypocrisy of the Euro-American colonial powers. The narrative implies that Western imperialism was solely responsible for the political chaos and the humanitarian crisis of the African state, and portrays China as a savior seeking to restore peace and prosperity. Leng Feng's rescue mission reinforces the ideal of a benevolent Chinese global empire that wields its power to protect Chinese

---

36. Hillenbrand and Starr, "Chinese Neo-Nationalism," 134.

and African civilians, develops a vaccine for an Ebola-like illness, and pours in investment and labor to aid Africa's infrastructure building. Far from a war enthusiast, Leng fights against Western mercenaries who collaborate with local insurgents to sabotage Sino-African friendship. Righteous anger provides the enmity and decisiveness that the exercise of an emerging Chinese power truly requires.

However, the vision of a righteous Chinese empire reveals a set of ambiguities that resemble the predicament of the American imperial vista in the post–Cold War era. As the neoconservative guru Irving Kristol (1920–2009) lamented, the conflict between the warrior and the businessman—the twin icons of the American hegemony—constantly deferred the actualization of a global American empire. The U.S. commitment to free trade and civil society made it difficult to wield its imperial military might with gravitas and authority.[37] As a result, the Homeric warrior degenerated into a greedy businessman. Likewise, President Xi has repeatedly vowed commitment to a free market ideology,[38] which renders the Wolf Warrior's righteous anger suspicious at best. Leng Feng does not seek to overthrow the colonial economic system. Rather, the warrior takes up "the white man's burden" to fight so that Chinese companies could safely drill for oil and gas in the African backyard. The rise of global China, as the authors of *Unhappy China* (*Zhongguo bu gaoxing* 中國不高興) foresaw in 2009, could be achieved only through the fusion of the warrior and the capitalist, under the masterful maneuvering of "doing business with a sword" (*chijian jingshang* 持劍經商).[39] Righteous anger, to begin with, is a Trumpian show to hammer out a better deal.

While *Wolf Warrior 2*'s phenomenal success created a multibillion-dollar cultural industry, it also exposes the commercialized nature of patriotism in the age of mass entertainment. Twenty years after the naysayers discovered the lucrative business of nationalism, cursing America has evolved into a gigantic ecosystem with an army of pro-government

---

37. For an analysis of Irving Kristol's vision of American empire, see Robin, *The Reactionary Mind*, 201–20.

38. Martin, Zhu, and Anstey, "Xi Jinping Vows Commitment to Global Trading Order as U.S. Deal Nears."

39. Song Xiaojun et al., *Zhongguo bu gaoxing*, 98–105.

public intellectuals, media performers, and publicity hunters jostling for attention. Instead of serving as pale copies of the Foreign Ministry spokesperson, however, these shrewd media practitioners frequently throw jaw-dropping remarks, create satirical tweets with punchy soundbites, and perform theatricalized anger or ridicule for the netizens' recreational consumption. The military-theorist-turned-comedian "Admiral" Zhang Shaozhong added a pseudoscientific flavor to the formula of America-bashing when he proudly declared that Beijing's cancer-inducing smog is thick enough to be "the country's top defense mechanism against American laser weapons"; the high-profile scholar-advisor Jin Canrong's lecture on Sino-U.S. relationship was refreshing precisely for his swagger and ineloquence, and for his (deliberate) misinterpretation of President Xi's promise of "win-win cooperation" with the United States as "China wins twice"; Fudan University's superstar professor Zhang Weiwei never failed to attract admiring fans with his tautological proclamation that the Chinese Dream is unique because China is unique.[40] This is the moment of amusing ourselves to death in the age of show business, when even the mindless observer could not get over the impression that these cheeky experts hardly mean what they say. Indeed, the performative nature of patriotism was exemplified by a notorious remark made by "China's No. 1 anti-America warrior" Sima Nan, who allegedly blurted out that "opposing America is my job but staying in America is my life" (反美是工作，赴美是生活) when netizens found out that he got on a flight bound for the United States to spend the Lunar New Year with his family.[41] If these wolf warriors did enchant their supporters with patriotic ire, they have also awakened no less public resentment against the hypocrisy of the nationalist business. As love and hate are two sides of the same coin, it can flip the other way at any moment.

Forty years after the death of Mao, no intellectual consensus about China's revolutionary experience has emerged out of the virulent memory debates and protracted cultural wars. In the Xi Jinping era, Chinese

---

40. See Jing Sun, *Red Chamber, World Dream*, 124.
41. Jing Sun, *Red Chamber, World Dream*, 103–4.

intellectuals have remained deeply divided about the meaning of revolution for twentieth-century China—its demonic power, its moral and ethical implications, and the price the Chinese people have paid to bring it into existence. Meanwhile, a cynical consensus has indeed begun to crystalize in response to the surge of patriotic passions in the age of the Chinese Dream. For the new generation of Chinese dreamers, the acrimonious debates about Mao's crimes and virtues could never reach a decision. Yet ideological polarization had made it difficult to normalize Chinese history and national consciousness in the new era of geopolitical competitions. As China and the West drift slowly but inevitably toward another Cold War, Chinese citizens must be inculcated with a sanitized account of a sacred national past to assert confidence against the lure of Western universalism. Even though liberals believed that the unveiling of Maoist catastrophes contributes to the moral strength of the Chinese identity, they have rendered China vulnerable to ideological attacks from the West. For cynical realists, the cunning of the Machiavellian was perhaps always better than the naivety of the idealist in the existential struggle for global supremacy.

Given the effervescence of nationalism in the public space, Chinese intellectuals are confronted with a difficult choice: between resignation and conformity. Nevertheless, the return of violent hatred should not be read as a death knell for independent thinking. As this epilogue shows, thinkers and writers have understood the Chinese Dream not simply under the rubric of national rejuvenation, but also through more ambiguous allegories and responses: amnesia, mourning, cynical conformity, and religious piety. The drama of these dreamers neither vindicates the heroism of dissent nor condemns the tyrannophilia of the intelligentsia-in-captivity. Rather, it illuminates the profound, if troubling, political passions and ideological convictions of the post-Mao generation caught between a failing socialist utopia and a rising neoliberal juggernaut.

Bibliography

Abbeele, Georges Van Den. "The Persecution of Writing: Revisiting Strauss and Censorship." *Diacritics* 27, no. 2 (Summer 1997): 2–17.
Adorno, Theodor W. "Late Style in Beethoven." In *Essays on Music*, edited by Richard Leppert, translated by Susan H. Gillespie, 564–68. Berkeley: University of California Press, 2002.
———. *Negative Dialectics*. Translated by E. B. Ashton. New York: Routledge, 1973.
———. "Resignation." *Telos* 35, no. 166 (Spring 1978): 290–93.
Adorno, Theodor W., Else Frenkel-Brunswik, Daniel J. Levinson, and R. Nevitt Stanford. *The Authoritarian Personality*. New York: Verso, 2019.
Agamben, Giorgio. "On the Uses and Disadvantages of Living among Specters." In *Nudities*, translated by David Kishik and Stefan Pedatella, 36–42. Stanford, CA: Stanford University Press, 2011.
Ames, Roger T., and Jinhua Jia, eds. *Li Zehou and Confucian Philosophy*. Honolulu: University of Hawai'i Press, 2018.
Anagnost, Ann. *National Past-Times: Narrative, Representation, and Power in Modern China*. Durham, NC: Duke University Press, 1997.
Anderson, Marston. *The Limits of Realism: Chinese Fiction in the Revolutionary Period*. Berkeley: University of California Press, 1990.
Anderson, Perry. *Considerations on Western Marxism*. New York: Verso, 1976.
Angle, Stephen C. "The Adolescence of Mainland New Confucianism." *Contemporary Chinese Thought* 49, no. 2 (April 2018): 83–99.
Apter, David E., and Tony Saich. *Revolutionary Discourse in Mao's Republic*. Cambridge, MA: Harvard University Press, 1998.
Arendt, Hannah. *Eichmann in Jerusalem: A Report on the Banality of Evil*. New York: Penguin, 2006.
Aron, Raymond. *The Opium of the Intellectuals*. New York: Routledge, 2001.

Ba Jin 巴金. "Wenge bowuguan" 文革博物館 [A museum of the Cultural Revolution]. In *Suixiang lu* 隨想錄 [Miscellaneous reflections], 601–4. Beijing: Renmin wenxue chubanshe, 1983.

Bao, Weihong. *Fiery Cinema: The Emergence of Affective Medium in China, 1915–1945*. Minneapolis: University of Minnesota Press, 2015.

Barmé, Geremie R. *In the Red: On Contemporary Chinese Culture*. New York: Columbia University Press, 1999.

———. "The Irresistible Fall and Rise of Chairman Mao." In *Shades of Mao: The Posthumous Cult of the Great Leader*, edited by Geremie R. Barmé, 3–74. Armonk, NY: M. E. Sharpe, 1996.

Barth, Karl. *The Epistle to the Romans*. Translated by Edwyn C. Hoskyns. Oxford: Oxford University Press, 1968.

Bartsch, Shadi. *Plato Goes to China: The Greek Classics and Chinese Nationalism*. Princeton, NJ: Princeton University Press, 2023.

Benedict, Ruth. *Chrysanthemum and the Sword: Patterns of Japanese Culture*. Boston, MA: Mariner Books, 2006.

Benjamin, Walter. "Left-Wing Melancholy." *Screen* 15, no. 2 (July 1974): 28–32.

———. *The Origin of German Tragic Drama*. Translated by John Osborne. New York: Verso, 1998.

———. "Theses on the Philosophy of History." In *Illuminations: Essays and Reflections*, translated by Harry Zohn, edited by Hannah Arendt, 253–64. New York: Schocken Books, 1968.

Berger, Thomas U. *War Guilt and World Politics after World War II*. New York: Cambridge University Press, 2012.

Berkson, Mark. "A Confucian Defense of Shame: Morality, Self-Cultivation, and the Dangers of Shamelessness." *Religions* 12, no. 1 (January 5, 2021): 32. https://doi.org/10.3390/rel12010032.

Berlin, Isaiah. *The Hedgehog and the Fox*. Edited by Henry Hardy. Princeton, NJ: Princeton University Press, 2013.

———. "Two Concepts of Liberty." In *Liberty: Incorporating Four Essays on Liberty*, edited by Henry Hardy, 166–217. Oxford: Oxford University Press, 2002.

Berns, Walter. *Freedom, Virtue, and the First Amendment*. Westport, CT: Greenwood Publishing Group, 1969.

Bernstein, Michael André. *Foregone Conclusions: Against Apocalyptic History*. Berkeley: University of California Press, 1994.

Bernstein, Richard. *China 1945: Mao's Revolution and America's Fateful Choice*. New York: Vintage, 2015.

Bernstein, Richard, and Ross H. Munro. *The Coming Conflict with China*. New York: Knopf, 1997.

Berry, Chris. "*Wolf Warrior 2*: Imagining the Chinese Century." *Film Quarterly* 72, no. 2 (Winter 2018): 38–44.
Berry, Michael. *A History of Pain: Trauma in Modern Chinese Literature and Film*. New York: Columbia University Press, 2008.
Blanchette, Jude. *China's New Red Guards: The Return of Radicalism and the Rebirth of Mao Zedong*. New York: Oxford University Press, 2019.
Bloom, Alan. *The Closing of the American Mind: How Higher Education Has Failed Democracy and Impoverished the Souls of Today's Students*. New York: Simon & Schuster, 1987.
Blumenberg, Hans. *The Legitimacy of the Modern Age*. Translated by Robert M. Wallace. Cambridge, MA: MIT Press, 1985.
Boggs, Carl. *Intellectuals and the Crisis of Modernity*. Albany: State University of New York Press, 1993.
Boswell, James. *The Life of Samuel Johnson*. Edited by Christopher Hibbert. New York: Penguin Classics, 1986.
Bourg, Julian. "Blame It on Paris." *French Historical Studies* 35, no. 1 (Winter 2012): 181–97.
———. *From Revolution to Ethics: May 1968 and Contemporary French Thought*. Montreal: McGill-Queen's University Press, 2017.
Boym, Svetlana. *The Future of Nostalgia*. New York: Basic Books, 2002.
Braester, Yomi. *Painting the City Red: Chinese Cinema and the Urban Contract*. Durham, NC: Duke University Press, 2010.
———. "Taiwanese Identity and the Crisis of Memory: Post-Chiang Mystery." In *Writing Taiwan: A New Literary History*, edited by David Der-wei Wang and Carlos Rojas, 213–32. Durham, NC: Duke University Press, 2007.
Branscombe, Nyla R., and Bertjan Doosje. "International Perspectives on the Experience of Collective Guilt." In *Collective Guilt: International Perspective*, edited by Branscombe and Doosje, 3–15. Cambridge: Cambridge University Press, 2004.
Breckman, Warren. *Adventures of the Symbolic: Postmarxism and Democracy*. New York: Columbia University Press, 2015.
———. *Marx, the Young Hegelians, and the Origins of Radical Social Theory*. Cambridge: Cambridge University Press, 1999.
Brown, Wendy. "Resisting Left Melancholia." In *Loss: The Politics of Mourning*, edited by David L. Eng and David Kazanjian, 458–66. Berkeley: University of California Press, 2003.
Buckley, Chris. "Nie Yuanzi, Whose Poster Fanned the Cultural Revolution, Dies at 98." *New York Times*, September 3, 2019. https://cn.nytimes.com/obits/20190905/nie-yuanzi-dead/.

Burnyeat, M. F. "Sphinx without a Secret." In *Explorations in Ancient and Modern Philosophy*, vol. 2, 289–304. Cambridge: Cambridge University Press, 2012.

Burton, Robert. *The Anatomy of Melancholy*. New York: New York Review Books, 2001.

Butler, Judith, Ernesto Laclau, and Slavoj Žižek. *Contingency, Hegemony, Universality: Contemporary Dialogues on the Left*. 2nd ed. New York: Verso, 2011.

Cai Yi 蔡儀. *Xin meixue* 新美學 [New aesthetics]. Beijing: Shehui kexue chubanshe, 1985.

Cai Yuanpei 蔡元培. "Yi meiyu dai zongjiao shuo" 以美育代宗教說 [Replacing religion with aesthetic education]. In *Cai Yuanpei meixue wenxuan* 蔡元培美學文選 [Selections of Cai Yuanpei's essays on aesthetics], 68–69. Beijing: Beijing daxue chubanshe, 1983.

Calhoun, Craig. *Neither Gods nor Emperors: Students and the Struggle for Democracy in China*. Berkeley: University of California Press, 1997.

Carrai, Maria Adele. *Sovereignty in China: A Genealogy of a Concept since 1840*. Cambridge: Cambridge University Press, 2019.

Cassirer, Ernst. *The Myth of the State*. New Haven, CT: Yale University Press, 1961.

Chai, Ling 柴玲. *A Heart for Freedom*. Carol Stream, IL: Tyndale Momentum, 2011.

———. "Interview at Tiananmen Square with Chai Ling." Accessed May 16, 2022. http://afe.easia.columbia.edu/special/china_1950_chailing.htm.

Chan, Anita. *Children of Mao: Personality Development and Political Activism in the Red Guard Generation*. Seattle: University of Washington Press, 1985.

Chan Chi-keung 陳志強. *Wanming wangxue yuanelun* 晚明王學原惡論 [Late-Ming Neo-Confucianism and the problem of prime evil]. Taipei: Taida chuban zhongxin, 2018.

Chang Hao 張灝. *Youan yishi yu minzhu chuantong* 幽暗意識與民主傳統 [Dark consciousness and democratic tradition]. Beijing: Xinxing chubanshe, 2006.

Chang, Sung-sheng Yvonne. *Literary Culture in Taiwan: Martial Law to Market Law*. New York: Columbia University Press, 2004.

———. *Modernism and the Nativist Resistance: Contemporary Chinese Fiction from Taiwan*. Durham, NC: Duke University Press, 1993.

Cheek, Timothy. *The Intellectual in Modern Chinese History*. Cambridge: Cambridge University Press, 2015.

Cheek, Timothy, David Ownby, and Joshua A. Fogel. "Mapping the Intellectual Public Sphere in China Today." *China Information* 32, no. 1 (2018): 107–20.
———, eds. *Voices from the Chinese Century: Public Intellectual Debate from Contemporary China*. New York: Columbia University Press, 2019.
Chen, Cheng. *The Return of Ideology: The Search for Regime Identities in Postcommunist Russia and China*. Ann Arbor: University of Michigan Press, 2016.
Chen Huaiyu 陳懷宇. "Chen Yinke yu Heerde" 陳寅恪與赫爾德 [Chen Yinke and Herder]. In *Zai xifang faxian Chen Yinke* 在西方發現陳寅恪 [Discovering Chen Yinke in the West], 320–54. Beijing: Beijing shifandaxue chubanshe, 2013.
Chen Jianhua 陳建華. "'Gonghe' zhuti yu simiwenxue" 「共和」主體與私密文學 [Republican subject and the literature of intimacy]. *Ershiyi shiji* 152 (December 2015): 65–83.
Chen, Ming. "On Confucianism as a Civil Religion and Its Significance for Contemporary China." *Contemporary Chinese Thought* 44, no. 2 (January 2013): 76–88.
Chen Pingyuan 陳平原. "Xuezhe de renjian qinghuai" 學者的人間情懷 [This-worldly temperament of scholars]. *Dushu* 5 (1993): 75–80.
Chen, Po-hsi. "Wang Anyi, Taiwan, and the World: The 1983 International Writing Program and Biblical Allusions in Utopian Verses." *Chinese Literature Today* 6, no. 2 (2017): 52–61.
Chen Sihe 陳思和. "Shilun Chen Yingzhen de chuangzuo yu 'wusi' xinwenxue chuantong" 試論陳映真的創作與「五四」新文學傳統 [On Chen Yingzhen's literary creation and the tradition of May Fourth new literature]. In *Chen Yingzhen: Sixiang yu wenxue* 陳映真：思想與文學 [Chen Yingzhen: Thought and literature], vol. 1, edited by Chen Guangxin and Su Shufen, 15–49. Taipei: Taiwan shehuiyanjiu zazhi, 2011.
Chen Wangheng 陳望衡. *Ershi shiji Zhongguo meixue bentilun wenti* 二十世紀中國美學本體論問題 [The problem of aesthetic ontology in twentieth-century China]. Wuhan: Wuhan daxue chubanshe, 2007.
Chen, Xiaomei. *Staging Chinese Revolution: Theater, Film, and the Afterlives of Propaganda*. New York: Columbia University Press, 2016.
Chen Xiyuan 陳熙遠. "Zongjiao—yige Zhongguo jindai wenhuashi shang de guanjianci" 宗教——一個中國近代文化史上的關鍵詞 [Religion—a keyword in the cultural history of modern China]. *Xin shixue* 13, no. 4 (December 2002): 37–65.
Chen Yingzhen 陳映真. *Chen Yingzhen zuopinji* 陳映真作品集 [A collection of Chen Yinzhen's works]. 15 vols. Taipei: Renjian chubanshe, 1988.
———. *Gui xiang* 歸鄉 [Homecoming]. Taipei: Kunlun chubanshe, 2001.

———. "Mountain Path." In *Stories from Contemporary Taiwan*, edited by Catherine Dai, translated by Nicholas Kass, 93–194. New York: Bookman Books, 1988.

———. "My Kid Brother Kangxiong." In *The Columbia Anthology of Modern Chinese Literature*, edited by Joseph S. M. Lau and Howard Goldblatt, 205–20. New York: Columbia University Press, 2007.

———. "Shilun Chen Yingzhen" 試論陳映真 [On Chen Yingzhen]. In *Chen Yingzhen wenxuan* 陳映真文選 [Selected works of Chen Yingzhen], 3–11. Beijing: Sanlian shudian, 2009.

Chen Yinke 陳寅恪. "Feng Youlan *Zhongguo zhexueshi* shangce shencha baogao" 馮友蘭中國哲學史上冊審查報告 [Review of Feng Youlan's *History of Chinese Philosophy*, vol. 1]. In *Jinming guan conggao erbian* 金明館叢稿二編 [Essays from the hall of golden illumination], 279–81. Beijing: Sanlian shudian, 2015.

———. "Feng Youlan *Zhongguo zhexueshi* xiace shencha baogao" 馮友蘭中國哲學史下冊審查報告 [Review of Feng Youlan's *History of Chinese Philosophy*, vol. 2]. In *Jinming guan conggao erbian* 金明館叢稿二編 [Essays from the hall of golden illumination], 284–85. Beijing: Sanlian shudian, 2015.

———. "Li-tang shizu zhi tuice houji" 李唐氏族之推測後記 [A postscript to my speculation on the imperial house of Li]. In *Jinming guan conggao erbian* 金明館叢稿二編 [Essays from the hall of golden illumination], 335–45. Beijing: Sanlian shudian, 2015.

———. *Liu Rushi biezhuan* 柳如是別傳 [An extended biography of Liu Rushi]. 3 vols. Shanghai: Shanghai guji chubanshe, 1980.

———. "Lun *Zaishengyuan*" 論《再生緣》[On *Love in Two Lives*]. In *Hanliu tang ji* 寒柳堂集 [The collection from the hall of icy willow], 1–107. Beijing: Sanlian shudian, 2015.

———. "Qinghua daxue Wang Guantang xiansheng jinianbeiming" 清華大學王觀堂先生紀念碑銘 [An epitaph for Mr. Wang Guowei]. In *Jinming guan conggao erbian* 金明館叢稿二編 [Essays from the hall of golden illumination], 246. Beijing: Sanlian shudian, 2015.

———. *Tangdai zhengzhishi shulungao* 唐代政治史述論稿 [A commentary on the political history of the Tang dynasty]. Beijing: Sanlian shudian, 2015.

———. "Wang Guantang xiansheng wanci bingxu" 王觀堂先生挽辭並序 [Elegy on Wang Guowei]. In *Chen Yinke ji: Shiji* 陳寅恪集：詩集 [Anthology of Chen Yinke: Poetry], 12–17. Beijing: Sanlian shudian, 2015.

———. *Yuan Bai shi jianzhenggao* 元白詩箋證稿 [A study of the poetry of Yuan Zhen and Bai Juyi]. Beijing: Sanlian shudian, 2015.

Ching, Leo T. S. *Anti-Japan: The Politics of Sentiment in Postcolonial East Asia*. Durham, NC: Duke University Press, 2019.

Chomsky, Noam. "The Responsibility of Intellectuals." *New York Review of Books*, February 23, 1967. https://chomsky.info/19670223/.

Chong, Woei Lien. "Combining Marx with Kant: The Philosophical Anthropology of Li Zehou." *Philosophy East and West* 49, no. 2 (April 1999): 120–49.

Chow, Rey. "Violence in the Other Country: Preliminary Remarks on the 'China Crisis,' June 1989." *Radical America* 22 (July–August 1998): 23–34.

Cook, Alexander C. *The Cultural Revolution on Trial: Mao and the Gang of Four.* New York: Columbia University Press, 2016.

———, ed. *Mao's Little Red Book: A Global History.* Cambridge: Cambridge University Press, 2014.

Cui Xiaosu 崔小粟. "Yinian sanci qinjin rujia, Xi Jinping weihe ruci qiangdiao chongshi chuantongwenhua" 一年三次親近儒家，習近平為何如此強調重拾傳統文化 [Why does President Xi Jinping place such emphasis on reviving traditional culture]. *Renminwang*, September 25, 2014. http://cpc.people.com.cn/n/2014/0925/c164113-25731729.html.

Culp, Robert. *The Power of Print in Modern China: Intellectuals and Industrial Publishing from the End of Empire to Maoist State Socialism.* New York: Columbia University Press, 2019.

Dahrendorf, Ralf. *Society and Democracy in Germany.* New York: W. W. Norton, 1976.

Dai Qing 戴晴. "Yetan chunxia zhijiao" 也談春夏之交 [On the turn of spring and summer]. *Huaxia wenzhai*, no. 12 (1993): 2–24.

Dai Yan 戴燕. *Wenxueshi de quanli* 文學史的權力 [The power of literary history]. Beijing: Beijing daxue chubanshe, 2002.

Dannhauser, Werner J. "Leo Strauss: Becoming Naïve Again." *American Scholar* 44, no. 4 (Autumn 1975): 636–42.

Davies, Gloria. *Worrying about China: The Language of Chinese Critical Inquiry.* Cambridge, MA: Harvard University Press, 2007.

de Man, Paul. *Allegories of Reading: Figural Language in Rousseau, Nietzsche, Rilke, and Proust.* New Haven, CT: Yale University Press, 1982.

Deng Xiaomang 鄧曉芒. "Ping Liu Xiaofeng de xueli" 評劉小楓的學理 [On Liu Xiaofeng's scholarly reasoning]. Accessed October 25, 2022, http://www.aisixiang.com/data/69423.html.

Denton, Kirk A. *Exhibiting the Past: Historical Memory and the Politics of Museums in Postsocialist China.* Honolulu: University of Hawai'i Press, 2013.

Derman, Joshua. *Max Weber in Politics and Social Thought.* Cambridge: Cambridge University Press, 2012.

Derrida, Jacques. *Specters of Marx: The State of Debt, The Work of Mourning and the New International.* New York: Routledge, 1994.

Diamond, Martin. "Democracy and 'The Federalist': A Reconsideration of the Framers' Intent." *American Political Science Review* 53, no. 1 (March 1959): 52–68.

Dirlik, Arif. "Confucius in the Borderlands: Globalization, the Developmental State, and the Reinvention of Confucianism." In *Culture and History of Postrevolutionary China: The Perspective of Global Modernity*, 97–156. Hong Kong: Chinese University of Hong Kong Press, 2011.

———. "Mao Zedong in Contemporary Chinese Official Discourse and History." *China Perspectives* 2, no. 90 (January 2012): 17–27.

Donald, Stephanie. "National Publicness." In *Public Secrets, Public Spaces: Cinema and Civility in China*, 59–64. New York: Rowman & Littlefield, 2000.

Doss, Erika. *Memorial Mania: Public Feeling in America.* Chicago: University of Chicago Press, 2010.

Drury, Shadia. *Leo Strauss and the American Right.* New York: St. Martin's Press, 1997.

Elgat, Guy. *Nietzsche's Psychology of Ressentiment: Revenge and Justice in "On the Genealogy of Morals."* New York: Routledge, 2017.

Engels, Jeremy. *The Politics of Resentment: A Genealogy.* University Park: Pennsylvania State University Press, 2015.

Fällman, Fredrik. "Hermeneutical Conflict? Reading the Bible in Contemporary China." In *Reading Christian Scriptures in China*, edited by Chloë Starr, 49–67. London: T&T Clark, 2008.

Fan, Chun-yen. "The Pavilion of Yüeh-yang." In *Inscribed Landscapes: Travel Writing form Imperial China*, translated by Richard E. Strassberg, 158–59. Berkeley: University of California Press, 1994.

Fang Fang 方方. *Ruanmai* 軟埋 [Soft burial]. Beijing: Renmin wenxue chubanshe, 2016.

Fang, Lizhi 方勵之. "The Chinese Amnesia." *New York Review of Books*, September 27, 1990. https://www.nybooks.com/articles/1990/09/27/the-chinese-amnesia.

Felski, Rita. "Suspicious Minds." *Poetics Today* 32, no. 2 (Summer 2011): 215–34.

Feng Yibei 馮衣北. "Yetan Chen Yinke xiansheng de wannianxinjing" 也談陈寅恪先生的晚年心境 [Reflections on the late state of mind of Chen Yinke]. In *Chen Yinke wannian shiwen ji qita* 陳寅恪晚年詩文及其他

[Chen Yinke's late poetry, essays, and other matters], 1–19. Guangzhou: Huacheng chubanshe, 1986.
Ferber, Ilit. *Philosophy and Melancholy: Benjamin's Early Reflections on Theater and Language*. Stanford, CA: Stanford University Press, 2013.
Fewsmith, Joseph. *China since Tiananmen: From Deng Xiaoping to Hu Jintao*. 2nd ed. Cambridge: Cambridge University Press, 2008.
Finchelstein, Federico. *Fascist Mythologies: The History and Politics of Unreason in Borges, Freud, and Schmitt*. New York: Columbia University Press, 2022.
Fisher, Philip. *The Vehement Passions*. Princeton, NJ: Princeton University Press, 2002.
Fitzgerald, John. "China and the Quest for Dignity." *National Interest* 55 (Spring 1999): 47–59.
Fletcher, Emily. "Two Platonic Criticisms of Pleasure." In *Pleasure: A History*, edited by Lisa Shapiro, 15–41. Oxford: Oxford University Press, 2018.
Forges, Roger Des, and Luo Xu. "China as a Non-Hegemonic Superpower? The Uses of History among the *China Can Say No* Writers and Their Critics." *Critical Asian Studies* 33, no. 4 (October 2010): 483–507.
Frazer, Michael L. *The Enlightenment of Sympathy: Justice and the Moral Sentiments in the Eighteenth Century and Today*. New York: Oxford University Press, 2010.
Freud, Sigmund. *The Future of an Illusion*. New York: W. W. Norton, 1989.
———. "Mourning and Melancholia." In *The Standard Edition of the Complete Psychological Works of Sigmund Freud*, vol. 14 (1914–1916), *On the History of the Psycho-Analytic Movement, Papers on Metapsychology and Other Works*, 237–58. London: Hogarth Press and the Institute of Psycho-Analysis, 1957.
Fukuyama, Francis. *The End of History and the Last Man*. New York: Free Press, 1992.
Fung, Edmund S. K. *The Intellectual Foundations of Chinese Modernity*. Cambridge: Cambridge University Press, 2010.
Furet, François. *The Passing of an Illusion: The Idea of Communism in the Twentieth Century*. Chicago: University of Chicago Press, 2000.

Gan Shaosu 甘少蘇. *Zongdai he wo* 宗岱和我 [Zongdai and me]. Chongqing: Chongqing chubanshe, 1991.
Gan Yang 甘陽. *Tong santong* 通三統 [Unifying three heritages]. Beijing: Sanlian shudian, 2007.
———. *Wenming, guojia, daxue* 文明・國家・大學 [Civilization, nation, university]. Beijing: Sanlian shudian, 2012.

---. *Zhengzhi zheren Shitelaosi: Gudian baoshouzhuyi zhengzhizhexue de fuxing* 政治哲人施特勞斯：古典保守主義政治哲學的復興 [Strauss, philosopher of politics: The revival of neoconservative political philosophy]. Hong Kong: Oxford University Press, 2002.
Gan Yang 甘陽, Tang Wenming 唐文明, Zhang Xiang 張翔, Bai Tongdong 白彤東, Yao Zhongqiu 姚中秋, Yao Yusong 姚育松, Chen Ming 陳明, Zeng Yi 曾亦, Gan Chunsong 干春松, Chen Bisheng 陳壁生, Chen Shaoming 陳少明, and Liu Xiaofeng 劉小楓. "Kang Youwei yu zhiduhua ruxue" 康有為與制度化儒學 [Kang Youwei and institutionalized Confucianism]. *Kaifang shidai* 5 (2014): 12–41.
Gao Mobo 高默波. *Gao Village: Rural Life in Modern China*. Honolulu: University of Hawai'i Press, 2007.
---. "Shuxie lishi: *Gaojiacun*" 書寫歷史：《高家村》[Writing history: Gao Village], *Dushu* 1 (January 2001): 9–16.
Garver, John W. *China's Quest: The History of the Foreign Relations of the People's Republic of China*. New York: Oxford University Press, 2016.
Gay, Peter. *The Enlightenment: An Interpretation; the Rise of Modern Paganism*. New York: Vintage Books, 1966.
Ge Zhaoguang 葛兆光. "Zuishi wenren buziyou" 最是文人不自由 [The unfreedom of literati]. *Dushu* 5 (1993): 3.
Gentile, Emilio. *Politics as Religion*. Princeton, NJ: Princeton University Press, 2006.
Gilburd, Eleonory. *To See Paris and Die: The Soviet Lives of Western Culture*. Cambridge, MA: Harvard University Press, 2018.
Gitlin, Todd. *The Twilight of Common Dreams*. New York: Holt, 1996.
Goldman, Merle. *China's Intellectuals: Advise and Dissent*. Cambridge, MA: Harvard University Press, 1981.
Goossaert, Vincent, and David A. Palmer. *The Religious Question in Modern China*. Chicago: University of Chicago Press, 2011.
Gordon, Peter E. *Adorno and Existence*. Cambridge, MA: Harvard University Press, 2016.
---. "Contextualism and Criticism in the History of Ideas." In *Rethinking Modern European Intellectual History*, edited by Darrin M. McMahon and Samuel Moyn, 32–55. New York: Oxford University Press, 2014.
---. *The Continental Divide: Heidegger, Cassirer, Davos*. Cambridge, MA: Harvard University Press, 2010.
---. "Critical Theory between the Sacred and the Profane." *Constellations* 23, no. 4 (December 2016): 466–81.
---. "Habermas, Derrida, and the Question of Religion." In *The Trace of God: Derrida and Religion*, edited by Edward Baring and Peter E. Gordon, 110–31. New York: Fordham University Press, 2015.

———. "Heidegger in Black." *New York Review of Books*, October 9, 2014. https://www.nybooks.com/articles/2014/10/09/heidegger-in-black/.

———. "A Lion in Winter." *The Nation*, September 13, 2016. https://www.thenation.com/article/archive/a-lion-in-winter/.

———. *Rosenzweig and Heidegger: Between Judaism and German Philosophy*. Berkeley: University of California Press, 2003.

———. "Weimar Theology: From Historicism to Crisis." In *Weimar Thought: A Contested Legacy*, edited by Peter E. Gordon and John P. McCormick, 150–78. Princeton, NJ: Princeton University Press, 2013.

Gordon, Peter E., and John P. McCormick. "Weimar Thought: Continuity and Crisis." In *Weimar Thought*, edited by Peter E. Gordon and John P. McCormick, 1–11. Princeton, NJ: Princeton University Press, 2013.

Graham, A. C. "The Meaning of Ch'ing [Qing]." In *Studies in Chinese Philosophy and Philosophical Literature*, 59–65. Albany: State University of New York Press, 1986.

Grieder, Jerome B. *Hu Shih and the Chinese Renaissance: Liberalism in the Chinese Revolution, 1917–1937*. Cambridge, MA: Harvard University Press, 1970.

Gries, Peter Hays. *China's New Nationalism: Pride, Politics, and Diplomacy*. Berkeley: University of California Press, 2004.

Gu, Edward, and Merle Goldman, eds. *Chinese Intellectuals between State and Market*. New York: Routledge, 2004.

Gu Lin 谷林. "Gu Lin zhi Zhi An han" 谷林致止庵函 [A letter from Gu Lin to Zhi An]. In Zhi An 止庵, *Liuchou biji* 六丑筆記 [Notes on six types of ugliness], 81. Beijing: Dongfang chubanshe.

Gu, Xin. "Subjectivity, Modernity, and Chinese Hegelian Marxism: A Study of Li Zehou's Philosophical Ideas from a Comparative Perspective." *Philosophy East and West* 46, no. 2 (April 1996): 205–45.

Guan Ruiwen 關瑞文. "Ping Liu Xiaofeng de hanyu jidushenxue" 評劉小楓的漢語基督神學 [On Liu Xiaofeng's Sino-Christian theology]. *Daofeng* 4 (1996): 220–39.

Guo Moruo 郭沫若. "Guanyu houjin bogu wenti" 關於厚今薄古問題——答北京大學歷史系師生的一封信 [On elevating the past over the present—a letter to the teachers and students of the history department at Peking University]. *Guangming ribao*, June 10, 1958.

Guo, Yingjie. *Cultural Nationalism in Contemporary China: The Search for National Identity under Reform*. New York: Routledge, 2004.

Guo, Yingjie, and Baogang He. "Reimagining the Chinese Nation: The 'Zeng Guofan Phenomenon.'" *Modern China* 25, no. 2 (April 1999): 142–70.

Habermas, Jürgen. *An Awareness of What Is Missing: Faith and Reason in a Post-Secular Age*, translated by Ciaran Cronin. New York: Polity, 2014.
Hall, David L., and Roger T. Ames. *Thinking through Confucius*. Albany: State University of New York Press, 1987.
Hamrin, Carol L., and Timothy Cheek. *China's Establishment Intellectuals*. Armonk, NY: M. E. Sharpe, 1987.
Han, Song. "I and the Dispatches on the Book *China Can Say No*." *Contemporary Chinese Thought* 30, no. 2 (Winter 1998–1999): 96–99.
Havel, Václav. "The Power of the Powerless." In *Vaclav Havel or Living in Truth*, edited by Jan Vladislav, 36–122. Boston, MA: Faber and Faber, 1986.
Haw, Stephen G. "The *History of a Loyal Heart (Xin shi)*: A Late-Ming Forgery." *Journal of the Royal Asiatic Society* 25, no. 2 (2015): 317–25.
Hayot, Eric. *The Hypothetical Mandarin: Sympathy, Modernity, and Chinese Pain*. Oxford: Oxford University Press, 2009.
He Guanghu 何光滬. *He Guanghu zixuanji* 何光滬自選集 [Selected works of He Guanghu]. Guilin: Guangxi shifandaxue chubanshe, 1999.
He Guimei 賀桂梅. *"Xinqimeng" zhishi dang'an* 「新啟蒙」知識檔案 [A knowledge archive of the "New Enlightenment"]. Beijing: Beijing daxue chubanshe, 2010.
Hershatter, Gail. *The Gender of Memory: Rural Women and China's Collective Past*. Berkeley: University of California Press, 2011.
Hillenbrand, Margaret, and Chloë Starr. "Chinese Neo-Nationalism." In *Documenting China: A Reader in Seminal Twentieth-Century Text*, edited by Hillenbrand and Starr, 132–46. Seattle: University of Washington Press, 2011.
Hochschild, Arlie Russell. *The Managed Heart: Commercialization of Human Feeling*. 3rd ed. Berkeley: University of California Press, 2012.
Hsia, C. T. "Obsession with China: The Moral Burden of Modern Chinese Literature." In *A History of Modern Chinese Fiction*, 533–54. New Haven, CT: Yale University Press, 1971.
Hu Shih 胡適. *Wenti yu zhuyi* 問題與主義 [Problems and isms]. Taipei: Yuanliu, 1986.
Hu Shouwei 胡守為, ed. *Chen Yinke yu ershishiji Zhongguo xueshu* 陳寅恪與二十世紀中國學術 [Chen Yinke and Chinese scholarship in the twentieth century]. Hangzhou: Hangzhou renmin chubanshe, 2000.
Hu Wenhui 胡文輝. *Chen Yinke shi jianshi* 陳寅恪詩箋釋 [An exegesis on Chen Yinke's poetry]. Guangzhou: Guangdong renmin chubanshe, 2013.
Huang, Martin. *Desire and Fictional Narrative in Late Imperial China*. Cambridge, MA: Harvard University Press, 2001.

Huang, Max Ko-wu. *The Meaning of Freedom: Yan Fu and the Origins of Chinese Liberalism*. Hong Kong: Chinese University of Hong Kong Press, 2008.
Huntington, Samuel P. *The Clash of Civilizations and the Remaking of World Order*. London: Simon & Schuster, 2011.

Ing, Michael. "Born of Resentment: *Yuan* 怨 in Early Confucian Thought." *Dao* 15, no. 1 (March 2016): 19–33.
Ip, Hung-yok. *Intellectuals in Revolutionary China, 1921–1949: Leaders, Heroes and Sophisticates*. New York: Routledge, 2009.

Jacoby, Russell. *The Last Intellectuals: American Culture in the Age of Academe*. New York: Basic Books, 2000.
Jaffa, Harry. *Crisis of the House Divided: An Interpretation of the Issues in the Lincoln-Douglas Debates*. Garden City, NY: Doubleday, 1959.
Jameson, Fredric. *The Political Unconscious: Narrative as a Socially Symbolic Act*. London: Routledge, 1983.
Jaspers, Karl. *The Question of German Guilt*. Translated by E. B. Ashton. New York: Fordham University Press, 2001.
Javeline, Debra. "The Role of Blame in Collective Action: Evidence from Russia." *American Political Science Review* 97, no. 1 (February 2003): 107–21.
Jay, Martin. *The Dialectical Imagination: A History of the Frankfurt School and the Institute of Social Research, 1923–1950*. Berkeley: University of California Press, 1996.
Ji Xianlin. *The Cowshed: Memories of the Chinese Cultural Revolution*. Translated by Chenxin Jiang. New York: New York Review Books, 2016.
Jia, Jinhua. "Li Zehou's Reconception of the Confucian Ethics of Emotion." *Philosophy East and West* 66, no. 3 (July 2016): 757–86.
Jiang Dongxian. "Searching for the Chinese Autonomy: Leo Strauss in the Chinese Context." Master's thesis, Duke University, 2014.
Jiang Qing 蔣慶. *A Confucian Constitutional Order*. Edited by Daniel A. Bell and Ruiping Fan. Translated by Edmund Ryden. Princeton, NJ: Princeton University Press, 2016.
———. *Zhengzhi ruxue* 政治儒學 [Political Confucianism]. Beijing: Sanlian shudian, 2003.
Jiang Qing 蔣慶, Chen Ming 陳明, Kang Xiaoguang 康曉光, Yu Donghai 余東海, and Qiu Feng 秋風. *Zhongguo bixu zairuhua* 中國必須再儒化 [China must be re-Confucianized]. Singapore: World Scientific Press, 2016.

Johnson, Ian. "Forget Marx and Mao. Chinese City Honors Once-Banned Confucian." *New York Times*, October 18, 2017. https://www.nytimes.com/2017/10/18/world/asia/china-guiyang-wang-yangming-confucian.html.
Joseph, William A. *The Critique of Ultra-Leftism in China, 1958–1981*. Stanford, CA: Stanford University Press, 1984.
Judt, Tony. *The Burden of Responsibility: Blum, Camus, Aron, and the French Twentieth Century*. Chicago: University of Chicago Press, 2007.

Kahn, Victoria. *The Future of Illusion: Political Theology and Early Modern Text*. Chicago: University of Chicago Press, 2014.
Kant, Immanuel. "An Answer to the Question: What Is Enlightenment?" In *Practical Philosophy*, translated and edited by Mary J. Gregor, 11–22. Cambridge: Cambridge University Press, 1999.
Kant, Immanuel. "What Does It Mean to Orient Oneself in Thinking." In *Religion within the Boundaries of Mere Reason: And Other Writings*, edited by Allen Wood and George di Giovanni, 1–16. Cambridge: Cambridge University Press, 1999.
Kearney, Richard. "Derrida and Messianic Atheism." In *The Trace of God*, edited by Edward Baring and Peter E. Gordon, 199–212. New York: Fordham University Press, 2015.
Khan, Sulmaan Wasif. *Haunted by Chaos: China's Grand Strategy from Mao Zedong to Xi Jinping*. Cambridge, MA: Harvard University Press, 2018.
Kubin, Wolfgang. "Introduction." In *Symbols of Anguish: In Search of Melancholy in China*, edited by Wolfgang Kubin, 7–16. New York: Peter Lang, 2001.

Laclau, Ernesto, and Chantal Mouffe. *Hegemony and Socialist Strategy: Toward a Radical Democratic Politics*. 2nd ed. New York: Verso, 2014.
Lai, Pan-Chiu, and Jason Lam, eds. *Sino-Christian Theology: A Theological Qua Cultural Movement in Contemporary China*. Berlin: Peter Lang, 2010.
Lambert, Andrew. "From Aesthetics to Ethics: The Place of Delight in Confucian Ethics." *Journal of Chinese Philosophy* 47, no. 3–4 (September 2020): 154–73.
Landsberger, Stefan R. "Mao as the Kitchen God: Religious Aspects of the Mao Cult during the Cultural Revolution." *China Information* 11, no. 2–3 (Autumn/Winter 1996): 196–214.
Lanza, Fabio. *The End of Concern: Maoist China, Activism, and Asian Studies*. Durham, NC: Duke University Press, 2017.
Larson, Wendy. *From Ah Q to Lei Feng: Freud and Revolutionary Spirit in 20th Century China*. Stanford, CA: Stanford University Press, 2009.

Lean, Eugenia. *Public Passions: The Trial of Shi Jianqiao and the Rise of Popular Sympathy in Republican China*. Berkeley: University of California Press, 2007.

Lee, Ching Kwan, and Guobin Yang, eds. *Re-envisioning the Chinese Revolution: The Politics and Poetics of Collective Memory in Reform China*. Stanford, CA: Stanford University Press, 2007.

Lee, Haiyan. "Mao's Two Bodies: On the Curious (Political) Art of Impersonating the Great Helmsman." In *Red Legacies in China*, edited by Jie Li and Enhua Zhang, 245–70. Cambridge, MA: Harvard University Press, 2016.

———. *Revolution of the Heart: A Genealogy of Love in China, 1900–1950*. Stanford, CA: Stanford University Press, 2007.

———. *The Stranger and the Chinese Moral Imagination*. Stanford, CA: Stanford University Press, 2014.

Leese, Daniel. *Mao Cult: Rhetoric and Ritual in China's Cultural Revolution*. Cambridge: Cambridge University Press, 2011.

Lefort, Claude. "The Permanence of the Theologico-Political?" In *Political Theologies: Public Religions in a Post-Secular World*, edited by Hent de Vries and Lawrence E. Sullivan, 148–87. New York: Fordham University Press, 2006.

Legge, James, trans. "Wei Ling Kung." In *The Chinese Classics: Confucian Analects, the Great Learning, and the Doctrine of the Mean*, 294–306. Hong Kong: Hong Kong University Press, 1960.

Levenson, Joseph. *Liang Ch'i Ch'ao and the Mind of Modern China*. Cambridge, MA: Harvard University Press, 1959.

Leys, Ruth. "The Turn to Affect: A Critique." *Critical Inquiry* 37, no. 3 (Spring 2011): 434–72.

Li, Cheng, and Barry McCarron. "A New Type of Major Power Relationship? An Interview with Cheng Li." *Georgetown Journal of International Affairs* 15, no. 2 (July 2014): 156–62.

Li, He. *Political Thought and China's Transformation: Ideas Shaping Reform in Post-Mao China*. New York: Palgrave Macmillan, 2015.

Li, Huaiyin. *Reinventing Modern China: Imagination and Authenticity in Chinese Historical Writing*. Honolulu: University of Hawai'i Press, 2012.

Li, Jie. "Discerning Red Legacies in China." In *Red Legacies in China*, edited by Jie Li and Enhua Zhang, 1–22. Cambridge, MA: Harvard University Press, 2016.

———. *Utopian Ruins: A Memory Museum of the Mao Era*. Durham, NC: Duke University Press, 2020.

Li, Jie, and Enhua Zhang, eds. *Red Legacies in China: Cultural Afterlives of the Communist Revolution*. Cambridge, MA: Harvard University Press, 2016.

Li, Jing. *China's America: The Chinese View the United States, 1900–2000*. Albany: State University of New York Press, 2011.

Li, Lu. *Moving the Mountain: My Life in China from the Cultural Revolution to Tiananmen Square*. New York: Macmillan, 1990.

Li, Wai-yee. "Introduction." In *Trauma and Transcendence in Early Qing Literature*, edited by Wai-yee Li and Wilt L. Idema, 1–70. Cambridge, MA: Harvard University Press, 2006.

———. "Nostalgia and Resistance: Gender and the Poetry of Chen Yinke." In *Xiang Lectures on Chinese Poetry*, vol. 7, 1–26. Montreal: McGill University Press, 2016.

———. *The Readability of the Past in Early Chinese Historiography*. Cambridge, MA: Harvard University Press, 2007.

———. *Women and National Trauma in Late Imperial Chinese Literature*. Cambridge, MA: Harvard University Press, 2014.

Li Xiguang 李希光 and Liu Kang 劉康. *Yaomohua Zhongguo de beihou* 妖魔化中國的背後 [Behind the demonization of China]. Beijing: Zhongguo shehui kexue chubanshe, 1996.

Li Zehou 李澤厚. *The Chinese Aesthetic Tradition*. Translated by Maija Bell Samei. Honolulu: University of Hawai'i Press, 2009.

———. *Huaxia meixue: Meixue sijiang* 華夏美學：美學四講 [The Chinese aesthetic tradition: Four lectures on aesthetics]. Beijing: Sanlian shudian, 2008.

———. "Kongzi zai pingjia" 孔子再評價 [A re-evaluation of Confucius]. In *Zhongguo gudai sixiangshi lun* 中國古代思想史論 [Treatises on ancient Chinese intellectual history], 1–49. Beijing: Sanlian shudian, 2008.

———. *Lishi bentilun* 歷史本體論 [Historical ontology]. Beijing: Sanlian shudian, 2008.

———. *Mei de licheng* 美的歷程 [The path of beauty]. Beijing: Sanlian shudian, 2009.

———. "Meixue san tiyi" 美學三題議 [Three treatises on aesthetics]. In *Zhongguo dangdai meixue lunwenji* 中國當代美學論文集 [A collection of essays on contemporary Chinese aesthetics], edited by Liu Changjiu and Pi Chaogang, 286–90. Chongqing: Chongqing chubanshe, 1988.

———. *Pipanzhexue de pipan: Kangde shuping* 批判哲學的批判：康德述評 [Critique of critical philosophy: A new approach to Kant]. Beijing: Sanlian shudian, 2007.

———. "Qimeng yu jiuwang de shuangchong bianzou" 啟蒙與救亡的雙重變奏 [The symbiotic variations of enlightenment and national salvation]. In *Zhongguo xiandai sixiangshi lun* 中國現代思想史論 [Treatises on modern Chinese intellectual history], 1–46. Beijing: Sanlian shudian, 2007.

———. "Qingnian Mao Zedong" 青年毛澤東 [On young Mao Zedong]. In *Zhongguo xiandai sixiangshi lun* 中國現代思想史論 [Treatises on modern Chinese intellectual history], 122–49. Beijing: Sanlian shudian, 2007.

———. *Shiyong lixing yu legan wenhua* 實用理性與樂感文化 [Pragmatic reason and culture(s) of pleasure]. Beijing: Sanlian shudian, 2008.

———. "Sixiang xueshu wenda" 思想學術問答 [A dialogue on my thoughts and scholarship]. In *Li Zehou xueshu wenhua suibi* 李澤厚學術文化隨筆 [Li Zehou's essays on culture and learning], 270–73. Beijing: Zhongguo qingnian chubanshe, 1998.

———. "Subjectivity and 'Subjectality:' A Response." *Philosophy East and West* 49, no. 2 (April 1999): 174–83.

———. *Youwu daoli, shili guiren* 由巫到禮，釋禮歸仁 [From shamanism to ritualism, from ritualism to humanism]. Beijing: Sanlian shudian, 2015.

Li, Zehou, and Jane Cauvel. *Four Essays on Aesthetics: Toward a Global Perspective*. Lanham, MD: Lexington Books, 2006.

Li Zehou 李澤厚 and Liu Zaifu 劉再復. *Gaobie geming* 告別革命 [A farewell to revolution]. Hong Kong: Tiandi tushu, 2011.

Liang Zhigang 梁志剛 and Hu Guangli 胡光利. *Ji Xianlin dazhuan* 季羨林大傳 [A biography of Ji Xianlin]. Harbin: Haerbin chubanshe, 2013.

Lifton, Robert Jay. *Thought Reform and the Psychology of Totalism: A Study of "Brainwashing" in China*. Chapel Hill: University of North Carolina Press, 1989.

Lilla, Mark. "Reading Strauss in Beijing." *New Republic*, December 17, 2010. https://newrepublic.com/article/79747/reading-leo-strauss-in-beijing-china-marx.

———. *The Reckless Mind: Intellectuals in Politics*. New York: New York Review Books, 2003.

———. *The Shipwrecked Mind: On Political Reaction*. New York: New York Review Books, 2016.

Lin, Yu-Sheng. *The Crisis of Chinese Consciousness: Radical Antitraditionalism in the May Fourth Era*. Madison: University of Wisconsin Press, 1978.

Liu Binyan 劉賓雁. *Di'erzhong zhongcheng* 第二種忠誠 [A higher kind of loyalty]. Hong Kong: Xuelin shudian, 1987.

Liu, Cixin. *The Dark Forest*. Translated by Ken Liu. New York: Tor, 2016.

Liu, Jianmei. "Liu Zaifu's Three Voyages of Life." *Prism* 17, no. 1 (March 2020): 183–98.

———. *Revolution Plus Love: Literary History, Women's Bodies, and Thematic Repetition in Twentieth-Century Chinese Fiction*. Honolulu: University of Hawai'i Press, 2003.

Liu Qing 劉擎. "Zhongguo yujing xia de ziyouzhuyi: Qianli yu kunjing" 中國語境下的自由主義：潛力與困境 [Liberalism in the Chinese context: Potential and dilemma]. *Kaifang shidai* 4 (2013): 106–23.

Liu Rushi 柳如是. "Jinming chi yong hanliu" 金明池詠寒柳 [A praise for the icy willow by the pond of golden illumination]. In *Liu Rushi shiwen ji* 柳如是詩文集 [A collection of Liu Rushi's poetry and essay], edited by Gu Huizhi, 220–21. Beijing: Zhonghua quanguo tushuguan wenxian weisuo fuzhizhongxin, 1996.

Liu Xiaobo. "That Holy Word 'Revolution.'" In *Popular Protest and Political Culture in Modern China*, edited by Jeffrey N. Wasserstrom and Elizabeth J. Perry, 309–24. New York: Routledge, 1994.

Liu Xiaofeng 劉小楓. *Bainian gonghezhiyi* 百年共和之義 [Essays on the making of a republic in China]. Shanghai: Huadong shifandaxue chubanshe, 2011.

———. *Gonghe yu jinglun* 共和與經綸 [Republic and statecraft]. Beijing: Sanlian shudian, 2012.

———. "Hanyushenxue yu lishizhexue" 漢語神學與歷史哲學 [Sino-Christian theology and the philosophy of history]. In *Shengling jianglin de xushi* 聖靈降臨的敘事 [The coming of the holy spirit], 1–108. Beijing: Sanlian shudian, 2003.

———. "Jilian Dongniya" 記戀冬妮婭 [Remembering Tonia]. In *Zheyidairen de pa he ai* 這一代人的怕和愛 [The fear and love of this generation], 40–52. Beijing: Huaxia chubanshe, 2012.

———. "Liuyi shengren zan" 六譯聖人讚 [Liao Ping's praise of the Sage]. In *Zheyidairen de pa he ai* 這一代人的怕和愛 [The fear and love of this generation], 155–70. Beijing: Huaxia chubanshe, 2012.

———. "Rujia gemingjingshen yuanliukao" 儒家革命精神源流考 [Research on the origin of Confucian revolutionary spirit]. In *Rujiao yu minzuguojia* 儒教與民族國家 [Confucian religion and nation-state], 85–194. Beijing: Huaxia chubanshe, 2007.

———. "Shangdi jiushi shangdi" 上帝就是上帝 [God is God]. In *Zouxiang shizijia de zhen* 走向十字架的真 [Toward the truth of the cross], 45–80. Shanghai: Huadong shifandaxue chubanshe, 2011.

———. *Shihua zhexue* 詩化哲學 [Poeticized philosophy]. Jinan: Shandong wenyi chubanshe, 1986.

———. *Shitelaosi de lubiao* 施特勞斯的路標 [Leo Strauss's pathmarks]. Beijing: Huaxia chubanshe, 2011.

———. "Weishu yu zuopai rujiaoshi" 緯書與左派儒教士 [Apocryphal writings and leftist Confucian priests]. In *Rujiao yu minzuguojia* 儒教與民族國家 [Confucian religion and nation-state], 1–84. Beijing: Huaxia chubanshe, 2007.

———. "Wenhua jidutu xianxiang de shehuixue pingzhu" 文化基督徒現象的社會學評註 [A sociological commentary on cultural Christians]. In *Zheyidairen de pa he ai* 這一代人的怕和愛 [The fear and love of this generation], 171–81. Beijing: Huaxia chubanshe, 2012.
———. *Xiandaixing shehuililun xulun* 現代性社會理論緒論 [Preface to social theory of modernity]. Shanghai: Sanlian shudian, 1998.
———. "Xushi yu lunli" 敘事與倫理 [Narrative and ethics]. In *Chenzhong de roushen* 沉重的肉身 [The unbearable weight of flesh], 1–11. Beijing: Huaxia chubanshe, 2007.
———. *Yimei weijian* 以美為鑒 [America as mirror]. Beijing: Huaxia chubanshe, 2017.
———. *Zhengjiu yu xiaoyao* 拯救與逍遙 [Salvation and easiness]. Shanghai: Huadong shifandaxue chubanshe, 2011.
Liu, Yu. "Maoist Discourse and the Mobilization of Emotions in Revolutionary China." *Modern China* 26, no. 3 (May 2010): 329–62.
Liu Zaifu 劉再復. "Lun wenxue de zhutixing" 論文學的主體性 [On the subjectivity of literature]. *Wenxue pinglun* 6 (1985): 11–26.
———. *Xingge zuhe lun* 性格組合論 [On the composition of human character]. Shanghai: Shanghai wenyi chubanshe, 1986.
Liu Zaifu 劉再復 and Lin Gang 林崗. *Zui yu wenxue* 罪與文學 [Guilt and literature]. Hong Kong: Oxford University Press, 2002.
Loewe, Michael. *Dong Zhongshu: A "Confucian" Heritage and the Chunqiu Fanlu*. Leiden: Brill, 2011.
Lu Jiandong 陸鍵東. *Chen Yinke de zuihou ershinian* 陳寅恪的最後二十年 [The last twenty years of Chen Yinke]. Beijing: Sanlian shudian, 1995.
Lu, Lucy Xing. "Rhetoric of Nationalism and Anti-Americanism: A Burkean Analysis of *China Can Say No*." *Intercultural Communication Studies* 2 (September 1998): 163–75.
Lü Peng 呂澎. "Zuishi wenren you ziyou" 最是文人有自由 [The freedom of literati]. *Dushu* 8 (1993): 63.
Lu Xun 魯迅. "Geming wenxue" 革命文學 [Revolutionary literature]. In *Lu Xun quanji* 魯迅全集 [The complete works of Lu Xun]. 18 vols. (Beijing: Renmin wenxue chubanshe, 2005), 3:567–70.
———. "Mujiewen" 墓碣文 [Tombstone inscriptions], in *Lu Xun quanji*. 18 vols. (Beijing: Renmin wenxue chubanshe, 2005), 2:207–8.
Lukács, Georg. *The Theory of the Novel*. Cambridge, MA: MIT Press, 1974.

Ma Guochuan 馬國川. *Wo yu bashiniandai* 我與八十年代 [The eighties and me]. Beijing: Sanlian shudian, 2011.

Ma Licheng 馬立誠. *Dangdai Zhongguo bazhong shehui sichao* 當代中國八種社會思潮 [Eight intellectual currents in contemporary China]. Beijing: Shehui kexue wenxian chubanshe, 2011.

Makeham, John. *Lost Soul: "Confucianism" in Contemporary Chinese Academic Discourse*. Cambridge, MA: Harvard University Press, 2008.

Mannheim, Karl. *Ideology and Utopia: An Introduction to the Sociology of Knowledge*. Translated by Louis Wirth and Edward Shils. New York: Harvest, 1936.

Mansfield, Harvey, Jr. *The Spirit of Liberalism*. Cambridge, MA: Harvard University Press, 1978.

Mao Zedong 毛澤東. "Beijianzhe zui congming, gaoguizhe zui yuchun" 卑賤者最聰明，高貴者最愚蠢 [The downtrodden is the most intelligent and the noble is the most stupid]. In *Jianguoyilai Mao Zedong wengao* 建國以來毛澤東文稿 [Mao Zedong's manuscripts since 1949], vol. 7, 236–38. Beijing: Zhongyang wenxian chubanshe, 1998.

Marasco, Robyn. *The Highway of Despair: Critical Theory after Hegel*. New York: Columbia University Press, 2015.

Marchal, Kai. "Modernity, Tyranny, and Crisis: Leo Strauss in China." In *Carl Schmitt and Leo Strauss in the Chinese-Speaking World*, edited by Kai Marchal and Carl K. Y. Shaw, 173–96. Lanham, MD: Lexington Books, 2017.

Marchal, Kai, and Carl K. Y. Shaw, eds. *Carl Schmitt and Leo Strauss in the Chinese-Speaking World: Reorienting the Political*. Lanham, MD: Lexington Books, 2017.

Marcuse, Herbert. *Eros and Civilization: A Philosophical Inquiry into Freud*. Boston, MA: Beacon Press, 1974.

Martin, Peter. *China's Civilian Army: The Making of Wolf Warrior Diplomacy*. Oxford: Oxford University Press, 2021.

Martin, Peter, Charlie Zhu, and Chris Anstey. "Xi Jinping Vows Commitment to Global Trading Order as U.S. Deal Nears." *Bloomberg News*, November 4, 2019. https://www.bloomberg.com/news/articles/2019-11-05/xi-says-countries-shouldn-t-put-their-interests-above-others.

Marx, Karl. "On the Jewish Question." In *Karl Marx: Early Writings*, translated by Rodney Livingstone and Gregor Benton, 211–42. New York: Penguin, 1992.

———. "A Contribution to the Critique of Hegel's 'Philosophy of Right.'" In *Karl Marx: Early Writings*, translated by Rodney Livingstone and Gregor Benton, 243–57. New York: Penguin, 1992.

Massumi, Brian. *Parables for the Virtual: Movement, Affect, Sensation*. Durham, NC: Duke University Press, 2002.

McCormick, John P. *Carl Schmitt's Critique of Liberalism: Against Politics as Technology.* Cambridge: Cambridge University Press, 1999.

———. "Fear, Technology, and the State: Carl Schmitt, Leo Strauss, and the Revival of Hobbes in Weimar and National Socialist Germany." *Political Theory* 22, no. 4 (November 1994): 619–52.

McGrath, Jason. *Postsocialist Modernity: Chinese Cinema, Literature, and Criticism in the Market Age.* Stanford, CA: Stanford University Press, 2008.

McIntosh, Janet. "The Trump Era as a Linguistic Emergency." In *Language in the Trump Era*, edited by Janet McIntosh and Norma Mendoza-Denton, 1–46. Cambridge: Cambridge University Press, 2020.

McMulian, Gordon, and Sam Smiles, eds. *Late Style and Its Discontents: Essays in Art, Literature, and Music.* Oxford: Oxford University Press, 2016.

McVeigh, Rory, and Kevin Estep. *The Politics of Losing: Trump, the Klan, and the Mainstreaming of Resentment.* New York: Columbia University Press, 2019.

Meinecke, Fredrich. *The German Catastrophe.* Boston, MA: Beacon Press, 1964.

Mitchell, Maria D. *The Origins of Christian Democracy: Politics and Confession in Modern Germany.* Ann Arbor: University of Michigan Press, 2012.

Mitscherlich, Alexander, and Margarete Mitscherlich, eds. *The Inability to Mourn: Principles of Collective Behavior.* New York: Grove Press, 1975.

Mitter, Rana. *A Bitter Revolution: China's Struggle with the Modern World.* Oxford: Oxford University Press, 2005.

Møllgaard, Eske J. *The Confucian Political Imagination.* London: Palgrave Macmillan, 2018.

Moody, Peter. *Conservative Thought in Contemporary China.* Washington, DC: Lexington Books, 2007.

Morson, Gary Saul. *Narrative and Freedom: The Shadows of Time.* New Haven, CT: Yale University Press, 1996.

Moses, A. Dirk. *German Intellectuals and the Nazi Past.* Cambridge: Cambridge University Press, 2007.

Mufson, Steven. "China Puts Forth Persistent, Caustic Anti-U.S. Themes." *Washington Post*, August 13, 1996.

Müller, Jan-Werner. "Concepts, Character, and the Specter of New Cold Wars." In *Isaiah Berlin's Cold War Liberalism*, edited by Jan-Werner Müller, 1–10. London: Palgrave Macmillan, 2019.

———. *A Dangerous Mind: Carl Schmitt in Post-War European Thought.* New Haven, CT: Yale University Press, 2003.

———. *What Is Populism?* Philadelphia: University of Pennsylvania Press, 2016.

Murong, Xuecun. "The Art of Xi Jinping." *New York Times*, November 21, 2014. https://www.nytimes.com/2014/11/22/opinion/murong-xuecun-china-the-art-of-xi-jinping.html.

Murthy, Viren. "Modernity against Modernity: Wang Hui's Critical History of Chinese Thought." *Modern Intellectual History* 3, no. 1 (April 2006): 137–65.

Nazar, Hina. *Enlightened Sentiments: Judgment and Autonomy in the Age of Sensibility.* New York: Fordham University Press, 2012.

Nelson, Eric. "Recognition and Resentment in the Confucian Analects." *Journal of Chinese Philosophy* 40, no. 2 (June 2013): 287–306.

Ni, Peimin. *Understanding the Analects of Confucius.* Albany: State University of New York Press, 2017.

Nie Yuanzi 聂元梓. "Da Ji Xianlin jiaoshou" 答季羡林教授 [My response to Professor Ji Xianlin]. *Ai sixiang*, May 9, 2005. http://www.aisixiang.com/data/6693.html.

Nietzsche, Friedrich. *Beyond Good and Evil: Prelude to a Philosophy of the Future.* Translated by Walter Kaufmann. New York: Vintage, 1989.

———. *On the Genealogy of Morals.* Translated by Walter Kaufmann and R. J. Hollingdale. New York: Vintage Books, 1967.

Norrie, Alan. "Justice on the Slaughter-Bench: The Problem of War Guilt in Arendt and Jaspers." *New Criminal Law Review* 11, no. 2 (April 2008): 187–231.

Nussbaum, Martha. *Anger and Forgiveness: Resentment, Generosity, Justice.* New York: Oxford University Press, 2016.

———. *Political Emotions: Why Love Matters for Justice.* Cambridge, MA: Harvard University Press, 2013.

———. *Upheavals of Thought: The Intelligence of Emotions.* Cambridge: Cambridge University Press, 2003.

Nylan, Michael. "On the Politics of Pleasure." *Asia Major* 14, no. 1 (January 2001): 73–124.

Olick, Jeffrey K. *The Sins of the Fathers: Germany, Memory, Method.* Chicago: University of Chicago Press, 2016.

Osnos, Evan. "Born Red." *New Yorker*, April 6, 2015. https://www.newyorker.com/magazine/2015/04/06/born-red.

Ost, David. *The Defeat of Solidarity: Anger and Politics in Postcommunist Europe.* Ithaca, NY: Cornell University Press, 2005.

Packer, Mark. "Kant on Desire and Moral Pleasure." *Journal of the History of Ideas* 50, no. 3 (July–September 1989): 429–30.

Pang, Laikwan. *The Art of Cloning: Creative Production during China's Cultural Revolution*. New York: Verso, 2017.
Parker, Emily. "Titanic Takes Chinese by Storm Following President-Led Ballyhoo." *Asian Wall Street Journal*, April 14, 1998.
Parkinson, Anna M. *An Emotional State: The Politics of Emotion in Postwar West German Culture*. Ann Arbor: University of Michigan Press, 2017.
Parsons, William B., ed. "The Letters of Sigmund Freud and Romain Rolland." In *The Enigma of the Oceanic Feeling*, 170–80. New York: Oxford University Press, 1999.
Peng Hsiao-yen 彭小妍. *Weiqing yu lixing de bianzheng: wusi de fanqimeng* 唯情與理性的辯證：五四的反啟蒙 [The dialectic of emotion and reason: The May Fourth counter-enlightenment]. Taipei: Lianjing chuban, 2019.
Peng Qian 彭謙. *Zhongguo weishenme shuobu* 中國為什麼說不 [Why China can say no]. Beijing: Xinshijie chubanshe, 1996.
Pensky, Max. *Melancholy Dialectics: Walter Benjamin and the Play of Mourning*. Amherst: University of Massachusetts Press, 1993.
Perry, Elizabeth J. *Anyuan: Mining China's Revolutionary Tradition*. Berkeley: University of California Press, 2012.
———. "China's (R)evolutionary Governance and the COVID-19 Crisis." In *Evolutionary Governance in China: State-Society Relations under Authoritarianism*, edited by Kellee S. Tsai, Szu-chien Hsu, and Chun-chih Chang, 387–96. Cambridge, MA: Harvard University Press, 2021.
———. "Missionaries of the Party: Work-Team Participation and Intellectual Incorporation." *China Quarterly* 248, no. s1 (November 2021): 73–94.
———. "Moving the Masses: Emotion Work in the Chinese Revolution." *Mobilization* 7, no. 2 (June 2002): 111–28.
Pippin, Robert B. "The Modern World of Strauss." *Political Theory* 20, no. 3 (August 1992): 448–72.
Pocock, J. G. A. "Prophet and Inquisitor: Or, a Church Built upon Bayonets Cannot Stand: A Comment on Mansfield's 'Strauss's Machiavelli.'" *Political Theory* 3, no. 4 (November 1965): 385–401.
Posner, Richard A. *Public Intellectuals: A Study of Decline*. Cambridge, MA: Harvard University Press, 2003.
Puchner, Martin. *Poetry of the Revolution: Marx, Manifestos, and the Avant-Gardes*. Princeton, NJ: Princeton University Press, 2005.
Puett, Michael. "The Ethics of Responding Properly: The Notion of Qing 情 in Early Chinese Thought." In *Love and Emotions in Traditional Chinese Literature*, edited by Halvor Eifring, 37–68. Leiden: Brill, 2004.
Pye, Lucian W. "After the Collapse of Communism: The Challenge of Chinese Nationalism and Pragmatism." In *The Study of Modern China*, edited by Eberhard Sandschneider, 31–51. New York: St. Martin's Press, 1999.

———. *The Mandarin and the Cadre: China's Political Cultures.* Ann Arbor: University of Michigan Press, 2000.

———. *The Spirit of Chinese Politics.* Cambridge, MA: Harvard University Press, 1992.

Qu Qiubai 瞿秋白. *Duoyu de hua* 多餘的話 [Superfluous words]. Nanchang: Jiangxi jiaoyu chubanshe, 2009.

Rancière, Jacques. *Althusser's Lesson.* London: Continuum, 1974.

———. *The Politics of Aesthetics: The Distribution of the Sensible.* Translated by Gabriel Rockhill. New York: Bloomsbury, 2004.

Reddy, William M. *The Navigation of Feeling: A Framework for the History of Emotions.* Cambridge: Cambridge University Press, 2004.

Remley, William L. "Nietzsche's Concept of *Ressentiment* as the Psychological Structure for Sartre's Theory of Anti-Semitism." *Journal of European Studies* 46, no. 2 (June 2016): 143–59.

Reys, Ruth. *From Guilt to Shame: Auschwitz and After.* Princeton, NJ: Princeton University Press, 2017.

———. "The Turn to Affect: A Critique." *Critical Inquiry* 37, no. 3 (Spring 2011): 434–72.

Robin, Corey. *The Reactionary Mind: Conservatism from Edmund Burke to Donald Trump.* New York: Oxford University Press, 2017.

Rojas, Carlos. *The Great Wall: A Cultural History.* Cambridge, MA: Harvard University Press, 2010.

Rose, Gillian. *The Melancholy Science: An Introduction to the Thought of Theodor W. Adorno.* New York: Verso, 2014.

Rošker, Jana S. *Following His Own Path: Li Zehou and Contemporary Chinese Philosophy.* Albany: State University of New York Press, 2020.

Said, Edward W. *On Late Style: Music and Literature against the Grain.* New York: Vintage, 2007.

———. "Traveling Theory." In *The World, the Text, and the Critic,* 226–47. Cambridge, MA: Harvard University Press, 1983.

Sandel, Michael. *Liberalism and the Limits of Justice.* 2nd ed. Cambridge: Cambridge University Press, 1998.

Santner, Eric L. *The Royal Remains: The People's Two Bodies and the Endgames of Sovereignty.* Chicago: University of Chicago Press, 2011.

Saxonhouse, Arlene W. "Aristotle on the Corruption of Regimes: Resentment and Justice." In *Aristotle's Politics: A Reader's Guide,* edited by Thornton Lockwood and Thanassis Samaras, 184–203. Cambridge: Cambridge University Press, 2015.

Scheler, Max. *Ressentiment*. Translated by Lewis B. Coser and William W. Holdheim. Milwaukee, WI: Marquette University Press, 1994.

Schmalzer, Sigrid. *Red Revolution, Green Revolution: Scientific Farming in Socialist China*. Chicago: University of Chicago Press, 2016.

Schmitt, Carl. *The Concept of the Political*. Translated by George Schwab. Chicago: University of Chicago Press, 2007.

———. *Political Theology: Four Chapters on the Concept of Sovereignty*. Translated by George Schwab. Chicago: University of Chicago Press, 2006.

Schneider, Axel. "Bridging the Gap: Attempts at Constructing a 'New' Historical-Cultural Identity in the People's Republic of China." *East Asian History*, no. 22 (December 2001): 129–44.

Schwarcz, Vera. *The Chinese Enlightenment: Intellectuals and the Legacy of the May Fourth Movement of 1919*. Berkeley: University of California Press, 1990.

Schwartz, Benjamin. *In Search of Wealth and Power: Yen Fu and the West*. Cambridge, MA: Harvard University Press, 1964.

Shambaugh, David. *Beautiful Imperialist: China Perceives America, 1972–1990*. Princeton, NJ: Princeton University Press, 1993.

Shen Jiru 沈驥如. *Zhongguo budang "bu xiansheng"* 中國不當「不先生」 [China doesn't want to be "Mr. No."]. Beijing: Jinri zhongguo chubanshe, 1998.

Sheppard, Eugene. *Leo Strauss and the Politics of Exile: The Making of a Political Philosopher*. Lebanon, MA: Brandeis University Press, 2007.

Sheridan, Michael. "Chinese Feed Their Fear of Foreigners." *Sunday Times*, August 11, 1996.

Shih, Shu-mei. "What Is Sinophone Studies?" In *Sinophone Studies: A Critical Reader*, edited by Shu-mei Shih, Chien-hsin Tsai, and Brian Bernards, 1–16. New York: Columbia University Press, 2013.

Shih, Shu-mei, Chien-hsin Tsai, and Brian Bernards, eds. *Sinophone Studies: A Critical Reader*. New York: Columbia University Press, 2013.

Shim, Tae-Shik. "The Aesthetic Thought of Zhu Guangqian (1897–1986)." PhD diss., University of Edinburgh, 2008.

Shoshan, Nitzan. *The Management of Hate: Nation, Affect, and the Governance of Right-Wing Extremism in Germany*. Princeton, NJ: Princeton University Press, 2019.

Slingerland, Edward. "Mind and Body in Early China: An Integrated Humanities-Science Approach." *Journal of the American Academy of Religion* 81, no. 1 (March 2013): 6–55.

Song Qiang 宋強, Zhang Zangzang 張藏藏, Qiao Bian 喬邊, Gu Qingsheng 古清生, and Tang Zhengyu 湯正宇. *Zhongguo haishi neng shuobu* 中國

還是能說不 [China can still say no]. Beijing: Zhongguo wenlian chubangongsi, 1996.
Song Qiang 宋強, Qiao Bian 喬邊, Caiwang Naoru 才旺瑙乳, Xia Jilin 夏吉林, and Liu Hui 劉輝. *Disidairen de jingshen* 第四代人的精神 [The spirit of the fourth generation]. Lanzhou: Gansu wenhua chubanshe, 1997.
Song Qiang 宋強, Zhang Zangzang 張藏藏, Qiao Bian 喬邊, Gu Qingsheng 古清生, and Tang Zhengyu 湯正宇. *Zhongguo keyi shuobu* 中國可以說不: 冷戰後時代的政治與情感抉擇 [China can say no: Political and emotional choices in the post–Cold War era]. Beijing: Zhonghua gongshanglianhe chubanshe, 1996.
Song Xiaojun 宋曉軍, Wang Xiaodong 王小東, Huang Jisu 黃紀蘇, Song Qiang 宋強, and Liu Yang 劉仰. *Zhongguo bu gaoxing* 中國不高興 [Unhappy China]. Nanjing: Jiangsu renmin chubanshe, 2009.
Sprinker, Michael, ed. *Ghostly Demarcations: A Symposium on Jacques Derrida's Specters of Marx*. New York: Verso, 1999.
Starr, Chloë. *Chinese Theology: Text and Context*. New Haven, CT: Yale University Press, 2016.
Straughn, Jeremy Brooke. "'Taking the State at Its Word': The Arts of Consentful Contention in the German Democratic Republic." *American Journal of Sociology* 110, no. 6 (May 2005): 1598–650.
Strauss, Leo. "Letters to Karl Löwith," *Constellations* 16, no. 1 (2009): 82–84.
———. *On Tyranny: Including the Strauss-Kojève Correspondence*. Edited by Victor Gourevitch and Michael S. Roth. Chicago: University of Chicago Press, 2000.
———. *Persecution and the Art of Writing*. Chicago: University of Chicago Press, 1988.
———. *Philosophy and Law*. Albany: State University of New York Press, 1995.
———. "Preface to the English Translation." In *Spinoza's Critique of Religion*, 1–31. New York: Schocken Books, 1965.
———. *Thoughts on Machiavelli*. Chicago: University of Chicago Press, 1995.
———. "What Is Liberal Education?" In *An Introduction to Political Philosophy: Ten Essays*, edited by Hilail Gildin, 311–20. Detroit, MI: Wayne State University Press, 1989.
Su, Yang. *Collective Killings in Rural China during the Cultural Revolution*. Cambridge: Cambridge University Press, 2011.
Sun, Anna. *Confucianism as a World Religion: Contested Histories and Contemporary Realities*. Princeton, NJ: Princeton University Press, 2013.

Sun, Jing. *Red Chamber, World Dream: Actors, Audience, and Agendas in Chinese Foreign Policy and Beyond*. Ann Arbor: University of Michigan Press, 2021.

Sun Yi 孫毅. "Hanyu shenxue yu 'jidu shijian'" 漢語神學與「基督事件」 [Sino-Christian theology and the "Christ Event"]. *Daofeng* 29 (Fall 2008): 183–98.

Tang Junyi 唐君毅. *Lun Zhonghuaminzu zhi huaguo piaoling* 論中華民族之花果飄零 [On the scattered flowers and fruits of the Chinese nation]. Taipei: Sanmin shuju, 1974.

Tanguay, Daniel. *Leo Strauss: An Intellectual Biography*. Translated by Christopher Nadon. New Haven, CT: Yale University Press, 2011.

Tomkins, Silvan S. *Affect Imagery Consciousness*. 2 vols. London: Tavistock, 1962–1963.

Traverso, Enzo. *Left-Wing Melancholia: Marxism, History, and Memory*. New York: Columbia University Press, 2017.

Tsu, Jing. *Failure, Nationalism, and Literature: The Making of Modern Chinese Identity, 1895–1937*. Stanford, CA: Stanford University Press, 2005.

Tsui, Brian. *China's Conservative Revolution: The Quest for a New Order, 1927–1949*. New York: Columbia University Press, 2018.

Tu, Hang. "Long Live Chairman Mao! Death, Resurrection, and the (Un)Making of a Revolutionary Relic." *Journal of Asian Studies* 81, no. 3 (August 2022): 507–22.

Tu, Weiming. "Cultural China: The Periphery as the Center." *Daedalus* 120, no. 2 (Spring 1991): 1–32.

Turner, Bryan S. "Max Weber and the Spirit of Resentment: The Nietzsche Legacy." *Journal of Classical Sociology* 11, no. 1 (February 2011): 75–92.

Tyler, Patrick E. "Rebel's New Cause: A Book for Yankee Bashing," *New York Times*, September 4, 1996. https://www.nytimes.com/1996/09/04/world/rebels-new-cause-a-book-for-yankee-bashing.html.

U, Eddy. *Creating the Intellectual: Chinese Communism and the Rise of a Classification*. Berkeley: University of California Press, 2019.

Van Dongen, Els. *Realistic Revolution: Contesting Chinese History, Culture, and Politics after 1989*. Cambridge: Cambridge University Press, 2019.

Veg, Sebastian. *Minjian: The Rise of China's Grassroots Intellectuals*. New York: Columbia University Press, 2019.

———. "The Rise of China's Statist Intellectuals: Law, Sovereignty, and 'Repoliticization.'" *China Journal* 82 (July 2019): 23–45.

Virág, Curie. *The Emotions in Early Chinese Philosophy*. Oxford: Oxford University Press, 2017.

Wakeman, Frederic. *The Great Enterprise: The Manchu Reconstruction of Imperial Order in Seventeenth-Century China*. Berkeley: University of California Press, 1985.

Waley, Arthur, trans. *The Book of Songs: The Ancient Chinese Classic of Poetry*, edited by Joseph R. Allen. New York: Grove Press, 1996.

Wang Anyi 王安憶. *Jishi yu xugou* 紀實與虛構 [Documentation and fabrication]. Taipei: Rye Field Publishing, 1996).

———. *Qimeng shidai* 啟蒙時代 [The age of enlightenment]. Beijing: Renmin chubanshe, 2007.

———. "Shushu de gushi" 叔叔的故事 [The story of my uncle]. In *Wang Anyi zixuanji* 王安憶自選集 [Selected works of Wang Anyi]. 6 vols. (Beijing: Zuojia chubanshe, 1996), 3:1–77.

———. *The Song of Everlasting Sorrow*. Translated by Michael Berry and Susan Chan Egan. New York: Columbia University Press, 2008.

———. "Utopian Verses." In *Years of Sadness: Autobiographical Essays by Wang Anyi*, edited by Wang Lingzhen, translated by Wang Lingzhen and Mary O'Donnell, 13–68. Ithaca, NY: Cornell University East Asian Program, 2009.

———. "Wenge yishi" 文革軼事 [A Tale from the Cultural Revolution]. In *Wang Anyi zixuanji*. 6 vols. (Beijing: Zuojia chubanshe, 1996), 3:425–501.

———. "Yingte naxiong nai'er" 英特納雄耐爾 [The Internationale]. In *Wutuobang shipian* 烏托邦詩篇 [Utopian verses]. Shanghai: Huadong shifandaxue chubanshe, 2011.

Wang, Ban. *Illuminations from the Past: Trauma, Memory, and History in Modern China*. Stanford, CA: Stanford University Press, 2004.

———. *The Sublime Figure of History: Aesthetics and Politics in Twentieth-Century China*. Stanford, CA: Stanford University Press, 1997.

Wang, David Der-wei 王德威. "Haipai zuojia, youjian chuanren" 海派作家，又見傳人 [An heir of Shanghai-style literature]. *Dushu* 6 (1996): 37–43.

———. *Hou yimin xiezuo* 后遺民寫作 [Post-loyalist writing]. Taipei: Rye Field Publishing, 2007.

———. *The Lyrical in Epic Time: Modern Chinese Intellectuals and Artists through the 1949 Crisis*. New York: Columbia University Press, 2015.

———. *The Monster That Is History: History, Violence, and Fictional Writing in Twentieth-Century China*. Berkeley: University of California Press, 2004.

———. "Red Legacies in Fiction." In *Red Legacies in China*, edited by Jie Li and Enhua Zhang, 184–213. Cambridge, MA: Harvard University Press, 2016.

———. "'Standing Alone Atop the Mountain, Walking Freely under the Sea:' On Liu Zaifu and *Five Autobiographical Accounts*." *Prism* 17, no. 1 (March 2020): 143–56.

———. "Utopian Dream and Dark Consciousness: Chinese Literature at the Millennial Turn." *Prism* 16, no. 1 (March 2019): 136–56.

———. "Worlding Literary China." In *A New Literary History of Modern China*, edited by D. Wang, 1–28. Cambridge, MA: Harvard University Press, 2017.

Wang Fan-sen 王汎森. "Anti-Ism Thinkers: The Post-May Fourth Schism in Political Thought." *Chinese Studies in History* 52, no. 3–4 (2019): 223–38.

———. "'Zhuyi shidai' de lailin—Zhongguo jindai sixiang shi de yige guanjian fazhan"「主義時代」的來臨－中國近代思想史的一個關鍵發展 [The coming of the age of ism: A turning point in modern Chinese intellectual history]. In *Sixiang shi shenghuo de yizhong fangshi: Zhongguo jindai sixiang shi de zai sikao* 思想是生活的一種方式：中國近代思想史的再思考 [Thinking as a way of life: Reconsiderations on modern Chinese intellectual history], 165–250. Taipei: Lianjing chuban, 2017.

Wang, Horng-luen. "Understanding Contemporary Chinese Nationalism: Institutions, Structures of Feeling, and Cognitive Frames." *Router*, no. 19 (Autumn 2014): 189–250.

Wang Hui 汪暉. *Ah Q shengming zhong de liuge shunjian* 阿Q生命中的六個瞬間 [Six moments in the life of Ah Q]. Beijing: Huadong shifandaxue chubanshe, 2014.

———. *China's Twentieth Century: Revolution, Retreat, and the Road to Equality*. New York: Verso, 2016.

———. "Contemporary Chinese Thought and the Question of Modernity." Translated by Rebecca E. Karl. *Social Text* (Summer 1998): 9–44.

———. *Diandao* 顛倒 [Reversal]. Beijing: Zhongxin chubanshe, 2016.

———. *The End of the Revolution: China and the Limits of Modernity*. Translated by Rebecca Karl. New York: Verso, 2010.

———. "Zhongguo jueqi de jingyan jiqi mianlin de tiaozhan" 中國崛起的經驗及其面臨的挑戰 [China's rise: Experiences and challenges]. *Wenhua zongheng* 2 (2010). http://www.aisixiang.com/data/33011.html.

Wang, Jing. *High Culture Fever: Politics, Aesthetics, and Ideology in Deng's China*. Berkeley: University of California Press, 1996.

Wang Mingming 王銘銘. *Chaoshehui tixi: Wenming yu zhongguo* 超社會體系：文明與中國 [Hyper-social system: Civilization and China]. Beijing: Sanlian shudian, 2015.

Wang, Ning. *Banished to the Great Northern Wilderness: Political Exile and Re-education in Mao's China*. Ithaca, NY: Cornell University Press, 2016.

———. "Victims and Perpetrators: Campaign Culture in the Chinese Communist Party's Anti-Rightist Campaign." *Twentieth-Century China* 45, no. 2 (May 2020): 188–208.

Wang Shan 王山. *Disanzhi yanjing kan Zhongguo* 第三隻眼睛看中國 [China through the third eye]. Taiyuan: Shanxi renmin chubanshe, 1993.

Wang, Tao. "Leo Strauss in China." *Claremont Review of Books* 12, no. 2 (Spring 2012). https://claremontreviewofbooks.com/leo-strauss-in-china/.

Wang Xiaobo 王小波. *Chenmo de daduoshu* 沉默的大多數 [The silent majority]. Beijing, China: Zhongguo qingnian chubanshe, 1997.

Wang Xiaodong 王小東. "Weilai de chongtu" 未來的衝突 [Future struggles]. *Zhanlue yu guanli* 1 (1993): 46–50.

Wang Xiaohui 王小慧. "Jiushiniandai de Chen Yinke xiangxiang" 九十年代的陳寅恪想象 [The cultural imagination of Chen Yinke in the 1990s]. *Xiaoshuo pinglun* 2 (2015): 70–78.

Wang, Xiaojue. *Modernity with a Cold War Face: Reimagining the Nation in Chinese Literature across the 1949 Divide*. Cambridge, MA: Harvard University Press, 2013.

Wang, Zhang. *Never Forget National Humiliation: Historical Memory in Chinese Politics and Foreign Relations*. Stanford, CA: Stanford University Press, 2012.

Watson, Rubie, ed. *Memory, History, and Opposition under State Socialism*. Santa Fe, NM: School of American Research Press, 1994.

Weber, Max. "Science and Vocation." In *The Vocation Lectures*, translated by Rodney Livingston, 1–31. Indianapolis, IN: Hackett, 2004.

Weigelin-Schwiedrzik, Susanne. "In Search of a Master Narrative for 20th-Century Chinese History." *China Quarterly*, no. 188 (December 2006): 1070–91.

Weigelin-Schwiedrzik, Susanne, and Cui Jinke. "Whodunnit? Memory and Politics before the 50th Anniversary of the Cultural Revolution." *China Quarterly* 227 (September 2016): 734–51.

Weiss, Jessica Chen. *Powerful Patriots: Nationalist Protest in China's Foreign Relations*. New York: Oxford University Press, 2014.

Wen Xin 溫馨. "*Zhongguo keyi shuobu* chuban yinqi hongdong" 《中國可以說不》出版引起轟動 [The publication of *China Can Say No* caused a sensation]. *Sina*, September 29, 2009.

White, Hayden. *Metahistory: The Historical Imagination in Nineteenth-Century Europe*. Baltimore, MD: Johns Hopkins University Press, 1973.

Williams, Raymond. *Marxism and Literature*. Oxford: Oxford University Press, 1977.

Wolin, Richard. *The Politics of Being: The Political Thought of Martin Heidegger*. New York: Columbia University Press, 1992.

———. *The Wind from the East: French Intellectuals, the Cultural Revolution, and the Legacy of the 1960s*. Princeton, NJ: Princeton University Press, 2017.

Wong Young-tsu 汪榮祖. *Shijia Chen Yinke zhuan* 史家陳寅恪傳 [A biography of Chinese historian Chen Yinke]. Taipei: Lianjing, 1984.

Wu, Shengqing. *Modern Archaics: Continuity and Innovation in the Chinese Lyrical Tradition, 1900–1937*. Cambridge, MA: Harvard University Press, 2014.

Wu Xuezhao 吳學昭. *Wu Mi yu Chen Yinke* 吳宓與陳寅恪 [Wu Mi and Chen Yinke]. Beijing: Qinghua daxue chubanshe, 1992.

Wu Yashun 吳亞順. "Ouxiang de huanghun" 偶像的黃昏 [The twilight of idols]. *Xin Jingbao*, June 22, 2013.

Wu Yiching. *The Cultural Revolution at the Margins: Chinese Socialism in Crisis*. Cambridge, MA: Harvard University Press, 2014.

Wurgaft, Benjamin Aldes. *Thinking in Public: Strauss, Levinas, Arendt*. Philadelphia: University of Pennsylvania Press, 2015.

———. "The Uses of Walter: Walter Benjamin and the Counterfactual Imagination." *History and Theory* 49, no. 3 (October 2010): 361–83.

Xi Jinping. *Xi Jinping: The Governance of China*. Beijing: Foreign Languages Press, 2014.

Xiong Shili 熊十力. *Lun Liujing* 論六經 [On the *Six Confucian Classics*]. Beijing: Renmindaxue chubanshe, 2006.

Xu Fuguan 徐復觀. *Zhongguo yishu jingshen* 中國藝術精神 [The spirit of Chinese art]. Beijing: Shangwu yinshuguan, 2010.

Xu Jian 徐戩, ed. *Gujin zhizheng yu wenming zijue* 古今之爭與文明自覺 [The quarrel of the ancients and the moderns]. Shanghai: Huadongshida chubanshe, 2010.

Xu Jilin 許紀霖. *Dangdai Zhongguo de qimeng yu fanqimeng* 當代中國的啟蒙與反啟蒙 [Enlightenment and anti-enlightenment in contemporary China]. Beijing: Shehuikexue wenxian chubanshe, 2011.

———. "Gu Zhun de daode Shijian" 顧准的道德實踐 [The moral practice of Gu Zhun]. In *Gu Zhun zaisilu* 顧准再思錄 [Reflections on Gu Zhun], edited by Luo Yinsheng, 120–22. Fuzhou: Fujian jiaoyu chubanshe, 2010.

———. "Xiandai Zhongguo de ziyouzhuyi chuantong" 現代中國的自由主義傳統 [The tradition of liberalism in modern China]. *Ershiyi shiji*, no. 42 (August 1997): 27–35.

Xu Shen 許慎. *Shuowen jiezi zhu* 說文解字注 [Discussing writing and explain characters]. Shanghai: Guji chubanshe, 1988.

Xu Youyu 徐友漁, Dang Guoying 黨國英, and Jiao Guobiao 焦國標. "Zhiyi *Gaojiacun*" 質疑《高家村》[Questioning *Gao Village*]. *Nanfang zhoumo*, March 29, 2001.

Yan Lianke. "On China's State-Sponsored Amnesia." *New York Times*, April 2, 2013. https://www.nytimes.com/2013/04/02/opinion/on-chinas-state-sponsored-amnesia.html.

Yang, Guobin. *The Red Guard Generation and Political Activism in China*. New York: Columbia University Press, 2016.

Yang Huilin 楊慧林. *Zai wenxue yu shenxue de bianjie* 在文學與神學的邊界 [At the boundary of literature and theology]. Shanghai: Fudan daxue chubanshe, 2012.

Yang, Huilin, and Daniel H. N. Yeung, eds. *Sino-Christian Studies in China*. Newcastle, UK: Cambridge Scholars Publishing, 2006.

Yeh, Wen-Hsin. *The Alienated Academy: Culture and Politics in Republican China*. Cambridge, MA: Harvard University Press, 1990.

———. "Historian and Courtesan: Chen Yinke and the Writing of *Liu Rushi Biezhuan*." *East Asian History*, no. 27 (June 2004): 57–70.

Yi Zhongtian 易中天. "Quanjun motan Chen Yinke" 勸君莫談陳寅恪 [Rationales for not talking about Chen Yinke]. In *Shusheng yiqi*, 226–30. Kunming: Yunnan renmin chubanshe, 2001.

Yu Quanyu 喻權域. "Fangmei guilai, geng you xinxin" 訪美歸來，更有信心 [I feel even more confident after visiting America]. In *Zhongguo keyi shuobu: Lengzhanhou shidai de zhengzhi yu qinggan jueze* 中國可以說不: 冷戰後時代的政治與情感抉擇 [China can say no: Political and emotional choices in the post–Cold War era], edited by Song Qiang et al., 427–35. Beijing: Zhonghua gongshanglianhe chubanshe, 1996.

Yu Ying-shih 余英時. "Chen Yinke de shixue sanbian" 陳寅恪的史學三變 [Three changes in Chen Yinke's historiography]. In *Chen Yinke wannian shiwen shizheng* 陳寅恪晚年詩文釋證 [An interpretation of Chen Yinke's late poetry and essays], 331–77. Taipei: Dongdai tushu gongsi, 1998.

———. "Chen Yinke 'Lun *Zaishengyuan*' shuhou" 陳寅恪《論再生緣》書後 [An afterward to Chen Yinke's "On *Love in Two Lives*"]. In *Chen Yinke wannian shiwen shizheng* 陳寅恪晚年詩文釋證 [An interpretation of Chen Yinke's late poetry and essays], 227–42. Taipei: Dongdai tushu gongsi, 1998.

———. *Chen Yinke wannian shiwen shizheng* 陳寅恪晚年詩文釋證 [An interpretation of Chen Yinke's late poetry and essays]. Taipei: Dongdai tushu gongsi, 1998.

———. "Chen Yinke yanjiu de fansi he zhanwang" 陳寅恪研究的反思和展望 [Reflections and prospects in Chen Yinke studies]. In *Chen Yinke yanjiu: Fansi yu zhanwang* 陳寅恪研究：反思與展望 [Chen Yinke studies: Reflections and prospects], edited by Yu Ying-shih, 1–19. Beijing: Jiuzhou chubanshe, 2013.

———, ed. *Chen Yinke yanjiu: Fansi yu zhanwang* 陳寅恪研究：反思與展望 [Chen Yinke studies: Reflections and prospects]. Beijing: Jiuzhou chubanshe, 2013.

———. "Lun Chen Yinke de xueshujingshen he wannian xinjing" 論陳寅恪的學術精神和晚年心境 [On the scholarly spirit and the late state of mind of Chen Yinke]. In *Chen Yinke wannian shiwen shizheng* 陳寅恪晚年詩文釋證 [An interpretation of Chen Yinke's late poetry and essays], 1–72. Taipei: Dongda tushu gongsi, 1998.

———. *Shi yu Zhongguowenhua* 士與中國文化 [Literati and Chinese culture]. Shanghai: Shanghai renmin chubanshe, 1987.

———. *Xiandai ruxue lun* 現代儒學論 [Treatises on modern Confucian learning]. Shanghai: Shanghai renmin chubanshe, 1998.

———. *Yu Ying-shih huiyilu* 余英時回憶錄 [A memoir of Yu Ying-shih]. Taipei: Yunchen wenhua, 2018.

———. "Zhongguo jindai sixiangshi shang de jijin yu baoshou" 中國近代思想史上的激進與保守 [Radicalism and conservatism in modern Chinese intellectual history]. In *Qian Mu yu Zhongguo wenhua* 錢穆與中國文化 [Qian Mu and Chinese culture], 188–222. Shanghai: Yuandong chubanshe, 1994.

Yue Daiyun 樂黛雲. "Chonggu Xueheng: Jianlun xiandai baoshouzhuyi" 重估學衡：兼論現代保守主義 [Reassessing the Xueheng School: On modern conservatism]. In *Lun chuantong yu fanchuantong* 論傳統與反傳統 [On tradition and anti-tradition], edited by Tang Yijie, 415–28. Taipei: Lianjing chuban, 1989.

———. "Youyu: Zhongguo shiye" 憂鬱：中國視野 [Melancholy: The Chinese vision]. In *Tang Yijie, Yue Daiyun suibi* 湯一介、樂黛雲隨筆 [Miscellaneous writings from Tang Yijie and Yue Daiyun], edited by Chen Huachang and Huang Daojing, 305–10. Xi'an: Taibai wenyi chubanshe, 2005.

Yuen, Samson. "Debating Constitutionalism in China: Dreaming of a Liberal Turn?" *China Perspectives*, no. 4 (2013): 67–72.

Yurchak, Alexei. *Everything Was Forever, Until It Was No More: The Last Soviet Generation*. Princeton, NJ: Princeton University Press, 2005.

Zarrow, Peter. *Abolishing Boundaries: Global Utopia in the Formation of Modern Chinese Political Thought, 1880–1940*. Albany: State University of New York Press, 2019.

———. *After Empire: The Conceptual Transformation of the Chinese State, 1885–1924*. Stanford, CA: Stanford University Press, 2012.

Zha Jianying 查建英. *Bashiniandai fangtanlu* 八十年代訪談錄 [The eighties]. Beijing: Sanlian shudian, 2006.

———. "China: Surviving the Camps." *New York Review of Books*, January 26, 2016. https://www.nybooks.com/daily/2016/01/26/china-surviving-camps-cultural-revolution-memoir/.

Zhang Liang 張亮 and E Fan 鵝帆. "Wenruo shusheng tiaozhan qiangquanlaoda, minjian qishu zhendong xifangshijie" 文弱書生挑戰強權老大，民間奇書震動西方世界 [Petty literati challenged the superpower, folk wisdom shocked the Western world]. In *Zhongguo haishi neng shuobu* 中國還是能說不 [China can still say no], edited by Song Qiang et al., 417–20. Beijing: Zhongguo wenlian chubangongsi, 1996.

Zhang, Longxi. "Western Theory and Chinese Reality." *Critical Inquiry* 19, no. 1 (Autumn 1992): 105–30.

Zhang, Qiang, and Robert Weatherley. "The Rise of 'Republican Fever' in the PRC and the Implications for CCP Legitimacy." *China Information* 27, no. 3 (November 2013): 277–300.

Zhang Qing 章清. *Hu Shi pai xuerenqun yu xiandai Zhongguo ziyouzhuyi* 胡適派學人群與現代中國自由主義 [The school of Hu Shih and modern Chinese liberalism]. Shanghai: Shanghai sanlian, 2015.

Zhang Qiuhui 張求會. *Chen Yinke congkao* 陳寅恪叢考 [An evidential approach to Chen Yinke]. Hangzhou: Zhejiang daxue chubanshe, 2012.

———. *Chen Yinke de jiazushi* 陳寅恪的家族史 [Chen Yinke's family history]. Guangzhou: Guangdong jiaoyu chubanshe, 2007.

Zhang Taozhou 張桃洲. *Zhongguo dalu xianfengshige jianshi* 中國大陸先鋒詩歌簡史 [A brief history of avant-garde poetry in mainland China]. Taipei: Xiuwei jingdian, 2019.

Zhang Xu 張旭. "Shitelaosi zai Zhongguo" 施特勞斯在中國 [Leo Strauss in China]. *Jishou daxue xuebao* 24, no. 4 (2003): 12–16.

Zhang, Xudong. *Chinese Modernism in the Era of Reforms*. Durham, NC: Duke University Press, 1996.

———. *Postsocialism and Cultural Politics*. Durham, NC: Duke University Press, 2008.

Zhang Xueli 張學禮. *Zhongguo heyi shuobu* 中國何以說不 [How China can say no]. Beijing: Hualing chubanshe, 1996.

Zhao, Dingxin. *The Power of Tiananmen: State-Society Relations and the 1989 Beijing Student Movement*. Chicago: University of Chicago Press, 2004.

Zhao, Suisheng. *A Nation-State by Construction: Dynamics of Modern Chinese Nationalism*. Stanford, CA: Stanford University Press, 2004.

Zhao Tingyang 趙汀陽. *Huici Zhongguo: Zuowei yige shenxing gainian de Zhongguo* 惠此中國：作為一個神性概念的中國 [China as a theological concept]. Beijing: China CITIC Press, 2016.

———. *Tianxia tixi: Shijie zhiduzhexue daolun* 天下體系：世界制度哲學導論 [All under heaven: The Tianxia system for a possible world order]. Beijing: Renmindaxue chubanshe, 2011.

Zhou Yiliang 周一良. "Xiang Chen xiansheng qingzui" 向陳先生請罪 [My confession to Mr. Chen]. In *Chen Yinke yu ershishiji Zhongguo xueshu,* 陳寅恪與二十世紀中國學術 [Chen Yinke and Chinese scholarship in the twentieth century], 8–12. Hangzhou: Hangzhou renmin chubanshe, 2000.

Zhu Dongli 祝東力. *Jingshen zhilü: Xinshiqi yilai de meixue yu zhishifenzi* 精神之旅：新時期以來的美學與知識分子 [A spiritual journey: Aesthetics and intellectuals in the New Era]. Beijing: Zhongguo guangbodianshi chubanshe, 1998.

Zhu Guangqian 朱光潛. "Wo de wenyi sixiang de fandongxing" 我的文藝思想的反動性 [The reactionary nature of my literary thoughts]. In *Zhu Guangqian quanji,* 朱光潛全集 [The complete works of Zhu Guangqian], vol. 5, 33–39. Hefei: Anhui jiaoyu chubanshe, 1987.

Zhu Xueqin 朱學勤. "Yijiujiuba: Ziyouzhuyixueli de yanshuo" 一九九八：自由主義學理的言說 [The emergence of liberalism in 1998]. In *Sixiangshi shang de shizongzhe* 思想史上的失蹤者 [Those who disappeared from intellectual history], 237–56. Guangzhou: Huacheng chubanshe, 1999.

Zhuangzi. "All under Heaven." In *The Wisdom of Zhuangzi on Daoism*, translated by Chung Wu, 423–38. New York: Peter Lang, 2008.

Zhuo, Xinping, ed. *Christianity: Religious Studies in Contemporary China*. Leiden: Brill, 2013.

Žižek, Slavoj. "Melancholy and the Act." *Critical Inquiry* 26, no. 4 (Summer 2000): 657–81.

Zuckert, Catherine H., and Michael P. Zuckert. *The Truth about Leo Strauss: Political Philosophy and American Democracy*. Chicago: University of Chicago Press, 2006.

Zweig, Stefan. *The World of Yesterday*. Lincoln: University of Nebraska Press, 2013.

Index

Locators in *italic* refer to figures.

Adorno, Theodor W.: on Beethoven's late style, 81–82n2; the double bind of melancholy, 133–34n19; epigram to chapter three, 125; on fascist propaganda, 17; on resignation, 131; writing poetry after Auschwitz was impossible, 68

aestheticism: aesthetic fever (*meixue re*), 51, 53–54, 64, 181; Great Debate of Aesthetics (*Meixue dabianlun*), 55; Kantian-Confucian "aesthetic education" proposed by Li Zehou, 39, 49–50, 51, 56, 57, 57n29; lyricism, 20, 21, 48. *See also* Li Zehou 李澤厚—Confucian aesthetics of this-worldly affection

affect: cultural loyalism as an affective syndrome, 82–83; reason emotion nexus, 23–24, 75, 189, 217, 221–22, 241–42; use of Chen Yinke's image in Chinese cultural and political debates, 117–19, 120–21

Agamben, Giorgio, 163

Anderson, Marston, 139

Anti-Rightist Campaign (*Fanyou yundong*): censoring by China's political elite, 29; "chain of prey" syndrome created by, 66; Chinese intelligentsia targeted during, 8–9

Aron, Raymond, 159n63

Assmann, Jan: conception of "cultural memory," 28

Ba Jin 巴金: the culture of contrition advocated by, 39, 50, 109; repentance consciousness (*chanhui yishi*) proposed by, 64–65, 69, 266

Barmé, Geremie R.: on Chai Ling's Maoist rhetoric, 4n7; on nostalgia for the Maoist years, 134; on patriotic ire inculcated by shame, 236

Barth, Karl: absolutist idea of religion, 191; on "God is God," 187; Liu Xiaofeng's interpretation of, 187–88, 189; Strauss's zeal for the radical otherness of God, 191

Beijing student movement (1989): Chai Ling's leadership of, 3, 3n3, 4, 4n7; hunger strike at Tiananmen Square, 1–3

Benedict, Ruth, 70

Benjamin, Walter, 130, 131, 153, 156

Berlin, Isaiah: on "foxlike intellectual," 105; on liberals' "state of wounded consciousness," 119; on negative liberty, 13, 86n14, 114
Bernstein, Michael André, 48, 110
Boym, Svetlana: restorative nostalgia defined by, 134, 134n20
Brown, Wendy, 127n4, 130
Burton, Robert, 264

Cai Yi 蔡儀, 55, 55n24
Cai Yuanpei 蔡元培, 20, 61, 182
Carr, E. H., 80
Cartesian rationalism: anti-intentionalism, 16; Li Zehou's emotive turn as a rebellion against, 57
Cassirer, Ernst, 62–63
Chai, Ling 柴玲: call to "awaken the Chinese people with blood and death," 4, 4n7; leadership in the Beijing student movement, 3, 3n4
Cheek, Timothy: on pluralization of Chinese intelligentsia after 1989, 30–31n74; on post-Mao intellectual camps, 8n16
Chen Boda 陳伯達, 91
Chen Duansheng 陳端生: authorship of *Love in Two Lives* (*Zaisheng yuan*), 81; Yu Ying-shih's postscript to Chen Yinke's "On *Love in Two Lives*" ("Lun Zaishengyuan"), 89–90
Chen Ming 陳明, 197, 258
Chen Pingyuan 陳平原, 107–8
Chen Yingzhen 陳映真: biographical details, 136–37; at the 1983 Iowa Writing Program, *149*; on utopian socialism, 41, 143–46
—"Mountain Path": plot summary, 145–46; on poetics of resistance, 145–47; Wang Anyi's criticism of, 148
Chen Yinke 陳寅恪: author of *An Extended Biography of Liu Rushi*, 81, 95-99, 111; death in the Cultural Revolution, 40, 117; denunciation by Marxist scholars, 81, 90–91, 109–10; former residence of, 99, *100*; hermeneutics of empathy, 33; as an inspirational figure for Chinese liberal thinkers, 38, 40, 83–84, 116; tomb of Chen Yinke and his wife Tang Yun, *116*; Wang Guowei's martyrdom praised by, 93–94, 104. *See also* Lu Jiandong 陸鍵東
—construction of his cultural loyalism: Feng Yibei's polemics against cultural loyalism, 83; Lu Jiandong's account of Chen as a liberal martyr, 40, 108–13, 116, 117, 118, 119; during the post-Mao "Chen Yinke fever," 84; Yu Ying-shih on his cultural loyalism, 40, 81–82, 89–94, 116
—liberal political imaginaries of: Lu Jiandong's account of Chen as a liberal martyr, 40, 108–13, 116, 117, 118, 119
"Chen Yinke fever" (*Chen Yinke re*): as an exemplary case of memorial mania, 88; impact on post-Mao liberalism, 40, 115–19; Li Zehou on scholarly fashions of the early nineties, 101; multifarious uses of Chen Yinke's image in the age of mass media, 120–21; in popular discourse since the early 1980s and into the 2000s, 83–84. *See also* Chen Yinke 陳寅恪
China Can Say No: banning of its sequel by Chinese officials, 242; contempt for the "spineless Americanophiles" expressed by Zhang Zangzang (Zhang Xiaobo), 237; international success, 212–13, *214*, 240–41; the naysayers' cynical performance of patriotism revealed by Wang Xiaobo, 244; official endorsement included in its afterward, 242; overview of its contents, 211–12; post–Cold War timing of its publication, 212, 240; rejectionism of its authors compared with a "Red Guard mentality," 242; *ressentiment* intertwined with nationalism

in, 39, 42, 213, 215, 225, 230, 239, 248–49; Song Qiang's autobiographical account of his transformation into a proud patriot, 228–29, 234, 237–39; Zhang Xiaobo's recruitment of co-authors, 227–28

Chinese Dream: enhancement by *Wolf Warrior 2*, 272, 275; impact of the legacy of *ressentiment* on, 248–49, 254, 271–73; impact on Chinese intellectual debates, 42, 252–53, 276; Lu Xun on dreams and dreaming, 250; portrayal in Xi Jinping's "Speech on Literature and Art" (2014), 252–53

Christianity: Christian culture of sin compared with the Maoist discourse of guilt, 71–72, 74; Christian notion of guilt, 39, 50, 64–65, 69–72, 109; "cultural Christianity" (*wenhua jidutu*), 168, 174–75, 185–86, 188–89, 189n51, 206–7, 255; other-worldly virtue of the Judeo-Christian tradition, 167; Sino-Christian theology, 174;

Christian transcendence: Barth on "God is God," 187–88, 189; prioritized by Liu Xiaofeng, 177; this-worldly mentality of Confucianism distinguished from, 62; ultimacy/ultimate value (*zhongji jiazhi*) sought by Liu Xiaofeng, 167–68, 169–70, 175, 177, 185, 195, 207–8

Confucianism and the Confucian literary tradition: allegorical criticism of *jituo*, 106; the Confucian term "religion" (*jiao*), 181–82; cultural expression of *yuan* related to *ressentiment*, 215n7; ideal of "scholar-officials" (*shidafu*), 30, 106, 131–32; introspection of *youyu* (the Chinese equivalent of melancholy), 131–32; Kang Youwei's vision of Confucian theocracy, 172, 194–95, 197, 257–59; Mainland New Confucianism (*dalu xinrujia*), 35, 37, 175 257; meritocratic ideal of the "four occupations" (*simin shehui*), 199–200, 256; Overseas Confucianism, 91, 175, 197, 256-58; this-worldly aesthetics of, 45, 63–64, 167. *See also* Li Zehou 李澤厚—Confucian aesthetics of this-worldly affection

conservatism: on indigenous sources of China's modernization, 9, 103, 167, 197, 208; the malleable and versatile nature of Chinese conservatism, 10n19, 11–12n23;

—cultural: of Confucian revivalists, 10, 11, 42, 50, 103, 196–97; desire to restore a traditionalistic social order, 11; the Xueheng School, 103–4

—neoconservatism: of Irving Kristol, 274; as a major intellectual cluster in the post-Mao era, 8, 8n16; rise among Chinese international-relations specialists, 233

—political: backlash against the liberal consensus, 9, 46–47, 102, 167, 196, 254; Burkean, 196, 207, 264; coexistence with cultural conservatism, 11–12n23; remolding of Mao's socialist legacy, 11; restoration of a traditionalistic social order, 11, 169; of Xi Jinping, 252. *See also* quasi-religious sentiment

contrition and apology: and the moral certainty of post-Tiananmen liberals, 6; repentance consciousness proposed by Ba Jin, 4–65, 69, 109, 266; restitution and compensation demanded by writers of scar literature, 70

COVID-19 pandemic: criticism of Fang Fang's *Wuhan Diary*, 268–69; social Darwinist rhetoric deployed by the CCP during, 270

Cultural Revolution: Ba Jin's repentance for his participation in, 64–65, 69, 266; Chinese intelligentsia targeted during, 8–9; Gao Mobo's revisionist account of, 6-7; Ji Xianlin's confession for his complicity during, 73–76; liberal indignation against the

Cultural Revolution (*continued*) atrocities of, 8, 22–23; Liu Daren's critique of, 143; Lu Jiandong's account of Chen Yinke during, 40, 108–13, 116, 117, 118, 119; sentimental education employed to address the trauma of, 254; the unrealized socialist ideals of, 8; Yan Lianke's satirization of, 6

Dahrendorf, Ralf, 53
Davies, Gloria: on "patriotic worrying," 13n27, 21, 132
de Man, Paul, 73
Deng Xiaoping: China's revisionist turn in the late 1970s, 143; criticism of Deng Xiaoping's reform program, 102, 233; Gan Yang's proposal to combine Mao's socialist egalitarianism and Deng's market reformism, 200; on "keeping a low profile and biding your time" (*taoguang yanghui*), 229; loosening of state regulation on the Protestant Church, 174; rehabilitation policy (*pingfan zhengce*), 2; "Resolution on Certain Questions in the History of Our Party since the Founding of the PRC" (1981), 5, 65; Southern Tour (1992), 108, 185, 224, 225; unleashing of the social and cultural imaginary by his reformist leadership, 9, 53, 86; and Xi Jinping's new orthodoxy, 6
Derrida, Jacques: call for a New International, 161; embrace of the spectrality of Marxism, 160; messanicity of, 161–62, 162n70
Dong Zhongshu 董仲舒: "three heritages" (*santong shuo*) of, 200; *xing* (inborn nature) pitted against *qing* (the delusionary state), 19
Doss, Erika: "memorial mania" coined by, 88
Dostoevsky, Fyodor, 184n40, 252

emancipatory promises of socialist ideals: the dystopian turn of intellectual thinking after 1989, 10, 41, 86, 128, 133–34, 143–46, 165; of melancholic Marxism, 127–28; melancholy as a form of resistance, 37, 41, 127, 144–45, 158–62, 254, 262; Wang Hui on the emancipatory potential of Maoist mass politics, 6, 13, 162. *See also* New Enlightenment movement
emotion: emotive turn of modern Chinese literary and cultural studies, 21. *See also* enlightened sentiments; melancholy; *qing* (emotion); reason emotion nexus; structure of feeling
emotion (*qing*): dynamic interplay with *li* (intellect), 18, 78; Virág on the semantic range of *qing* in pre-Qin philosophy, 19n42
enlightened sentiments: aesthetic inculcation called for by Cai Yuanpei, 20, 61, 182; criticism of liberals' faith in, 42, 229–30; as crucial for the May Fourth generation's efforts, 50, 78; defined as the cultivation of aesthetic sensibility and moral emotion, 48; new tensions and confrontations generated by the cult of, 79; revolution plus romance as a key trope for articulating a new national community, 21; Zhu Guangqian's aesthetics of feeling: 20, 54, 55, 55n24

Fang Fang 方方: controversy surrounding her novel *Soft Burial* (*Ruanmai*), 265–68; criticism of her *Wuhan Diary*, 268–69; liberal intelligentsia epitomized by, 266; as a "trembling in the presence of illiberalism," 270
Feng Yibei 馮衣北: on Chen Yinke's late poems, 82–83; his true identity as Liu Sifen, 83n4
Fewsmith, Joseph: on pluralization of Chinese intelligentsia after 1989, 30–31n74; on political conservatism,

11; on post-Mao intellectual camps, 8n16; on resurgence of authoritarian politics in the post-Tiananmen era, 102; on rise of popular books on foreign policy in the 1990s, 226

Fragrant Youth: Mao's revolutionary art troupe featured in, 260–61, 262, 263–64; melancholy-turned-anger in, 262–64; socialist nostalgia of, 260, 261–63

Freud, Sigmund: as a cultural hero of the post-Mao generation, 54; distinction between mourning and melancholia, 127; "oceanic feeling" coined by, 171, 171n7

Fukuyama, Francis, 159n63

Furet, François, 125, 159n63

Gan Yang 甘陽: Boya College at Sun Yat-Sen University established by, 199; conviction that Strauss's classicism restored Confucian-imperial models, 199; didactic Straussianism of, 197–99; revival of the political mythology of "three heritages" (*santong shuo*), 200

Gao Mobo 高默波: *Gao Village*, 6–7, 120

Garver, John W.: analysis of the patriotism of overseas returnees, 246n95

Ge Zhaoguang 葛兆光, 106–7

Goldman, Merle: analysis of China's "dissident intelligentsia," 30

Gordon, Peter E.: on Adorno's "paradoxical simultaneity," 133–34n19; on Barth's crisis theology, 187; on Cassirer, 63; on the issue of reductive historical narratives, 35; on utopian promise of past ideas, 34

Gu Qingsheng 古清生: *China Can Say No* co-authored by, 211n1, 227

Gu Zhun 顧准: as a moral icon, 13, 109, 109n79

guilt (*zui*): the Christian culture of sin compared with the Maoist discourse of guilt, 71–72, 74; collective guilt, 65n47; exoneration implied by the recognition of, 73; "literature of contrition" related to, 39–40, 51, 69–70, 109; Liu Zaifu on quasi-religious guilt, 50, 52–53, 68–72

Guo Moruo 郭沫若, 91, 112

Habermas, Jürgen: call to "think with Heidegger against Heidegger," 33–34, 173; employment of his "constitutional patriotism" by Chinese liberals, 196, 267

Havel, Václav, 30, 266

He Guanghu 何光滬, 174

Heidegger, Martin: dangerous liaison with the Nazi regime, 31; reception of his philosophy in the PRC in 1980s, 180

Hochschild, Arlie Russell, 216, 218

Hsia, C. T., 132

Hu Shih 胡適, 85

Hu Yaobang 胡耀邦, 56

Huntington, Samuel P., 233

intelligentsia (*zhishifenzi*): engagement in truth-seeking criticism inspired by Havel, 30, 266; the modern intellectual as a cultural and political ideal, 29–30, 87–88; moral imperative to "serve the public good" (*weigong*), 30, 31–32; radical break with China's revolutionary past, 2; soul-searching mood of humanist writers in the 1980s of, 180. *See also* conservatism; the Left; liberalism; nationalism; New Enlightenment movement; post-Mao intelligentsia; *wenxue* (literature)

—political campaigns against: after the crackdown in Tiananmen Square, 46–47; targeting by the Maoist regime, 4–5, 8–9; the White Terror in postwar Taiwan, 136–37. *See also* Anti-Rightist Campaign

318　INDEX

Jaffa, Harry, 203
Jaspers, Karl, 45, 69, 70–71, 252, 267
Ji Xianlin 季羨林: advocation of a "culture of contrition" grounded in the Christian notion of guilt, 39, 50, 109; as a confessor, 73–76; *The Cowshed* (*Niupeng zayi*), 72–73; denunciation by Nie Yuanzi 聶元梓, 73, 73n66
Jiang Qing 蔣慶: political Confucianism advocated by, 197, 205, 258; on the utilitarianism of Confucian learning, 260
Jiang Zemin, 5, 242

Kang Youwei 康有為: on "Confucian religion" (*kongjiao*), 172, 194–95, 197, 257–59
Kant, Immanuel: Kantian-Confucian "aesthetic education" proposed by Li Zehou, 39, 49–50, 51, 56, 57, 57n29; Li Zehou's *Critique of Critical Philosophy: A New Approach to Kant*, 56
—initial orientation: political conviction informed by, 23, 217; the term *Gefühl* (feeling) to, 22
Kierkegaard, Søren, 184n40, 208
Kristol, Irving, 274

land reform campaign (1950s): as the setting of Fang Fang's *Soft Burial*, 265–66, 268; "speaking bitterness" (*suku*) during, 66
Lee, Haiyan: on "class racism," 49; on May Fourth sentimentalism, 23, 50–51; on the quasi-religious dimensions of Mao's image, 170; on "revolution plus romance," 21
Lefort, Claude, 77
the Left: the dystopian turn of intellectual thinking after 1989, 10, 41, 86, 128, 133–34, 165; insight into the contradictions of capitalism by the cultural left, 160; liberal-*versus*-leftist battles, 12–13, 86, 142; as a major intellectual cluster in the post-Mao era, 8, 8n16; parting of ways with the liberals re the New Enlightenment, 46. See also Chen Yingzhen 陳映真; May Fourth Movement (1919); Wang Anyi 王安憶
—New Left (*xin zuopai*): deployment of Maoist and neo-Marxist theories, 9; distinguished from its Western counterpart, 9–10n18; emergence in 1997 of, 6; melancholia of, 129–30; utopianism of, 164. See also Wang Hui 汪暉
Levenson, Joseph, 20n45
li 理 (intellect): Dai Zhen's justification of human desires against *li*-centered public morality, 19; dynamic interplay with *qing* (emotion), 18, 78
li 禮 (ritual propriety), 59, 63
Li, Wai-yee: on Ming loyalists, 93, 98; on "romantic loyalists of Jiangnan" (*Jiangnan fengliu yimin*), 97
Li Xiguang 李希光, 245
Li Zehou 李澤厚: biographical details, 55–56; as the embodiment of the 1980s New Enlightenment, 56–57; *A Farewell to Revolution* published with Liu Zaifu, 46–47, 48; as an inspirational figure for Chinese liberal thinkers, 38; Liu Zaifu as his close ally, 66, 67; *The Path of Beauty* (*Mei de licheng*), 54–55, 57; on scholarly fashions of the early nineties, 101
—Confucian aesthetics of this-worldly affection: Cai Yuanpei's aesthetic thinking compared with, 61; "culture of pleasure" (*legan wenhua*) identified as a core Confucian aesthetic, 39, 49, 58–59, 60, 76, 181; on "emotional-rational structure" (*qingli jiegou*), 57; Judeo-Christian culture of guilt distinguished from, 60–61; merging with Liu Zaifu's other-worldly guilt, 40, 50, 52–53, 64, 76–78; transcendence placed within the realm of human relations, 45, 62, 64, 77

liberalism: association with neoliberalism, 10-11, 130, 159; Chen Yinke as an inspirational figure for Chinese liberal thinkers, 38, 40, 83–84, 108–14, 116, 117; Chinese context of the term "liberal," 9n17; consensus politics of liberal reform, 9; conservative backlash against the liberal consensus, 9, 46–47, 102, 167, 196, 254; crushing of their dream of constitutional governance, 201; disorientation of liberal thinking in the immediate post-Tiananmen era, 102, 107; failure of post-Mao liberalism, 86, 169; Hu Shih's promotion of liberal values, 85; as a major intellectual cluster in the post-Mao era, 8, 8n16; moral-psychological dimensions of the liberal temperament, 87–89, 117–18, 119; mourning viewed as the most appropriate moral-emotional response, 254; parting of ways with the Left re the New Enlightenment, 46

Lifton, Robert Jay, 71

Lilla, Mark: on reactionaries, 166, 216; on tyrannophilia, 31n78, 202

Lin Zhao 林昭, 88

Liu Binyan 劉賓雁: "Between Man and Monster" (1979), 180; "a higher kind of loyalty" (di'erzhong zhongcheng), 30

Liu Cixin 劉慈欣, *The Three Body Problem* (*Santi*), 269–70

Liu Daren 劉大任, *Azaleas Cry Out Blood* (*Dujuan tixue*), 143

Liu Rushi 柳如是: Ming loyalist spirit of resistance, 81, 95–99. *See also* Chen Yinke 陳寅恪

Liu Xiaobo 劉曉波, 26, 171–72

Liu Xiaofeng 劉小楓: biographical details, 167–68; Center for Classic Studies at Renmin University established by, 199; on Confucian sage-king, 168, 206; conservative transvaluation of Maoist ideals, 178, 197–99, 204–7; cross-cultural engagement with religion, 177, 206–7; as the founder of the Chinese Straussian School, 41; *geming* (revolution) explained by, 200–201; on Mao as the founding father of the Chinese nation, 201
—Christianity: Christian transcendence prioritized by, 177; "cultural Christianity" (*wenhua jidutu*) of, 167–68, 174–75, 185–86, 188–89, 189n51, 206–7, 255; ideological conversion and deconversion, 36; Liu's abandonment of, 168, 190–91, 206; the transcendent God of the Bible, 181; ultimacy/ultimate value (*zhongji jiazhi*) sought by, 167–68, 169–70, 175, 185, 195, 207–8

Liu Zaifu 劉再復, 67; culture of contrition advocated by, 39, 50, 69–70, 109; *A Farewell to Revolution* published with Li Zehou, 46–47, 48

lived experience of socialism: Chinese liberals' reflection on, 267; Gao Mobo on the socialist memory of the underprivileged masses, 120; its saturation with personal memories, ideals, and pursuits, 12–13, 22, 127, 254; nostalgia for it, in the mise-en-scène of *Fragrant Youth*, 261; Wang Anyi's reflections on, 133, 150; Yurchak's distinction between "living socialism" and "state rhetoric," 27n60, 261

loyalism and loyalists (*yimin* 遺民): Bo Yi 伯夷 and Shu Qi 叔齊 distinguished from "ermetic subjects" (*yimin* 逸民), 92–93; cultural loyalism (*wenhua yimin*) as an affective syndrome, 82; Liu Rushi's Ming loyalist spirit of resistance, 81, 95–99; loyalist pathos, 21, 93; Ming loyalists, 82, 93, 98; Song loyalist Zheng Sixiao 鄭思肖, 95. *See also* Chen Yinke 陳寅恪—construction of his cultural loyalism

320   INDEX

Lu Jiandong 陸鍵東: on Chen Yinke's interactions with the socialist state, 119; on Chen's death in the Cultural Revolution, 40; moral desire to mend historical injustices, 118; publication of *The Last Twenty Years of Chen Yinke*, 108; transformation of Chen into a liberal martyr, 108, 110–14, 117

Lü Peng 呂澎, 107

Lu Xun 魯迅 : call to arms (*nahan*) expressed by, 136; on dreams and dreaming, 250; on leftist literature as a form of distraction, 139; *The True Story of Ah Q*, 163

Lukács, Georg, 130

Mannheim, Karl, 235

Mao Dun 茅盾, 132, 139

Mao Zedong: complication of his vision by his mournful writing, 131; enshrinement as the Great Helmsman, 6, 51, 170; glorification by Xiong Shili as a democratic saint, 203–4; Li Zehou's study of Mao's early thought, 59; Maoist sublime, 53–54, 76–78; quasi-religious yearning for the return of, 8, 171; on *ressentiment*, 220–21. *See also* Liu Xiaofeng 劉小楓

Mao's revolution: Chen Yingzhen's reflection of, 145–47; Chen Yinke's defiance of, 40, 80, 88, 111–14; class-status (*chengfen*) system as part of, 49; defined as a generic term, 4; Liu Xiaobo on the holy word "revolution," 171–72; the lived experience of it contrasted with the utopia imagined by Sinophone Marxists, 27. *See also* Anti-Rightist Campaign; Cultural Revolution; land reform campaign (1950s); political campaigns

Mao's socialist egalitarianism: as the centerpiece of PRC official ideology, 200; the Confucian social hierarchy shaken by, 256; Gan Yang's proposal to combine it with Deng's market reformism, 200; Liu Xiaofeng's criticism of it, 206–7

Marasco, Robyn: deployment of Adorno's rethinking of aporia, 133–34n19

Marcuse, Herbert, 131

Massumi, Brian, 16

May Fourth generation: enlightened sentiments of, 23, 50; historicizing Confucian literature, 175, 258; moral imperative to "serve the public good" (*weigong*), 30; the Xueheng group's dissatisfaction with the anti-traditionalist spirit of, 104

May Fourth Movement (1919): Chinese intelligentsia (*zhishifenzi*) associated with, 2; criticized by Liu Xiaofeng, 205; the dilemma of literary realism in the era of, 139; its cultural-intellectualist approach compared with the post-Mao intelligentsia, 47–48; Li Zhehou's proposal to "creatively transform" the legacy of liberal pluralism, 57; liberalism associated with, 84, 85–86; literary realism during, 139; patriotic worrying of May Fourth writers, 132

McCormick, John P.: on the issue of reductive historical narratives, 35; on Schmitt's Hobbesian understanding of fear, 205

melancholy: of Chen Yingzhen and Wang Anyi, 158–61, 164–65; Confucian emphasis on the introspection of *youyu* (the Chinese equivalent of melancholy), 131–32; the "culture of defeat" among left-wing intellectuals after 1989, 126, 126n2; distinguished from mourning by Freud, 127; distinguished from nostalgia with respect to memory, 134–35; impact on the post-Mao reason and emotion nexus, 14; melancholia transformed into a poetics of resistance in Chen Yingzhen's "Mountain Path," 145–47;

melancholic Marxism, 40–41, 128–30, 160–61, 164; melancholy as a form of resistance, 37, 41, 127, 144–45, 158–62, 254, 262; melancholy-turned-anger in the epilogue of *Fragrant Youth*, 262–64; patriotic worrying of May Fourth writers, 132; for unrealized socialist ideals, 8, 14, 27, 160, 264; Wang Anyi's reflections on the lived experience of socialism, 133, 150

memory debates and politics: ideological polarization evident in, 6–7, 21–22, 88; impact of remembrances of Maoist violence and destruction, 14; parallelism of moral sentiments and ethical reasoning in, 15; selective remembering, 27–29, 32, 253–54

Mitscherlich, Alexander, and Margarete Mitscherlich, 52n18

Mou Zongsan 牟宗三, 257

mourning: of Chen Yinke's tragic fate, 40, 83, 113, 115, 117, 255; of the decline of public authority of the cultural elite in the neoliberal era, 31; impact of the culture of apology on the liberal politics of mourning, 14, 40, 79, 116–17; "inability to mourn," 51–52, 70, 72, 114, 117, 266; melancholy distinguished from mourning by Freud, 127; the mournful tone of critical theory, 162; Wang Anyi's mourning for socialist culture, 129, 152–53

nationalism: anti-Japanese sentiments of, 222n33; diffusion of *ressentiment* through grassroots nationalism, 42, 213, 221–24, 239, 243–45, 247–49; as a major intellectual cluster in the post-Mao era, 8, 8n16; patriotic sentiment of naysayers, 235–36; represented by the say-no genre, 42, 215–16, 222, 242–43, 248–49; *ressentiment* underlying its rise in the post-Tiananmen era, 213–15, 248–49, 254, 271–73; wolf warrior diplomacy, 271

neoconservatism. *See* conservatism—neoconservatism

neoliberalism. *See* liberalism

New Culture Movement, 57, 61

New Enlightenment movement: break with the myth of Mao's revolution, 85, 169; collapse of, 3, 101, 235, 248; conflict between pleasure and guilt in, 78–79; Fang Fang, *Soft Burial* as part of the spiritual milieu of, 266; *A Farewell to Revolution* associated with, 46–47; legacy of, 46–48; Li Zehou as the embodiment of, 56; wounded consciousness associated with, 164–165. *See also* enlightened sentiments

New Left. *See* the Left—New Left

Nie Yuanzi 聂元梓, 73, 73n66

Nietzsche, Friedrich: as a cultural hero of 1980s college students, 54; phrase "twilight of the idols," 202; "will to power," 198

—discourse of *ressentiment*: Confucian cultural expression of *yuan* compared with, 215n7; the corrosive affect borne by *ressentiment* condemned by Scheler, 42; diffusion of its moral psychology through grassroots Chinese nationalism, 42; on the moral psychology of, 217–18; quote from *Beyond Good and Evil*, 220n29; Song Qiang's embrace of nationalism precipitated by nihilism compared with, 239; weakness claimed as a moral virtue by *Say No* authors contrasted with, 213, 221, 243–44

1989 Tiananmen crackdown: criticism of Deng Xiaoping's reform program in the wake of, 102, 233; the end of the New Enlightenment movement signaled by, 3, 78–79, 101; neoliberal market embraced by liberals in the wake of, 86

Nora, Pierre: "sites of memory" (*lieux de mémoire*), 28

322 INDEX

nostalgia: for the bourgeois modernity of prerevolutionary Shanghai, 151; distinguished from melancholy with respect to memory, 134–35; socialist nostalgia of *Fragrant Youth*, 260, 261–63; willful socialist nostalgia among the post-Mao generation, 37
Nussbaum, Martha, 16–17

Parkinson, Anna M.: distinction between affect and emotions, 17–18; on memory politics, 32; on resentful subjects, 247
Perry, Elizabeth J.: on the CCP's "emotion work" (*yuqing gongzuo*), 219; on "cultural positioning," 260; on Ji Xianlin's Maoist demand for confession, 74
Plato: fantasy of being able to advise a tyrant and produce a perfect regime, 32, 202; on *logos*, 63; Platonic conception of pleasure, 58, 58n31
political campaigns: bystanders and informers during, 66, 266; complicity of Chinese intellectuals during Mao's mass campaigns, 52. *See also* Anti-Rightist Campaign; Cultural Revolution; intelligentsia (*zhishifenzi*)—political campaigns against; land reform campaign (1950s); Mao's revolution
political persecution: "chain-of-prey" syndrome, 66; during the land reform campaign as the subject of *Soft Burial*, 265–68; of intellectuals in the course Chinese history, 25–26. *See also* Cultural Revolution
political theology: coined by Schmitt, 176; Liu Xiaofeng's obsession with, 41, 168, 170; the quasi-religious dimensions of Mao's image, 170
post-Mao intelligentsia: aesthetic fever (*meixue re*) of the post-Mao cultural milieu, 51, 53–54, 64, 181; four major intellectual clusters, 8, 8n16; "inability to mourn," 51–52, 70, 72, 114, 117, 266. *See also* conservatism; the Left; liberalism; nationalism
post-Tiananmen era: anti-Western sentiment during, 211–12, 213, 230, 232–33; conservatism of Confucian revivalists, 10, 11, 42, 50, 103, 196–97; disorientation of liberal thinking in the immediate post-Tiananmen era, 102, 107; grassroots nationalism in the post-Tiananmen era, 10, 10n20, 42, 212, 215–16, 222, 242–43, 248–49; Gu Zhun 顧准 as a moral icon, 13, 109, 109n79; impact of the culture of apology on the liberal politics of mourning, 40, 79, 116–17; liberals' imaginary nostalgia for republican China, 37, 196; Liu Xiaofeng's Straussian conversions during, 177; rhetoric of *ressentiment* during, 215–17, 248, 273; rightward turn of intelligentsia during, 11. *See also China Can Say No*; say-no literature
Pye, Lucian W., 219

Qian Mu 錢穆, 89, 257
Qiao Bian 喬邊: *China Can Say No* co-authored by, 211n1, 227
qing (emotion). *See* emotion (*qing*)
Qu Qiubai 瞿秋白, 136
quasi-religious sentiment: conservatives' quest for a sacred national past associated with, 24; discourse of guilt replete with Maoist political connotation, 72; impact of a passion for a mythic narrative to invest post-secular society with a sacred cultural-political tradition, 15

Rancière, Jacques, 125
reason emotion nexus: critical lyricism, 21, 48; the lacuna in liberals' emotionally charged reasoning merits,

118; the meaning of "sentimental republic," 15; pitfalls of the reason emotion nexus, 16; political emotions underpinning Chinese intellectual polemics, 14; "revolution plus romance" identified as a key literary-affective trope, 21; tripartite framework of, 23-24, 255

Reddy, William M.: on "emotional utterances," 16; exploration of the "emotional regime," 17

Red Guard generation (*laosanjie*): lived experience of socialism of, 27, 36

Red Guard movement: awareness of their atrocities among the Taiwanese public, 143; bloody factional warfare among Red Guards, 25-26; "collective guilt" used to shield them from moral anxiety or guilt, 65n47; Ji Xianlin physically and mentally abused by, 72-73; *Say No* authors' rejectionism compared with, 242; Song Binbin's apology, 7

reform and opening-up (*gaige kaifang*): disassociation of the Chinese intelligentsia from, 2

ressentiment: cultural expression of *yuan* in the Confucian tradition related to, 215n7; diffusion through grassroots nationalism, 42, 213-17, 220-24, 239, 243-45, 247-49, 254, 271-74; intertwined with nationalism in *China Can Say No*, 39, 42, 213, 215, 225, 230, 239, 248-49; lingering hate associated with, 213, 220, 243-44, 271; pivotal role of storytelling in the discursive politics of, 222-23; the "psychological dynamite" of, 218; as the repression of shame, 42, 247-48. See also Nietzsche, Friedrich—discourse of *ressentiment*

Rolland, Romain, 171, 171n7

Rose, Gillian: on Adorno's melancholy science, 133-134n19

Rousseau, Jean-Jacques, 50, 73

Said, Edward W.: on Beethoven's late style, 81-82n2; travelling theory, 36

Sartre, Jean-Paul, 31, 54

Say No. See *China Can Say No*

say-no literature: criticism of it by liberal Chinese intellectuals, 244; grassroots nationalism in the post-Tiananmen era represented by, 42, 215-16, 222, 242-43, 248-49; the moral psychology of *ressentiment* diffused through, 42, 213-15, 220-24, 245, 247-49; as an outward manifestation of a xenophobic Boxer mentality, 213-15, 240, 244. See also *China Can Say No*

scar literature (*shanghen wenxue*): assault on Mao's legacy, 52, 66, 179; restitution and compensation demanded by writers of, 70; Wang Anyi's "The Story of My Uncle" contrasted with, 151

Scheler, Max, 184n40; on "naïve self-confidence" of noble persons, 235; on *ressentiment*, 218, 239

Schmitt, Carl: as the "Crown Jurist of the Third Reich," 172; fear as the primary source of political order endorsed by, 205-6, 208; on the friend-and-foe dichotomy, 236-37, 237n65; "political theology" coined as a term, 176

Schwartz, Benjamin, 84

search-for-roots literary movement: criticism of, 128; cultural nostalgia for ancestral origins, 128

sentimental education: as the emotive underpinning of enlightenment rationality, 38, 50; failure of, 4; historical trauma addressed by, 254; transformation of society steeped in ideological fanaticism as its goal, 266

sentimentalism: definition, 50; the exploration of sentimental public space in modern Chinese literary and cultural

sentimentalism (*continued*)
studies, 21; its reflexive character celebrated in the May Fourth literary field, 50; Mao's critique of, 141; the meaning of "sentimental republic," 15. *See also* enlightened sentiments; melancholy; nostalgia; quasi-religious sentiment

Shen Jiru 沈驥如, 242–43

Sinophone: defined, 35–37; Mao's utopian revolution imagined by Sinophone Marxists, 27

social Darwinism: as international order, 230; Mao's social-Darwinian vision of a chaotic universe, 59; of the rhetoric deployed by the CCP during the COVID pandemic, 269; vision of a future global order in Liu Cixin, *The Three-Body Problem*, 269–70

socialist realism: criticism of *Serve the People* by socialist realist writers, 6; Li Zehou's dissatisfaction with, 56; the socialist-realist gaze defined, 126n1

Soft Burial. *See under* Fang Fang 方方

Song Qiang 宋強: account in *China Can See No* of his transformation into a proud patriot, 228–29, 234, 237–39; *China Can Say No* co-authored by, 211n1, 227; patriotic sentiment identified as the driving force of his salvation consciousness, 235–36

"speaking bitterness" (*suku*): impact on *Say No* authors, 220; introduced, 66

Starr, Chloë: on Chinese cultural Christians, 189n50; on contemporary Chinese theological writings, 174n17; repressed shame related to Chinese nationalist pride, 248

Strauss, Leo: appropriation by American neoconservatism, 197–98; Chinese Straussians inspired by, 168–69, 200–202, 207; critique of liberalism, 166, 172; the Schmitt-Strauss exchange, 168. *See also* Liu Xiaofeng 劉小楓; Gan Yang 甘陽

structure of feeling: coined by Raymond Williams, 23; enlightenment structure of feeling of the May Fourth generation, 23, 50; of the post-Mao intelligentsia, 15, 36; of Wang Anyi's reclaiming of her memories of socialism, 161

Tang Junyi 唐君毅, 91, 91, 257, 257
Tang Wenming 唐文明, 258
Tang Zhengyu 湯正宇: *China Can Say No* co-authored by, 211n1, 227
Tanguay, Daniel, 193, 202–3
this-worldly pleasure (*cishi zhi le*): Li Zehou's cultivation of "new sensibilities" (*xin ganxing*) grounded in, 51. *See also* Li Zehou 李澤厚—Confucian aesthetics of this-worldly affection

Thought Reform (*Sixiang gaizao yundong*): Chinese intelligentsia targeted during, 8–9; religious conversion as an essential ingredient of thought reform, according to Lifton, 71

Tomkins, Silvan S., 16
Traverso, Enzo, 126n2
Tu, Weiming, 37

Ulysses' Gaze (Theo Angelopoulos, 1995), 125–26, 165

Veg, Sebastian: on *minjian*, 243; on post-Mao intellectual camps, 8n16
Virág, Curie: *le* 樂 translated as "delight," 58n30; on the semantic range of *qing* in pre-Qin philosophy, 19n42; on the Western fascination with the Confucian holist heart-mind, 18n41

Wang Anyi 王安憶: *The Age of Enlightenment* (*Qimeng shidai*), 164–65; criticism of Chen Yingzhen's "Mountain Path," 148; friendship with Chen

Yingzhen, 41; melancholy associated with her literary narrations of politics, 158–61, 164–65; at the 1983 Iowa Writing Program, *149*; reflections on the lived experience of socialism, 133, 150; "The Story of My Uncle," 151

Wang Bing 王兵, *West of the Tracks* (2003), 264

Wang, David Der-wei: on "critical lyricism," 21, 48; on Li Zehou's Confucian "original substance of feeling," 57n29; on "revolution and enlightenment," 29, 48; on "the tradition of literature as manifestation," 25

Wang Guowei 王國維: Chen Yinke's elegy for, 93–94, 104; Li Zehou on his place in scholarly fashions of the early nineties, 101

Wang Hui 汪暉: on "downward transcendence" (*xiangxia chaoyue*), 13, 162; on the emancipatory potential of Maoist mass politics, 6, 13, 162; reading of Lu Xun's *The True Story of Ah Q*, 163

Wang Shan 王山, 227n42

Wang Shuo 王朔, 108, 226

Wang Xiaobo 王小波, 244

Weber, Max and Weberian academicians: characteristics of Weberian academicians, 101, 107; Chen Yinke contrasted with, 106, 107; "value-free" scholarship, 105; Weberian rationality, 117, 146, 176

wenxue (literature): impact of the commercialization of the culture industry on, 225–27; "literariness of ideas" (*sixiang de wenxuexing*), 25; Lu Xun on leftist literature as a form of distraction, 139; public discussion of and intellectual engagement with politics via, 25–26; "revolution plus romance," 21, 260; Xi Jinping's "Speech on Literature and Art," 252–53. *See also* Confucianism and the Confucian literary tradition; say-no literature; scar literature (*shanghen wenxue*)

Wolf Warrior 2: commercial success of, 270, 274–75; enhancement of Xi Jinping's Chinese Dream, 272, 275; the final duel between "Big Daddy" and Leng Feng, 272, *273*; the moral psychology of *ressentiment* diffused through, 271–74; wolf warrior diplomacy, 271

Xi Jinping: as general secretary of the Chinese Communist Party (2012), 251–52; the new orthodoxy of, 6; as a sent-down youth during the Cultural Revolution, 250–51. *See also* Chinese Dream

Xiong Shili 熊十力, 203–4

Xu Fuguan 徐復觀, 257

Xu Jilin 許紀霖: on Gu Zhun and Chen Yinke, 109n79; on the "parting of ways" between the liberals and Left re the New Enlightenment, 46; on post-Mao intellectual camps, 8n6, 11

Yan Fu 嚴復, 84

Yan Lianke 閻連科: *Serve the People* (*Wei renmin fuwu*), 6

Yi Zhongtian 易中天, 120–21

Yu Quanyu 喻權域, 242

Yu Ying-shih 余英時: on Chen Yinke's refusal to "leave the parental state" (*qu fumu zhi bang*): 40, 89–94, 116, 82; identification with Chen's "empathic understanding" (*liaojie zhi tongqing*), 40, 92; impact of Chen's "On Love in Two Lives" ("Lun *Zaishengyuan*") on, 89–90, 91

Yue Daiyun 樂黛雲, 103–4, 179

Yurchak, Alexi, 27n60, 261

Zeng Guofan 曾國藩, 102–3, 196

Zha Jianying 查建英, 75

Zhang Meng 張猛, *The Piano in a Factory* (2010), 264

Zhang Qiuhui 張求會, 109, 113
Zhang Shaozhong 張召忠, 275
Zhang Taiyan 章太炎, 162
Zhang Xiaobo 張小波 (Zhang Zangzang 張藏藏 as his pen name): *China Can Say No* co-authored by, 211n1; contempt for the "spineless Americanophiles" expressed in *China Can Say No*, 237; patriotic sentiment exploited in his marketing of books, 225, 228; publishing industry experience of, 225; recruitment of co-authors to write *China Can Say No*, 227–28
Zhang Zangzang 張藏藏. *See* Zhang Xiaobo 張小波 (Zhang Zangzang 張藏藏 as his pen name)
Zhao, Suisheng, 219–20
Zhou Yiliang 周一良: remorse over his politically motivated attacks against Chen Yinke, 114
Zhu Guangqian 朱光潛, 20, 54, 55, 55n24
Zhu Xueqin 朱學勤, 115
Žižek, Slavoj, 131, 150
Zong Baihua 宗白華, 54, 179
Zweig, Stefan, 79

Harvard East Asian Monographs
(most recent titles)

432. Kenneth J. Ruoff, *Japan's Imperial House in the Postwar Era, 1945–2019*
433. Erin L. Brightwell, *Reflecting the Past: Place, Language, and Principle in Japan's Medieval Mirror Genre*
434. Janet Borland, *Earthquake Children: Building Resilience from the Ruins of Tokyo*
435. Susan Blakely Klein, *Dancing the Dharma: Religious and Political Allegory in Japanese Noh Theater*
436. Yukyung Yeo, *Varieties of State Regulation: How China Regulates Its Socialist Market Economy*
437. Robert Goree, *Printing Landmarks: Popular Geography and* Meisho zue *in Late Tokugawa Japan*
438. Lawrence C. Reardon, *A Third Way: The Origins of China's Current Economic Development Strategy*
439. Eyck Freymann, *One Belt One Road: Chinese Power Meets the World*
440. Yung Chul Park, Joon Kyung Kim, and Hail Park, *Financial Liberalization and Economic Development in Korea, 1980–2020*
441. Steven B. Miles, *Opportunity in Crisis: Cantonese Migrants and the State in Late Qing China*
442. Grace C. Huang, *Chiang Kai-shek's Politics of Shame: Leadership, Legacy, and National Identity in China*
443. Adam J. Lyons, *Karma and Punishment: Prison Chaplaincy in Japan*
444. Craig A. Smith, *Chinese Asianism, 1894–1945*
445. Sachiko Kawai, *Uncertain Powers: Sen'yōmon-in and Landownership by Royal Women in Early Medieval Japan*
446. Juliane Noth, *Transmedial Landscapes and Modern Chinese Painting*
447. Susan Westhafer Furukawa, *The Afterlife of Toyotomi Hideyoshi: Historical Fiction and Popular Culture in Japan*
448. Nongji Zhang, *Legal Scholars and Scholarship in the People's Republic of China: The First Generation (1949–1992)*
449. Han Sang Kim, *Cine-Mobility: Twentieth-Century Transformations in Korea's Film and Transportation*
450. Brian Hurley, *Confluence and Conflict: Reading Transwar Japanese Literature and Thought*

451. Simon Avenell, *Asia and Postwar Japan: Deimperialization, Civic Activism, and National Identity*
452. Maura Dykstra, *Uncertainty in the Empire of Routine: The Administrative Revolution of the Eighteenth-Century Qing State*
453. Marnie S. Anderson, *In Close Association: Local Activist Networks in the Making of Japanese Modernity, 1868–1920*
454. John D. Wong, *Hong Kong Takes Flight: Commercial Aviation and the Making of a Global Hub, 1930s–1998*
455. Martin K. Whyte and Mary C. Brinton, compilers, *Remembering Ezra Vogel*
456. Lawrence Zhang, *Power for a Price: The Purchase of Appointments in Qing China*
457. J. Megan Greene, *Building a Nation at War: Transnational Knowledge Networks and the Development of China during and after World War II*
458. Miya Qiong Xie, *Territorializing Manchuria: The Transnational Frontier and Literatures of East Asia*
459. Dal Yong Jin, *Understanding Korean Webtoon Culture: Transmedia Storytelling, Digital Platforms, and Genres*
460. Takahiro Yamamoto, *Demarcating Japan: Imperialism, Islanders, and Mobility, 1855–1884*
461. Elad Alyagon, *Inked: Tattooed Soldiers and the Song Empire's Penal-Military Complex*
462. Börje Ljunggren and Dwight H. Perkins, eds., *Vietnam: Navigating a Rapidly Changing Economy, Society, and Political Order*
463. En Li, *Betting on the Civil Service Examinations: The Lottery in Late Qing China*
464. Matthieu Felt, *Meanings of Antiquity: Myth Interpretation in Premodern Japan*
465. William D. Fleming, *Strange Tales from Edo: Rewriting Chinese Fiction in Early Modern China*
466. Mark Baker, *Pivot of China: Spatial Politics and Inequality in Modern Zhengzhou*
467. Peter Banseok Kwon, *Cornerstone of the Nation: The Defense Industry and the Building of Modern Korea under Park Chung Hee*
468. Weipin Tsai, *The Making of China's Post Office: Sovereignty, Modernization, and the Connection of a Nation*
469. Michael A. Fuller, *An Introduction to Literary Chinese (Second Edition)*
470. Gustav Heldt, *Navigating Narratives: Tsurayuki's* Tosa Diary *as History and Fiction*
471. Xiaolu Ma, *Transpatial Modernity: Chinese Cultural Encounters with Russia via Japan (1880–1930)*
472. Yueduan Wang, *Experimentalist Constitutions: Subnational Policy Innovations in China, India, and the United States*
473. M. William Steele, *Rethinking Japan's Modernity: Stories and Translations*
474. Judith Vitale, *The Historical Writing of the Mongol Invasions in Japan*
475. Hang Tu, *Sentimental Republic: Chinese Intellectuals and the Maoist Past*

2776